CREDIT
MANAGEMENT

ROBERT BARTELS

The Ohio State University

THE RONALD PRESS COMPANY • NEW YORK

Library of Congress Catalog Card Number: 67–11256
PRINTED IN THE UNITED STATES OF AMERICA

Robert Bartels, Ph.D., The Ohio State University, is Professor of Business Organization at that institution. He previously taught at the University of Washington and lectured at the University of Iowa, University of Colorado, University of California, and, under a Fulbright grant, at the University of Salonica in Greece. He was a Distinguished Visiting Professor at the University of Southern California in 1961, and was a Cultural Exchange Lecturer at the University of Moscow in 1963. Dr. Bartels has authored several books in business and marketing and has written many articles on credit, marketing theory, and international marketing.

To
Ida Mae Bartels

Preface

It has been said that to understand the composition of a drop of water is to understand the ocean. While that may be true of a qualitative analysis of water, one could miss the environmental setting which the water provides for the activity which occurs within, upon, and around the sea by concentrating too narrowly on a microscopic view. Lack of perspective may cause one to be swamped by water in its larger aspects while presuming to become master of its elemental character.

This analogy may be applied to the phenomenon of credit. Historically and traditionally, credit has been approached elementally, with the single credit transaction of credit risk as the basic unit of study. Credit was collectively interpreted as the equivalent of the sum of individual credit transactions, as the sea might be the sum of the drops of its water. This concept does not reveal credit as an environmental institution embracing multiple social and economic currents, supporting business systems, and interrelating islands of interests among individuals participating in this sociobusiness function. Credit must be comprehended both elementally and collectively to achieve either a managerial or a social mastery.

Throughout this book, credit is viewed as both a social and a technical phenomenon. Both its elemental and its collective aspects are considered on the assumption that, in our society today, the institution of credit is of interest to other than business managers. Credit managers and general managers must understand the broad social, as well as the economic, aspects of credit in order to perform their technical functions effectively.

Part I deals with basic credit concepts, with essential vocabulary and fundamental ideas which custom and scientific thinking have woven into the structure of credit thought and practice.

Part II develops the idea that credit, as it is found in our economy—in fact, as it is found in any economy—is a product of broad social influences, rather than merely the creation of businessmen. Every society nourishes or restricts opportunities for the growth of a credit system through the character of its culture.

Part III considers the idea that the production of a credit service involves the performance of certain functions. These include: the investment of capital, the bearing of credit risk, and the performance of a routine of technical activities. The business costs which arise from these functions, and the means in which they are referred to users of credit service in terms and charges, are also considered.

Part IV shows that the need to perform elemental credit functions results in the emergence of agencies and institutions which perform them. The institutional system is a complex of establishments either integrated with or separated from the performance of merchandising functions, and variously integrated or specialized in the performance of the credit functions themselves. For analytical purposes these establishments are classified as primary and auxiliary, full-function and limited-function.

Part V develops the idea that certain organizational policies are particularly relevant to management of the credit functions, and that credit management is a responsibility which must be accommodated on several organizational levels.

Part VI relates to credit management technology, including all of the activities which comprise the routine of the credit operation. This consists mainly of analysis of creditworthiness, the use of diverse sources of information, authorization of credit transactions, and problems and procedures in collecting. Finally, standards for appraisal of the credit function are proposed.

Appreciation is expressed to Professor William M. Morgenroth, The Ohio State University, for his helpful suggestions made while teaching the book in manuscript form.

ROBERT BARTELS

Columbus, Ohio
January, 1967

Contents

V   INTERNAL ORGANIZATION FOR CREDIT OPERATION

VI   THE MANAGEMENT OF CREDIT BUSINESS

I

INTRODUCTION

1

The Nature of Credit

To understand credit once is not necessarily to understand it for all times, for the nature and uses of credit have differed at various times and places in history. Its present character in our society is related to what it was in the past, but at any time it is more closely related to the character of contemporary society than to anything else. The elements of any credit system are inherent in individual credit transactions which are similar in different circumstances. In its totality, however, the nature and significance of credit differ widely in diverse social settings. The nature of credit may be discussed, therefore, in terms of four separate concepts: the credit transaction, credit management, credit economics, and social aspects of credit.

THE TRANSACTIONAL CONCEPT OF CREDIT

Credit is basically related to transactions which involve, in addition to the use of credit, also credit service, creditworthiness, purchasing power, debt, credit redemption, and credit volume.

Credit Defined

The term "credit" is used to designate a type of transaction, a type of commercial relationship between individuals or business organizations. When credit is used, values pass from one party to another with the understanding that payment will be made at a future time. A promise serves as the medium of exchange, goods or services being offered by the one party, a promise of payment by the other. Credit exists only at the time of transaction or exchange, not before or after it. While the credit transaction may mark the consummation of a sale, it represents only a partially completed transaction. Title may pass upon agreement, but the exchange is completed only with ultimate payment—with fulfillment of the promise upon which the credit transaction was based.

Credit Service

It is commonly said in connection with credit transactions that a vendor "gives credit." Notwithstanding long and widespread usage of this expression, strictly speaking it is not true, and its persistence has clouded the understanding of credit. The fact is that in an exchange the *buyer gives his credit* (promise) which the seller accepts as consideration for the surrender of the commodities and services which he provides. In no sense can it be accurately said that the vendor gives *credit*—or that he *gives* anything. Rather he offers products and services, including *credit service,* which provides the buyer an opportunity to use his credit. Credit service is a commercial offering as tangible as guarantees, adjustments, or delivery, as valuable as physical products, and it involves similar costs of performance and charges. Thus a credit transaction is made possible by the *performance of a credit service.*

Creditworthiness

Another common but somewhat unclear notion is that an individual *has* credit. Prior to the actual use of credit at the time of a credit transaction, there is neither assurance nor evidence that "credit" exists. What may exist, however, is the basis upon which the credit promised is deemed credible, namely, qualities of integrity, responsibility, etc. These are attributes which make one's promise, or credit, worthy of acceptance and together constitute one's creditworthiness.

Creditworthiness is different from credit; a person may have one without having the other. Frequently persons of moral and financial integrity whose promise to pay would be commercially acceptable make no use of that qualification in buying on credit.

Thus there may be creditworthiness without actual credit. Vendors recognize this and attempt to effect the conversion through sales attractions intended to stimulate credit buying. Conversely, creditworthy individuals may at times seek in vain to prove their creditworthiness. In strange cities, if unknown to bankers or merchants, the most creditworthy buyer may be refused the privilege of credit transactions. The opposite experience is also common: individuals with no creditworthiness are accepted on credit terms, thus effecting credit without creditworthiness. Such situations create dilemmas not only for the sellers and the buyers individually, but for society in general, as defaults, bankruptcies, suits, and losses follow in their wake. Much of the technical work of credit management consists of the ascertainment of creditworthiness and of the transmission of this potentiality into credit.

Purchasing Power

It is commonly believed that creditworthiness constitutes purchasing power and that by the use of credit, purchasing power is increased. Those who hold this belief regard credit as a means of augmenting purchasing power, and they sometimes fear the inflationary effects of credit business. The fact is that under certain circumstances creditworthiness may constitute purchasing power; under others it does not. The difference usually depends upon whether credit is in the hands of personal or business users, whether its long- or short-run effects are considered, and whether it is used in a static or dynamic economy.

For consumers, purchasing power is usually equated with income, because relatively few individuals have liquid wealth which they may spend in excess of their income. Income for a week, a month, or a year, therefore, is essentially the limit of their purchasing power—and of their purchasing during a given period. When buying is shifted to a credit basis, *purchasing power* is still related to income, although *purchasing* based upon long-term income may be accelerated, giving an impression that credit augments short-run purchasing power far above short-run income. Thus this issue is a question of timing, but the normal fact is that creditworthiness is *based upon purchasing power,* rather than purchasing power being based upon credit.

The credit of a business enterprise, however, differs in this respect from personal credit. The creditworthiness of a business enterprise rests largely upon the ability of its management to operate effectively and profitably. This ability in turn depends somewhat upon management's ability to use its credit, in purchasing as well as in borrowing. Consequently, acceptance of the credit of a business firm by a vendor or lender *creates* purchasing power for that business. Business credit, therefore, is based not upon a fixed amount of purchasing power, such as personal income, but upon the expected ability to use profitably that which is obtained on credit.

The impact of credit upon general purchasing power varies also with the vitality of the economy. The behaviors already noted are typical of a static economy—one in which there is no over-all growth. In a dynamic economy, on the other hand, use of credit may increase *general* purchasing power although it may not so affect *individual* purchasing power. This is created through the increased spending resulting from the use of credit and from the purchasing power created by those whose incomes are increased by the greater volume of credit business. This multiplying effect of credit has been both favored and feared by economists. As the business and personal segments of the economy affect differently the creation of purchasing power through the use of credit, their respective effects upon economic stability are also dissimilar.

Debt

When creditworthiness gives rise to credit transactions, so long as the promise of payment is not fulfilled, the outstanding obligation is termed "debt." Debt is a residual; it is the balance or remainder of transactional promises made but not fulfilled. It is credit spent but purchases unpaid. A debtor may exhaust his creditworthiness by the amount of his credit expenditure; thus debt is in effect a complement of creditworthiness—one increases as the other declines.

To the debtor, debt is represented by payables—usually accounts or notes payable. Creditors represent debt as a receivable. In either case it is a quantifiable item, whereas creditworthiness is not so measurable. The total of creditors' receivables is the total of outstanding debt. Information concerning debt is accumulated from creditors as an index of general economic condition. As published in the *Federal Reserve Bulletin,* that portion of all consumer debts arising from the sale of goods and services and from consumer loans is designated "consumer credit."

Credit Redemption

The cycle of the credit transaction is not completed until the promised payment is made, the debt discharged, and credit-worthiness redeemed. In the initial step in a credit transaction, payment for goods obtained is made in the form of credit; ultimate payment of money obtains not the goods but the restoration of creditworthiness. One thus in effect buys back the credibility of his promise for future use. This occurrence is a determinant of future and total transactions which may occur between the debtor and creditor, for the possibility of doing business with one whose creditworthiness is intact (redeemed) is greater than with one who has spent his potentiality and carried an obligation for past purchases.

Credit Volume

A measurement of credit activity is "credit volume," other-wise stated as volume of credit sales or loans made, depending upon the nature of the operation. From the standpoint of the user of credit, credit volume represents the total value of credit transactions in which he has participated during a period of time.

Credit volume has a multiple relationship to both credit-worthiness and debt. One's creditworthiness is re-established and his credit made respendable when they are redeemed by payment of debt. Thus as one buys on credit, pays his debt, and again uses his credit, he transacts with his credit a volume of business, during a period, which may be vastly greater than his creditworthiness at any given instant. Similarly, a creditor may transact a volume of credit sales many times the amount of the investment he makes in receivables (debt) carried.

The relationships among these variables are significant indexes for credit management, from the standpoints of both creditors and debtors. They indicate something of the quality of the credit operation, the nature of risk carried, the profitability of utilization of funds in credit operation, and effectiveness in inducing cus-tomers to use their credit.

THE MANAGERIAL CONCEPT OF CREDIT

When management undertakes to provide credit service, it must assume the attendant responsibilities. Certain functions must be performed, and a unit of the business organization must be manned and managed.

Credit Functions

From the standpoint of management, the rendering of credit service is a unique management function. It corresponds with some other functions in that it is a means for accomplishing business objectives; it differs from others in the nature of the management problems and processes which it poses.

For maximum success, the performance of credit service must be regarded as a function of total management responsibility. Top, middle, and technical management alike share responsibility for coordination of credit in over-all business activity. Unless this service contributes to general corporate goals, lesser credit objectives may be in conflict with broad aspirations of the company. As a part of the whole enterprise, credit service contributes to both the service objective of the firm and to its profit and efficiency objectives.

The distinctiveness of credit service management lies in the variables which it presents for management. Like other operations, it requires the investment of working capital. Such capital invested in receivables is subject to risks differing from those related to any other asset or other part of the business venture. Furthermore, the personnel, facilities, and processes required by a credit operation differ from those in other parts of a business. Thus the providing of credit service is, from the management standpoint, a functional operation consisting of three inherent activities: investment of capital, bearing of credit risk, and performance of the routines of credit analysis, promotion, collection, etc.

Credit Organization

A credit operation is an organized unit of credit activity. Such operations are both specialized and nonspecialized. The nonspecialized operations are those in which credit service is offered in conjunction with a merchandising operation. These are typified by the credit departments of retailers, wholesalers, and manufacturers. Their credit operations are generally regarded as "sales-supporting" and are often offered as a "free" service. The nonspecialized credit operations may perform part or all of the credit functions.

Specialized credit operations are organizations which are separate from merchandising establishments and which provide credit service, in whole or in part, as a distinct and separate service. All lending agencies are such specialized credit operations. So also are such sales-facilitating operations as sales finance companies, factors, credit card companies, etc. Together these specialized and nonspecialized credit operations constitute the credit structure of our economy.

All credit functions are performed either by credit specialists or by nonspecialized credit operations. The functions, however, are shiftable, and the division and allocation of functions among the various organizations are the effects of individual management decisions based usually on considerations of costs and efficiency. A manufacturer, for example, may perform all functions inherent in providing credit service, or he may shift them in part or in total to other specialists. Even those specialists may in turn shift some of their functions to other specialists, as when finance companies resort to banks for capital. Through their differentiated offerings, various credit operations attempt to provide the assortment of services needed in our credit economy.

Business Policy

A number of business policies are dependent upon the concept of credit held by management.

Amassing of Capital. It is often the policy of a business to use its credit for providing the capital of the business. In capitalistic systems, people with investable funds do not always have ideas and talent for using those funds, while people with technical and managerial talent do not always have the capital for effectuating their ideas. Long-term or permanent investment may be achieved through the sale of stock or equity certificates; it may also be obtained through a business firm's use of its credit—by borrowing. Thus credit is a means by which business financial structures are formed and shaped. One responsibility of management is to use its credit to the optimum advantage in this type of financing.

Financing of Flows.   Not all capital used in business is in the form of a steady, continuing investment; some of it is for the purpose of financing flows of assets and activities through the enterprise in irregular patterns.   Credit performs the function of facilitating the financing of these flows.   For example, the business operation may be characterized by seasonal variations in inventory, accounts receivable, sales personnel, or advertising expenditures.   Each of these circumstances imposes demands for supplemental funds.   Credit is a means of providing such additional increments which might be unobtainable in any other way.

Creating a "Product."   When it is realized that a credit service is a distinct part of one's offering to his market, it is recognized as part of the "product" or "product package" which he presents. Like any other part of the product mix, credit service is provided only if there is a market for it, and the particular character of the service offering depends upon the segment of the market to be served.   Markets for credit service differ in a number of respects: some are markets for long-term credit service, others for short-term; some are for large sums, some for small; some are excellent credit risks, others poor.   In consideration of these differences in the market, management undertakes to provide the type of credit service—and provide it under the proper cost circumstances— which will constitute a marketable and profitable product offering.

Contribution to Profit.   The contribution which credit service makes to total profit may be made through either direct or indirect means.   When used in connection with the sale of merchandise, credit service may increase profit by stimulating sales. Such credit selling (also called sales credit service) thus becomes part of the "marketing mix," being one of the variables at the disposal of marketing management, along with advertising, personal salesmanship, branding, etc., by which sales objectives may be achieved.   Credit management in this role contributes to sales profit, as does sales management.

In addition to facilitating the sale of merchandise offered on credit terms, credit service may itself constitute a salable service and thus make a direct contribution to operating profit.   Increasingly the utility of this service is being recognized, and increasingly it is being offered as a distinct service, both in lending and merchandising establishments. Many retail stores have adopted credit plans whereby a charge is collected for this service, whereas formerly retail credit was merely an aid to making sales. Numerous specialists taking over the credit function have also arisen to provide this service for a charge. Likewise the number and variety of lending agencies have increased, all of which render credit service which is paid for.

Credit Costs and Charges

Whether directly or indirectly contributing to profit, through charges or through merchandising profit, credit service is provided only with the incurrence of costs which must be passed on to customers in one form or another. When credit service is employed mainly as a sales stimulant and no direct charge is made, an impression is created that such credit service is "free." Actually, it is free only of the direct charge, as in retail and mercantile open accounts, but performance costs must be compensated, and they are passed to customers in the over-all price of products sold. Loan credit service is never "free"; a charge is always made for it.

When direct credit charges are made, they are usually expressed in one of three forms: as a percentage, as a flat dollar amount, and as a credit price differing from a cash price by what is called a "time–price differential." Because historically charges for credit service were made mainly for loans, for which the charge was termed "interest" and which were regulated by usury laws, all credit charges came to be regarded as identical with interest. In contemporary credit practice, however, interest, or the cost of money involved, is not the only cost, and the term "credit service charge" is employed to designate this broader charge that is made.

The credit service charge is actually a composite charge, including charges for the money involved (interest) and for other elements. The range of credit service charges is much wider than the range of capital costs in the money market. Among the other elements included in the broader charge are the following: the degrees of risk in different types of credit users; the merchandising service of making credit service available conveniently, intelligently, and securely; and counseling and personal relations service. Usury concepts applicable to interest are not equally applicable to credit service charges.

THE ECONOMIC CONCEPT OF CREDIT

From the standpoint of management, credit is a means for the accomplishment of certain business objectives. From the standpoint of the general economy, credit is a phenomenon with significance exceeding its role in an individual enterprise.

Of particular importance as an economic contribution of credit is the fact that it represents the creation of a type of economic value. Production, economically considered, consists of the creation of value or utility. In simple production economies, form utility, or the creation of value through the making and shaping of physical products, is the principal type of value. With increasing complexity of developed economies, the contribution of marketing service to value formation has been acknowledged, especially in the production of time and place utilities. Still other changes in market circumstances have induced the performance of additional services, also regarded as utilities, and one of these is the production of *possession utility* through credit service.

Possession and use are always the objects of exchange wherever the processes of production and consumption are separated. Exchange effects the transfer of the total of accumulated values or utilities produced. In the past, it was generally assumed that exchange is accompanied by cash payment. With the rise of circumstances leading to the present use of credit, that assumption became less valid, for although supply and desire of buyers may be present the means of payment often are not. Social expectations place a premium upon immediate satisfaction of desire, and the possibility of obtaining through credit earlier possession of goods, whose acquisition for cash would otherwise be delayed, was accompanied by a willingness to pay more for having such goods *at once* than for the *same goods* at a later time. Satisfaction of this sense of value in the market is achieved through the provision of credit service, and the utility thereby created might well be designated "possession utility."

Possession utility is an attribute of credit service in both business and consumer credit offerings. No businessman would deny the value of capital provided by lenders. Most of them would admit also that the ability to obtain merchandise inventory on credit terms also has a value, for such possession is the means of conducting business and making a business profit. That possession utility is a value recognized by ultimate consumers is attested in their willingness to pay for it in the various charges which are made for credit service.

THE SOCIAL CONCEPTS OF CREDIT

Credit in contemporary United States cannot be adequately described merely as a type of transaction, as a function of business management, or as an economic activity. Credit itself is a social phenomenon of this period. It is a pervasive characteristic of our way of life, an expression of our values, our expectations, our demands upon the whole system of business. It is a vast network of practices and relationships which have been conceived, developed, and institutionalized. Credit represents an elaborate frame of thought. History will mark the twentieth century as an era of business achievement, and the phenomenon of credit will be seen as a distinguishing characteristic of our times. This view of credit must be held by businessmen as well as by citizens in general, for only in the context of our environment can the contributions or the potentialities of credit be realized.

An Economic Institution

It is generally conceded that ours is a credit economy. By this is meant that the character of our economic system is determined in large measure by our use of credit. Every business organization and most personal consumers use credit in some form. The continuity of business operation is dependent upon the continuing availability of credit. Credit instruments in the form of checks constitute a principal portion of our medium of exchange. In certain respects even our monetary system is based upon contractual promises of the government. The banking system is designed to provide and to regulate the volume of credit service in the economy. Other financing establishments too have arisen to provide for credit needs. The institution of credit is manifest not only in systems of establishments, but also in a variety of markets for credit service, in the social control of credit, and in systematized procedures of credit administration. The market for credit service is nationwide, and it includes many categories of business and personal users of credit, depending upon the purpose for which credit is used, the degree and nature of risk in-

volved, the amount and duration of the financing involved, etc.
Competition, performance records, consumer reaction, and laws
combine as controls of credit.

A Social Institution

Credit, however, is broader than an economic phenomenon;
it reflects non-economic as well as economic ideals of a people.
In some societies credit has little place, partly because prevailing
beliefs and customs exclude it. In the United States, particularly
in the past quarter of a century, attitudes toward credit have
changed so as to make acceptable what had formerly been a less
acceptable social practice. To buy on credit, to borrow money,
and to be in debt are now widely regarded as normal. Acting in
accord with this belief, people have achieved a standard of living
dependent upon credit. Young married couples with children
are among the heaviest users of credit, for by it they may obtain
the consumer goods deemed essential to a minimum standard of
living. Credit aids in the formation of families and in the unification of the manner of living among different social groups.

The prevailing system of credit, its established debtor–creditor
relationships, its behavior patterns, and attitudes held toward it,
all combine to create in credit a social phenomenon for which
history has no precedent. Evidence of debt is found in antiquity,
and selling on credit as well as lending has increased in prominence during the past century, but never before have the circumstances of a society flowered in such a manifestation of commercialized confidence as our present credit system. Without
denying that credit practices and agencies have visible effects
upon social behavior today, it cannot be overemphasized that
these uses of credit are primarily a *product* of society.

Credit has been both widely praised and condemned, but the
fact remains that underlying the institution of credit are some
traits of a people of which any nation might be proud. Credit is
based upon confidence. It is in a sense a manifestation of a pervasive confidence existing among individuals, businesses, social
groups. Where confidence does not characterize commercial
practices, credit does not exist or develop. Even in our own
credit system the floods and ebbs of confidence in the economic
outlook have an expanding or contracting effect upon credit.

Confidence, in turn, is the result of other circumstances. First, it is dependent upon general prevalence of such qualities as honesty, lawfulness, responsibility, and industry. Neither individual credit transactions nor a system of credit business can occur in the absence of these qualities. Personal honesty is essential, but more so honesty in commercial transactions.

Honesty in and toward business is a product of a second circumstance necessary for the emergence of a credit system: education. The American people are particularly well informed concerning the nature and operation of business. In a mass-production and mass-consumption economy they learn the impersonality of business policies and conduct themselves in compliance with rules, regulations, laws, and business principles. In an exchange economy they learn how to manage their personal budgets, to equate income and expenditure, to save and to borrow. Without the millions of instances of self-regulation in the use of credit which occur daily, no amount of business facilities or personnel would be adequate to administer the volume of credit business now conducted in this country.

A third requisite to our credit system is the business ingenuity for which American businessmen are universally known. By both trial and error and by scientific methods they have developed such organizations as credit information bureaus; such facilities as credit identification and authorization systems; such forms of credit as charge account banking plans, revolving credit plans, travelers' credit card plans, and the like.

Human nature being basically uniform, people everywhere possess honesty, intelligence, and originality. Yet they do not make use of credit as it has developed in the United States, nor has their use of credit assumed the proportions of an economic or social institution for them. The credit system in the United States is a unique conception.

DISCUSSION QUESTIONS

1. What is meant by the statement that the importance of credit in our economy exceeds the importance of the individual credit transaction?

2. Individuals with creditworthiness sometimes find their credit unacceptable. Cite reasons for this. If use of credit is desirable, what remedies would you propose for this?

3. Outline or diagram the circumstances under which the use of credit increases purchasing power.

4. Explain the statement that the management of credit does not rest wholly with credit managers.

5. What more is there to credit management than appraisal and approval of the individual credit transaction?

6. From an economist's viewpoint, does the value termed "possession utility" exist in the mind of the user of credit or in the expenses incurred by the supplier of credit service?

7. Both possession utility, as related to credit, and time utility, as related to storage, express value creation relative to time. Distinguish between them.

8. What qualifies credit to be regarded as an "institution" in our society?

9. Identify the terms used in this chapter which have a technical meaning that may be somewhat apart from the meaning of the word in common usage.

II

THE INSTITUTIONAL CHARACTER OF CREDIT

2

Social Orientation
of Credit

In the previous chapter some of the social aspects of credit were briefly sketched. In this chapter the idea that credit in the business system is determined by cultural conditions of the society in which it is found is further elaborated. Wide variations in the use of credit in different countries cause one to question why such differences exist. They have generally been attributed to the initiative of business entrepreneurs, as though uses of credit were mainly an effect of business practice. The point of view taken here is that credit practices are themselves an effect of more fundamental social circumstances. Dissimilarities in the use of credit are pointed out and credit in the United States is related to its own surrounding environment.

Society as an Environment

To understand environmental influences on credit, one must first understand what constitutes environment. Physical characteristics of environment are readily recognized, but the less obvious psychosocial aspects are often even more important. And so they are in the interpretation of credit. Not only is society a product of its own physical environment, but society—its structure, relationships, customs, laws, values, etc.—in turn constitutes the environment in which business in general, and credit business in particular, take place. From the standpoints of both the supplier and the user, credit occurs in a realm of thought which is affected by many human factors. Credit is accepted or rejected in relation to social values. It is private or professionalized, serviceful or predatory, regulated or free, specialized or homogeneous, depending upon the general characteristics of the society. The anatomy of a society, therefore, must be understood in order to comprehend how the processes of credit business are performed.

Credit and other business processes are part of a larger pattern of ways in which any society meets needs common to all people. In some societies the means are more technical, more sophisticated, than in others, but in all societies the processes involve interaction among related individuals, and those interactions are governed by general social values. These behavior patterns constitute the major social institutions. The providing of credit service is a function of the economy, but the relations and interactions of all those engaged in supplying such service are affected by the relationship of economic activity to other social activity.

The principal social institutions and their functions are as follows:

> *The family,* providing mainly through biological relationships the nurture, care, personal protection, and affection needed by mankind for its perpetuation, survival, and personal development. Family processes are carried on through relationships of individuals in such roles as husband, wife, parents, sons and daughters, brothers and sisters, in-laws, etc.

> *The school,* providing for the intellectual needs, not merely through teacher-student relationships but also through an elaborate system of academic and technical specialization, as well as through administrative organization.

> *The church,* serving the needs of the individual for recourse to spiritual resources outside himself, to a theistic identification. The organization of this institutional process usually relates individuals in a variety of roles differentiated by authority, function, intercession, etc., such as Leader, Master, Pope, rabbi, priest, pastor, layman.

> *The economy,* supplying the consumption needs of men. The economic processes are performed through participants interacting in the roles of manager, employee, owner, other financier, consumer, intermediate customer, resource, competitor, government,

and community. The supplying of credit service is one of the economic processes; it is one of the ways conceived and sanctioned by society for achieving its consumption goals.

The military, supplying defense for a people from opponents both within and without. The institutional relationships of the military process are among the most clearly defined and highly disciplined of a society.

The government, acting from the standpoint of principle and justice, serving the collective interests of society as arbiter, initiator, coordinator, and protector of the common interest. Government has long acted as regulator of economic processes, and in this role has both encouraged and curtailed economic participants in the supplying of credit services. As in other instances when voluntary economic interests have failed to supply social needs, government has acted directly in an economic role, supplying credit service through its farm or home financing agencies, or through its export credit insurance program.

Leisure, consisting of role relationships whereby the human need for aesthetic self-expression, beauty, relaxation, and play is satisfied. Most recently identified by sociologists as a major social institution, leisure is a set of relationships in which human behavior is increasingly finding expression.

The social environment of credit practice consists of all of the systems of social behavior, which influence creditors and debtors alike. Rates and types of family formation and division, degrees of literacy and intelligence, religion-based attitudes toward abstinence and prodigality, governmentally administered concepts of justice, morality, and fairness, and all such non-economic aspects of society have direct bearing upon credit business. This perception somewhat invalidates the long-held assumption that creditors and debtors act simply as "economic" men—motivated largely or wholly by economic considerations. They are both products of their *total* environment.

The Economy and Credit

Fuller analysis of patterns of credit usage is made in the following chapter; here, however, consideration is given to some of the social aspects of the economy, of which the credit systems are a part.

Every society has an economy, for all people have systematic means of supplying their common consumptive needs. Whatever the processes or however organized, those systems constitute the economy of the society. While credit is generally associated with delayed payment in an exchange economy, sequential unilateral exchanges, often involving the trust and confidence inherent in credit transactions, are also found elsewhere. Thus the character of credit is more fundamental than any particular manifestation of credit, as a means of serving certain social goals. In non-market economies, such as those characterized by reciprocity or gift giving, the equivalence of an offering is understood from custom, and confidence in compliance with the expectation of reciprocity is fully supported by prevailing social systems. In no other society, however, even in those with advanced exchange economies, have the elements of credit blossomed into such elaborate expression as in the United States.

The character of the economy, with its component of credit, in the United States has been determined mainly by principles upon which this society has been built: democratic self-determination, personal property, private initiative, market exchange, economic specialization, management initiative, consumer orientation, and government regulation. Acting from these bases, in the aforementioned roles of participants in the economic process, this society has produced a unique structure of credit establishments and distinctive patterns of economic behavior relative to credit.

The structure of establishments offering credit service includes a variety of enterprises accommodating long-, intermediate-, and short-term credit needs. They are differentiated as to the service or combination of services they provide, as well as in their charges and in the competitive initiative they take. Some are sponsored by the users of credit service, most by investors, some by government.

Perhaps most distinctive of credit in the American economy are the types of participants in the credit processes and their culture-born expectations, which determine the interactions among these participants and the patterns of their behavior. As our economy and business system have evolved, the following roles have become identified among the individuals involved in the credit activity:

1. Managers
2. Employees
3. Owners
4. Other financiers

5. Consumers
6. Intermediate customers
7. Resources
8. Competitors
9. Government
10. Community

In our type of economy, initiative is taken by managers in ascertaining and supplying consumer wants. Consumers expect this, and response of managers to this anticipation nurtures expectations of consumers as to how this credit service should be provided. So too do the general customs and attitudes of the society. Such culture-born expectations, therefore, distinguish the competition, cooperation, and conflict among participants in the United States from those found in other countries.

Consumers expect, for example, that credit service for both business and personal use will be supplied in the variety of forms needed by the market, and that offerers of credit service will take initiative in conceiving and supplying such service. They expect also that charges made therefor will at least be legal, or that where no law is involved charges will be "fair" and "reasonable." They expect debt and debtors to be handled with businesslike dignity, and humanity. They expect disclosure of truthful information upon which intelligent decisions concerning a complex negotiation can be made.

Creditors, or credit managers, on the other hand, also have culture-based expectations of those with whom they deal. They expect credit obligations to be honored with integrity, with legal compliance where law governs, or with personal honesty otherwise. They expect of their competitors the freedom of innovation and the opportunity to excel by superiority, which are vouchsafed and required by the competitive, capitalistic system. The community expects of the credit industry and of the government the creation, mainly through legalized rates, of a structure of credit service offerings adequate for the needs of both business and consumers.

These expectations are not always fulfilled, but to the extent that they are sanctioned by society they constitute obligations upon others in the systems of credit relationships. The interplay among those holding the various expectations is the functioning of the credit system as a social process.

Credit in Historical Perspective

In historical perspective, the role of credit has varied at times even as it does among societies today, for in both time or space, societies are differentiated by the same variables. In general, credit has occupied an increasingly prominent position. The need for it has almost universally existed, but prevailing attitudes have ranged from almost complete exclusion to popular acceptance. A few examples will illustrate the changing role of credit.

In the world of the ancient Hebrews, some types of credit were approved, but in general the Mosaic codes for civil life placed rigid restrictions upon its use. "Credit" consisted mainly of loans, and they were made to relieve the pressures of personal poverty, not for commercial purposes.[1] From the borrower's standpoint, the loan represented a misfortune; from the lender's, charity. Usury, or the taking of interest, was forbidden in all codes as profiteering at the expense of the distressed. Taking usury from foreigners, however, was sometimes permitted. And consonant with the seventh-year cessation of agriculture, provision was made for a year's suspension of creditors' right to demand payment. Notwithstanding the strict attitudes toward debtor–creditor relations, the need for credit continued and increased, indicating perhaps the dominance of consumer expectations and the relative impotence of outmoded attitudes in the face of changing circumstances.

With the emergence of exchange economies in contrast to those characterized by barter, trade, and self-sufficiency, and with the increased use of money, opportunities for credit relationships increased. So long as loans continued to be predominantly for personal rather than business purposes, theologians and economists appraised credit and condemned usury mainly on the grounds of the sterility of money. Industrialization changed this. Increased opportunity for profitable employment of money in manufacturing and commercial ventures proved the profitability of investable money and furnished justification for charging interest. This view has continued to have credence.

Throughout the history of credit, the institution of personal property has also been important, for property rights have given

---

[1] James Hastings, *Dictionary of the Bible* (New York: Charles Scribner's Sons, 1944), p. 183.

dominance to creditors in the debtor–creditor relationship. As a creditor's right, Shylock claimed a "pound of flesh." Other creditors have claimed the person of the debtor as slave or indentured servant, while others have demanded his imprisonment. Even today the stigma cast on creditors by long abuse of property rights continues to color behavior, and modern creditors often bend over backward to avoid the impression of excessive reliance upon this right. More equality in the relationship has been attained as creditors have come to regard a claim less as absolute property than as a means to a commercial end, which may be achieved in general notwithstanding individual losses in particular.

Social change has altered credit selling as well as lending. Starting also from a legal basis, credit selling was early placed on a personal—almost friendship—basis as some of the larger retail stores accepted credit from their known, better customers. Attitudes toward borrowing, however, colored somewhat those toward buying on credit, particularly instalment purchasing, but this yielded gradually to the opportunity and the necessity to use credit. As business became impersonalized and as the mass economy of the middle-income class evolved, attitudes toward credit began to change. Buyers saw credit as a medium of exchange; sellers saw the credit market as a definable and divisible segment of the general market. An increase in the size of the market for credit service caused further shift of management attitude from the legal and personal to the administrative and impersonal, so that both lending and vending on credit have become functions comparable to other business functions.

Contemporary Determinants of Credit

The social environments in which credit emerges are differentiated by basic philosophies, organization, technology, and customs. More specifically, the credit environment consists of the prevailing economic and non-economic attitudes relative to credit. Some of those which determine the role of credit in the United States today are briefly discussed in the following pages.

Economic Conditions. Of principal importance are the prevailing economic conditions of the mid-twentieth century, which have several distinguishing characteristics. First, the economy is relatively stable, and continually expanding. Cyclical variations are less pronounced than formerly. Consequently this has resulted in the reduction of uncertainty in both business and consumer credit risks and has encouraged increased use of credit. Second, the distribution of personal income has been widened and the average income increased. This has produced not only a greater number of persons with significant purchasing power in the market, but also an increase of discretionary purchasing power—that which exceeds the requirements for basic necessities and which can be used more at the discretion of the spender. Much of this portion of income is available for the purchase of services, including credit service, and for the purchase of more expensive goods requiring the use of credit. Third, opportunities for personal economic advancement have made people confident of their ability to liquidate debt out of earnings and have encouraged credit buying. Fourth, impetus has been given credit by various social programs which have increased the stability of incomes, such as workmen's compensation insurance, unemployment relief, social security benefits, and retirement plans. All of these have provided creditworthiness. Fifth, the availability of capital in our economy, provided by both personal and institutional savings and by the facilities of the banking system, has made possible the carrying of receivables required by credit business.

Social Conditions. Many non-economic conditions of our society also have contributed to present uses of credit. Early marriages, personal independency, and kinship relationships are a few factors which have affected credit. Early marriages have advanced family formation and accelerated demand for homes and home furnishings, as well as for children's supplies. It is during early years of marriage that demand for credit service is greatest. Moreover, in our society many unmarried men and women live separate from their families, and many older people maintain independent residence, also increasing the need for and use of credit. The size of cities, the growth of suburbs, and the mobility of the general population have accentuated the need for transportation and given rise to credit business. Literacy, education, and, particularly, knowledge of business processes and practices facilitate credit, for they have given rise to favorable attitudes toward it. Finally, increasing leisure, effected by shorter working hours and by household labor-saving devices, has opened markets for new commodities and for transportation service, which in turn have augmented the demand for credit service.

Social Attitudes. Along with changing social conditions, new attitudes toward living are also linked with the increased use of credit. According to students of society,[2] older people, for example, are more conservative toward personal finances than the younger generation, who have never experienced a depression. Younger people, in an expanding economy, are inclined to believe that future prosperity will pay for debt incurred today. There is little respect for self-denial, either as a virtue or as a means of capital accumulation. Saving is a practice which must be disciplined, as through payroll deduction plans or Christmas Club plans, which, incidentally, are often used for paying taxes rather than for Christmas purchases. Planned spending rather than planned saving is the objective of some people, with income being fully budgeted and budgets geared to a thirty-day cycle. There is wide indifference to money but considerable concern for goods, little knowledge of credit charges but some familiarity with interest on savings. Much reliance is placed on protective credit legislation of the last thirty years.

The concept of equality is commonly applied to enjoyment of "the good things of life," and people widely believe that they have a "right" to the conveniences and luxuries which heretofore only abstinence and frugality made possible. This expectation is held not only by young people but also by their elders, who wish their children to begin family life with all the advantages which they have experienced in their parental home.

Attitudes Toward Credit. New attitudes toward credit have also had a marked effect upon its use. The need for credit was formerly thought to be evidence of prodigality, poor personal financial management, and wantonness. Indeed, when the need for credit service sprang more from necessity, these implications were sometimes warranted, but the attitude was accentuated by theological convictions of the virtue of thrift and the sinfulness of want and debt. Moralistic evaluation of credit and debt continued after the beginning of the twentieth century, but objective appraisal of the social and economic circumstances produced a more impersonal attitude toward credit. Today, personal in-

[2] See William H. Whyte, Jr., *The Organization Man* (New York: Doubleday & Company, Inc., 1957), pp. 352–64.

debtedness is generally not regarded derogatorily; rather in some instances it has become an accepted status symbol of conformity. Increasingly credit is regarded as a service which is valuable and worthy of a charge, although a distinction is not always made between the commodity purchased on credit and the credit service itself. Credit and debt have attained social respectability, a businesslike character, and impersonality.

From the business point of view, also, changes in attitude have occurred. Because of creditor dominance inherent in ownership, creditors have often entered grudgingly or negatively into the credit relationship. Gradually the promotional opportunities inherent in credit business were recognized, and more recently an attitude that credit service is a marketable product has evolved. Thus providers as well as users of credit service have attained a viewpoint which has facilitated the development of credit in our economy.

Technological Developments. The developing use of credit, however, has not been wholly a result of general attitudes and conditions. It has resulted also from a type of business ingenuity not heretofore found elsewhere in the world. Recognizing an opportunity for service and being free to exploit it for personal gain, businessmen have devised a technology relative to credit without which the present system would be inoperative. Some of this technology is conceptual; some of it is mechanical.

Essential to the credit system, for example, are several basic concepts, such as the idea that a credit operation is not merely a risk but a calculated risk, one willingly assumed in consideration of the gain to be realized. So too is the assumption of the fundamental honesty of men in their dealings with others. Credit is based not on confidence alone, but upon the concept of commercialized confidence—confidence in honesty translated into business enterprise. Another basic concept concerns the anatomy of the credit risk, that its composition consists of payment variables termed *character, capacity,* and *capital.* A few other technical concepts upon which the credit system is founded are that creditworthiness is based upon purchasing power available in a given period, that a time-sale charge is different from interest, and that mercantile credit is self-liquidating. Such concepts have evolved through the creativity of businessmen.

In addition to such concepts, a number of technical instruments or mechanisms have also fostered the development of credit. They include certain credit institutions, such as credit bureaus and agencies, collection specialists, and credit insurance and credit life insurance companies. Specialized filing and authorization systems, assorted credit terms, and a variety of credit instruments are also examples of technological developments which have aided the growth of credit.

Social Control of Credit [3]

Inasmuch as the activities of society inhere in relationships which involve rights and expectations of various roles, there is possibility of conflict among them. Society reserves the authority to arbitrate between individuals and to act against individuals on behalf of society in general. The function of control which all societies perform, and which generally exists in some form of governmental authority, has long been extended to credit practices. Credit relates individuals in many role positions, each possessing rights and each having obligations, and society attempts to harmonize all interests in terms of the basic principles.

Society has acted through government to control credit practices with both qualitative and quantitative restraints. Laws governing charges have long set a framework in which credit participants have been expected to act. Legal interest rates are determinable by the states, whose intent is to protect customers against abusive charges in a market where demand and supply alone may not effect a just price.

Regulatory power has not been employed in only a negative way, however, for through enabling legislation, sanction has been given for a range of charges by an assortment of legalized credit service agencies. The federal government has even stepped from its position of arbiter into that of participant in the credit process by performing itself some credit services.

Charges, however, are not the only aspect of credit which society through government channels has controlled. The content of communications in the debtor–creditor relationship is another, for because of the complexity of credit conditions facts concerning charges may be stated in different ways, and misimpressions can be given unbeknown to customers. It is the ob-

---

[3] For an extensive study of credit regulation, see Barbara A. Curran, *Trends in Consumer Credit Legislation* (Chicago: University of Chicago Press, 1965).

jective of social control to reduce the chance of error or misstatement through requirements that credit charges be stated separately from the principal involved, and that total debtor liability, number of payments, and length of credit period also be stated. Such controls have been incorporated mostly in state legislation pertaining to consumer loans and sales financing, although many have been voluntarily set up by trade groups and associations interested in protecting themselves as competitors as well as for the protection of customers.

Perhaps the most ambitious effort to effect controls has been a proposed "Truth-in-Lending" Bill (88th Congress: S. 750) sponsored by Senator Paul H. Douglas. Intended to substitute federal for state regulation of credit practices, this bill would require that credit users be informed in advance of the charge for credit in terms of simple annual percentage rate. It differs from the typical state laws in requiring disclosure of credit charges in percentages, not merely in dollars. Strong opposition to the bill has been presented by both merchants and lenders, who regard the computation of percentage rates in advance of sale as unfeasible, if not impossible.[4]

It is significant that as credit practices have increased in other countries, problems and controls have arisen there as here. In Alberta, Canada, for example, a rate disclosure act was passed in 1963, but its enforcement was thwarted because of failure of even a government-sponsored committee to find a formula by which the effectual rate, required by the act, could be easily ascertained.[5]

It is not uncommon in a period of rising social consciousness of need for control that unnecessary diversity characterizes control efforts. So it has been to some extent with state legislation regulating consumer credit. At the same time, efforts to achieve uniformity have been made. In the early decades of this century both the lack of legitimate consumer loan services and the variety of illegal lending schemes stimulated the promulgation of a model uniform small loan act. Although adoption of modified versions of this recommendation resulted in some uniformity, throughout

[4] Robert W. Johnson, *Methods of Stating Consumer Finance Charges* (New York: Columbia University Press, 1961), pp. 103–19.

[5] "Death Knell for Alberta Disclosure Law?" *The Industrial Banker and Time Sales Financing*, February, 1965, p. 15.

ensuing years wide diversity again appeared both in the consumer
lending field and in other forms of consumer credit. Consequently, in 1964 the National Conference of Commissioners on
Uniform State Laws—in existence since 1892 and responsible for
the completion of the Uniform Commercial Code in 1952—began
an exhaustive study of the entire field of consumer credit for the
purpose of drafting comprehensive uniform or model state legislation.[6]

Governmental controls of credit have been largely qualitative
controls, on the presumption that in a free enterprise system if the
practices are fair it is not the government's prerogative or responsibility to determine the amount of debt or credit business.
Selective efforts to control credit are made by the government
mainly through the open market operations, the rediscount rate,
and the reserve requirements of the Federal Reserve System.
Exceptional measures were taken to control the quantity of credit
indirectly during World War II in Regulation W imposed by the
Executive Office of the President, 1941. Thus the size of down
payments and the repayment terms were specified for instalment
purchases and loans. This act was finally terminated in 1952.

DISCUSSION QUESTIONS

1. What difference is implied in regarding credit as each of the following: a business process, an economic process, a social process?
2. Why is the market behavior of individuals not fully explainable in
   terms of the concept of the "economic man"?
3. Cite influences derived from the non-economic social institutions
   which influence both consumers and credit managers in their credit
   relationships.
4. Show the social orientation of the use of credit in the United States
   and in another country by contrasting the cultural conditions of each.
5. Explain what is meant by the following terms: "economic participant," "social role," "role expectations," "behavior pattern." Show
   their relevance to the understanding of credit in our society.
6. Does the use of credit in America today differ from its use in earlier
   periods in degree or in kind? Explain.

[6] "The Uniform Consumer Credit Law Project," *The Credit World,* April,
1965, p. 5, and "Consumer Credit Project," *The Industrial Banker and Time Sales
Financing,* April, 1965, p. 3.

7. Distinguish between the basic roots of our society which are conducive to credit and the contemporary circumstances which give it its present form.

8. What is meant by "credit technology," and what place has it in the emergence of a credit system in an economy?

9. What justification is there for the idea that credit managers have a "social responsibility"? How is this idea related to governmental regulation of credit?

3

Markets for Credit Service

The concept of credit service as a marketable product relates credit management to portions of marketing theory concerned with product development and market identification.

A *product* is variously defined. According to classical economic theory it is an embodiment of inherent qualities, mainly the physical qualities represented by its form. Utility theorists see a product as the service or satisfaction which is provided in the experience of the user. Marketing theorists see a product, in terms both of users' perception and of inherent characteristics, as including not only physical form but also availability in terms of time and place, packaging, assortment, associated services, and the atmosphere of its environment.

Similarly viewed, credit service also is a product. Although less tangible than a physical product, it nevertheless has form in the terms on which it is offered, in the value or amount of service made available, in the accessibility of the credit office, and in the atmosphere of the place and the attitude of the persons associated with the offering.

In marketing theory, a *market* may be a place, a group of customers, or the particular relationship of demand and supply which gives expression to price. The classical economist thinks of markets as homogeneous and uniform, characteristics consistent with the concept of pure competition. Modern marketing theorists emphasize the importance of differences in the general market as well as uniformities. When the market is not reduced to homogeneity by the minimization or elimination of differences, it is seen to consist of distinct segments or differentiated submarkets. These are often so dissimilar that the offering of entirely different products to each is warranted. Products, therefore, in their broader sense, are adapted or made to conform to the specific market segment for which they are intended. Modern marketing begins with the identification of market segment characteristics and translates these demand factors not only into product characteristics but also into the entire marketing program.

Similarly, the market for credit service is not a uniform, homogeneous market but rather a composite of many market segments with many distinctly differentiated demands for credit service. The types of markets for credit service and their implications for management are the subject of this chapter.

CHARACTERISTICS OF MARKETS FOR CREDIT SERVICE

Although the market for credit service is segmented, it has some characteristics which must be considered as relating to the market in general.

Separate Versus Joint Demand

Demand for credit service is sometimes linked with demand for products; on the other hand, it is sometimes entirely separate from demand for products. In the first instance, it is usually the commodity that is desired primarily, and credit service is desired when acquisition of the commodity would otherwise be delayed for lack of cash. In such cases the joint demands may be equal, except where down payments are involved. When the demand for credit service is derived from the need for cash, however, it may be wholly apart from the market for products.

Separate Versus Joint Offering

Similarly, credit service may be offered with or apart from products, and buyers may or may not have the option to pay for them separately. In most retail stores selling on open account, there is no choice, so far as price is concerned, to take or to leave credit service. It is provided as a general service of the store, its costs are included in the one price for which goods are sold, and customers who qualify for credit accept this "free" service as a convenience, rather than as a separate purchase.

Alternative Sources of Service

Credit service offerings have become so diversified and specialized that a choice is usually available to a customer in the market. This choice may be made not only between competitors providing similar offerings, but also between suppliers of cash and sales credit service, or between vendors and other specialists offering credit service. The substitutability of both similar and dissimilar service offerings brings into direct competition a variety of suppliers.

Product Packaging

When their products are essentially similar, competitors attempt to differentiate them. These efforts range from product containers, such as uniquely packaging the product, to product environments, including the convenience and attractiveness of store locations. Some of these differentiations are important and real to customers; others are only minor psychological influences.

Markets for credit service are also influenced by the "product package" in which the service is offered. Credit service is not only the money involved, but also the manner in which it is presented. The service extras, the management personality, the creditor image, the promised user satisfaction—these are elements of the product and are presented to influence and to correspond with the assumed characteristics of the market.

Leadership in business is sometimes associated with product innovation. In credit business such innovations do not occur often; throughout the history of credit there has been little change in offerings. Some noteworthy innovations in retail credit have been instalment terms, budget and optional accounts, credit card services, and consumer credit life insurance.

Nature of Competition

The market for credit service is characterized by both price and non-price competition. Among mercantile vendors, price competition is mainly in the credit terms offered. Inasmuch as discounts are generally uniform in an industry, credit price differentiation has taken the form of variations allowed in the net or discount periods—providing for moderate delinquency, for taking discounts after expiration of discount periods, or for additional deductions for payment in advance of the discount period. Among retail vendors and lenders, there has been much more price competition, especially among agencies acting under different rate laws. Rate differences are presumed to be allowed in consideration of costs involved in serving different market segments, but the overlapping of those segments and the availability of choice among users of credit have thrown suppliers into direct price competition.

In general, there has been a tendency to subordinate price competition in supplying credit service. When the only legal lenders operated under the legal usury rate, avoidance of price competition strengthened the impression of the legality of their operation. When vendors operated mainly through "free" open accounts, this non-charge service completely avoided "price" comparison, for the charge for credit service was buried in the price of the goods and services combined. Price competition has been further avoided by suppliers whose terms made computation of comparable rates difficult. By variation of payments and credit periods, and nominal rates, an illusion of price competition has been created where there was none, or price competition has been avoided when actually there was some. Every effort seems to have been made to avoid competition on price alone.

CLASSIFICATION OF MARKETS FOR CREDIT SERVICE

The market for credit service consists of all who use their credit in the market for goods and services. Inasmuch as this market is segmented and not homogeneous, it is more accurately said that the markets for credit service are made up of users of credit who have similar characteristics. Their commonalities may be classified on several bases reflecting the expectations and relations among various debtor–creditor groups and the interaction patterns among them. The following are the most useful bases, and the categories commonly identified thereon:

Basis	Type
Nature of user	Public, private
Motive of user	Business, personal
Value acquired	Commodities, credit service, cash
Service required	Funds, risk, operations
Length of time	Long-, intermediate-, short-term
Manner of payment	Single-payment, instalment
Quality of risk	Low, medium, high

When used to divide and subdivide the market, these classifications identify market segments which may be studied in different relations to each other and to the agencies providing the specific services to meet the various market needs.

Thus while the total market is divisible into public and private (business and personal) segments, each of them in turn is divisible into more specialized markets, as for sales or cash credit service. With the variables stated, the possibilities of market segmentation are illustrated by the matrices shown in Fig. 3–1.

From these matrices it will be seen that personal users of credit constitute markets quite distinct from businesses and public agencies. It is not enough merely to identify ultimate consumers as one large market for credit service, however; they actually seek a variety of types of such service, classified as to whether they are

Value Acquired	Nature of User		
	Public	Private	
		Business	Personal
Sales credit			
Cash credit			

Length of Time	Personal Users of Credit	
	Sales Credit	Cash Credit
Short term		
Intermediate term		
Long term		

Quality of Risk	Personal Users of Cash Credit		
	Short Term	Intermediate Term	Long Term
High			
Medium			
Low			

Fig. 3–1. Selected matrices of market segments for credit service.

in connection with a purchase or a loan. For each of those types
there are short-, intermediate-, and long-term needs. Sales credit
service of short-term duration may be illustrated by thirty-day
charge account credit; intermediate-term, by one- or two-year
instalment credit; and long-term-, by twenty-year mortgage credit.
For each of these categories, moreover, there may be a range of
risk characteristics extending from high to low quality, each
constituting markets which require different treatment and possibly served by separate agencies.

In addition to the differences which such market types represent, there are other characteristics which distinguish markets for
credit service. A few of these are shown in Table 3–1 wherein
contrasts are made between the public, business, and personal
sectors of the market. Other characteristics might be considered
for specific purposes of analysis.

Table 3–1. Characteristics of Selected Segments
of the Market for Credit Service

Characteristic	Public	Private	
		Business	Personal
Use of credit	For purposes of government	For purposes of business	For consumption
Motivation	Shift deficit financing	Shift financing, risk, operation	Convenience, need
Risk quality	Generally good	Range	Range
Instruments	Bonds, notes, bills, certifi- cates, accounts	Notes, drafts, contracts, accounts	Accounts, notes
Security	Promise	Mortgage, assets, promise	Mortgage, assets, promise
Elasticity	None	Some	Some
Limit	Legal limit	Profit potential	Capacity to pay, earnings
Behavior patterns	Institutional interaction, organized markets	Cost–price important	Payment terms important

From this it may be noted that when in the market for credit
service, the government through the issuance of long- and short-
term credit instruments, seeks funds and materials for the func-

tions peculiar to government, such as maintenance of defense, research in space, building of highways and dams, providing postal service, assisting agriculture, industry, and labor, etc. Government has not repaid its obligations to creditors as fast as it has used its credit. Consequently, its residual debt has increased, and Congress has repeatedly raised the limit of its legal indebtedness.

By contrast, business organizations in the market for credit service are pursuing typical business objectives: obtaining inventories, supplies, equipment, etc.; acquiring working or investment funds for carrying on the business processes; etc. This use of credit constitutes shifting a financing function—and sometimes the risk and operations functions as well—to credit specialists and other suppliers of credit service. Their demand for credit service is somewhat elastic, influenced to a degree by interest rates, but demand is more often determined by the prospects for profitable employment of that which is obtained on credit. As charges for credit service are one of the total business costs, the rational economic motivations of entrepreneurs cause them to seek the most favorable credit terms.

Consumers' use of credit provides further contrast of behavior in the market for credit service. Their objective is consumption, not production. Their motivations are convenience, provision for emergency, or to take advantage of opportunities to improve the level of their living. The wide range of risk quality among them excludes some from the market and causes others to be offered an assortment of terms, instruments, and services commensurate with the risk involved. Some are more willing to pay for credit service than others, and even among the willing ones there is often more concern with payment terms—down payment and monthly payments—than with the stated charge. Although there is some elasticity of demand, depending upon the terms of credit service available, demand is more largely a function of earning power, income, and capacity to pay.

TRENDS IN MARKETS FOR CREDIT SERVICE

As the use of credit results from prevailing social conditions and attitudes, trends in the latter affect trends in markets for credit service. It is these changing circumstances, therefore, both in consumption and in business practice, that suppliers of credit service have looked to for their markets, and to which they have adapted their offerings.

Several developments in the consumer market have influenced this marketing of credit service. The market has increased with the increase of population, but as credit is used differently at different age levels, the market is disproportionately affected as the age composition of the total population changes. The most active market for personal credit service is among younger families, those under 45 and with children under 18. With early and rapid family formation, the market for homes and household goods is greatly increased. The Federal Reserve Board's Surveys of Consumer Finances have indicated that between 50 and 65 per cent of consumers under 45 use instalment credit. Consequently, with the large percentage of the population entering the 20–30-year age group prior to 1970, markets for credit service in connection with certain types of merchandise will be expanded. Simultaneously, an increased number and percentage of the population are now in the upper age group. Their need for credit service diminishes quantitatively, but it continues and even increases for such items as travel, medical service, education, and other cultural services.

Another trend in personal consumption has stemmed from the mobility of our people. With greater use of automobiles, the purchase of supplies at other than the home base has encouraged the use of gasoline credit cards issued by petroleum companies. Increased travel has been accompanied by increased purchasing away from home of all types of services and products, indicating a market for a type of credit service hitherto non-existent, namely, that which has been supplied by the issuers of universal credit cards. Furthermore, increased travel by airplane has shown in the service field a market for instalment credit service, which originally was confined to tangible and durable goods. Thus, distinct markets have emerged, and perceptive entrepreneurs have fashioned credit services to accommodate them.

During the past several decades, new concepts of market convenience have appeared among consumers as cities have expanded, use of autos has increased, and purchasing has become more diversified. The former "around-the-corner" convenience has given way to "convenience-by-driving." At the same time, convenience has also been defined as the ability to make assorted (related and unrelated) purchases at one place. The results of these trends have been twofold: (1) a proliferation of vending places in suburban branches of downtown stores and in shopping centers and (2) the "scrambling" of merchandise, or the offering of several product lines together as in drugstores, groceries, auto supply stores, and the like.

Accompanying these merchandising trends have been two parallel developments in consumer credit. First, established credit customers have been buying away from stores where their account records were, and they have been buying increasingly where they were not known and where vendors were often unable for economic reasons to provide the credit service desired. This condition in the market for consumer credit has led to several innovations among suppliers of credit service: use of credit identification acceptable in all branches or units of a chain, and the rise of specialists providing credit service for small unrelated merchants. The invention of new systems and processes has accompanied the adaptation of the credit product to new markets.

Second, the trend of merchants providing for the assorted needs of consumers has also had a parallel in credit servicing. Two or more forms of credit service are now often offered by lenders and vendors who formerly offered only one. Many retailers provide not only regular open accounts but also revolving or optional accounts and instalment credit. Some engage in lending. Lenders have diversified into sales financing; industrial banks have extended their markets by taking out commercial bank charters; commercial banks have undertaken factoring; and savings and loan companies have made loans for purchase of household equipment. Thus credit service suppliers have sought to cater to different markets, primarily among different individuals. Correlated to this market diversification is the fact that a given individual or family constitutes a market for different kinds of credit service at any one time, and also at different times in his life cycle.[1] Consideration is therefore increasingly being given to meeting not only the assorted but the continually changing needs of the market. Trends in the use of credit by business organizations have also affected the credit policies of vendors, lenders, and others supplying credit service. The business market for credit service, however, differs from the consumer market

[1] For enlargement of the concept of the life cycle and its implications for credit service suppliers, see Robert W. Johnson, "Consumer Credit Forecast for 1965," *Consumer Finance News*, December, 1964, p. 24. See also by the same author, "The Credit Market," *The Credit World*, December, 1965, p. 10.

in that such service is sought not only for purchasing and borrowing, but increasingly to assist in the supplying of credit service to its own customers.

Normal markets for credit service to business always vary with cyclical changes in business conditions, affecting changing needs for working capital. Secular trends alter needs for fixed investments, equipment, etc. Policy trends also affect the need for credit, as have the policies of leasing equipment and of lease-back of real estate. Expansion of foreign business has required establishing credit relations with banks for discounting drafts. Establishment of sales branches and distribution point warehouses relates marketing policies to credit service needs, as does the decision to shorten or lengthen distribution channels. All of these trends which have occurred within recent decades have altered the market for credit service.

In addition, the growing prominence of the credit function in business has itself created markets for credit service. Lenders and credit vendors do not always assume full responsibility for performing all the functions and assuming all the risks of their credit operations. They pass them on to other specialists, thus presenting a market for credit service connected with the credit service they are in turn supplying to other markets. The rise of such secondary markets has encouraged the development of factoring, sales financing, bank charge plans, and commercial financing. These services will be discussed more fully in a later chapter; it is sufficient at present merely to indicate that they represent evidence of adaptiveness on the part of credit service suppliers to the various and varying needs or markets for this service.

Credit Market Research

Because credit has generally not been regarded as a marketable service, but rather as a financing function in the distribution of other products, little attention has been given to research into markets for it. Some state laws have required proof of need for additional lending offices as a prerequisite to licensing them, and this has stimulated some research into markets in terms of population, income, building starts, and mortgages. Classifications have been made of the credit customers of some lenders and vendors as a basis for understanding who are their clientele. Neither qualitative nor quantitative aspects of credit service markets, however, have been very carefully detailed.

Perhaps the main hindrance to research has been the lack of distinction between products sold on credit and credit service itself. Credit service has not been thought of as a separate item. Classification of customers has served a descriptive rather than an analytical or promotional purpose. Prevalence of a sellers' market for credit service has also placed less premium upon exact knowledge of markets. Moreover, differentiation of suppliers by rates of charge sanctioned for them by the states has served somewhat as a market selection device and need for others has not been felt.

However, the research techniques used in other market analyses are applicable to the study of markets for credit service. Qualitative studies may be made to define market segments needing service. These may be made from external studies of motivation, customer behavior, and competitive offerings. They may also be made from the study of internal data evidencing customer types by risk classes, location, delinquencies, size and volume of orders, etc. Quantitative studies may also be made based upon population and industry trends, sales forecasts, money rates, competitors, and trade credit experiences.

Summary and Conclusions

If credit service is a marketable product, then it must be intended for markets. The production orientation of business has obscured this aspect of credit service, but contemporary marketing theory brings it into view. The market for credit service, as for physical products, can be segmented so far as it seems worthwhile to the supplier. Basic use characteristics mainly distinguish market segments, but underlying social, economic, and administrative trends influence credit use habits. To the extent that the business system is responsive to such change, new agencies and new services have been created to serve the changing market. The market viewpoint in supplying credit service should enhance interest in research into credit markets.

DISCUSSION QUESTIONS

1. Define "product" as it might be understood by the following: production manager, marketing manager, advertising manager, economist, consumer. What relevance has each to the definition of credit service as a "product"?

2. What are the different ways in which "product differentiation" may be applied to credit service offerings?

3. Illustrate the concept of "market" for credit service as the following: a place, a group of traders, demand and supply forces, a state of mind.

4. Explain the concepts of "homogeneity" and "heterogeneity" as they apply to the market or markets for credit service.

5. Of what use is product differentiation if there is no market segmentation?

6. Construct several experimental matrices illustrating the use of different bases of market classification for the identification of market segments.

7. Explain how an individual or a business may be simultaneously in different markets for credit service. How may each evolve from one market to another throughout its life cycle?

8. What effect upon competition in the offering of credit service have specialization and diversification of offerings?

4

Patterns in the Use of Credit

In previous chapters some social and managerial aspects of credit were shown. Equally important is an economic view of credit, whereby are seen in aggregate the components and proportions of the credit mechanism, the interaction of its parts, and trends in its performance. These subjects are considered in this chapter.

For several reasons, the economic aspects of credit are especially important. First, while every society has its economy, often involving deferred payments, ours is characterized by the use of credit. The economic life of almost every person, and certainly every business and non-business organization, is touched by credit. The participation of individuals in credit processes, both as debtors and as creditors, is directly affected by the capitalistic, free, market nature of our economy. Second, being capitalistic, the credit system provides its participants as creditors with a degree of dominance or power over economic activities. Changes in the use of credit are watched as evidence of changes in general economic conditions. Third, the emergence and survival of credit power centers reflect the creativity of our entrepreneurs, the vitality of our competition, and the resiliency of our economic system to adapt itself to changing needs.

SECTORS OF THE CREDIT ECONOMY

Macro economic analysis is concerned not with individual credit transactions, but with interaction patterns among major groups of participants, or sectors, engaged in the credit processes. The financial sectors of the economy are the various types of suppliers of credit service and the types of users of credit. In our economy, however, creditors and debtors are not two different groups; they are two roles both of which the same individuals act. Thus the flow of credit service is not unidirectional; there is no one source of credit service or of the funds invested in credit operations, no one group of suppliers of credit service to another group of users of credit. The flows are multidirectional and circular. As depicted in Fig. 4–1, participants may simultaneously

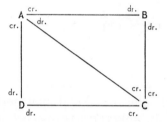

Fig. 4–1. Paired credit relationships.

be both creditor and debtor, in more than one relationship, and at the same time. Figure 4–2 shows how participants in different credit sectors may be sequentially related, forming a chain of creditors and debtors until the first creditor becomes the final debtor.

This multiple-role behavior of participants in our credit proc-

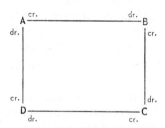

Fig. 4–2. Circular credit relationships.

esses results from the nature of our economy and is one of its special characteristics. It is a condition of capitalism, in which financial assets are mainly in private hands and widely distributed. It reflects economic specialization, in which individuals engage in numerous types of credit transactions—cash and sales credit, business and personal, short- and long-term. It suggests economic affluence and discretionary use of financial assets, whereby participants are found to be simultaneously in opposite credit roles.

The financial sectors of the whole economy reflect these role characteristics of individuals in their credit activities. First, the sectors may be classified like individuals, as follows:

Private	Public
Personal	Business
Financial	Non-financial
Bank	Non-bank
U.S. Government	State and local governments
Monetary	Credit

Second, each sector has both financial assets and liabilities—is at the same time both creditor and debtor. Third, private sectors are predominant; the U.S. Government, its monetary authorities, and the state and local governments together hold only 8.0 per cent of all financial assets and 24.1 per cent of all liabilities. Fourth, in addition to the non-financial suppliers of credit service, a sector of financial specialists has arisen to facilitate serving the credit needs of both private and public markets for credit service.

The financial statement of the entire economy, as shown in Table 4–1, includes $2,710.5 billion of financial assets and $2,053.4 billion of liabilities. These sums are unequal because this is a statement of *financial assets* and liabilities, not of *receivables* and liabilities. The assets include holdings of corporate stock, gold stock and foreign exchange, Treasury currency, and lendable but unloaned funds of financial institutions, which are unmatched by liabilities. When these non-credit elements are excluded, the credit assets and liabilities of all sectors are approximately $2,000 billion. This, however, is not the total of debt outstanding in our economy, for it does not include many unreported personal and institutional credit relationships. The published data nevertheless present a substantial record of credit and other financial activities from which some deductions may be drawn.

Table 4–1.　Financial Assets and Liabilities, December 31, 1964
(amounts in billions of dollars)

Sector	Assets		Liabilities	
Private domestic				
non-financial sectors	$1,671.0	61.6%	$ 859.9	41.9%
Households	1,305.2	48.2	313.4	15.3
Business	292.8	10.8	416.4	20.3
State and local				
governments	73.1	2.7	130.1	6.3
U.S. Government	84.7	3.1	303.3	14.8
Financial sectors	874.7	32.3	802.7	39.1
Monetary authorities	60.8	2.2	60.8	3.0
Commercial banks	306.8	11.3	284.0	13.8
Non-bank finance	507.1	18.7	457.8	22.3
Rest of world	80.0	3.0	87.6	4.3
All Sectors	$2,710.5	100.0%	$2,053.4	100.0%

SOURCE: *Federal Reserve Bulletin,* November, 1965, p. 1618.

In the rest of this chapter, three groups of sectors engaged in credit processes are discussed: private non-financial, financial, and U.S. Government.

PRIVATE NON-FINANCIAL SECTORS

The usual distinction between private and public sectors is not made in this analysis, nor is it in the government statistics upon which this is based, for, in addition to households and business, state and local governments are dealt with as a private sector. The reason is that in credit markets these public agencies act like private entities, selling their credit instruments and acquiring those of other debtors. The U.S. Government does the same thing, but it is distinguished by the character of its credit and by the influence it has over the entire credit system through its monetary authority, banking regulations, and financial agencies. Thus while from one viewpoint all government credit represents public responsibility, from another viewpoint only the federal government credit activities are "non-private."

Additional distinction is made between "non-financial" and "financial" sectors, the former using credit in personal consumption and in merchandising and service operations, the latter using their credit in providing cash credit service and in facilitating sales financing operations. (Further classification of credit operations is made in Chapter 11.)

Households

As non-financial private participants in the market for credit service, households possess 48.2 per cent of all financial assets and have 15.3 per cent of all liabilities. Households are comprised of individuals engaged in the processes of personal life. They are the principal owners of the economy, holding many types of assets: business enterprises, real estate, and personal property, in addition to *financial assets* including corporate securities and various credit claims—demand and savings deposits, claims against insurance and pension funds, and bond notes, and other receivables. Against more than $1,300 billion of financial assets, households have liabilities of $313 billion. Their financial assets reflect the range of private financial interests in an economy such as ours. Their liabilities reflect mainly the processes of living and consumption—the acquisition of residences and of consumption goods. Between 1951 and 1964, the financial assets of households increased 179 per cent; their liabilities increased 291 per cent.

The financial status of households has long been of special interest to economic analysts, for the relation of their debt to their means of liquidating their debt has been regarded as affecting economic stability. Proof of this influence, however, requires some understanding of the composition of households' assets and liabilities. The fact that households own financial assets of $1,000 billion in excess of their liabilities bespeaks their solvency. It does not, however, give assurance that they are able to liquidate their debts in accord with expectations nor that the economy is secure because of this margin of difference. Each type of asset has its intended use; life insurance reserves are an unlikely fund for paying short-term debt, although borrowing on those reserves for such purposes has increased. Moreover, the maturity cycles of different assets and liabilities progress at different rates, and mortgage debt cannot be equated with demand deposits nor consumer credit with government securities held. The uses of funds must be related to the sources of funds for different purposes, and consumer debt is usually related to consumer income rather than to consumer financial *assets* as a criterion of creditworthiness and of economic stability.

While mortgage debt is the largest single item in household liabilities, and while construction activity is a major factor in the economy, more significance is attached to volume and rate of production and distribution activities which are reflected in the portion of household liabilities termed "consumer credit." This represents the debt related to acquisition of consumer goods—automobiles, other durable goods, soft goods, and services—and to the loans which are obtained either for purchasing these items or for realigning the personal debt structure. These acquisitions are the ultimate objective of economic activity, and economic stability depends upon the ability of households to pay for its consumption debt.

As shown in Table 4–2, household liabilities outstanding in the form of consumer credit obligations were $76.8 billion at the end of 1964. This total is divided into its components in Table 4–3, $59.4 billion, or 77.3 per cent, being owed on instalment debt and $17.4 or 22.7 per cent on non-instalment. Divided on the basis of acquisitions, 60.0 per cent was for commodities purchased, 6.0 per cent for services, and 34.0 per cent for loans made. Debt for automobiles is the largest single item in the statement,

Table 4–2. Financial Assets and Liabilities of Households, 1964 (amounts outstanding at end of year in billions of dollars)

Total financial assets		*$1305.2*	*100.0%*
Demand deposits and currency		83.8	6.4
Savings accounts		253.0	19.4
Life insurance reserves		101.0	7.7
Pension fund reserves		136.6	10.5
Credit market instruments		714.4	54.7
U.S. Government securities	$ 76.0	5.8	
State and local obligations	36.6	2.8	
Corporate and foreign bonds	4.1	.3	
Corporate stock	586.5	44.9	
Mortgages	11.2	.8	
Security credit		1.2	.1
Miscellaneous		15.3	1.2
Total liabilities		$ *313.4*	*100.0%*
Credit market instruments		299.7	95.6
1- to 4-family mortgages	$188.1	60.0	
Other mortgages	13.1	4.2	
Consumer credit	76.8 ᵃ	24.5	
Bank loans n.e.c.	12.2	3.9	
Other loans	9.5	3.0	
Security credit		8.4	2.7
Trade credit		2.3	.7
Miscellaneous financial transactions		3.0	.9

ᵃ See Table 4–3.
SOURCE: *Federal Reserve Bulletin,* November, 1965, p. 1622.

Table 4–3.   Composition of Consumer Credit, 1964
(amounts outstanding at end of year in billions of dollars)

Acquisition	Manner of Payment					
	Instalment		Non-instalment		Total	
Commodities	$39.8	67.0%	$ 6.3	36.2%	$46.1	60.0%
Automobiles	24.5	41.2			24.5	31.9
Other consumer goods	15.3	25.8			15.3	19.9
Charge account items			6.3	36.2	6.3	8.2
Services			4.6	26.4	4.6	6.0
Loans	19.6	33.0	6.5	37.4	26.1	34.0
Repair and modernization	3.5	5.9			3.5	4.6
Personal loans	16.1	27.1			16.1	21.0
Single-payment loans			6.5		16.5	8.4
Total	$59.4	100%	$17.4	100%	$76.8	100%
	77.3%		22.7%		100%	

SOURCE: *Federal Reserve Bulletin,* November, 1965, p. 1592.

constituting almost one-third of the total. Personal instalment loans and other durable goods bought on instalment rank second and third in the array. Non-instalment charge account debt amounted to $6.3 billion or 8.2 per cent of the total. This is not to say that instalment *purchases* exceeded non-instalment credit purchases; the more rapid turnover of non-instalment accounts produces the relatively small residual outstanding.

A remarkable fact about consumer credit liabilities of the household sector is their rate of increase during the past two decades. Since 1950, the total of instalment and non-instalment debt increased from $21.4 billion to $86.0 billion in 1965, or an index increase from 100 to 402. During that time, the index of instalment debt increased to 460 and non-instalment debt to 262. (See Table 4–4.)

Table 4–4.   Index of Consumer Credit Outstanding, 1950–1965
1950 = 100

Year	Total	Instalment	Non-Instalment
1946	100	100	100
1965	402	460	262

SOURCE: *Federal Reserve Bulletin,* selected years.

This rise in consumer credit debt has been attributed to two influences: (1) changing environmental conditions affecting the use of credit and (2) the changing quality of consumer credit itself. It is unquestionable that changes in our economy and society have increased the use of credit and the amount of outstanding debt. This is a phenomenon to be observed. There continues a question, however, whether consumer credit terms have become so liberal, and whether consumer attitudes toward debt have so deteriorated, that the aggregate debt constitutes a collective threat to the economy.

Answers to this question have been sought in the relation of consumer debt to the size of the population, to changes in the price level, to changes in consumer purchasing power and to changes in consumption habits. Concurrent with the growth of consumer debt from $8.4 billion to $74.4 billion, the population of the United States increased from 141 million to 193 million (see Table 4–5). The per capita debt increased from $59 to $385, or an index increase from 100 to 652, in contrast to the total debt increase to a level of 884. During that period the consumer price index (1957–1959 = 100) rose from 68.0 to 108.1. When adjusted to price change, per capita debt rose from $87 to $356, or, expressed as an index, from 100 to 409. This is to say that more people were buying more commodities and services on credit than formerly.

This fact is self-evident to even a casual observer. Its explanation lies in the changes which have occurred in personal living in the decades following World War II and in the changes in buying habits as disposable income and discretionary purchasing power have increased. One need only consider the additional products which have become commonplace in personal and family living: high-fidelity and stereo equipment, television, power mowers, second cars in the family, boats, underwater and skiing equipment. Purchase of these postwar items would have been impossible, however, had after-taxes income not increased to the point where such purchases beyond basic consumption needs could be made.

After-taxes or disposable personal income has increased fourfold since 1946, while consumer credit outstanding has increased ninefold, with the result that as a percentage of spendable income that form of debt increased from 7.9 per cent to 17.1 per cent. It is known that as incomes increase, spending patterns change.

Table 4–5. Consumer Credit Outstanding in Relation to Population, Price Level and Disposable Personal Income, 1946–1966

(1) Year	(2) Instalment (billions)	(3) Non-Instalment (billions)	(4) (2)+(3) Total Consumer Credit (billions)	(5) Population (millions)	(6) (4)÷(5) Per Capita Debt (dollars)	(7) Consumer Price Index (BLS) 1957–59 = 100	(8) (6)÷(7) Adjusted Per Capita Debt	(9) Personal Disposable Income (billions)	(10) (4)÷(9) Consumer Debt as Per Cent of Disposable Personal Income (per cent)
1946	$ 4.2	$ 4.2	$ 8.4	141.4	$ 59	68.0	$ 87	$107	7.9
1947	6.7	4.9	11.6	144.1	80	77.8	103	170	6.8
1948	9.0	5.4	14.4	149.2	97	83.8	116	189	7.6
1949	11.6	5.7	17.3	151.1	115	83.0	138	190	9.1
1950	14.7	6.7	21.4	153.6	139	83.8	166	208	10.3
1951	15.3	7.3	22.6	156.3	145	90.5	160	228	9.9
1952	19.4	8.0	27.4	159.0	172	92.5	186	239	11.5
1953	23.0	8.2	31.2	161.7	193	93.2	207	253	12.3
1954	23.5	8.9	32.5	164.6	197	93.6	210	257	12.6
1955	28.9	9.9	38.8	167.5	232	93.4	248	274	14.2
1956	31.7	10.6	42.3	170.6	248	94.7	262	293	14.4
1957	33.9	11.1	44.9	173.5	259	98.0	264	309	14.5
1958	33.6	11.3	45.1	176.5	256	100.7	254	318	14.2
1959	39.2	12.3	51.5	179.4	287	101.5	283	337	15.3
1960	42.8	13.2	56.0	182.3	307	103.1	298	350	16.0
1961	43.5	14.2	57.7	185.3	311	104.2	298	364	15.9
1962	48.0	15.1	63.2	188.2	337	105.4	320	384	16.5
1963	53.7	16.1	69.9	190.8	366	106.7	343	404	17.3
1964	58.1	16.3	74.4	193.1	385	108.1	356	436	17.1
1965	67.4	18.6	86.0	195.6	440	110.6	398	465	18.5

SOURCES: *Federal Reserve Bulletin; United States Department of Commerce, Business Statistics, 1965; Statistical Abstracts of U.S.*

53

Basic necessities require a progressively smaller percentage of income, and relatively large amounts are left to the discretionary spending of the individual. This increment of income is directed toward the purchase of items generally bought on credit, specifically instalment credit. The question of the soundness of consumer debt in the household sector, therefore, relates to the adequacy of discretionary income to meet debt resulting from the purchase of so-called "non-essentials." [1]

In a study of consumer debt related to discretionary income, as computed by the J. Walter Thompson Company and by the National Industrial Conference Board, Reavis Cox observes [2] that consumer debtors have behaved in ways which suggest the soundness of their debt. Their fixed commitments, both short-term and long-term, have increased but not at a faster rate than their spending power. Their payments combining interest and debt retirement have never since 1945 exceeded 12 per cent of consumers' personal income. Their indebtedness has never exceeded by more than 20 per cent what consumers have paid out as principal and interest payments in one year. In other words, outstandings could be liquidated in little more than one year if payments to service present consumer debts were applied to the extinction of those debts. Their total consumer credit obligations do not exceed more than from 50 to 65 per cent of discretionary income, leaving cushion for their debt. Accordingly, Cox concludes, "In the aggregate, consumers could take a very drastic cut in their incomes without finding that they had to choose between defaulting on their obligations and cutting down on expenditures for 'essentials' or 'necessities,' even if these terms are defined very liberally." [3]

Business

The private business sector of the economy is a second major complex of credit patterns. Business establishments constitute a primary market for credit service—they use their credit in acquiring commodities and cash which are essential to the performance of the functions they undertake. At the same time, they

[1] See Arno H. Johnson, "Discretionary Spending Power and Consumer Credit," *The Credit World*, April, 1965, p. 12; and *Industrial Banker and Time Sales Financing*, March, 1965, p. 3.

[2] Reavis Cox, *Consumers' Credit and Wealth* (Washington, D.C.: National Foundation for Consumer Credit, 1965), pp. 41–42.

[3] *Ibid.*, p. 42.

Table 4–6. Financial Assets and Liabilities of the Business Sector, December 31, 1964
(amounts outstanding in billions of dollars)

Financial Assets			Liabilities		
Deposits	$ 60.1	19.6%	Corporate bonds	$ 92.4	21.5%
Government securities	20.7	6.8	Mortgages	70.2	16.3
Consumer credit	18.4	6.0	Bank loans	60.3	14.0
Loans	5.9	1.9	Other loans	20.8	4.8
Trade credit	144.9a	47.3	Taxes payable	17.6	4.1
Miscellaneous financial			Trade debt	110.9a	25.9
transactions	56.3	18.4	Miscellaneous financial		
			transactions	57.6	13.4
	$306.3	100.0%		$429.8	100.0%

a *Total* debts and receivables stated for all categories.
SOURCE: *Federal Reserve Bulletin,* November, 1965, p. 1623.

are suppliers of credit service to other private and public sectors which buy their products and services. The relative proportions of their debt and their credits reflect changes in business policies and economic circumstances over the years.

The credit of the business sector includes all receivables and payables carried on the books of business enterprises. Farm business and non-corporate and corporate non-financial business establishments comprise this sector. As reported by the Federal Reserve Board, the business sector in 1964 had financial assets (credits) of $306.3 billion and liabilities (debts) of $429.8 billion.[4] This represented 11 per cent of all financial assets and 20 per cent of all liabilities. The business sector, in other words, uses more credit in its acquisitions than it supplies credit service to other sectors of the economy. This indicates the extent to which the business sector is dependent upon credit, for the performance of its own credit service and for its other functions.

The uses of credit by business are observable in the composition of its financial assets and liabilities, as shown in Table 4–6. Chief among its financial assets—its claims against others to whom private non-financial business establishments supply credit service—are the following: demand and time deposits, government securities, consumer credit accounts, trade credit, loans on open market paper, and receivables from miscellaneous financial transactions. Foremost among its liabilities, representing use which

[4] "Flow of Funds," *Federal Reserve Bulletin,* November, 1965, p. 1623. Adjustment has been made to include *all* non-corporate non-financial business trade debt and trade receivables, rather than only *net* trade credit assets.

business has made of its own credit for acquiring cash, commodities, and service, are the following: corporate bonds, mortgages, bank and other loans, taxes payable, trade debt, and miscellaneous financial transactions. Of all private sectors, business alone has more liabilities than financial assets, re-emphasizing the importance of credit service in the conduct of business, but suggesting also the adequacy of other financial sectors for meeting these needs in business.

Although business uses many types of credit service, the trade, or business itself, is the principal supplier *and* user of business credit service. In 1964, the business sector held credits from the trade amounting to $144.9 billion, or 47.3 per cent of all its financial assets. At the same time, this sector owed $110.9 billion to the trade. It will be noted that whereas the business sector is a net *debtor* in the economy, it is a net *creditor* with respect to trade transactions. More than 53 per cent of the financial assets of the business sector consist of claims against consumers and business establishments resulting from the movement of goods and services through trade channels. Funds for carrying this surplus of receivables are obtained from various forms of equity and debt financing.

As indicated in Table 4–7, the role of the business sector in

Table 4–7. Trade Credit and Trade Debt Held by the Business Sector,[a]
1951–64
(amounts outstanding at end of year, in billions of dollars)

Year	Trade Credit	Trade Debt	Net Trade Credit	Ratio—Trade Credit: Debt
1951	$58.0	$47.0	$11.0	123.4
1952	62.7	50.2	12.5	124.9
1953	62.6	51.9	10.7	120.6
1954	67.2	56.2	11.0	119.6
1955	78.3	66.0	12.3	118.6
1956	87.2	72.8	14.4	119.8
1957	89.7	74.1	15.6	121.1
1958	98.3	80.1	18.2	122.7
1959	104.9	85.5	19.4	117.3
1960	110.9	89.4	21.5	124.0
1961	120.6	96.9	23.7	124.5
1962	128.4	101.6	26.8	126.4
1963	136.1	107.7	28.4	126.4
1964	144.9	110.9	33.6	130.0

[a] Includes trade receivables and debt of farm business, non-corporate non-financial business, and corporate non-financial business.

SOURCE: *Federal Reserve Bulletin,* November, 1965, p. 1623.

financing trade credit is increasing. Between 1951 and 1964, trade liabilities of the business sector increased 136 per cent from $47 billion to $110.9 billion. At the same time, receivables held due from the trade increased 155 per cent from $58 billion to $144.9 billion. In 1964, credit held exceeded business debt to the trade by 30 per cent.

Three explanations are offered for this increase of net trade credit. One is that, willingly or unwillingly, the business sector is assuming increased responsibility for financing trade. If it did not do this, trade and trade increases would be financed by financial rather than by non-financial institutions, whether by banks or non-banks. The widening gap of trade credit over trade liabilities held by business indicates that it has assumed this function in some measure and thus has evolved a new credit pattern.

The magnitude and character of this credit trend are best shown by comparisons with some others. Between 1950 and 1964, the following trends are reported: [5]

	Per Cent
Trade receivables held by corporations	+ 208.1
Corporate manufacturers' trade notes and accounts receivable	+ 124.4
Total commercial bank loans	+ 215.1
Bank loans to business	+ 151.6
Inventories held by corporations	+ 101.8
Net working capital of corporations	+ 95.3
Sales by corporate manufacturers	+ 75.3

Trade receivables held by corporate business increased 176 per cent, while those held by non-corporate business increased only 28 per cent. Receivables held by manufacturers increased less than those held by all trade establishments; trade credit expanded twice as fast as inventories; and receivables became second in importance to plant investment in many corporation statements.[6] According to the National Bureau of Economic Research,[7] trade credit during the period of 1954–1957 represented 16 per cent of the assets of manufacturing companies, 33 per cent of the assets of wholesale companies, and 48 per cent of the assets of construction companies. Assumption of this responsibility has presented busi-

[5] Statistics of the Securities and Exchange Commission and of the U.S. Treasury, Internal Revenue Service.

[6] Otto Steinhaus, "Is Credit Dangerously Swollen?" *Credit and Financial Management,* February, 1964, p. 10.

[7] "Trade Credit Zooms Up," *Business Week,* April 25, 1964.

ness with new problems of financing its additional investment in trade credit.

A second explanation of growing trade credit financing by business lies in the basic responsibility business has always had to supply credit service to the trade. Ability to carry receivables has characterized wholesalers, and a prerequisite to engaging in wholesaling has been the possession of funds or access to lines of credit. Corporations have qualified for this better than non-corporate businesses, so that corporations not only supply non-corporate businesses with credit service in normal times but give additional support in recession periods.[8] Net credit extended to unincorporated businesses by corporations tended to increase sharply during the recessions of 1949, 1954, and 1958, when at the same time bank loans to the smaller businesses were below normal. Thus the business sector follows a trade credit pattern different from that of the financial sectors. Within the long-run secular trend of increasing trade credit moves a cyclical trend which may be counter to short-run business conditions.

A third explanation for trade credit trends of the business sector lies in the quality of trade credit as influenced by both creditor and debtor circumstances. The increase of trade receivables is attributed to (1) greater leniency in credit granting and (2) unwillingness or inability of trade customers to pay as promptly as previously. Leniency is found in lengthened credit terms, in decreased ratios of receivables to sales, and in diminished collection rates.[9] These effects are often voluntarily produced in the effort to increase credit sales, but they may also be accompanied by lower quality receivables. The fact that receivables rose from 35 days to 45 days for all manufacturers from 1955 to 1962 has been linked with another fact: that business failure liabilities were at an all-time high in 1963.

Evidence of a trend toward increased supplying of credit service to the business sector through trade credit carried by the business sector is no proof that new credit patterns are a sign of credit deterioration. Like new patterns of consumer credit, this may reflect only new ways of conducting credit business, which in turn may result in changed debtor–creditor relationships, new credit institutions, and new charges for credit service.

[8] Robert W. Johnson, "More Scope for Credit Managers," *Harvard Business Review*, November–December, 1961, p. 113.
[9] *Ibid.*, pp. 109–20.

FINANCIAL SECTORS

A second segment of the economy consists of financial sectors, whose purpose is to provide credit service to the non-financial sectors: to households and businesses (private sectors) and to local and state governments and the U.S. Government (public sectors). The financial sectors, facilitating the processes of production, distribution, and consumption, include non-bank financial institutions, banks, and monetary authorities or agencies of the U.S. Government. They assemble and create funds and make them available to primary markets for credit service and to other financial institutions.

The role played by financial sectors is measured by the fact that in 1964 they had financial assets of $874.7 billion and liabilities of $802.7 billion. This represented 33 per cent of all financial assets in the economy and 38 per cent of all liabilities. Whereas the business sector has liabilities in excess of the financial assets, indicating that debt financing is relied upon heavily for other than financial assets, banks and non-bank sectors have financial assets in excess of liabilities, indicating that (1) equity capital provides much of their lendable funds and (2) member banks by reason of their reserves with the Federal Reserve Bank can lend funds for which there is no comparable equity or debt source.

Commercial Banks

A principal financial sector of the economy is the commercial bank. Larger than any other type of the financial institutions, it has 11 per cent of the financial assets and 13 per cent of the liabilities of the economy. Its magnitude reflects the multiple role which it plays in credit systems serving public and private, business and household, financial and non-financial sectors. The commercial bank is a financial middleman, obtaining its funds mainly through deposits placed with it and dispensing them through loans.

The financial assets of commercial banks are derived almost equally from demand and time deposits. These two types of funds, however, are not obtained equally from the same depositors, nor are loans made to sectors proportionate to their contribution of funds. As is shown in Table 4–8, 68 per cent of the

Table 4–8.   Sources and Uses of Funds in Commercial Banks,
by Sectors, 1964
(amounts outstanding at end of year, in billions of dollars)

Sectors	Sources of Funds				Uses of Funds— Loans Made	
	Demand Deposits	Time Deposits	Total			
Households	$ 83.8	$ 94.8	$178.6	68%	$ 56.4	24%
Business	44.6	15.4	60.0	23	77.6	34
Governments	6.5	10.1	16.6	6	100.2	42
U.S.	6.5	.3			66.7	
State and local		9.8			33.5	
Foreign		6.7	6.7	2	—	
Total	$134.9	$127.0	$261.9	100%	$234.2	100%

SOURCE: *Federal Reserve Bulletin*, November, 1965, p. 1625.

demand and time deposits are contributed by households and 23
per cent by businesses. Businesses have three-fourths of their
deposits in demand accounts, while households have a preponderance of time accounts. Similarly, the U.S. Government
holds mainly demand deposits, while state and local governments
place their funds in time deposits.

The loan portion of the financial assets of commercial banks
differs also from its liabilities. Whereas households contribute
68 per cent of the deposits of the commercial banks, they account
for only 24 per cent of the loans made, divided almost equally between consumer credit debt and debt on 1–4 family mortgages.
The business sector contributes 23 per cent of the deposits but
takes 33 per cent of the loans. A larger discrepancy occurs in relations with government sectors, for whereas both the U.S. and
state and local governments make 6 per cent of the deposits they
have 42 per cent of the loans. The proportions of these market
segments have changed; the percentage of loans made by commercial banks to the various sectors in 1951 and 1964 were:

Loans Made	1951	1964
To households	15%	24%
To business	26	33
To governments	59	43
	100%	100%

These shifts in the patterns of credit services reflect the fact
that during this interval U.S. Government obligations to commercial banks, on the whole, remained stable, although their
composition often changed greatly from year to year. At the

same time, the borrowing of state and local governments from commercial banks increased fourfold, but the total of government loans did not increase at the rate of private borrowing. During this period, commercial bank loans to private sectors increased for all purposes: for consumer credit and home mortgages and for business loans and mortgages. This was a period in which commercial banks significantly extended their instalment credit loans and financing and in which their loans to non-corporate non-financial businesses were trebled, while other business loans more than doubled.

Non-Bank Sectors

The non-bank financial institutions of the economy likewise play a distinct and unique role in the nation's credit system. Using mainly funds of individuals collected through savings accounts and through payments to pension and insurance reserves, they supply credit service almost entirely to the private sectors of the economy. The financial institutions of this group include insurance companies, private pension funds, savings and loan associations, mutual savings banks, finance companies, credit unions, and a few others of lesser credit significance.

The total non-bank financial group holds 18 and 22 per cent of the financial assets and liabilities of the economy, respectively. The sources and uses of these funds, however, differ from other sectors and present distinct credit patterns. Whereas only 15 per cent of their $457.8 billion of liabilities are obtained through credit market instruments, 93 per cent of their financial assets consist of loans made through the use of such instruments. The principal sources of their funds are insurance and pension funds (40 per cent) and time and savings deposits (35 per cent); about 10 per cent are obtained through issuance of corporate bonds and stock. Only 2 per cent of their liabilities are in the form of bank loans. Thus the importance of their function in channeling *saved* funds into credit channels is apparent. As shown in Table 4–9, the uses of their funds are equally distinct. As percentages of the total financial assets of this sector, they rank as follows:

	Per Cent
Mortgage loans	40.0
Corporate stock and bonds	33.0
Government securities	10.0
Consumer credit	5.7
Trade credit	0.5

Table 4–9. Use of Funds Made by the Non-bank Financial Sectors, 1964
(per cent of sector's financial assets)

Non-bank Financial Sectors	U.S. Government Securities	State and Local Government Securities	Corporate Stock and Bonds	Consumer Credit	Trade Credit	Mortgages
		Financial Assets Held to Non-bank Financial Sectors				
Insurance companies	6.3	8.0	45.5	None	1.3	38.0
Private pension funds	6.1	None	87.8	None	None	4.3
Savings and loan associations	6.4	None	None	1.1	None	84.9
Mutual savings banks	12.0	Nil	8.1	Nil	None	75.0
Finance companies	None	None	None	57.3	None	10.8
Credit unions	None	None	None	79.2	None	Nil

SOURCE: *Federal Reserve Bulletin*, November, 1965, p. 1619.

The evident purpose of this sector is to provide long-term credit service to private users of credit—to business through investment in corporate stocks and bonds and to both households and business through mortgage loans. Loans to the public sector and short-term credit services to the private sector are minimal. Within this general framework, there is further specialization of certain sectors. The financial assets of insurance companies consist mainly of corporate stocks and bonds and of mortgages; private pension funds, of stocks and bonds; savings and loan associations and mutual savings banks, of mortgages; and finance companies and credit unions, of consumer credit. These financial sectors are chiefly suppliers of credit service to the primary markets.

There have also been several trends in the credit patterns of the non-bank sectors, as shown in Table 4–10. Between 1951 and

Table 4–10. Financial Assets and Liabilities of Non-bank
Financial Sectors, 1951 and 1964
(year-end outstandings in billions of dollars)

Sectors	Financial Assets				Liabilities			
	1951		1964		1951		1964	
Insurance companies	$ 74.1	48.8%	$182.3	36.0%	$ 63.2	47.5%	$142.5	31.5%
Private pension funds	7.4	4.8	62.3	12.3	7.4	5.5	62.3	13.6
Savings and loan associations	19.2	12.6	119.3	23.5	17.8	13.3	111.4	24.2
Mutual savings banks	23.5	15.5	54.2	10.7	21.1	15.8	49.8	10.9
Finance companies	9.8	6.4	36.3	7.1	6.1	4.5	31.3	6.8
Credit unions	11.8	11.7	8.2	1.6	17.4	13.1	8.2	1.8
Others			44.5	8.7			52.3	11.4
Total	$151.8	100.0%	$507.1	100.0%	$133.0	100.0%	$457.8	100.0%

SOURCE: *Federal Reserve Bulletin*, November, 1965, pp. 1618, 1619, 1625, 1626.

1964, insurance companies and mutual savings banks had a declining portion of the financial assets and liabilities of this group. Private pension funds, savings and loan associations, finance companies, and credit unions had an increasing portion. These changes are attributable to the increased popularity of consumer instalment credit, to rate differentials among competing sectors, to the growth of pension plans, and to the increasing prevalence of savings throughout the economy.

GOVERNMENT SECTORS

Although the U.S. Government and state and local governments are public agencies, their roles in the credit market differ. Both use their credit for obtaining goods and services needed for the performance of their functions. Both have liabilities in excess of their financial assets. Both issue their own securities and credit obligations. Apart from these similarities, they differ in that the state and local governments behave much like private sectors, whereas the U.S. Government acts to augment the service of other credit sectors. The U.S. Government not only backs the private banking system with the Federal Reserve System to assure flows of funds as needed by the economy; it also provides credit service directly through its several agencies and indirectly through its guarantee and underwriting of credit risks.

State and local governments in 1964 had financial assets of $73.1 billion and liabilities of $130.1 billion. Seventy per cent of their obligations resulted from issuance of their own notes and bonds; another 23 per cent from holding pension funds. When not put to other uses, and to provide necessary liquid reserves, their financial assets were distributed like those of other private sectors, in time and demand deposits at commercial banks, in government and corporate obligations.

The U.S. Government, on the other hand, with financial assets of $84.7 billion and liabilities of $303.3 billion, had 88 per cent of its debt outstanding in the various forms of government securities. Its principal financial assets consisted of mortgage and other federal loans, claims against taxes payable, currency, and international monetary and credit balances.

DISCUSSION QUESTIONS

1. What circumstances of our economy produce the effect of all sectors being both debtors and creditors? Is this true of all individuals presented by the sectors?
2. Prepare a matrix relating financial and non-financial sectors with private and public sectors. Insert current statistics for each classification.

3. Explain the financial assets and liabilities of households in terms of the concept of market segmentation.
4. Appraise the consumers' indebtedness in terms of the fact that their debt is paid out of income rather than out of other assets—financial or otherwise.
5. Examine and appraise recent articles concerning consumer indebtedness in the light of the analysis made in this chapter.
6. Why, when liabilities of the business sector, in general, exceed its financial assets, do trade receivables held by businesses exceed trade debt?
7. Compare or contrast the factors which have led to the increase of both consumer debt and business debt.
8. What role is played by commercial banks in the credit system?
9. To what extent, and in what ways, are the sectors supplying credit service either competitive or non-competitive?
10. What unique characteristics has the behavior of governments in credit markets?

III

THE FUNCTIONAL
CHARACTER OF CREDIT

5

Objectives and Functions of Credit Management

Although credit is a phenomenon found in certain social and economic circumstances, it is also a process to be managed in the firm, and this aspect of credit is of primary immediate concern. As a management process, credit is a means of attaining determined ends; it is not undertaken for its own sake. In this respect, credit management is comparable to the management of other business processes. Yet, like each, the management of credit is unique in that it has distinct objectives and particular functions or processes for attaining them. These ends and means in the use of credit are the subject of this chapter.

MANAGEMENT OBJECTIVES

The performance of credit services is undertaken as a means of attaining objectives of the business organization. As seen previously, society has its objective in sanctioning and encouraging credit business: to be provided the assortment and volume of credit service requisite to meet the varied needs of business and personal consumption. Management likewise has its objectives in supplying credit service, whether in conjunction with the sale of a product or only in the sale of credit service alone. Pursuit of its objectives commits management to the performance of certain functions and to the assumption of related responsibilities. Management, however, has not a single objective in the use of credit. Its objectives are multiple, distributed among all levels of management. The objectives of management on three organizational levels are here considered.

Objectives of Top Management

Top management alone is charged with certain responsibilities in business, and it is therefore to top management that fall decisions in providing credit service which affect the over-all character and operation of the business. In general, management objectives fall into three categories, depending upon whether they relate to the needs of consumers, owners, or others. These objectives are sometimes identified as primary service objectives of the organization, profit objectives, and efficiency objectives. However stated, the first two types are directly the responsibility of top management, for it is they who must decide the character of the business, as determined by its product, services, and markets, and they who must conceive, innovate, and administer ways of turning a service objective into a profit for owners.

It is the prerogative of top management, therefore, to select objectives which are attainable through the offering of credit service. To supply or not to supply such service is the basic consideration. However this is decided, it affects the character of the business, determines its competition, its total product offering, its costs, its image in the mind of the public, its responsibility to public authorities. Such a decision rests primarily upon perception of market opportunity and confidence in one's ability to supply it.

When the existence of a market opportunity is assured, top management is responsible not only for the decision to exploit it but also for selection of the manner in which this is to be done profitably. Thus selection of forms of credit service, credit terms, degree of calculated risk assumption, services to be performed or purchased, and means of financing the operation are decisions for top management which are inseparable from its overriding objectives to perform a service and to do so profitably. In the making of these decisions, several factors are taken into consideration:

Market Analysis. In determining its objectives, top management requires an analysis of the market for credit service, as it would for any other product it offered for sale. Evidence of customers' preferences for credit service may be discovered. Some expect it as a convenience; others as a necessity. Buying motives of customers may be analyzed. The amount of service required by customers may also be ascertained. Customers' needs depend in part upon the type of goods sold. Expensive consumer goods are usually sold in connection with credit service; convenience goods infrequently require credit. Industrial customers also have needs and preferences relating to credit service.

As a basis of decisions concerning credit promotion, the market analyst attempts to ascertain the elasticity of demand for credit and for products sold on credit. Demand that has a credit elasticity expands with the increasing availability of credit service; contrariwise, it contracts. Thus management attempts to determine whether an offering of credit would substantially, or only slightly, alter the demand schedule for its products. Both mercantile and retail demand have a factor of response to credit, and in some circumstances it is more pronounced than in others.

Differential Advantage Sought. The decision of top management to offer credit service is sometimes no decision; circumstances provide no choice. If credit is commonly offered in a line of trade, not to so do would put a business at a competitive disadvantage. Profit objectives would thereby be affected by reticence to supply a market demand. On the other hand, although competitors may be on a par with respect to their credit offerings, the manner in which they offer or administer this service may provide them a differential advantage. It may give them a uniqueness in customers' eyes which contributes to achievement of their objectives.

Break-even Point. The offering of a credit service is a costly undertaking, and this must be recognized in deciding whether this is a suitable means of accomplishing corporate objectives. As retail food stores during the so-called chain store era undertook to reduce prices and costs, credit service along with some other services was eliminated. Similarly, manufacturers have refused to give cash discounts on the grounds that their profit was insufficient to permit it. Normally, the offering of credit service involves costs which must be borne in the operating margin. Whether these are passed on to customers in the form of higher prices depends upon the elasticity of demand and the point in volume of sales where, credit costs included, the firm will make a profit. Management must make some effort to ascertain the relation of a credit policy to the break-even point when making its credit decisions.

Ability To Perform. Even though the adoption of a credit policy may be highly desirable, consideration must be given to the ability to carry out the policy. Not the least important is the availability of funds. Adoption of a credit policy imposes a demand for increased working capital. Moreover, the competence of existing staff or additional personnel to handle the credit operation must be considered. The human element is large in credit management, and the right individual for the position may determine the difference between success and failure in the operation. Finally, attention must be given to the availability of services needed, such as credit bureaus and agencies, which play an important part in successful credit management.

Objectives of Middle Management

Depending upon how a business is organized, individuals in middle management positions also have objectives achievable through credit. Two positions on the middle management level which have such an interest are the manager of finance and the marketing manager. To the extent that they have been delegated responsibilities which concern primarily top management, their interests are identical. To middle management, however, usually falls some responsibility for achieving efficiency and economy. Thus one finds on this level a blending of service, profit, and efficiency objectives.

As credit consigns working capital of a business to certain uses, the financial manager, consistent with expectations of owners, and consistent with the broad objectives of top management, undertakes to make the best utilization of funds. Whether they be on hand or obtained, he is concerned with the productive and economical use of them. Traditionally, the financial manager has objectives which reflect caution rather than promotion. He expects through the offering of credit service to account satisfactorily to investors of funds in the business.

The marketing manager is another position with distinct objectives contributing to the use of credit. Credit to him is a means of achieving sales goals, reaching markets, developing customers, meeting competition, differentiating his offering, providing talking points, etc. His objectives are more promotional than cautious.

Objectives of Credit Manager

Depending again upon the organization of a business, objectives for the use of credit may be found on the operational level of credit management. In Chapter 18, attention is given to the division of credit management among several levels of responsibility. Here emphasis is placed upon the objectives held in positions outside the credit organization which are attainable through the offering of credit service. The manner in which the broad service and profit objectives are implemented in operations varies, but in every company providing credit service responsibility for efficiency objectives must be clearly assigned. Such objectives usually become those of the manager of the credit operation, whose concern is efficiency and economy in the utilization of personnel, supplies, resources, working capital, and time. Whereas other levels of management have objectives attainable *through* the offering of credit service, those of the operational manager are objectives attainable *in* the offering of credit service.

MANAGEMENT FUNCTIONS AND STRATEGY

Whatever the level of management, attainment of its objectives relative to credit service depends upon *management* of the requisite processes and resources. This calls for skill in the application of general management concepts and theory and understanding of the particular functions of credit to be managed.

Basically, management is the process of planning, organizing, and controlling activity. Applied to credit business, these processes occur on all levels of administration. Planning entails formulation of policies, rules, goals, and objectives; laying out of procedures; construction of models of performance and appraisal. Organizing involves the development of work groups and facilities, training of personnel, acquisition of funds, establishment of contacts with external services and suppliers, and direction and supervision of activities. Controlling is the relating of performance to plans and performance standards, determination of corrective action, administration of rewards and penalties, and adjustment of standards and plans.

Management may also be regarded as a process of combining

and coordinating a variety of factors which contribute to achievement of objectives. These factors, or variables, are the means or causal influences which produce certain results. Management skill is evidenced by the success attained through the selection and combination of these variables. Factors may be combined in varying proportions, with differing degrees of emphasis, and in different sequence; their specific combination constitutes what is sometimes termed a "mix" of variables. The factors to be managed and the particular combination of them is considered a "management mix," which represents a manager's judgment as to how his objectives can be achieved.

Each level of credit management has its own objectives, its own sets of factors relating to these objectives, its own "mix." Top management, for example, in accomplishing the credit objectives for which it is responsible, has at its disposal credit service (or the absence of credit service), products, working capital, fixed assets, and peers among resources, competitors, and market organizations. The role which credit plays in the mix of top management factors depends upon the philosophy, business acumen, innovativeness, and general outlook of the management executives.

On the middle management level, credit plays another, although related, role in achievement of marketing objectives. Marketing managers in seeking to attain sales and profit goals have at their command a number of means by which they seek to accomplish their objectives. Among them are products and product assortment, packaging, brand names and trademarks, advertising, personal selling, sales promotion, distribution channels and outlets, and—not the least—credit. Credit is thus combined with other elements in the marketing mix, in proportions and with emphasis deemed most appropriate, as a means of producing results. Marketing strategy in one instance may be built upon minimal emphasis of credit and maximum promotional effort; in another, upon liberal credit terms and credit authorization reflecting a generous policy of credit. Credit, however, is the *means;* it is not the end or objective.

Finally, the position of credit manager has its own objectives, means factors, and credit mix. Its objectives are largely efficiency and economy objectives, except as it shares or assumes service and profit objectives of others. Its means for accomplishing these objectives include personnel, paper forms, files, equipment, outside resources, and capital. These, too, are combined in varying proportions in different credit operations, illustrating the diversity of management strategies applicable to this phase of business.

Still another approach by which the functions of credit management may be interpreted is that, in addition to representing the application of general management principles to a specialized function, or combining variables in mixes appropriate to management levels, it consists of the performance of functions inherent in the credit process. As named before, they are the utilization of funds allocated to and invested in receivables, the assumption of a calculated credit risk, and the performance of a routine of credit departmental activities. Each of these is subject to management strategies which undertake to perform them or to shift the performance of them to other credit specialists. The management of these functions is the subject of the three following chapters.

DISCUSSION QUESTIONS

1. Explain the concept "management by objective" in terms of the management of credit.
2. Relate the management concept of "objectives" with the sociological concept of "role expectations."
3. Trace the objectives of management in offering credit service through the past century. Compare them with the objectives found in different industries, companies, and nations today.
4. Distinguish between the managerial objectives related to credit which might be delegated to lower levels of management and those which cannot be.
5. Correlate for several levels of management or managerial positions (1) its objectives and (2) the means available to it through the use of credit service of accomplishing these objectives.
6. Illustrate the idea that the elements in the marketing mix, including credit service, are variously combined and proportioned by equally competent managers.
7. Prepare a matrix of management variables, one side of which consists of the functions of planning, organizing, and controlling, and the other side of which is the three functions inherent in credit management. Illustrate the management activity which would be found in each of the coordinate boxes.
8. What correlation is there between the objectives of credit managers and those of other participants in the credit processes?

6

Capital Investment
Required by Credit

Although the three functions inherent in credit business are inseparable, the investing of funds in receivables resulting from credit transactions is principal. It is the substance of the credit relationship. Risk and operations are ancillary. Risk is the risk of return of the capital; operations is the process of administering the allocation and transfer of the capital.

Investment of funds in credit business, however, cannot be thought of merely as a *finance* function. It is, rather, a *financing* function—the financing of markets and marketing. Until credit transactions are consummated, the investment resides in "merchandise inventory"; thereafter it is in inventory which has moved on into the market, either as users or distributors of the goods. It is the implications of the investment in the credit process with which this chapter is concerned.

While the credit financing function has always been important, recognition of its importance is increasing. Formerly, the capital requirements for receivables were not always planned; they were accommodated as they arose. Today, in both mercantile and retail credit, needs for credit capital have increased to the point where they must be handled as an integral part of the financial structure of the organization. In many large retail establishments, receivables now are the largest asset item, exceeding real

76

estate and even merchandise inventory. The position of the investment in receivables made by one of the nation's largest retailing firms [1] illustrates its relative importance:

	Per Cent	
Cash	7.1	
Accounts receivable	34.0	
Merchandise inventory	25.0	
Supplies and prepaid expenses	1.3	
Total current assets		67.4
Investment in subsidiaries	.9	
Real estate not used in operations	1.8	
Miscellaneous	.9	
Property and equipment	29.0	
Total other assets		32.6
Total assets		100.0

The increase of instalment and revolving accounts has contributed to this. The accounts receivable included in this statement are actually only 70 per cent of the total receivables generated by their credit business. About 26 per cent had been sold without recourse, thus shifting the financing and risk functions to other credit specialists; the remaining 4 per cent represented a provision for future losses. Such an investment in receivables has been made necessary in retailing by the increase of sales volume, as well as by the increased use of instalment and other deferred payment credit.

Similarly, manufacturers are also today making larger capital investments in receivables. This has resulted less from new forms of accounts than from a larger percentage of business done on credit and from the lengthening of the collection period. In 1955, manufacturers' accounts receivable were 36.6 per cent of their total sales; in 1963, 48.9 per cent, and in 1965, 45.3 per cent. During the same period, the average number of days that sales were outstanding increased from 32.9 in 1955 to 44.0 in 1963.[2] Both factors indicate pressure on financing which increased manufacturers' investment in accounts receivable from $29 billion in 1955 to $52.9 billion in 1964. In response to this need, many manufacturers have established subsidiary finance companies to facilitate term-credit operations. Although many of them operate on borrowed capital, this gives further evidence of the function of cus-

[1] Federated Department Stores, Inc., Balance Sheet, 1962.
[2] "Newsletter," *Credit and Financial Management*, April, 1965, p. 23.

tomer financing settling upon vendors and becoming an increasingly important management responsibility.[3] The function of financing, which ultimately falls to buyers, and which at times has been assumed by banks and other finance specialists, seems increasingly today to devolve upon manufacturers and merchandisers. They, of course, have the choice of managing this investment function themselves in the form of their own receivables, or of shifting it to specialists who serve them rather than serving the vendors' customers directly.

CREDIT IN THE FINANCIAL STATEMENTS

The decision to conduct business on a credit basis imposes an obligation which is felt throughout the financial structure of the organization and is evidenced in both the balance sheet and the profit and loss statement.

Both lenders and vendors add to their balance sheet a current asset item which is generally designated as "receivables." Depending upon the type of business, several types of receivables may be identified. One is the "accounts receivable," which usually represent an open relationship between the seller and the buyer, whereby repeated credit transactions and payments are made on the same contractual understanding. Some vendors make further distinction between types of accounts receivable, identifying regular or 30-day accounts; extended accounts; and instalment accounts, which are usually evidenced by a note but which may have add-on purchase privileges. The capital required for each depends upon the character of the business and the turnover rates of the respective accounts.

Notes receivable represent another type of receivable held by both vendors and lenders. These are of single payment or instalment types. Acceptances, including sight and time drafts and trade acceptances, are still another form of receivable sometimes carried in the assets of manufacturers and wholesalers.

In anticipation of carrying receivables, creditors must be prepared to finance them. This requires that sufficient capital be available or accessible for supplying the receivables as they

[3] See "The Great Credit Pump," *Fortune*, February, 1963; Robert W. Johnson, "More Scope for Credit Managers," *The Harvard Business Review*, November–December, 1961; and David W. Christopher, "When Manufacturers Become Bankers," *Credit and Financial Management*, May, 1964, p. 10.

emerge, but it does not imply that a specific fund must be obtained at the time of each credit transaction. On the contrary, the fund which becomes a receivable for any specific transaction may already be in the balance sheet at the time of the transaction and is transposed to a receivable. With vendors, for example, assets move from inventory to receivables, and thence to the cash account. If the flow is normal, the turnover rates for each item will approximate the standard for the type of business. If sales are slow, the capital investment may linger longer in the form of inventory until management makes the necessary adjustment. On the other hand, if receivables are on long terms or if they mature sluggishly, investment will linger there longer until management adjusts the circumstance.

In contrast to merchandise vendors, vendors of services find that receivables emerge out of other working capital assets—wages are paid out of cash, and supplies are taken out of an inventory. Similarly, lenders transfer funds from "cash" to "receivables" as they consummate loans. In a going business, therefore, provision must be made for an amount of receivables consistent with the character of the business, but credit management is concerned not only with the funds actually on that account but also with the rates at which other assets are converted into the receivables for which he is primarily responsible.

Providing funds for the investment in receivables is itself a distinct part of the management of credit. It is a function not usually delegated to the manager of the operational credit function, but one more often reserved for a higher level financial manager or for a top executive officer. In general, such funds may be obtained in either or both of two ways: through equity investment or through borrowing. Provision needs to be made not only for the minimum of receivables to be carried but also for short-term supplements and for long-term growth. Taken together the funds obtained from all sources constitute the "financial structure," sometimes also called the "total funds." That portion of the financial structure which is contributed by owners, and the non-current loans made by creditors, is known as the "capital structure," sometimes called merely "capital."

Several sources of owners' equity furnish funds for the credit operation: common and preferred stock, earned and capital surplus, and net worth reserves. Long-term indebtedness in the form of bonds and notes also provides for receivables financing.

Short-term funds which assist in carrying receivables are obtained mainly through the issuance of notes to banks and other types of finance companies. Such notes may be offered with the security either of the general assets and credit of the firm or of the particular receivables for which financing is required. The investment in inventory made by merchandise creditors is usually not regarded as a source of funds for carrying receivables. If, however, a fast turnover of inventory can be achieved on credit sales, the investment made by the first seller may overlap the sale of the second seller and thus constitute a substitution for funds which might otherwise have to be obtained elsewhere.

In summary, the need for funds to be invested in receivables results from six factors: (1) the volume of sales made on credit, inasmuch as all must be run through as receivables; (2) terms of sale stating the duration of the credit period; (3) the rate at which outstanding receivables are collected; (4) seasonal fluctuations in the use of credit service in the particular industry or trade; (5) long-term growth pattern of the company; and (6) changing patterns in requirements for credit service among customers.

The choice of sources from which creditors obtain funds to invest in receivables is also influenced by several factors: (1) availability of funds; (2) degree of control desired over the investment; (3) rates of charge; (4) need for other services provided by the supplier of funds.

Credit managers may expect evidence of the credit operation in their profit and loss statement as well as in their balance sheet. Hopefully, of course, its principal effect will be upon sales, income, or gross profit. The only measure of this may be in the expanded merchandise sales on credit, but it may also be in the form of earnings from the sale of credit service. For lenders, the cost of lendable funds might be considered the equivalent of cost of "goods" sold for a merchandiser, but for others it is more probably an expense item.

The expenses connected with a credit operation are of several types. Inevitably there is the cost of funds invested in receivables. This cost varies depending upon the source and the character of the user. Both equity and loan sources are tapped. Loan rates range from the prime commercial rate extended to the largest and most creditworthy operators to the competitive open market rate on short-term instruments. There appears to be an increasing tendency to obtain funds for this purpose by borrowing, thus in effect shifting the function of financing but giving clearer evidence of costs of money. Spiegel, Inc., for example, in 1961 reported gross receivables of $246 million, against which they had short-term borrowings of $50 million and long-term borrowings of $120 million.[4] Similarly, in a study of five major consumer finance companies it was found that their total debt averaged 72.3 per cent and their capital stock 27.7 per cent of their total financial structure.[5] During the period 1947 to 1957, their non-current debt and minority interest increased from 25 per cent to 53 per cent of their financial structure while short-term borrowings decreased from 40 to 23 per cent. Simultaneously, net worth decreased from 35 to 24 per cent,[6] and interest expense increased from 5.9 to 12.6 per cent of the operating expenses of the companies.[7] The long-term and short-term debt interest rates during that period increased from 2.9 to 3.9 per cent and from 1.7 to 3.8 per cent, respectively.[8]

Many creditors cannot rely so heavily upon borrowings for their pool of funds which must supply an investment in receivables as well as for other assets. It is no less important that the cost of equity capital also be ascertainable. In the opinion of one authority,[9] the cost of equity capital is a function of the number of times earnings the public will pay for the company's stock —the price-earnings ratio. The higher this ratio—the more its stock can be sold for relative to its net earnings—the lower the cost of equity capital, and vice versa. Both net earnings and pre-tax earnings must be considered. Net earnings represent "cost" with respect to both the dividends paid therefrom and the earnings necessarily retained for growth and expansion. Moreover, the relation of pre-tax earnings to net earnings must be considered, for more effort and expense must be incurred to generate a given net earnings in the light of present tax structure. All

[4] Carl Rieser, "The Monster Spiegel Keeps Keeps Spiegel," *Fortune*, June, 1961, p. 150.

[5] *Composite Earnings Performance of the Major Consumer Finance Companies* (Menlo Park, Calif.: Stanford Research Institute, 1959), p. 8.

[6] *Ibid.*, p. 18.

[7] *Ibid.*, p. 30.

[8] *Ibid.*, p. 31.

[9] John F. Lebor, Vice-President, Federated Department Stores, Inc., as reported in *Papers Presented at the Gulf Coast Consumer Credit Conference, November 12–13, 1959* (Houston, Tex.: University of Houston, Bureau of Business and Economic Research, 1960), pp. 26–29.

things considered, according to this source, it seems improbable that few department stores in this country can obtain common equity capital at a pre-tax cost of less than 20 per cent per annum. Considering furthermore that some capital could be borrowed at lower rates, it was doubted that most department stores could get their pre-tax cost of capital much below 15 per cent and still maintain a healthy ratio of equity capital to borrowed capital.[10]

In another study of the cost of funds used by four bank and non-bank finance companies, it was found that the cost of non-equity funds ranged from 1.2 per cent to 4.6 per cent of receivables outstanding, and that the cost of equity funds ranged from 5.0 per cent to 12.1 per cent, expressed in terms of net profit, and from 3.4 per cent to 7.7 per cent, expressed in terms of dividends paid to owners. These costs experienced by four types of institutions are shown in Table 6–1.

In addition to the cost of capital, operating expenses and losses from uncollectable accounts also appear in the profit and

Table 6–1.   Average Cost of Funds by Source and
Type of Institution, 1959
(per cent of average outstanding balances)

Type of Institution	Debt and Deposits	Total Non-equity Funds	Equity Funds	
			Ratio of Net Profits (or Net Income) to Equity Funds	Ratio of Dividends to Equity Funds
Nine commercial banks, total	1.3	1.2	7.6	4.5
Interest on time deposits	2.7	—	—	—
Cost of handling deposits	0.7	—	—	—
Nine consumer finance companies	5.0	4.6	12.1	7.7
Ten sales finance companies	4.5	4.2	10.3	5.9
All federal credit unions	3.8	3.1	5.0	3.4

SOURCE: Paul F. Smith, *Consumer Credit Costs, 1949–59,* A Study by The National Bureau of Economic Research, Princeton: Princeton University Press, 1964, p. 88.

[10] See *Study of Consumer Credit Costs in Department Stores* (New York: National Retail Merchants Association, 1963), Appendix.

loss statement. Some analysis of costs allocable to those functions is made in the following chapters.

MEASURES FOR THE CONTROL OF CAPITAL INVESTED IN RECEIVABLES

Management implies control, and responsibility for management of the investment represented by receivables depends upon knowledge of how this investment is faring in the total operation of the company. To provide this information, a number of specific statistical devices have been conceived. The following are but a few which are appropriate for vendors and lenders and which can be supplemented by others of significance to the individual creditor.

Measures for Vendors

The measures most widely used by vendors relate outstanding receivables to circumstances inherent in this particular investment.

Turnover of Receivables. Turnover is a rate measure, the number of times that annual sales are a multiple of average receivables outstanding. This is a measure of utilization of the investment made in receivables and gives evidence of the profitability of that investment. It is derived by dividing net credit sales by average receivables. The quotient of this turnover rate then divided into the number of days in the year expresses the number of days the average receivables are outstanding.

$$\frac{\text{Net credit sales}}{\text{Average receivables}} = \text{Turnover of receivables}$$

$$\frac{365 \text{ days}}{\text{Turnover rate}} = \text{Day receivables are outstanding}$$

As profit from the credit operation is usually derived from the merchandise markup, an increased rate of receivables turnover would indicate either that more sales (and unit profit) were being generated with a given investment or that a given volume of business was being achieved with smaller receivables investment. This ratio is not primarily a measure of collection activity and should not be confused with the measure of that function, which is also expressed in a number of days outstanding.

Cost of Receivables. When a rate of charge is applicable to the investment in receivables, the cost of this investment is the product of this rate and the receivables involved. Two measures may be derived from this computation, however, and they should not be confused. One is the cost of investment in the average receivables for the span of a year; the per annum rate is applied to the average receivables:

$$\text{Average receivables} \times \text{per annum rate} = \text{annual cost}$$

The other is related to the cost of carrying the average receivables for the span of a turnover period. The rate of charge for a turnover period is derived by dividing the annual rate by the turnover rate:

$$\frac{\text{Per annum rate of charge}}{\text{Receivables turnover rate}} = \text{Rate of charge per turnover period}$$

Thus if a charge of 12 per cent per annum is assigned to the invertment in receivables, with a turnover rate of 6, a 2 per cent rate would be multiplied times the average receivables to ascertain the cost of the investment in them for the span of their duration.

Composition Analysis of Receivables. When there are different types of receivables, some usually bear a different return, if any, than others. Consequently, it is helpful to visualize the extent of the investment which is made in each. Total receivables, however, may be classified on several bases. They may be divided into (1) types of customers, i.e., trade and personal, (2) notes and accounts receivable, or (3) 30-day, revolving, and instalment accounts. As 30-day accounts and personal obligations of business employees seldom are income bearing, and as different types of receivables turn over at different rates, a composition analysis is a useful gauge of investment utilization.

Age Analysis of Receivables. The value of an investment in receivables is affected by the age of the individual accounts, particularly when they are outstanding beyond their due date. Consequently, a helpful management tool is a classification of all accounts in terms of currency and past due, with the latter being further classified as to length of delinquency. Some individual debts may fall wholly into one classification; others may be divided among several, as illustrated by the following:

| Accounts | Total Debt | Current Debt | Past Due Debt | | | Over 90 |
			1–30	31–60	61–90	
Jones	$ 75	$ 75				
Smith	200	25	$50	$125		
Walker	100					$100
Total	$375	$100	$50	$125		$100
Percentage	100	27	13	33		27

Experience indicates what per cent of accounts in the different categories is usually collectible, and by applying the appropriate percentage to the accounts in each group, the approximate residual value of the total investment can be determined. Also, by observing trends in the subdivisions of the whole, both credit granting and collection policies can be appraised.

Bad Debt Analysis. Bad debts of themselves are not necessarily undesirable, except when their relationship to sales becomes unsatisfactory. This can be determined from the ratio of bad debts to sales:

$$\frac{\text{Bad debts}}{\text{Credit sales}} = \text{Bad debt index}$$

The object of credit operation is to generate profit-producing sales. Credit business cannot be conducted, however, without exposure to risk, and loss can be expected. So long as loss increases less rapidly than the profits added by credit sales, assumption of the calculated risk is having its desired effect. Some evidence of this can be gained from the Bad Debt Index.

Inasmuch as some vendors provide for ultimate bad debt losses through periodic setting aside of a reserve for bad debts, the index may be expressed as the relation of the reserve to sales. Ultimately the reserve and the actual losses have to be reconciled, but unless extraordinary circumstances occur both can be fairly closely calculated in advance and should not differ widely.

Measures for Lenders

Because of the character of their assets and differences in accounting terminology for lenders, some of their measures for controlling investment in receivables differ from those of vendors. The following are some more commonly used by them.

Loans Outstanding. As money is their stock in trade, lenders are concerned with the portion of their total funds which is outstanding, and therefore income producing.

$$\frac{\text{Total loans outstanding}}{\text{Total funds (equity and debt)}} = \text{Funds used index}$$

As all funds involve some cost, and only those outstanding produce a return, the burden upon loans outstanding is evident.

A related measure is that showing the relationship between funds loaned and funds lendable, the latter being that portion of working capital which is more or less "on the shelf" awaiting customers. Some portion of the working capital will always be unproductive, for lendable funds must always be on hand. But the degree to which they are out and working is important to know.

$$\frac{\text{Funds loaned}}{\text{Funds lendable}} = \text{Working funds index}$$

Loan Income. Investment in receivables is measurable also relative to the income it produces. Such income, however, is a function of two variables: the loans *made,* and the loans *outstanding.* Income is derived from the time or continuance of loans outstanding, and a measure of average return may be expressed as follows:

$$\frac{\text{Gross income}}{\text{Average loans outstanding}}$$

On the other hand, there is significance in the relationship between income and loans made, for this is equivalent to an index of gross margin on merchandise sales. All expenses are paid out of gross income on loans—loans outstanding—but many expenses vary with loans made rather than with the duration of the loans.

$$\frac{\text{Gross income}}{\text{Total loans made}}$$

Still further information can be gained from the relationship between the average loans outstanding and the total loans made, for this is an approximation of the merchant's receivables turnover rate.

$$\frac{\text{Total loans made}}{\text{Average loans outstanding}} = \text{Loan receivables turnover}$$

Net Earnings.   The ultimate object of interest is net, not gross, earnings, and for lenders they are meaningfully related to both the capital invested and to the total funds used. As costs of funds vary with different sources, the relation of net earnings to total funds will reflect the efficiency of management in obtaining both equity and debt funds at attractive rates.

$$\frac{\text{Net earnings}}{\text{Total funds}}$$

On the other hand, an evidence of skill in management of investment is in the effectiveness with which debt funds can be employed to the ultimate benefit of owners. Consequently, the earnings derived from use of total funds accrue to equity interests and can be expressed as follows:

$$\frac{\text{Net earnings}}{\text{Total capital invested}}$$

Interest Rates.   Still another basis of investment management control is a knowledge of trends of interest rates, or credit service charges. Where such rates vary appreciably with money market conditions, management problems may be posed by changes in the spread between cost of capital employed and charges made on loans outstanding. Contracts made at an earlier time may work either for or against current commitments, and knowledge of the respective rate trends will be helpful in controlling profit factors.

DISCUSSION QUESTIONS

1. Examine the financial statements of several companies and observe the relation of the investment of capital in receivables to the investment in other assets.
2. Diagram the monthly need for capital invested in receivables to show the changing seasonal need for such funds in several types of business.
3. Outline the sources from which funds may be obtained for investment in receivables, and compare your list of potential sources with the sources actually used in a specific company to which you have access.
4. Identify at least four qualities of the investment in receivables which need to be watched and controlled. Suggest measures or means by which such control may be exercised.

5. Contrast the sources of non-equity funds available to commercial banks, other loan companies, and vendors. As rates for non-equity financing vary, what effect has this upon competition among suppliers of credit service?

6. Appraise the factors which determine the cost of equity funds used for financing receivables.

7. Contrast the significance of receivables turnover to vendors and to lenders.

7

Credit Risk Management

The second function of credit management is the management of credit risks. Risk implies exposure to loss, or the chance of experiencing loss. In business there are many types of risk, and much of the work of management consists of dealing with risk situations. There are, for example, property risks, relating to physical assets of the company; liability risks, or claims made for personal injury to others; price risks, or loss due to changing market conditions; marketing risks, or loss from misinterpretation of market needs; competitive risks, the risk of comparative management ineffectiveness; and, among others, credit risk, or the risk of loss from unfulfillment of the credit promise. More specifically, the credit risk is of a threefold nature: the chance of losing the capital invested in the receivables; the chance of having to incur unexpected expenses in safeguarding or in recovering that asset; and the chance of not increasing profit after having invested effort and money in this means of sales stimulation.

THE ROOTS OF CREDIT RISK

Each type of risk has its own contributing factors and, therefore, its unique management problems. When through a credit transaction merchandise inventory moves into a debtor's hands, the resulting "receivables" represent exposure to a wholly different set of risk circumstances. The possibilities of physical destruction, theft, deterioration, obsolescence, and market change have then passed. In their place arise the possibilities of loss from three types of circumstances: ineffective credit management, debtor circumstances, and environmental circumstances.

Ineffective Credit Management

Some credit risk is attributable to conditions created by credit managers themselves. Incompetence, a peril in all business functions, in credit management takes several forms. One is misjudgment of creditworthiness. Inability to interpret correctly the evidence at hand creates risk of one's own making. So too does lack of skill in gathering or ferreting information upon which a proper credit appraisal should be based. Subsequent default may be attributed to the debtor's behavior, but the cause of such loss would be the creditor's.

Another type of credit risk stems from the calculated credit risk policy of the creditor. Willingness to accept excessive risk in the hope of achieving highly uncertain ends is a common creditor fault. Calibration of credit risk is difficult, and risk gradations cannot always be precisely scaled to reveal safe cutoff points, but general distinctions can be found between policies made intentionally strict or liberal for planned purposes. The essence of such risk lies, therefore, in the management decision, not in credit market circumstances.

A third risk-producing fault of management is its failure correctly to interpret the market for credit service. This may result in not offering forms of credit and credit terms which are desired, or in offering those which are not in demand. Thus continuance of a cash policy when the market desires credit service, or the issuance of liberal terms for customers deserving more stringent terms, or the offering of uncompetitive cash discount terms—these actions induce risks. In substance, this would be failure to supply the market with a properly prepared and packaged credit service product.

Still another management fault in credit operations is that of failing to achieve its secondary objectives of efficiency in obtaining capital at suitable cost, achieving normal loss ratios and operating expenses, or making timely and economical collections. These are risks or eventualities related to the credit operation which lie wholly within the management responsibility.

Another risk related to credit but one which is actually a property risk arises from failure of management to protect the physical property of the receivables ledger. Destruction of such records through fire poses a risk which would have been non-existent except for the undertaking of a credit operation.

Debtor Risk Circumstances

On the other hand, credit risk is more commonly attributed to debtor circumstances than to those of the creditor; to the extent that this is warranted this constitutes another type of credit risk management problem. If it be assumed that management is efficient—that it obtains and correctly interprets the necessary information on creditworthiness, that its risk-acceptance policy is well calculated, and that its own operating performance is well executed—then risks of three types may derive from debtors' conditions. These represent conditions, changes of which are presumed to be within debtors' control, or for which they may be held responsible. These conditions relate to capacity, character, and capital, amplified in Chapter 20, but which are presented briefly here as a root of credit risk.

Capacity. Even well-founded credit approval may subsequently be reversed by change in the debtor's ability to fulfill his credit promise. Changes in his employment, earning capacity, or indebtedness mitigate against the integrity of his promise and produce an unexpected specific risk. Such circumstances may be unforeseen in any particular case, although a number of them are expected in general as part of the calculated risk policy of the creditor.

Character. Changes also occur in the willingness of debtors to comply with their purchase contracts. Dissatisfaction with products, conviction of having been oversold, marital disagreements, and displeasure with creditors' collection tactics change the degree of risk inherent in the credit relationship.

Capital. Debtors' circumstances may also change due to destruction and loss of assets, upon which creditworthiness is partially based. Fire, flood, and other hazards change the likelihood of gaining payment on an indebtedness.

Environmental Circumstances

Some bases of credit risk are found neither in the creditor nor in the debtor, but rather in the environmental circumstances in which both of them come together. General social and economic conditions constitute the environment of and are beyond the control of any individual. Business recessions, progressive automation, union strikes, disasters, droughts, and the like add unexpectedly to the other risks inherent in the credit relationship. In international trade credit, wars, inconvertibility of currencies, expropriation, and political repudiation of debts also are environmental factors determining credit risk.

RISK MANAGEMENT ALTERNATIVES

The means of managing credit risk are of three broad types: (1) to eliminate it entirely by selling for cash and not credit; (2) to shift it to insurance companies and others performing some combination of the credit functions; and (3) to control it through the application of devices which enable management to achieve selected goals. The first is an alternative not so much as a general policy but as a policy in selective selling. Analysis of credit-worthiness as a means of risk control is discussed in Chapter 20 as one of the operational processes. The use of various types of credit insurance is the subject of Chapter 15. The remainder of this chapter is concerned with the control of risk through the use of credit terms and instruments, as outlined in Table 7–1.

Credit terms are to the credit customer the statement of conditions under which credit service is provided him, specifying time, payments, and charges; to the credit service supplier they are a

Table 7–1.   Degrees of Credit Risk Obtainable Through
Credit Terms and Instruments

Type of Credit	Most Risk	Less Risk	Least Risk
Consumer	Regular open account Regular promissory note Negotiable Non-negotiable	Revolving account Cognovit note	C.O.D. Secured note
Business	Open account	Consignment C.O.D. Time draft Trade acceptance Promissory note	C.O.D. C.B.D.
	Time draft	Sight draft	Sight draft—letter of credit
	Revocable letter of credit	Irrevocable letter of credit Authority to purchase	Confirmed letter of credit
	Personal check	Certified check Personal check with letter of credit	Bank draft

statement of his expectations in the relationship. Every instance of credit service involves the statement of terms. Some are explicit; others are "understood." Some have such formality as to be embodied in legal documents, like notes and drafts. Their origins are as old as the institution of credit itself, and their present expression has evolved as "tradition" in various trades, industries, and types of business. Individually they are a statement of relationship; collectively they represent means which have evolved for the gradation of risk in the credit relationships.

Consumer Credit Terms

In the field of consumer credit, two general types of terms or instruments are used in common practice: accounts and notes. In themselves they represent different degrees of risk, for notes are a more definite evidence of indebtedness. Despite this fact, they are not always alternative devices of risk control in the eyes of management. Account terms are usually used where the credit relationship invites frequent, repeated transactions; notes, for the larger single transaction. Accounts are generally the more risky of the two, but both accounts and notes have variations which scale the risk involved.

Accounts Receivable. The typical or regular account is the open account of 30 days duration. It represents a contractual agreement made at the time the account is opened. The risk which characterizes it arises from the fact that unauthorized use of the account by others is possible; it involves no better evidence of the indebtedness than the sales slip; it is subject to a shorter period of legal collectibility than the note; and the administration of it is not always adapted to the more risky customers.

To compensate for these risk disadvantages, several variations of the regular account have been devised. One is the revolving account (a type of charge account payable in instalments) which was conceived originally to employ a moderate, fixed limit, more careful authorization of use, and a service charge as compensation for the risk and for the expenses of risk management. Such accounts, found in a number of variations, reduce the risk inherent in the regular account, and at the same time they permit the rendering of credit service to more risky customers without the bearing of undue risk by management.

When neither the regular nor the revolving account is a suitable safeguard against the inherent credit risks, C.O.D. or layaway terms may be offered. These do not involve credit, for no value is exchanged for a promise, and consequently no credit risk is borne.

Notes Receivable. In transactions where notes are a customary and acceptable instrument, several varieties of them also permit scaling the credit risk.

All promissory notes have certain features in common: they state unequivocally the promise which is the essence of credit; they constitute written evidence of the debt; the drawer or maker is the debtor and the payee is the creditor; and they have a statutory life exceeding that of accounts. They differ, however, with respect to negotiability, actionability, and security, and therefore represent varying degrees of risk to credit managers.

The simplest type of written promise to pay is a type of promissary note. It may be worded, in effect: "On March 10, I promise to pay John Jones ten dollars. Signature." While such an instrument is legal and actionable, in the eyes of credit managers it has the disadvantage of being non-negotiable. It cannot be passed with an endorsement to another holder or payee, and thus it obligates the original creditor to hold the instrument until its maturity. He thereby incurs all the risks which arise during the period of the indebtedness. This may be avoided by the use of a negotiable instrument which, in addition to being a signed and delivered promise to pay a definite sum at a stated time, is also made payable not to a specific individual but "to the bearer" or "to the order of" the individual named as payee. By the use of such an instrument in credit terms requiring a promissory note, the creditor not only minimizes certain risks, but also places himself in a position where he may shift the financing function by the sale or assignment of the note.

A promissory note thus worded, negotiable or non-negotiable, is actionable through the normal procedures of suit in court. Such action, however, involves the risk of disputation, time, and additional expense. When the creditor alleges default on a debt, the court notifies the debtor, invites refutation, and if necessary provides a hearing or trial before a judgment concerning the case is rendered. These disadvantages to the creditor are eliminated in some states where cognovit or judgment notes are recognized.[1] Such notes incorporate a statement which obviates, not the need

---

[1] The states recognizing the cognovit note are Colorado, Delaware, Illinois, Maryland, Ohio, Oklahoma, Pennsylvania, Rhode Island, Utah, Virginia, Wisconsin, and Wyoming.

for obtaining a judgment, but the need for the notification and trial which normally occur between the filing of the plaintiff's petition and the judgment. This statement, signed by the debtor along with other aspects of his promise, says essentially this: "I hereby authorize any Attorney at Law to appear in any Court of Record in the United States, after the above obligation becomes due, and waive the issuing and service of process and confess a judgment against me in favor of the holder hereof for the amount then appearing due, together with costs of suit, and thereupon to release all errors and waive all right of appeal."

The risk inherent in even negotiable cognovit notes may be further reduced by incorporation in the note of a statement of the security pledged behind the promise of the note. Secured notes offer tangible assets against which the creditor has a preferred claim, thus making them preferred creditors when other liens may be obtained against the general assets of the debtor. Such security may consist of mortgages, certificates of title, securities, valuable objects, and the like.

In selling or lending to consumers on credit, managers may thus elect to use such instruments and terms as suit the risk involved and their willingness and ability to bear that degree of credit risk. Alternatives offer options, which are usually exercised at the discretion of the creditor, although in practice the alternatives often become identified as the types of credit service offered different market segments, rather than the variety of services (terms) offered a given market segment.

Mercantile Credit Terms

In the process of supplying credit service to business users of credit, the same problems of risk management arise, and similar, although more elaborate, devices are used to effect control. These devices involve the use of accounts, drafts, letters of credit, and checks.

Open Accounts. Accounts opened by producers and distributors for their business customers, like retailers' regular accounts, provide credit service where risk falls within a customary span of magnitude. The concept of "regular" account is less applicable, however, for terms vary widely among customers to whom credit service is extended on an account. Terms differ by type not so much because of other needs of customers, as because of need for convenience in making payment, need for inspection of goods before making payment, and need for time to turn their own inventory before making payment. Thus there have arisen open account terms with varying discounts, discount periods, and credit periods as follows:

Regular: Both discount and net credit periods begin with date of invoice, which is usually the date of shipment from the vendor creditor: i.e., "2/10, net 30."

E.O.M.: Both discount and net credit periods begin with the end of billing month in which shipment was made. An accumulation of invoices may thus be billed and paid simultaneously, i.e., "2/10, net 30, E.O.M."

M.O.M.: The same as E.O.M., except that payment dating begins as of the middle rather than the end of the month.

R.O.G.: While net credit period begins with date of invoice, as in regular terms, the discount period begins with the receipt of goods, in order that the consignee may inspect the goods before making payment, and not be deprived of his cash discount because of the expiration of the discount period while the goods are in transit; i.e., "2/10, net 30, R.O.G."

Extra: Additional days introduced between invoice date and beginning of credit and discount periods, as an accommodation for seasonal business or for competitive reasons; i.e., "2/10, net 30, 60 extra," or "2/10, net 30, from March 1."

Proximo: A term used with a date to indicate that payment is due on that date of the next month; i.e., "2/10 proximo," meaning that payment with a 2 per cent discount is due on the 10th of the following month.

All such terms are regarded as credit terms and all offer a discount, but not all can be regarded as cash discount terms. A cash discount is one provided, not to induce *prompt* payment, for that is payment at the expiration of the credit period, but *prompter* payment—payment within the number of days specified. Consequently, proximo terms resemble a trade discount in some respects, for only a net credit period is stated.

The value of discount payments in reduction of risk and expenses is evident in the magnitude of the discounts offered. The familiar 2/10, net 30 terms, for example, provide a 2 per cent discount for paying 20 days earlier than otherwise required by the credit terms. As a rate, 2 per cent for 20 days is equivalent to 36 per cent for 360 days (2 : 20 = X : 360). The inducement implicit in any of the other credit terms may be similarly computed.

Open accounts, however, entail more credit risk than vendors are sometimes willing to assume. Open account terms are in fact perhaps the most risky of the mercantile terms. They not only permit the buyer to obtain possession of the goods without payment, but they expose the vendor to unrecompensed shipping charges and to subsequent collection expenses. One alternative to the open account terms is C.O.D.—collection on delivery, before the buyer acquires physical possession. Another is consignment terms—retention of title to goods by the seller even when the merchandise is in the hands of a consignee for resale. Still another is C.B.D.—cash payment required before shipment is made, thus avoiding futile shipping expenses. As occasions conducive to the use of open accounts do not coincide with the characteristics of promissory notes, the latter, as in consumer credit, are not really alternatives to the open account, with one exception. That exception is in relation to delinquent open accounts, for which notes are sometimes accepted as better evidence, in all ways that the note provides, of the debt. Another instrument with risk characteristics similar to the note and which is sometimes a substitute for account terms is the commercial draft.

Commercial Drafts. A draft is an order to pay a stated sum, drawn by one party upon another requesting that payment be made by them to a specified party, often the drawer himself. In a commercial relationship, the drawer is usually the seller and the drawee the buyer. Such drafts are distinguished from bank drafts (i.e., checks), which are identical instruments drawn upon a bank, rather than upon a commercial firm. The drawer of a bank draft (check) is usually the buyer, not the seller, in a commercial relationship.

Commercial drafts may be either time drafts or sight drafts. Time drafts are a written demand for payment at the end of whatever credit period is offered. They are honored by acceptance, by signature evidencing acceptance of the terms. When used in connection with the sale of commodities, they are essentially what is also termed a "trade acceptance." Such a signed document has much of the legal value of a promissory note for purposes of collection. Both reduce the credit risk by substituting a written evidence for an open understanding, yet both are vulnerable to all the circumstances which lead to risk through default.

Sight drafts narrow the risk one step further. They are requests for payment at sight, or upon presentation of the draft. Therefore they actually represent a type of C.O.D. term. The advantage of this particular instrument is that when it is accompanied by shipping documents they are not surrendered, and possession of the goods not gained, until payment is made. Thus while the vendor has reduced the risk inherent in an outright credit sale, or through the use of a time draft, he nevertheless has exposed himself to the possibility of non-payment upon presentation. Although the goods may yet be in the seller's possession, they may be in a disadvantageous location and he will have incurred useless transportation expenses.

Letters of Credit. Letters of credit are a means by which non-payment risk in the use of commercial drafts may be further reduced by substituting the creditworthiness of a bank for that of the purchaser when, because of the excessive credit risk factors both in the buyer and in his environment, the buyer's bank will, for a fee, guarantee payment in the form of a letter of credit. By this action the bank announces to the vendor who will be drawing a draft that if the draft, accompanied by appropriate documents, presented within a specified time, and not in excess of a stated amount, is drawn upon the bank instead of upon the customer, the draft will be honored. As banking institutions are more creditworthy than most of their clients, the opportunity to draw upon them is an improvement in the credit risk situation.

Not all letters of credit, however, are equally risk free. In what is known as a revocable letter of credit, the issuing bank may at any time before presentation of the draft revoke its assurance of payment. The drawer then has little more assurance than when his drafts, without a letter of credit, would be drawn directly upon the purchaser. By an irrevocable letter of credit, however, this risk is avoided and the objective of the letter of credit is achieved.

There are circumstances, moreover, where the bank issuing such a letter or the national environment in which it operates are so uncertain as to cast doubt upon either its willingness or its ability to fulfill its commitment. In such cases confirmation of the initiating bank's guarantee by another bank, particularly in the seller's country, gives the ultimate assurance which the vendor seeks. The confirmed, irrevocable letter of credit, therefore, affords the minimum of credit risk in draft transactions (see Fig. 7–1). Such measures are frequently employed in international credit transactions but rarely in the domestic market where, if conditions warrant even this, documentary drafts alone are used.

Distinction should be made between the letters of credit which are furnished sellers and those which are furnished buyers, both at the buyer's initiative. The former, at the request of a buyer, is sent to the seller who then draws his commercial drafts upon the buyer's bank requesting payment to himself. The other is furnished buyers who may be traveling abroad for the purpose of establishing their creditworthiness for cashing, in correspondent banks, checks (drafts) drawn upon the issuing, home bank. Thus the letter of credit may be used for drafts drawn by sellers and by buyers, for commercial drafts and for bank drafts. Their common feature is that in both cases the drafts are drawn upon the bank and not upon another commercial party.

Another distinction should be made between a letter of credit and an *authority to purchase*. The latter is an endorsement sent by a bank, at the request of an importer in its country, to a foreign seller endorsing the buyer's credit. It does not guarantee payment, and drafts drawn under such authority are drawn upon the buyer instead of his bank. Such a recommendation does little more for a credit manager than indicate that the buyer has relations with it and presumably that he has some credit standing.

Checks—Bank Drafts. The term "bank draft" is used in two meanings: (1) drafts drawn by a bank upon another bank and (2) drafts drawn by anyone upon a bank. The latter is the use preferred here, for it differentiates such drafts from those drawn upon commercial drawees, and it furnishes a common base for scaling the risk involved in an assortment of bank drafts.

Because of the fulfillment uncertainties inherent in checks, from the standpoint of both the drawer and the drawee bank, they must be regarded as credit instruments although the incidence of default is small relative to the volume of checks used. The risk which they involve stems mainly from the drawer having no account at the bank upon which he draws, from his having insufficient funds deposited, and from the insecurity of the bank itself. Ordinary personal checks carry all three types of risk. The possibility of no account and of insufficient funds is removed by certification of a personal check by the drawee bank, whereby

The First National City Bank of New York

ESTABLISHED 1812

CABLE ADDRESS "CITIBANK"

55 Wall Street, New York 15, N.Y.

CONFIRMED IRREVOCABLE STRAIGHT CREDIT   DATE

ALL DRAFTS DRAWN MUST BE MARKED:
DRAWN AS PER ADVICE

DEAR SIRS:
     WE ARE INSTRUCTED BY

TO ADVISE YOU THAT IT HAS OPENED ITS IRREVOCABLE CREDIT No.   IN YOUR FAVOR

FOR ACCOUNT OF

FOR A SUM OR SUMS NOT EXCEEDING A TOTAL OF

AVAILABLE BY YOUR DRAFT(S) AT   ON US TO BE ACCOMPANIED BY

     EXCEPT AS OTHERWISE EXPRESSLY STATED HEREIN. THIS ADVICE IS SUBJECT TO THE UNIFORM
CUSTOMS AND PRACTICE FOR COMMERCIAL DOCUMENTARY CREDITS FIXED BY THE THIRTEENTH CONGRESS
OF THE INTERNATIONAL CHAMBER OF COMMERCE.
     THE ABOVE-NAMED OPENER OF THE CREDIT ENGAGES WITH YOU THAT EACH DRAFT DRAWN UNDER AND
IN COMPLIANCE WITH THE TERMS OF THE CREDIT WILL BE DULY HONORED ON DELIVERY OF DOCUMENTS AS
SPECIFIED IF PRESENTED AT THIS OFFICE ON OR BEFORE
WE CONFIRM THE CREDIT AND THEREBY UNDERTAKE TO HONOR EACH DRAFT DRAWN AND PRESENTED AS
ABOVE SPECIFIED.

                              YOURS VERY TRULY.

COM 511A (L) REV. 11-56
ART 904

Fig. 7–1.   Confirmed, irrevocable letter of credit.

it sets aside a portion of the deposit sufficient to cover the draft when it is presented. A similar effect is achieved by the use of a cashier's check, whereby with cash is bought a draft drawn by the bank's cashier upon his own bank, from an account earmarked for this purpose. Still another type of bank draft is that drawn by one bank upon another in which it has deposits, this too being sold for cash to one whose personal checks may be regarded as too risky.

MEASURES OF RISK CONTROL

Credit risk is difficult to measure and more difficult to control inasmuch as some of the factors causing risk lie outside the authority of credit management. An effort can be made, however, to recognize the risk variables and the evidences, internal and external, which disclose the nature of credit risk. Some of the measures proposed below relate to material in later chapters, yet they are presented here to give a full picture of credit risk management. As credit risk is an effect of creditor risk policy, debtor circumstances, environmental conditions, insurance service, and managerial efficiency, all of these factors must be considered in the measurement of risk control.

Creditor Risk Policy

Credit risk should be accepted as a matter of policy and not merely as a consequence of performing a credit operation. Such policy, however, is not always formulated objectively, for decisions are often made in terms of the merits of individual cases rather than in terms of broad risk criteria. Nevertheless, statement can be made of the creditor's general policy, whether it be to accept only better risks or also poorer ones, whether to cater to one class of customers or several, whether to pursue a fixed policy or one varying with circumstances. If such a statement of objectives and policy is formulated, the entire credit operation can be judged in terms of this risk standard.

Debtor Circumstances

The total characteristics of an acceptable risk are not easily defined, but selected characteristics are sometimes evidence of a general risk policy. Thus a creditor may control his risk by refusing to accept the credit of persons or firms who have recently been declared bankrupt, whose total indebtedness is a determined portion of income, whose paying record has been deteriorating, whose current and quick ratios are of certain quality. With increased use of numerical valuation of creditworthiness, a rationalized cutoff point is also taken as summary evidence of credit risk. In all these instances, creditor policy represents a model of means–ends factors considered by management for controlling credit risk.

Environmental Conditions

As credit risk reflects environmental conditions, measures thereof are useful for control purposes. Thus indexes of unemployment, collections, delinquencies, credit extensions and debt reductions, retail sales, population trends, etc., are useful types of control information.

Insurance Service

Objective consideration of one's credit insurance program should also be made as a guide to risk control. Not all types of credit operations can avail themselves of all forms of credit risk insurance, but the availabilities and the terms of one's own policy should be understood.

Credit insurance, for example, which is available for mercantile credit risks, is not a complete coverage of all risk, but of abnormal risk, as determined by past losses, types of accounts, and the extent of the insurance contract. Retail instalment credit risk arising from death and disability may be covered by credit life insurance policies written either as individual policies or as group insurance policies. Finally, export credit risk arising from adverse foreign and international circumstances may be shifted to existing agencies. Knowledge of the potentialities of such insurance is essential to risk control.

Management Efficiency

Within the credit operation there are also measures providing information upon which sound risk management can be based.

These consist of statistical ratios which reveal the composition of the risk and its relation to other aspects of the credit operation.

Application Rejection Index. Credit policy concerning risk is evident in the extent to which applications for credit recognition are accepted or rejected. The relationship is expressed in a ratio as follows:

$$\frac{\text{Applications rejected}}{\text{Applications received}} = \text{Credit rejection index}$$

The index quotient may vary either with increase of applications received or with a change in the standards and rate of acceptance. Changes in either may stem from external circumstances or from internal policy changes.

Loss Index. Loss anticipated from acceptance of credit risk is usually provided for in a reserve established for this purpose. This provision for credit loss, however, is often made in an accounting period prior to the actual writing off of the individual accounts as bad debts. Consequently, trends in risk are indicated by the discrepancy between anticipated loss and actual loss, inasmuch as anticipation is the normality of previous experience and any departure from this in actual loss represents a change in risk which would be important to know. The formula for this computation is as follows:

$$\frac{\text{Bad debts written off}}{\text{Bad debt reserve established}} = \text{Loss index}$$

Age Analysis of Receivables. The procedure for analyzing receivables by currency and age was explained in the previous chapter as an interpretation of investment in receivables. The same analysis serves also to indicate something of the changing pattern of risk among the receivables.

Collection Index. Risk changes effect changes in the collectibility of outstanding accounts, as shown by the following formula:

$$\frac{\text{Collections during month}}{\substack{\text{Receivables outstanding at} \\ \text{beginning of month}}} = \text{Collection index}$$

This is an indication of risk easily computed from readily available data and may be used for immediate management decisions concerning collections.

DISCUSSION QUESTIONS

1. Contrast the concepts of "risk" and "calculated risk" in business. Illustrate the difference with several examples of each. Show what factors enter into the "calculation" so far as credit risk is concerned. Is the "calculated risk" the same as a "calculatable risk"?

2. In the management of credit risk, how does the selection of credit instruments on the basis of risk gradation differ from the selection of customers on the basis of their creditworthiness? Explain the differences and their implications.

3. What factors should be considered by management in deciding whether to assume and manage credit risk or shift it to credit risk specialists?

4. Tabulate the circumstances which affect credit risk, and match with them examples of risk management policies.

5. Although credit instruments may be ranked relative to their risk characteristics, not all are usable in every type of credit transaction. List the main types of situations in which different instruments are used, and show the range of choices available to a person operating in those circumstances.

6. Identify the factors which tend to cause one type of credit terms or instrument to be more risky than another.

7. Identify the parties in a business transaction who are the drawer, drawee, and payee in the following instruments: promissory note, commercial sight draft, commercial draft drawn under a letter of credit, draft drawn under a traveler's letter of credit, a certified check, a cashier's check, a bank draft.

8. Identify the principal causes of credit risk, and propose corresponding risk control measures which would serve to guide credit managers in their decisions.

8

Management of the Credit Operation

The third major function of credit management is the performance of processes necessary for the actual supplying of credit service.

Risk is an intangible to be managed and capital is an impersonal factor, but the credit operation consists of the relationships and interactions of the role participants in the use and supplying of credit service.

The operational function relates to that portion of the credit work for which the credit manager per se has been primarily responsible: for contacts with customers, information sources, peers, employees, and superior executives. Under the credit manager the work of risk analysis has been the focus of management activity, whereas persons on higher levels of management have been concerned more with the capital and credit risk functions.

In the management of the credit operation, efficiency and economy are principal objectives. Service to credit customers is also a consideration, but service policies are usually formulated apart from the routine of operational performance, as are also profit objectives.

This chapter is concerned with the processes of the credit operation, classified as to the management relationships and arranged approximately in the chronological order in which they occur. These processes, in some degree, are found in every credit operation, the extent and management of them differing due to type of market, type of credit service, and management policies. Like the other credit functions, operations are also divisible and shiftable.

MANAGEMENT—CUSTOMER RELATIONSHIPS

Most of the operational processes are found in management—customer relationships, where patterns of initiation, interaction, cooperation, conflict, and resolution are evolved.

Soliciting New Accounts

Although in the past those who were in need of credit service generally sought out lenders, initiative in modern credit business usually is taken by vendors and lenders themselves. This is typical of merchandising activities in a capitalistic, competitive, consumer-oriented market, and the advocation of the use of credit service is no exception.

In its more aggressive form, account solicitation extends to actual opening of accounts for potential customers, without their request or knowledge. Department stores sometimes open accounts in the name of creditworthy citizens, particularly newcomers to a community. Gasoline companies and car rental agencies do the same on a wider scale. Even wholesale distributors invite customers to deal with them on a credit basis. In most such instances of vendor initiative, the account is one for "free" credit service, where profit is realized from subsequent sales through use of the account.

There are, of course, more moderate forms of vendor solicitation through advertising whereby customers are invited to apply for an account, use the loan services, or buy "on easy terms" specific merchandise. Such solicitations begin unilaterally, and if they succeed they result in response or interaction between the supplier and user of credit service.

Receiving Credit Applications

By merely receiving credit applications and not openly soliciting them, creditors have appeared to preserve their dominance in the debtor–creditor relationship through a passive role. But whether it is solicited or not, an application for credit is almost always received as part of the credit process. Some are received as individual letters. Generally they are submitted in standard forms designed to meet the inquiry needs of the creditor. Their design is a function of the type of business, other sources of information used, competition, and the image which the creditor attempts to convey.

Interviewing the Applicant

Face-to-face contact between creditors and debtors at the time credit is approved has definite advantages, but, although desirable, this contact is not always achieved. When interviewing is part of the credit process, it provides both problems and opportunities for the credit manager: problems of providing space and personnel; opportunities to personalize the credit relationship for the benefit of both parties. As the number of credit customers increases, investigation tends to become more routinized, more dependent upon standard data from other sources, and interviewing is regarded as less essential.

Approving Credit and Setting Limits

The act of approving creditworthiness and setting credit limits is an evaluative act which requires of the credit manager a consideration of the objectives and limitations imposed by his own business environment, as well as by the qualifications of the applicant. When internal factors have been weighed and a decision reached, the conclusion defines the relationship, the terms, and the expectations between the two parties.

Notifying Credit Customers

Notification that credit has been approved is a communication function for management, and it provides an opportunity for statement or reiteration of terms and expectations. It is an occasion, too, for encouragement to use the credit established and to welcome the patronage of the new credit customer.

Identifying Credit Customers

When credit business becomes impersonalized to the point that neither credit nor sales personnel would recognize all customers whose credit has been established with the company, some device for identifying them is useful and is frequently employed. The credit cards, plates, coins, tags, etc., which identify, however, serve other functions as well: reducing risk of misrepresentation, facilitating credit sales authorization, and solidifying the debtor–creditor relationship with a visual symbol. Management in selecting a means of identification considers costs, risks, and time spent in other functions which are dependent upon identification.

Promoting Use of Credit

In its customer relations, credit management takes initiative not only in soliciting accounts but also in promoting business through the use of accounts that have been previously opened. Although a sales department function, this means of building business has increasingly engaged credit managers as their work has come to be regarded more as creative and less as only protective.

Authorizing Use of Credit

Authorization is the process of validating an already established credit relationship at the time of a particular transaction. Management's tasks are to devise such a system as will separate approved from unapproved customers; to place responsibility for on-the-spot decisions with duly authorized employees; and to minimize the costs of time, personnel, and facilities involved.

Billing; Receiving; Adjusting

The processes of billing, receiving payment, and adjusting claims that are often made by customers constitute a recapitulation of the credit transaction. Transfer of goods to the buyer and payment for the goods by him are, by the definition of credit, actions separated by time. With the fulfillment of the credit period, billing reminds the debtor of the creditor's expectation. Because of the many variables in human experience, payment may or may not be promptly received, but facilities must be provided for handling personal and mailed payment. Procedures must also be established for rediscussing the transaction, inasmuch as faults of both parties sometimes unsettle the original understanding, and further interaction, reconsideration of objectives, and new demonstrations of cooperation or conflict may be needed.

Collecting Delinquent Accounts

In collecting, the creditor takes the initiative because the debtor has failed to do so by not making proper payment. Collection effort is required for a small proportion of the credit accounts, but they involve sums essential to the profitability of the business. At stake is not only the capital already outstanding in the account but also the customer relationship which will yield future business. Collecting is a unique and inevitable process in the credit operation.

MANAGEMENT—SUPPLIER RELATIONSHIPS

Management of the credit operation requires interaction with other than customers. Also important in the management process are contacts with suppliers of credit information.

The development of patterns of information interchange is a responsibility of credit management. Both quality of information and cost are involved. Standard sources and relationships have been established to facilitate the routine of investigation of credit-worthiness, but resourcefulness and innovation are also not without reward. This relationship with suppliers of information provides opportunity for interaction initiated by either party. It is sometimes an agent–client relationship; it is also a competitor-peer relationship when exchange is made between credit managers.

Collecting, as well as information gathering, also presents a management–supplier relationship, for in this work, too, agents and specialists are engaged for specific purposes. Maintaining contacts with the individuals involved, reciprocating with them, and integrating their services into one's own needs is an integral part of operations management.

MANAGEMENT—EMPLOYEE RELATIONSHIPS

Some credit departments are one-man operations, but when others than the manager are employed organizational functions become part of the credit manager's responsibility. In that case, management–employee relations must be considered. Employee relations may arise in connection with several processes: interviewing, authorizing, billing, collecting, and adjusting. Much of the work delegated to credit department employees is routine and clerical, but even for such personnel, training, supervising, and counseling responsibilities must be assumed.

MANAGEMENT—OWNER RELATIONSHIPS

Credit management has responsibilities and obligations not only to customers and to employees but also to owners, whose profit expectations depend upon competence in credit techniques, integration of credit functions, and coordination of credit objectives and those of the business as a whole.

Management of credit operations requires effective cooperation with executive officers in planning general credit objectives, in conferring on sources and uses of required funds, on risk standards, and on limits in specific cases. It requires coordination with the sales, bookkeeping, personnel, and facilities maintenance departments. It requires diligence in watching account records, and in planning, scheduling, and evaluating processes and performance. Credit management's responsibility to owners, and to superior executives who represent owner interests, is to perform and to coordinate all activity to the best interests of all.

MEASURES OF OPERATIONAL PERFORMANCE

Operational performance, like that of other credit functions, must be appraised in terms of measures and standards of performance. As these are mainly efficiency measures, they involve elements of time and cost relative to output. Many specific ratios and trend analyses can be proposed to suggest the efficiency of operation; only a few of these are discussed here. Further consideration will be given the subject of cost analysis in the following chapter.

Cost: Credit Sales

The generation of credit sales is the primary management objective of the credit operation; therefore, cost of producing this effect must be known, if the effort is determined to be worthwhile. Total costs include both direct and indirect costs; allocation of the latter should be made on the same bases as when other performance analyses are made. Considering the current knowledge of credit cost analysis and of credit contribution to sales and profits, it is unlikely that many useful analyses of the contribution of credit operations are now made.

Cost: Income from Credit Sales

A similar analysis may be made of the relation of cost input to earnings output. When credit service is sold and a measurable income derived from it, operational costs should be judged in terms of such income.

Direct Cost Analysis

The direct expenses incurred in the administration of the credit department themselves furnish a basis for classification and analysis of costs. Trends in the proportions required for salaries, information services, rent, utilities, postage, and maintenance serve as a guide for controlling the intradepartmental activity.

Information Cost: Applications Processed

Some credit functions and costs may be reduced to meaningful ratios, such as the average cost of information for each application processed or approved. This may furnish evidence of need for more selective use of credit reports; for increased use of interviews, references, etc.; or for better coordination of account solicitation and the acceptance policy.

Time Required for Application Approval

Not all input factors need be measured in terms of dollar costs; time too is a factor. Reduction in time per investigation accelerates use of accounts, reduces backlog of work, and improves competitive image.

Time Required for Authorization

Nor is time a factor only in credit approval; it is important too in the authorization process. It is credit management's responsibility to devise such authorization facilities, organization, and policies as to produce the most speedy authorization commensurate with the risk involved.

DISCUSSION QUESTIONS

1. Analyze the work for which the credit operation is responsible, and suggest classifications for its functions.
2. Diagram the contacts which the credit manager has with individuals inside and outside of the credit operation in his performance of the credit work.
3. Analyze each of the relationships in which the credit manager interacts from the following standpoints: who takes initiative, who is the dominant participant, the relation of power and authority, loyalties, and conflict of interests.
4. Which of the functions of the credit operation are subject to mechanization?
5. Relate the functions of the credit operation to the objectives of the credit manager discussed in Chapter 5.
6. Which of the operational functions probably have to be performed together, and which could be separated and shifted?
7. What changes in the operational functions have occurred during the last few decades?
8. To what extent are the operational functions separable from investment and risk bearing?

9

The Cost of Credit Service

Performance of the credit functions discussed in the three preceding chapters involves costs on the part of the supplier of credit service. The steady increase of such costs as a part of our gross national product and their increase as a corporate expense in serving the markets for credit service have awakened new interest in them. The long neglect of understanding the cost of credit operations is one of the strange dark spots in scientific management, but much of its explanation lies in the lack of recognition given to the entire credit function. As in recent years the role of credit has gained prestige, as alternatives to the performance of the credit functions by specialists have increased, and as charges for credit service have become more common, a greater desire to understand credit costs has been expressed. This knowledge has been found useful both to individual suppliers of credit service and to regulative agencies charged with the establishment of their rates of charge.

At a time when business has long been cost conscious, conducting its performance on the basis of elaborate cost analyses, it is surprising that very little information is available concerning credit costs. A study of credit department expenses for the years 1947 and 1948 made by the Credit Research Foundation of the National Association of Credit Men was then identified as the first survey of its kind.[1] Respondent members of the Association

[1] *Study on Credit Department Expenses* (New York: National Association of Credit Men, Credit Research Foundation, 1950).

could furnish little information of their credit costs, explaining that the segregation of such costs had never been thought worthwhile, and that they were carried in general administrative expense, as operations expense at warehouses, or as combined with bookkeeping expense.[2] Others regarded them not even as an "expense" but as "promotional, the same as the sales department."[3] Data submitted differed so widely among the diversified industries that no generalizations could be made. A recommendation of the study was that credit department expense controls should be set up to provide a more accurate measurement of expenses.

Similarly, cost studies of retail credit operations have also been inconclusive. One survey published as early as 1941[4] concluded that most stores did not charge general overhead or the interest on money invested in accounts receivable to the credit department, nor did they keep cost data so as to permit comparison between instalment and open account costs. Credit department expenses reported for 1938, however, were shown to amount to from 0.72 to 4.08 per cent of credit sales. Adding interest on average outstandings, the total expense ranged from 1.33 to 5.03 per cent of credit sales. Deducting income from past-due accounts and from instalment sales, net expense was from 0.57 to 5.03 per cent of credit sales.[5]

The accounting methods reported in that study were consistent with those generally adopted by the Credit Management Division of the National Retail Merchants Association whose *Credit Management Year Book* contains annual information on credit operating costs. They, too, however, report only direct costs of the credit operation, showing the cost as a per cent of net credit sales to range from 1 per cent to 4 per cent, varying with the size of the department store and with the character of its credit operation. No overhead costs nor cost of invested funds were included in these figures.

Further study of department store credit was undertaken for the National Retail Merchants Association in 1963 by an independent research organization. This study, too, was said to be

[2] *Ibid.*, pp. 18–19.
[3] *Ibid.*, p. 25.
[4] John Reid Roller, *Retail Credit-Office Expense in Ohio Department Stores,* Research Monograph Number 29 (Columbus, Ohio: The Ohio State University, Bureau of Business Research, 1941).
[5] *Ibid.*, p. 29.

the first definitive research into retail customer credit costs. The objective of the study was to give a fair examination of *all* credit costs and to relate them to income produced from the credit operation. Eight categories of credit costs were identified: (1) new account costs, (2) account servicing costs, (3) account collection costs, (4) interest at 6 per cent on receivables outstanding, (5) space and equipment costs, (6) cost of additional sales people required to handle credit customers, (7) management expenses, and (8) other miscellaneous credit costs.[6] The application of this cost analysis was made to regular 30-day, revolving, and instalment accounts.

The conclusion of this study was that retail credit was not a "business venture" but a "selling tool," for credit operating costs almost without exception exceeded income from credit service. Profit came from the merchandise markup rather than from the credit service charge. Thus this study not only allocated other than direct costs to the operation, it also related them to earnings, which in the past were not so important as they are today.

The finding of this study was that in 80 retail stores studied, involving 730,000 regular 30-day accounts and 663,000 revolving credit accounts, the total cost of the credit operation was $22 million annually and receipts from service charges $15.8 million, leaving a deficit of $6.2 million, or 2.55 per cent of credit sales. The cost of handling the average 30-day account was $6.73 per year; the revolving account, $11.82; and the instalment account, $17.25. As 30-day accounts earn only late charges, the net cost for them amounted to 3.76 per cent of sales on such accounts. Revolving credit accounts had a deficit of 1.31 per cent of such credit sales; instalment accounts, 0.05 per cent of instalment credit sales.[7]

Studies have also been made of the earnings and expenses of consumer finance companies, sales finance companies, commercial banks, and federal credit unions.[8] In 1959, their operating expenses measured in terms of credit outstanding were 14.25, 7.74, 4.17, and 3.30 per cent, respectively. In terms of the type of their business, these expenses ranged from 2.84 per cent of credit outstanding on automobile paper acquired directly by commercial

---

[6] *Study of Customer Credit Costs in Department Stores* (New York: National Retail Merchants Association, 1963).

[7] *Ibid.* See also Victor H. Brown, "Customer Credit Costs in Department Stores," *The Credit World,* February, 1965, p. 7.

[8] Paul F. Smith, *Consumer Credit Costs* (Princeton, N.J.: Princeton University Press, 1964).

banks to 14.42 per cent on personal loans of finance companies.[9] Differences in operating costs among lenders were attributed to several factors: method of acquiring business, character of the risks assumed, average size of contract, type of credit, and institutional differences.

CLASSIFICATION OF CREDIT COSTS

The analysis and control of costs in the credit operation necessitate the grouping or classification of expense items and the definition of variables which cause costs to differ, from time to time within a company and at a given time among various credit service suppliers. Classifications must have meaning, however, and the information sought influences the choice of base upon which expenditures are classified. The following are some of the more useful bases.

Direct Versus Indirect Costs

Credit costs have customarily been classified for purposes of analysis as direct and indirect costs. Only the former have been given much attention; the latter have often neither been identified as credit department costs nor allocated to the credit function. Direct costs are those resulting from the existence of a credit department, and for which the credit manager per se is held responsible. There is no indisputable distinction between direct and indirect categories, however; they reflect the policy and attitude of the individuals employing them. At best they express degrees by which different types of expenses have been brought into the credit analysis.

Basic to all cost analyses is a detailed itemization of costs according to bookkeeping usage. In Table 9–1 are listed most of the types of expenditures involved in the credit operation. Many creditors maintain such a grouping of costs, and they have been the basis of cost analyses made by both mercantile and retail credit study groups. The costs most often directly charged against the credit operation are those in Group I. Credit managers have usually been responsible for each of the functions represented therein, but they are not always responsible for expenditures in the other groups. According to this, when consideration is given only to such costs, the credit performance is more or less judged as an end in itself, a self-contained operation with

[9] *Ibid.*, p. 82.

a small number of cost variables the allocation of which is unquestionable.

Costs listed in Group II include those which, while directly related to the credit operation, are not always incurred at the discretion of the credit managers. They involve decisions of others and the application to credit operations of accounting

Table 9–1. Classification of the Costs of Credit Operation

GROUP I

Payroll	Postage and express
Credit approval	
Credit authorization	Credit information
Collecting	Dues
Account servicing	Reports and reference books
Social Security payment	Periodicals
Insurance and retirement	
Supplies and materials	
Stationery	Bad debt loss
Printing	
Supplies	

GROUP II

Advertising and promotion	Utilities
	Heat
Travel and entertainment	Light
	Power
Rent and occupancy	Refrigeration
Maintenance and depreciation	Services
Office furniture and equipment	Bonding
Tabulating equipment	Insurance
Air conditioning	Credit insurance
Authorization equipment	Auditing
Mail equipment	Collection agency service
Data-processing equipment	Legal service
	Teletype service
Taxes and licenses	Charge-plate franchise
Interest on invested funds	Telephone and telegraph
Interest on borrowed funds	

GROUP III

Administrative personnel	Central information files
Legal service	Purchasing
Floormen	Research
Additional salesmen	Timekeepers
Mail department	Institutional advertising
Exchange department	Donations
Comptroller's department	Bank examinations
	Franchise tax

principles more commonly applied elsewhere, as in the allocation of space and service costs on some rational basis. Although the traditional credit manager may not have had authority to originate promotion, depreciation, and service policies, the complete credit performance must be judged in terms of these criteria.

The third class of costs, Group III, consists of those incurred by the business as a whole, some part of which could reasonably be assigned to the credit operation. This group has been least allocated to credit analysis, but its inclusion is essential.

Functional Cost Allocation

The same expenses may be grouped along lines of the three functions of credit management: investment of funds, credit risk bearing, and performance of the routine of the credit operation. Some of the considerations for each have already been suggested in preceding chapters, along with measures for appraising their performance. The most detailed of the three is the departmental performance itself. Costs there incurred may be classified as best serves the purpose of management, but the following are several approaches to this analysis:

Direct Versus Indirect. Distinction is here made between costs which vary directly with number of applications, accounts, credit transactions, bad debts, etc., and those which continue almost independent of variations in credit business. Such information may aid in budgeting departmental expenditures, in computing a break-even point for credit operations, or in estimating the contribution which credit earnings make to general overhead.

Personnel Versus Mechanical. Expenditures may be divided between those made for people and those made for things. Automation increases the cost of the latter while reducing the former. At the same time, the extent of personnel costs related to given processes is often underestimated unless all of the personal expenditures of time and effort are considered.

Self-generated Versus Bought. One of the purposes of credit cost analysis is to aid decisions as to whether services should be performed by the credit department or bought from other specialists. Credit information, for example, if gathered completely by every creditor would cost each much more than that which can be bought from a credit bureau or agency. Costs of self-insurance might be considered in contrast to purchased insurance. The cost of self-generated service is also a measure of the value which the creditor is adding to the "product" of the firm, and correspondingly what he is adding to the total national output of value.

Explicit Versus Implicit. Explicit costs being those which are spent out of pocket, these are the obvious ones which have engaged the attention of management as "direct" costs. They are not the only direct costs, however, for costs of funds may be equally direct, yet unallocated because they do not involve an immediate outlay. Assets which may be depreciated for accounting purposes, as well as rent for space used, may be implicit rather than explicit costs. Both should be considered in making an appraisal of the credit operation.

Time of Cost Incurrence

Of great importance to credit cost control is a knowledge of the time in the process of the credit operation when the costs are incurred. This knowledge serves for timing their control, for making charges, and for calculating refunds. On the basis of time, credit costs are incurred in four periods:

Prior to the Credit Transaction. Expenditures for advertising, account solicitation, and investigation of prospective credit customers may be made prior to any contact with the customer, and they may result in no returns to the creditor. Such expenditures are general, indirect expenditures, unallocable to specific accounts or business. Some credit service suppliers engage more in this activity than others. Certainly this is not an expenditure which can be directly charged to a customer in a credit transaction, nor for which he may be directly charged once he has entered into a credit relationship.

Acquisition or Opening Costs. Another group of expenditures are incurred at the time that applications are made, investigated, and approved. These include the costs of interviewing, investigating, notifying, preparing identification plates, setting up account records, billing and filing legal notice where that is essential. Such costs relate solely to the identity of the account and do not vary with either the amount of it or the length of time that it will be outstanding. Creditors expect to amortize such fixed costs during the life of the credit relationship, but they are not always recouped when that relationship is of short duration.

In those cases efforts are made by the use of formulas to allocate a reasonable portion of the costs to the customer in the form of a credit charge.

Maintenance or Carrying Costs. A third set of costs occurs after the account has been acquired and during the life of it. Such costs are continuing and recurring. The principal continuing cost is the interest on funds invested in the account. Among the recurring costs are those for billings, receipt of payment, counseling, encouraging further use of the account, record keeping, and the costs of authorization. Some of these costs are more directly allocable to the individual accounts than are others. Provision is sometimes made through non-payment penalties for assessing the customer for part of these costs.

Termination Costs. Still other costs occur at the end of a credit relationship. Then are incurred the costs of collecting if payment is not made according to terms. Collection costs may include fees paid to collection agencies and attorneys, as well as the creditor's own collection costs. Then too are incurred some bookkeeping costs. In the normal course of affairs, these costs bear a planned relationship to the total costs anticipated and to earnings or profits from the credit transaction. When the debt is terminated prematurely, such costs may become disproportionate to earnings collectible, and an economic problem for the creditor results.

Illustration of Credit Costs

The classification and range of credit costs in department stores are shown in Table 9–2. For all types of credit in the eleven stores studied, the average cost of rendering credit service was 5.84 per cent of credit sales. Regular 30-day accounts had the lowest cost, 3.76 per cent; revolving credit accounts, 7.50 per cent; and conventional instalment accounts, 8.46 per cent of credit sales.

CREDIT COST VARIABLES

Costs of rendering credit service differ (1) among the transactions and relationships of a given creditor and (2) among different types of credit service suppliers. Whether their costs be considered from one or another standpoint discussed above, cost differences are attributable to variables which it is the responsi-

Table 9–2.   Credit Costs and Service Charges in Eleven Department Stores, as Per Cent of Credit Sales, 1962

		Type of Account		
	Total	30-Day Charge Accounts	Revolving Credit Accounts	Conventional Instalment Accounts
Credit sales	100.00	100.00	100.00	100.00
Service charge revenue	4.21	.11	7.05	9.12
Total credit costs	5.84	3.76	7.50	8.46
New account costs	.47	.28	.63	.84
Account servicing costs	1.62	1.45	1.98	1.29
Account collection costs	1.00	.43	1.55	1.65
Interest at 6% on account receivable investment	2.19	1.04	2.65	4.29
Credit space and equipment costs	.14	.12	.17	.13
Additional salespeople's costs due to credit	.21	.25	.27	.04
Management costs	.21	.19	.25	.22
Other credit costs	–	–	–	–
Excess (deficiency) of revenue over costs	(1.63)	(3.65)	(.45)	.66

SOURCE: "The True Costs of Customer Credit in Department Stores," *Stores*, November, 1963, pp. 8 ff.

bility of management to manage. The manner in which credit managers combine these variable factors influences their operating cost, determines their competitive position, and affects the charges which they make for credit service.

The following are the variables affecting credit costs:

1. Degree of risk deemed acceptable
2. Number of accounts serviced
3. Size of credit transaction
4. Size of account outstanding
5. Duration of receivable outstanding
6. Rate paid for capital in receivable
7. Extent of credit promotion
8. Occupancy charges assessed
9. Administrative overhead allocated
10. Cost of services purchased

As the variables in one relationship differ from those in another, the costs of serving different customers will not be the same. Such cost differences must be understood for management control and for assessing to customers appropriate charges. Because for expediency not every item of cost can be allocated specifically to every credit customer, a policy of assessing each an "average" cost is usually adopted. When the average costs of different creditors are arrayed, those performing one kind of credit service will be found having costs significantly different from those rendering another type of service, or catering to another segment of the credit market. Such institutional cost differences may be illustrated by the matrix of variables and combinations thereof shown in Table 9–3.

Table 9–3. Hypothetical Relation of Institutional Credit Costs to Credit Cost Variables

Institution Representing Combination of Variables	Credit Cost Variables [a]										Total Cost
	A	B	C	D	E	F	G	H	I	J	
1	1	1	1	1	1	1	1	1	1	1	10
2	2	2	2	2	2	2	3	2	2	2	21
3	1	1	1	1	1	2	2	2	1	1	13
4	1	1	1	2	1	1	1	1	1	1	11
5	3	4	4	3	1	1	2	2	2	3	25
6	1	1	1	1	2	2	1	1	1	1	12

[a] Key to variables:

A = credit risk accepted
B = number of accounts serviced
C = size of credit transaction
D = size of account outstanding
E = duration of receivable outstanding
F = rate paid for capital in receivables
G = extent of credit promotion
H = occupancy charges assessed
I = administrative overhead allocated
J = cost of services purchased

DISCUSSION QUESTIONS

1. What similarity or difference would there be between retail and mercantile credit operations in the application of cost analysis methods?

2. Account for the standards of cost accounting which have been applied to credit costs during the past few decades.

3. Identify the bases upon which credit costs may be classified to provide better information upon which to base credit decisions.

4. Construct a table or schedule of credit costs for different types of operations for comparison with charges, to be studied later, made by specialists to whom credit functions (and costs) might be shifted.

5. From the contents of Table 9–2, prepare a paper or discussion entitled "Factors in Department Store Credit Costs."

6. Explain Table 9–3 in terms of the following: elements of the "credit" mix," competitive advantage in credit operation, price competition in credit services, need for control of credit costs.

7. Make a comparative study of the credit costs of the following: a savings and loan association, a consumer loan company, a wholesale or manufacturing establishment, and a department store.

8. Who in a company should be interested in and responsible for cost analysis of its credit operation?

9. Prepare an analysis of the costs incurred at different times during the life of a credit relationship. What factors cause this incidence of cost to differ among credit operations?

10

Charges for Credit Service

Because credit service has not always been provided as a marketable product, charges have not always been made for it. Yet with increasing use of credit in all its forms, the problems of pricing it in the market have multiplied. Charging for credit service has in fact presented some unique pricing problems. It has been linked with age-old attitudes concerning exploitation and usury. It has confused the pricing of a service with the pricing of money alone. It has involved pricing credit service both separately and in conjunction with product sales. It has spread over the markets of those who sought credit service through necessity and those who sought it from choice. And it has been posed in price terms which have made communication between creditors and debtors difficult, misunderstandable, and sometimes abused. Nevertheless, understanding of the factors involved in charges for credit service is essential alike to suppliers who have incurred credit costs, users of credit who would appraise market offerings, and regulatory agencies who expect in this market the standard of behavior demanded elsewhere.

THE NATURE OF CREDIT CHARGES

In the following explanation of credit charges, distinction will be made between calculation, statement, and collection.

Calculation of Credit Charges

The calculation of credit charges represents the effort to determine the value of such service in the market. Value exists both as a utility concept in the mind of the buyer and as a cost input in the records of the seller. Both are taken into consideration in the setting of credit charges, but, as is common in a competitive capitalistic economy, prices tend to gravitate toward input costs, allowing for cost differentials in supplying different types of credit service. Both suppliers of credit service and regulatory agencies have related charges to costs, and both the legal and commercial structure of charges appear to reflect this fact.

Charges for credit service are generally calculated in one of three ways, or as a combination thereof: as a per cent of the principal involved, computed either on the amount outstanding or on the initial sum; as a flat dollar charge; and as a time–price differential.

The Percentage Charge. Perhaps the most common type of credit charge is that by which a percentage of the value involved is assessed as the charge. This has historic antecedence and is related to the calculation of interest on money loans. It is a method of charge which seems understandable to users of credit, who, in their respective credit service markets, find a percentage rate acceptable—the "prime rate" for commercial borrowers, a "savings account rate" for depositors, a "mortgage rate" for borrowers, etc.

Percentage rate charges, however, are not all of the same type. Some rates are applied to the original indebtedness involved; others are applied to the remaining balance outstanding. Moreover, some rates are applicable to the total value of a transaction; others are applicable only to that portion of the transaction which required investment in a receivable. Furthermore, some rates apply equally to an entire credit transaction; others employ a progressive scale of rates applied to different portions of the sum involved. The objectives of these rates are, respectively, (1) to provide compensation for different risks and costs inherent in dissimilar credit relationships, (2) to provide for risk and operational costs apart from capital costs, and (3) to compensate suppliers for fixed costs which may be the same for small credits as for large.

The rates for most types of credit charges have been legalized. Within the legal framework, competition may determine the going market rate. Outside the legal structure, credit transactions still occur at illegal rates. Basically, the *legal rate*, determined individually by the states, is that which is collectible without consent, as when a judgment is obtained with interest henceforth on a claim which until then carried no rate of charge. By contrast, a *legal contract rate* is that which is collectible with agreement of the debtor. In some states where the legal rate is 6 per cent, the contract rate may be 8 per cent. In addition to these legal rates, however, are several others granted to licensed types of creditors whose needed credit services can be supplied only with the incurrence of higher costs and higher charges. Both bank and non-bank creditors are governed by such provisions, although not all rates charged by non-bank creditors are subject to legal regulation.

The Dollar Charge. Because uniform, flat dollar charges bear little relationship to transactions of various magnitudes, they seldom serve as the whole charge for credit service. There are, however, several ways in which flat charges are made. One is when a minimum charge is made for a volume of credit business too small to warrant use of a rate, thus providing for some of the fixed expenses involved. Another is when certain specific costs are passed on to the customer, as filing charges or an investigation fee. Still another is when an arbitrary charge is made, as by an illegal lender, to obscure the rate of the charge. Nevertheless, while the charge may not be computed in terms of a flat charge, it may be so quoted to the customer, as will be discussed later.

The Time–Price Differential. In credit selling, the charge for credit service is not always differentiated from the charge for merchandise; rather, they are together quoted at one price known as the time price, distinguished from the cash price. The differential is called the "time–price differential." In earlier years, when sales financing charges obviously exceeded legal interest rates, the concept of a time–price differential was used to avoid accusations of illegality. Even when usury has been found, the courts recognize that a vendor may sell an article at one price for cash and at a higher price on time and that the difference is not interest and therefore not usurious.

Recently, however, an interpretation of the time price has evolved which further refines the concept. When the price of a commodity is agreed upon and thereafter an additional amount is added for credit charge, it is held that the agreement pertained to the cash price only and not to the time price.[1] Only when

---

[1] See Robert L. Oare, "Time Selling and Usury," *Time Sales Financing*, June, 1950, reprinted in *The Industrial Banker & Time Sales Financing*, April, 1965, p. 8.

explicit agreement is reached concerning the price of *both* commodity and credit charge is the creditor free of possibility of guilt for usury. Otherwise, it has been held, the higher price in the sales contract is merely a device to conceal a usurious charge. Notwithstanding this interpretation, the time–price concept is widely used and is incorporated into the sales financing legislation of many states.

Statement of the Credit Charge

How a vendor computes his price and how he states it to his customer are two different things. In the sale of credit service, the charge may be stated as computed, expressed in some arbitrary way, or not quoted at all.

"Free" Credit Service. Regardless of the costs involved in connection with the regular 30-day charge account, usually no direct charge is made for credit service. Costs are included in general overhead and covered by the merchandise markup. While there is no objection to such practice, cash customers are thereby obliged to pay as much as credit customers, and no inducement is provided credit customers to pay early.

Additional Charges. When specific credit charges are stated, they are usually added to the cash price of the merchandise. In such a case, there are three ways in which the additions may be expressed. First, it may be added as a lump sum to be paid, as a charge payable at the termination of a single-payment loan. Second, it may be added to the principal and both made payable in equal payments, each of which would include a different proportion of credit charge. Many personal loans and sales finance contracts are arranged in this way. Third, the credit charge may be added to the payable portion of principal in unequal payments.

Discount Charges. Not all credit charges are literally *added* to the principal. Some, computed as a percentage of the principal, are stated as subtractions or discounts, rather than as add-ons. Some commercial bank loans are expressed in this manner, with the charge deducted from the sum borrowed before the balance is given to the customer as a loan. Mercantile cash discount terms are also expressed as a discount from a due amount. Charges made by factors, charge account banks, credit card companies, and some others also are stated as a deduction from the principal amount involved.

Collection of the Credit Charge

The computed credit charge represents an estimate of the total charge for credit service. Neither the computation nor the statement of charge, however, gives assurance either that the total costs will be reimbursed in every case or that they can be collected when they are incurred. The collection of charges does not coincide with credit costs for several reasons. In the minds of customers, costs incurred do not always represent service rendered, prior to the completion of the credit relationship. Heavy initial charges would be psychologically adverse to creditors' interests. And the coincidence of costs and charges cannot always be scheduled, because debtor behavior cannot always be anticipated. Consequently, several collection plans are employed by creditors.

Some charges are collected at the beginning of the credit relationship, as in the case of real estate mortgage closing fees, filing fees, investigation charges, and, in a sense, the discount on commercial loans. Factors' charges and bank charge plan charges are also deducted from invoices advanced at the beginning of the credit period.

Other charges are collected throughout the credit period, particularly in instalment contracts. Usually the total charge is divided into portions payable with the periodic repayments of principal. Penalties for delinquency are also collected during the life of the contract. Still other charges are collected at the end of the credit period, as in the case of interest on single-payment loans.

As creditors' costs may not coincide with customers' sense of service rendered, and as charges collected may not coincide with charges earned, attempts have been made to reconcile costs, earnings, and collections in fairness to all. In Table 10–1 are illustrated six plans for collecting charges which express different ideas about the relationship of these three factors. The illustration presents six arrangements for paying charges of 8 per cent on an instalment contract for $1,200 repayable in 12 months.

Plan 1 is that in which the charge is "collected" at the outset by deducting $96 interest for the year from the $1,200 borrowed. Plan 2 is for the payment of $96 at the end of the 12th month along with $1,200 principal due. Plan 3 is for the collection of charges each month, computed as a per cent of the balance out-

Table 10–1. Six Plans for the Collection of Credit Charges
(terms: $1200 at 8 percent, repayable in 12 months)

	(1)	(2)	(3)		(4)		(5)			(6)	
							Payment on Original Balance				
	Single Payment Loan, Discounted	Single Payment Loan	Payment on Balance Outstanding		Equal Divisions		Arbitrary Allocation			Rule of 78ths	
Month			Principal	Interest	Principal	Interest	Principal	Interest	Charge	Principal	Interest
1	($96)	—	$100	+ $8.00	100	+ 8	100	+ 8.00	+ 30.80	100	+ 14.77
2	—	—	100	+ 7.33	100	+ 8	100	+ 7.33	+ 1.20	100	+ 13.54
3	—	—	100	+ 6.67	100	+ 8	100	+ 6.67	+ 1.20	100	+ 12.31
4	—	—	100	+ 6.00	100	+ 8	100	+ 6.00	+ 1.20	100	+ 11.08
5	—	—	100	+ 5.33	100	+ 8	100	+ 5.33	+ 1.20	100	+ 9.85
6	—	—	100	+ 4.67	100	+ 8	100	+ 4.67	+ 1.20	100	+ 8.62
7	—	—	100	+ 4.00	100	+ 8	100	+ 4.00	+ 1.20	100	+ 7.38
8	—	—	100	+ 3.33	100	+ 8	100	+ 3.33	+ 1.20	100	+ 6.15
9	—	—	100	+ 2.67	100	+ 8	100	+ 2.67	+ 1.20	100	+ 4.92
10	—	—	100	+ 2.00	100	+ 8	100	+ 2.00	+ 1.20	100	+ 3.69
11	—	—	100	+ 1.33	100	+ 8	100	+ 1.33	+ 1.20	100	+ 2.56
12	$1200	1200 + 96	100	+ .67	100	+ 8	100	+ .67	+ 1.20	100	+ 1.23
Total	$1200	$1296	1200	+ 52.00	1200	+ 96	1200	+ 52.00	+ 44.00	1200	+ 96.00
			$1252		1296		1296			1296	

standing. Such a charge relates earnings directly to funds invested. In this case the total charge is only $52. Plan 4 provides for the same rate applied to the original rather than to the outstanding balance and for an equal division of the $96 add-on charge. Both plans 3 and 4 may be unsatisfactory to the creditor, for the former does not provide for other than money costs and the latter does not provide for his unequal incurrence of costs at different periods in the credit relationship. Plan 5 represents an effort to correct both of these deficiencies by making, in addition to the $52 interest charge, a $44 service charge covering the risk and the operating costs. It is assumed that acquisition and opening costs amount to $30.80 and that carrying costs thereafter are $1.20. In other words, if the customer should terminate the debt at the end of the first month, the creditor would feel that charges of $38.80 were due. Because the customer may object to paying 40 per cent of a year's charges for use of credit for 8.3 per cent of a year (1 month), still another plan of allocation known as the Rule of 78ths is illustrated in Plan 6.

Underlying the Rule of 78ths is the assumption that collections should be related to the length of time that each dollar of credit is outstanding. On a $1,200 credit repayable at $100 monthly, money is outstanding as follows:

12	units	of	$100	are	used	the	1st	month
11	"	"	"	"	"	"	2nd	"
10	"	"	"	"	"	"	3rd	"
9	"	"	"	"	"	"	4th	"
8	"	"	"	"	"	"	5th	"
7	"	"	"	"	"	"	6th	"
6	"	"	"	"	"	"	7th	"
5	"	"	"	"	"	"	8th	"
4	"	"	"	"	"	"	9th	"
3	"	"	"	"	"	"	10th	"
2	"	"	"	"	"	"	11th	"
1	unit	"	"	is	"	"	12th	"
78	units	of	$100	are	used	for	one	month

Thus at the end of the first month $12/78$ths of $1,200 advanced for one year would have been used. At the end of the second month, $23/78$ths would have been used, etc. Accordingly, any charge computed on the original $1,200 ($1,200 \times 8\% = $96) should be scheduled and collected accordingly. Therefore, $14.77 ($96 \times 12/78$) would be due at the end of the first month, and other portions accordingly thereafter. Contracts longer than one year would be expressed in terms of more than 78 month-units. Fifteen-month contracts would involve the "Rule of 120ths"; of eighteen months, the "Rule of 171sts," etc.

The Rule of 78ths is widely used for adjustments in lending and sales financing where charges have been based upon an original balance but where repayment has not been as originally scheduled. Validity for use of this method has been gained through its incorporation into the instalment laws of many states.

Selection of a plan for collecting credit charges depends upon the nature and timing of costs incurred, the payment terms of the contract, and the likelihood of deviations from the original payment schedule.

TRUE RATES IN CREDIT CHARGES

The complexity of credit costs and the multiplicity of credit terms have resulted in both incomparability and the incomprehensibility of credit charges. Correction of this condition has been an objective of regulatory agencies, but even their good intentions in the interests of credit customers have not completely simplified credit terms or reduced the number of variables complicating them. For both customer and competitive reasons, complete uniformity of terms may be as undesirable as unattainable, but for the benefit of all, the confusion associated with them should be removed. This can be achieved to a large extent by the reduction of charges to rates and the expression of rates in terms of a common base. The comparability of rates converted to an annual basis, however, would not alone convey all information needed concerning charges, for knowledge of charges made in dollars is sometimes more useful than knowledge of rates. Nevertheless, familiarity with rate conversion methods is essential to judgment of credit practices, institutional credit differences, and social measures for the control of credit. A few of the main problems in true rate computation are discussed in the following pages.

Flat Rates

Credit charges are often quoted simply in terms of flat rates, which may or may not be on an annual basis. More reputable credit service suppliers usually quote rates on a time basis, as 6 per cent per annum, 1.5 per cent per month, 0.019178 per cent per day. Annual rates therefore may easily be obtained by multiplying the period rate by the number of period units in a year: 12 for months, 365 for days. Thus a 1.5 per cent monthly rate becomes an annual rate of 18 per cent; the 0.019178 daily rate a 7 per cent annual rate. Less reputable creditors may obscure true rates by quoting dollar charges for given lengths of time, such as a $10 charge for use of $200 for 3 months. A thinking customer would readily see that the nominal rate quoted is 5 per cent ($10 : $200 = 5%), and that inasmuch as this is for 3 months the annual rate would be 20 per cent (5% × 4 = 20%).

Mercantile cash discount terms pose a similar conversion problem, but their method of computation is different. Terms of $\frac{2}{10}$, net 30 indicate that a 2 per cent discount (charge) is given for paying 20 days early (30 days − 10 days). The annual rate of such a charge or discount, therefore, is 36 per cent (2% × 18 periods of 20 days).

Discount Terms

When discount terms are employed by financial organizations, they present still another problem of true rate determination. Banks which quote flat rates of 6 per cent per annum, if they discount the charge and advance to the customer the remainder of the principal, are actually charging a true rate of something in excess of 6 per cent. For example, on a $1,000 credit at 6 per cent discount, $940 would be advanced [$1,000 less $60 ($1,000 × 6%)]. Therefore, a charge of $60 on $940 principal used would be a 6.38 true rate ($60 : $940 = 6.38%). This same effect is created by banks' requirement that a compensating balance be left in a loan account. The true rate would be increased in proportion to the amount of the principal which could not be withdrawn.

Similarly, the true rate charged by finance companies which advance less than the amount on which their charge is based is higher than their nominal charge. One which charges 0.019178 per day or 7 per cent per annum would actually be charging 10 per cent per annum if it advanced only 70 per cent of the funds borrowed (7% : 70% = 10%).

Instalment Add-on Charges

When charges are computed on an original principal which is repaid in instalments, still another computation of true rate is required. The problem presented by instalment payments is that outstanding principal is continually being reduced while charges based on the original balance are necessarily increasing in relation to the balance in use. Many formulas have been devised for the conversion of nominal rate to true rate for instalment contracts,[2] but most of them are based upon the facts that the contract begins at the first of the 12-month period and is completed at the end of the 12th month (the beginning of the 13th), and that the number of dollars in use throughout 12 months is equivalent to half the original principal in use continuously for 6 months. The application of the formulas, however, presupposes a precise statement of the facts which go into the formula.

Determination of Credit Charge. It has already been shown that charge may be computed in many ways. In practical cases, it sometimes must be determined by deducting the cash price or original principal from the product of the payments and the number of payments. Increasingly credit charges are separately stated in instalment contracts, but in appraising promotional material a knowledge of ways to compute charges is useful.

Determination of Amount of Credit Service Used. The credit charge is made in consideration of the credit services used. There are several ways of looking at this. If no down payment is required, the purchase price of a commodity is probably the amount of credit service used. One might question, however, whether that sum is represented by the cash price or the credit price. From one standpoint, inasmuch as the commodity is the value sought, its price should represent the investment which the vendor has made, and therefore the capital involved in the transaction. On the other hand, when credit service is regarded as a service bought, as well as the merchandise, the credit costs incurred by the vendor also become an investment and expense for which the credit charge is compensation. The choice of one viewpoint or the other determines the length of time necessary

[2] See Milan V. Ayres, *Instalment Mathematics Handbook* (New York: The Ronald Press Co., 1946).

for repayment of the obligation. This is a point on which theory and credit practice do not exactly coincide.

To illustrate this point, let it be assumed that a commodity selling for $1,000 is sold on credit with a charge of 8 per cent, or $80, with the total obligation to be repaid in 12 instalments. That means that $1,080 is repaid in 12 instalments of $90 each. Question: How much credit service is involved? Only $1,000 if one considers just the vendor's investment in merchandise, but $1,080 if his investment in both merchandise and credit service is considered. Question: At the rate of repayment, how long will it take to pay for the credit service used? It would take 11.11 months ($1,000 : $90 = 11.11 months) from the one standpoint; 12 months from the other. Therefore, if $1,000 is regarded to be the amount of credit service used, 11.11 months should be thought of as the length of time needed for its repayment. (The other 0.89 month is for payment of the credit charge.) However, if $1,080 is the amount of credit service used, 12 months would be needed for its repayment.

When the problem of computing this true rate was first considered, the value of the merchandise alone was thought to be the value of credit service used. That was consistent with the failure to allocate all costs to a complete statement of credit costs involved. Notwithstanding this, in practice while the value of the merchandise was taken to be the amount of credit used, the length of the total contract was thought to be the length of time for computing the rate. Court decisions have been based upon this method in determining true instalment rates. Something might be said further for the third possibility: that the amount of credit service was the sum of the charge for the goods *and* the charge for credit service, and that the time for repayment was the total contract time for the repayment of both. Theoretical consistency suggests that the third proposition is most tenable and that the difference between a cash price and credit price is a differential charged for the purchase of two values instead of one (goods only). For practical consistency, however, inasmuch as the second method is the more generally used, that is the one that will be used in subsequent illustrations in this book.

When a down payment is required, the amount of that payment must be deducted from the cash price in order to determine the amount of credit service used.

Determination of Nominal Rate.   When both the credit charge and the amount of credit service used have been ascertained, the quotient obtained by dividing the former by the latter is the nominal rate of charge. This is sometimes a quoted rate. At other times it must be derived from other facts at hand. In either case, it is a rate in terms of time, whatever time is required for repayment of the total contract. In the formula given below, this length of time is symbolized by the letter n.

Computation of Nominal Annual Rate.   Only when an instalment contract is repayable in exactly one year, either by monthly or weekly payments, is the nominal rate also an annual rate. In all other instances it must be converted to an annual rate. This is done by dividing the nominal rate by n and multiplying by the number of time units in a year—12 if by months, 52 if by weeks. Thus in the illustration given above if $80 had been charged for $1,000 on a contract repayable in 16 months (instead of 12), the nominal rate would still have been 8 per cent, but the nominal annual rate would have been 6 per cent (8% : 16 × 12 = 6%). In the formula below, the nominal annual rate is symbolized by the letter r.

Computation of True Annual Rate.   When the computations listed above have been made, the true annual rate (symbolized by R) can be determined by use of the following formula: [3]

$$R = \frac{r\,(2n)}{n+1}$$

In carrying the above illustration to its conclusion, the following substitution of values would be made:

$$R = \frac{6\,(2 \times 16)}{16+1} = \frac{192}{17} = 11.3\%$$

Variations in Terms

The foregoing are the principal methods of computing true rates of charge, but there are some variations in credit terms which present other problems. One is in connection with the revolving charge account. The charge of 1.5 per cent per month

[3] This formula was developed by Theodore N. Beckman in 1924 and published in his *Credits and Collections in Theory and Practice* (2d ed.; New York: McGraw-Hill Book Co., Inc., 1930).

commonly made applies not to the *average* balance outstanding on this variable type of account, but to the *beginning* of month balance. Additions to and payments made on the account during the month may not be shown in the beginning of month balance on which the charge is made. Thus for an expression of true rate, over which the customer received credit, the numbers of days and dollar-days are related to furnish an average daily balance. This average balance when related to the charge for the month would yield a simple or nominal rate which could then be converted to an annual rate.[4]

Another variation in charges is that in which a combination charge is made, as by a factor, whose dual charge consists of one rate for funds advanced and another for other credit service performed. The former is a time rate; the latter is not. However, computation of a true rate would require that both charges be considered in relation to the amount of credit, for the length of time involved in the credit relationship. Except for the combination of the charges, the methods of computation previously discussed would be the same.[5]

DISCUSSION QUESTIONS

1. Distinguish clearly between calculation of the credit charge, statement of the charge to the customer, and allocation of the charge for collection purposes. Illustrate these three concepts with the charges of a real estate mortgage firm, a consumer finance company, a sales finance company, and a department store.
2. Is the addition of a charge to the principle involved always an "add-on" charge? Explain.

[4] For detailed illustration of this method, see Richard F. Vancil, "Calculating Simple Annual Rates," *The Credit World*, May, 1965, p. 20.

[5] Additional expressions of interest in this subject may be found in the following articles: Robert W. Johnson, "How Should Finance Charges Be Expressed?" *Consumer Finance News*, April, 1964, p. 3; Richard L. D. Morse and Theresa Courter, "Are Credit Terms Quoted Accurately?" *Consumer Finance News*, October, 1963, p. 3; M. R. Neifeld, "Yields and Longer Contracts," *Time Sales Financing*, July–August, 1963, p. 7; D. G. Mutch, "Interest Rates: 'True' Method?" *The Christian Science Monitor*, April 7, 1962; and Ralph A. Milliman, "A New Look at an Old Subject," *Time Sales Financing*, March–April, 1962, p. 5. For extensive coverage of the subject, see: Robert W. Johnson, *Methods of Stating Consumer Finance Charges* (New York: Columbia University Press, 1964); and M. R. Neifeld, *Neifeld's Guide to Instalment Computations* (Easton, Pa.: Mack Publishing Co., 1953).

3. To what extent is there justification for the collection of charges at the time and to the extent that costs are incurred by the supplier of credit service?

4. Diagram several plans of costs and charges in different credit situations so as to show the problems which arise when full payment is made before the expected duration of the contract.

5. What justification is there for charges made on a graduated scale, depending upon amount of credit involved; for charges combining two or more rates or types of charges; for charges expressed as so many dollars per hundred, rather than as rates; for charges made pro rata, rather than charges which are the same for "units or fractions thereof"?

6. What means other than the Rule of 78ths are there for adjusting charges when a refund is required?

7. In computation of actual rates, of what significance is it whether it be assumed that charges are paid before payments are made on principal, after all principal is repaid, or simultaneously with principal payments?

8. Obtain a schedule of credit charges from a local vendor or lender and compute the true annual rates involved, using the formula for R where necessary.

IV

THE STRUCTURE
OF CREDIT
ESTABLISHMENTS

11

The Emergent Credit Structure

The supplying of credit service to the economy is not simply an abstract performance of three basic credit functions; it is an institutionalized operation which has grown into elaborate credit systems. These institutions, linked in systems, constitute the framework in which credit management performs its work. They are the business forms which with competitive, social, and legal sanction have evolved as our prevailing credit structure. The emergence and operation of these institutions is the subject of Chapters 11–17.

THE NATURE OF CREDIT STRUCTURE

When a social need for an economic service exists, as the need for credit service in an exchange economy, certain activities must be performed. In credit business these have been identified as the investing of capital in receivables, the bearing of credit risk, and the performance of the routine of credit operation. The need to perform functions then gives rise to functionaries—parties who perform them. While the emergence of the functionary is a product of the function, the form of the functionary is not inherent in the function, and numerous types of business enterprises emerge to perform essentially the same function. Taken collectively, all forms of functionaries performing credit functions constitute the credit structure.

Any unit of business performing credit functions is *a credit operation*, whether it be a single individual, a credit department, or an entire business organization devoted to supplying credit service. The identity of each credit operation must be recognized and seen as part of the collective structure engaged in the performance of the total credit work. Whether the operating unit be one man behind the scenes of a manufacturing establishment, a credit department in a retail or wholesale concern, a bank, or a credit bureau, each is attempting, in its way, to meet some part of the need of the market for credit service. Each exists to perform one or more of the three credit functions; each incurs operational costs; each stands in a relationship to the organization within its own enterprise and to peers and competitors outside.

If the credit departments of vendors have not always been regarded as part of the credit structure, that has been because of the subordination of them to the merchandising activity. The tendency to regard the departmentized credit operation as more closely related to the merchandising performance than to the total system performing credit functions has obscured the basic credit functions, hampered the comparison of costs incurred by different operations, and prevented appreciation of the divisibility and shiftability of credit functions among the various functionaries.

Recognition of the functional relationship of all credit functionaries integrates the system, identifies their differences, and reveals new areas of credit management decision making.

Emergence Versus Stasis

Whatever the nature of the credit structure today, it has not always been so nor will it ever so be. The credit structure is an emergent phenomenon, not one of stasis. Its development has been characterized by specialization, integration, and diversification.

Structural Specialization. One of the emergent trends among credit operations has been that of increasing specialization. This development is characteristic of our economy, where entrepreneurial initiative often leads to division of tasks for improvement of performance. Moreover, in a growing market, progressive segmentation provides profitable opportunities for performance either of fewer functions or of different combinations of them. In the credit field these factors have produced an assortment of institutions differentiated in a number of ways.

DEPARTMENTIZED VERSUS INSTITUTIONALIZED. Credit operations within established business organizations—producers, distributors, or service facilities—are distinguishable from those which exist for the performance of credit service alone. The former are units of the structure, whereas the latter involve different management problems and provide a different service to the economy.

SALES VERSUS LOANS. Specialization occurs also on the basis of whether the promotion and financing of sales or the supplying of the needs for cash funds is the primary objective. Departmentized operations are usually concerned mainly with promoting the sale of products through the use of credit, but this promotional emphasis is sometimes a deterrent to shifting credit functions to specialists outside the parent establishment. The making of loans, however, both commercial and personal, is a distinctly different kind of business, differentiated by laws, by customers, and by competition.

BUSINESS VERSUS CONSUMER. Both departmentized and institutionalized creditors, and both those making sales and lending money, are classified as to whether they cater to business or personal markets for credit service. Mercantile creditors' activities are distinguished from those of retailers, and commercial lenders from consumer lenders.

HIGH- VERSUS LOW-RISK. Among the commercial and consumer lenders and credit vendors are an array of credit operations classified by the degree of risk entailed in providing service to their segment of the credit market. The assortment is wider among lenders, particularly in the consumer field, for there the degrees of risk specialization are most pronounced. Risk scalation among vendors is provided for more generally by the instruments and the forms of credit employed within the operation.

SHORT-TERM VERSUS LONG-TERM. The structure is also differentiated by some creditors having a longer relationship than others with customers. Thus real estate mortgage companies are in contrast to sales finance companies, and both with vendors on

30-day accounts. Each presents its own unique operations, relationships, and problems.

FUNCTIONAL SPECIALIZATION. Still another classification of credit establishments is made on the basis of function performed. Some perform all three of the functions; some only one or two, and not always the same combination of the three. Thus there are information specialists, risk specialists, financing specialists, and others who perform all or two of the functions.

Structural Integration. Some credit operations represent not a separation of credit performance from other operations, but an integration of the two. One example is the sales finance operation, integrated as a subsidiary with manufacturers of automobiles, consumer durable goods, and industrial equipment. Another is the credit union, established in an organization as an adjunct of its personnel activity. There are also plans whereby manufacturers' credit operations are integrated with those of distributors to facilitate credit service to dealers and consumers. All of these represent a combination into one operation of activities which have generally through specialization been assumed by separate business enterprises.

Functional Diversification. While specialization has occurred, so also has a counter trend of diversification of activities under one management. Whereas specialization offers an advantage of emphasis and concentration of effort, diversification offers possibilities of economy through the allocation of overhead to a greater variety and volume of business. Diversification is also undertaken to supply the varied credit needs of individuals.

Several prominent examples of diversification may be noted, and others are likely to be forthcoming. Department stores, for example, now generally offer two and three forms of credit service, whereas they formerly offered only one—the 30-day open account. Industrial banks have sought charters as commercial banks, in order to engage in commercial as well as consumer financing. Commercial banks have expanded their services to consumers along both lending and sales financing lines, while serving primarily commercial customers. Both personal finance and sales finance companies have diversified by obtaining licenses to engage in the business of the other. Mutual savings banks and savings and loan associations are currently undertaking to engage in the financing of instalment sales. This trend also is found today in merchandising, where the diversification of lines in a store is known as "scrambled merchandising." It has arisen from both external circumstances and internal policy decisions.

Primary and Auxiliary Suppliers of Credit Service

Although each of the classifications of credit operations discussed above is useful, still another, not generally made, is particularly pertinent to the analysis of the credit structure. It is that which identifies credit operations as primary or auxiliary suppliers of credit service.

Primary suppliers are those providing credit service to customers using their credit, as consumers, for the acquisition of consumption goods, or businesses, for acquisition of any asset except the financing of receivables. Auxiliary suppliers of credit service perform the credit functions for other business establishments, who otherwise would have to perform them themselves. All who serve in a primary capacity normally perform the three credit functions, although they may shift them to someone who performs them for them.

Characteristics of the two types of credit service suppliers may be summarized as follows:

Primary Suppliers	*Auxiliary Suppliers*
Their market consists of customers for credit service, who use the money or merchandise involved for *general consumption or business purposes.*	Their market consists of customers for credit service, who use this service in support of their *own credit service activities.*
Their market consists of users of credit who are only *debtors* in a credit relationship.	Their market consists of users of credit who are or would be *creditors* in another credit relationship.
Their market for credit service grows out of *personal* or *business* activity.	Their market for credit service grows out of the needs of that market to *provide credit service* for others; it is a derived, not a direct, demand for credit service.
They perform credit functions growing out of *their own needs* to provide a credit service.	They perform credit functions growing out of the performance of *credit operations in their customers' businesses.*

The structure of the credit system is set forth in Table 11–1, wherein both classes of credit establishments and the functions they perform are shown.

Although most suppliers of credit service operate as one or the other type, some perform in a dual capacity as both primary and auxiliary operations. The supplying of credit service to personal consumers is a function of primary operators. Retail stores selling on all types of accounts are primary credit service suppliers. So too are all types of lenders serving the market of personal consumers. The supplying of credit service to business establish-

Table 11–1. The Credit Structure and Related Functions

Type		Establishment		Functions Performed		
				Financing	Risk Bearing	Operations
Primary credit service operations	Vendors	Retailers		X	X	X
		Wholesalers		X	X	X
		Producers		X	X	X
	Lenders	Banks	Commercial	X	X	X
			Industrial	X	X	X
		Personal finance companies		X	X	X
		Savings and loan associations		X	X	X
		Credit unions		X	X	X
		Pawnbrokers		X	X	X
Secondary credit service operation Vendor and creditor auxiliaries	Full-function auxiliaries	Factors		X	X	X
		Charge account companies		X	X	X
		Sales finance companies		X	X	X
		Credit card companies		X	X	X
	Functionally specialized auxiliaries	Commercial finance companies		X		
		Banks		X		
		Credit insurance companies			X	
		Credit life insurance companies			X	
		Export credit insurance companies			X	
		Credit checking companies				X
		Credit information companies				X

ments, on the other hand, is of a twofold nature. Vendors selling on open account to business customers are primary suppliers. So too are banks and other lenders supplying funds for purchasing inventory or assets or for financing production or distribution. The auxiliary suppliers are those credit operations which perform for other lenders and vendors the functions which they would have to perform in supplying *their* credit customers. Banks and commercial finance companies advancing funds on the security of receivables are of this group. So are credit insurance companies taking over the credit risk, credit bureaus supplying credit information, and various organizations like sales finance companies, factors, charge account services, and credit card companies which take over all of the vendors' credit functions.

Credit Flows and Channels

While the credit structure may be thought of as institutions performing certain activities, like the business structure in general, it consists of *processes* carried on in numerous sets of relationships. These processes are sometimes termed flows, and the sets of relationships channels.

The need which impels the use of credit determines the nature of the flows which take place between the parties to the credit transaction. As reciprocity characterizes business, flows are balanced by counterflows, usually of an equal but different nature. For example, a credit purchase represents a flow of credit from the buyer to the seller, and a counterflow of merchandise. Later cash flows in payment of the debt, and creditworthiness is redeemed by an opposite flow. Thus it is seen that the substance of the flow is sometimes tangible, sometimes intangible. Much depends upon who takes the initiative in the relationship, for whether the seller refuses a request for credit, the buyer defaults on payment, or an intermediary intercedes for one or the other determines the patterns of flows and the sets of relationships which must be managed in the credit business.

The flows which occur in the relationships required for the distribution of a manufactured product are shown in Fig. 11–1. Upon receipt of an order, the manufacturer may pass it to a factor whom he engages to perform his credit functions. If the customer's creditworthiness is acceptable, a flow of cash will move from the factor to the manufacturer. Between the factor and the

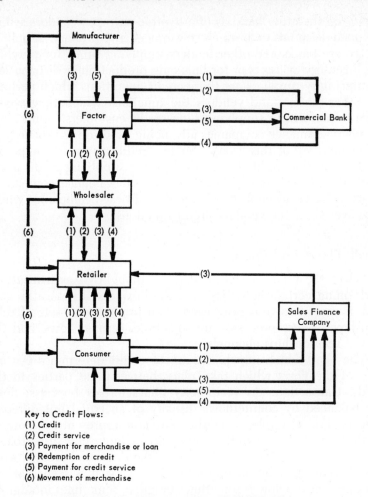

Key to Credit Flows:
(1) Credit
(2) Credit service
(3) Payment for merchandise or loan
(4) Redemption of credit
(5) Payment for credit service
(6) Movement of merchandise

Fig. 11–1. Flows through credit channels.

wholesale customer will flow credit service in one direction and ultimately payment in the other; similarly between the wholesaler and his retail dealer, and between the retailer and his ultimate customer. The factor, in turn, might borrow working capital from a commercial bank, in which case credit flows to the bank in exchange for cash; later payment flows to the bank in exchange for retirement of the debt and re-establishment of creditworthiness. Likewise, between the retailer and consumer the services of a sales finance company may be interposed. Then as credit flows from the consumer to the finance company, cash flows from it to the retailer; later a flow of payment cancels the debt.

The channel is the set or sets of relationships through which the flows take place. Relationships in sequence comprise the credit system. Credit channels, however, are parallel as well as sequential, and it is often the choice of management—or its obligation—to work through not one but many. Fig. 11–2 shows, for

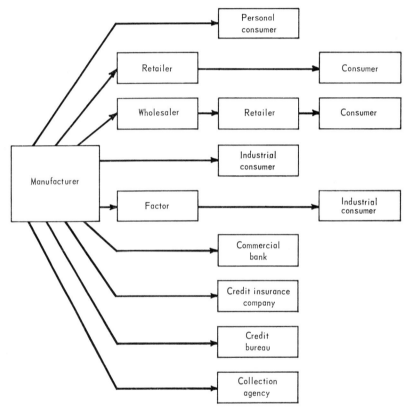

Fig. 11–2. Assortment of credit channels for a manufacturer.

example, the many sets of credit relationships which might exist for a manufacturer who is selling to several types of consumers, several distributive levels, and using the services of such credit specialists as a factor, commercial bank, credit insurance company, credit bureau, and a collection agency. Credit channels are sometimes determined by distribution policy. They are also determinants of distribution methods, which may depend upon the vendors' ability to provide credit service, through his own activity or that of someone else.

Adaptivity of Credit Structure

The existing credit structure is a twentieth century phenomenon peculiar to the United States. All business institutions represent a management concept of the best means of meeting what is presumed to be an economic need. This concept changes from time to time and reflects management's perception of its environment, on the one hand, and its ability to manage, on the other. Throughout history both have changed, with the result that credit institutions have evolved in a perceptible pattern.

Environmental influences are of principal importance, for they stem from prevalent social and economic conditions. Operations supplying consumers with credit service have changed with market conditions. The predominance of soft goods and food products in nineteenth century consumption caused the regular charge account to be about the only form of consumer credit. The appearance of automobiles and other durable products in the first quarter of this century gave rise to instalment credit plans and to sales financing agencies. The growth of the middle-income class and increased economic stability enlarged the market for consumer loan services, providing markets for consumer loan companies, credit unions, etc. Similarly, expansion of the wholesale market and pressures upon working capital have encouraged the development of factors and commercial finance companies in a variety of industries. The existing credit structure, therefore, is the product of many circumstances which have evolved in an orderly fashion.

It is also the product of management response to changing conditions. New opportunities influence the business structure only when and insofar as management develops techniques for turning those opportunities to profitable business. Thus in the competitive interplay in a free economic system entrepreneurs are continually innovating and emulating, seeking differential advantages and conforming to what others work out. Significant product differentiation has generally characterized the product offerings of credit service suppliers in the American system, but trends in the credit structure give evidence that lines of differentiation have become somewhat blurred, as diversification of services has progressed and as alternative offerings in the credit market have become more numerous.

CREDIT STRUCTURE AND MANAGEMENT DECISIONS

Business management today faces more decisions relative to credit operation than formerly. Whereas it was more or less taken for granted that if one undertook to render a credit service he would perform the credit functions—the alternative to performing them being not to render a credit service—today the functions are not inseparable. The credit structure is evidence that the credit functions are both divisible and shiftable, and a knowledge of this is essential to management concerned with credit.

The widening choice of services available to organizations which operate on a credit basis—as well as to those which do not —is a phenomenon of technological change in the credit economy. Like all such change, new procedures and new agencies cause alarm to vested interests and established operators. Consequently, traditional credit managers have sometimes shown reluctance to integrate themselves with developments in the credit structure. The shiftability of functions, however, is less a threat to conventional credit management than it is a boon to those who can profit by shifting, and an incentive to others who have not used credit service to do so. As population, incomes, spending, and the demand for credit service increase, so will the variety of credit service offerings, the institutions providing such service, the interrelationships among credit managers and other executive roles, and the opportunities for employment in the credit profession.

In the following chapters are discussed in more detail the primary and auxiliary types of credit service suppliers.

DISCUSSION QUESTIONS

1. Distinguish between "credit operation" and "credit establishment," "credit operation" and "credit structure," "credit structure" and "credit system." Which of these terms may be used in the plural as well as in the singular?

2. Examine a local directory to identify the types of credit operations which comprise the local credit structure.

3. Compare the trends recognizable in credit establishments with those in manufacturing and distribution in recent years.

4. Appraise trends in the credit structure from the standpoint that they are a response to market segmentation, or simply competitive differentiation.

5. Compare types of distributive establishments with credit service establishments as they are classified primary and secondary, full-function and limited-function. Is this sort of specialization in the credit structure unique?

6. Diagram channels and flows of credit service which illustrate the position and relations of all types of credit establishments and operations.

7. What constitutes innovation in credit management? Has innovative management produced new institutional types?

8. Of what practical management value is a knowledge of credit structure and of the concept of divisibility and shiftability of functions?

12

Primary Credit Service Establishments: Vendors

A large portion of the credit structure consists of vendors who perform credit functions in connection with the sale of merchandise and service. They include retailers, wholesalers, producers, and service establishments. Their credit service is rendered through the work of their credit departments. Being thus integrated with commercial activities, they usually operate without specific legal sanction or license, although some of their credit activities may be subject to functional if not institutional regulation. Also, as commercial activities, management of this type of credit operation is governed by policies which in the eyes of management seem best in the seller–customer relationship. Owner interests have been predominant guides to credit manager behavior, inasmuch as the performance objective of the credit unit has often been to serve the seller rather than the buyer. The turning of perspective in recent years, however, has identified the departmental credit operation increasingly with the total credit structure.

Vendors' credit operations have generally exemplified the category of primary credit service establishments. They perform the three basic credit functions. They are not confined to this status, however, and increasingly they are affiliated with other credit specialists in providing the flow of credit service which the market desires. They are sometimes in contrast to full-function auxiliary establishments which assume the entire credit work for other similar vendors. The auxiliary establishments which serve vendors in this way are the subject of Chapter 13. This chapter is concerned with the role of vendors' credit departments in the credit structure. Inasmuch as they have similarities in their organization, position in the corporate structure, lack of legal authorization, and their expression of commercial policies, attention here will be directed to some bases of the differences in this type of credit operation. Such differences may be found in the dual relationship of credit management in this type of operation to the market, on the one hand, and to superior management objectives, on the other. These relationships are embodied in the forms of credit service offered by vendors.

THE OPEN ACCOUNT

The credit operation for which vendors are most often responsible as primary credit service establishments is that providing open account service. An open account is that relationship between vendor and customer whereby an initial determination of creditworthiness serves as the basis for repeated credit transactions. It is a credit service inseparable from the sale of merchandise and service, and it is so integrated with vendors' sales policies as not often to be entrusted to administration by outsiders. For these reasons this portion of the credit structure is found inside institutions which are mainly of a non-credit nature. Moreover, because this function has traditionally been so sales related that it was not appraised fairly in its own rights, the relationship of this type of credit service supplier to the remainder of the credit structure has not always been appreciated.

The supplying of open account service has a history involving a variety of institutions in which this credit operation has been performed. They reflect the trends of social change and the efforts of creditors to manage the open account for more profitable results. As changes in the economy have evolved new types of retail establishments, their managers have faced the decision of whether or not to engage in the credit operation. Some have undertaken it; others have not. The short- and long-run necessities for delayed payment in consumer transactions first produced informal sales credit. Vendors had no choice—they performed the credit functions: carried the accounts, bore the risk, made collections. There was no one to whom such functions could have been shifted.

Formalization of the open account relationship accompanied the increase in size of business organizations and the impersonalization of the seller–buyer relationship. Growth of markets and growth of marketers increased the separation of creditors from their customers and led to standardization of terms but diversification of types of open accounts. Retail department stores were among the first to offer the regular open charge account "as a matter of policy." It was a gesture to customers' desire for convenience, but it was also a systematization of a competitive offering. The open account became one of the services of the so-called service retailers.

From the standpoint of management, the open account is a technique as well as a service in itself. It is generally believed that the provision of the open account has certain definite effects on retail business. It attracts customers to the store, for the open account is essential as an instrument of convenience. Moreover, inasmuch as the open account is usually a "free" form of credit service, it is one of many merchandising features which make the store an attractive, interesting, and desirable place to shop. Customers with charge accounts tend to shop the store more than those without accounts.[1] They also make cash as well as credit purchases when they are in the store. Furthermore, the open account has been claimed as a means to increase both unit sales and total sales per customer, to stabilize sales throughout the week and month, and to reduce buyer resistance.

Other retail establishments have also built reputations by offering or not offering credit service. The larger the volume and the more repetitive the use of the account, the greater the likelihood of importance attached to the open account. Success based on an opposite policy was demonstrated, however, in the experience of grocery store chains. They eliminated the open account long offered by the neighborhood grocery, removing the credit operation entirely from their organization. Likewise, so-called discount retailers of both hard and soft goods avoided the credit offering, relying upon price appeal rather than service as a customer attraction. Yet from time to time chain stores, super-

---

[1] "How Charge Accounts Affect Cash Sales," *The Credit World*, November, 1964, p. 18.

markets, and discounters alike have experimented with open accounts, depending upon the character of their market and the nature of their competition.

Retail open accounts are not limited to establishments of the types mentioned. A complete list would include the door-delivered products such as milk and baked goods; services such as dry cleaning and laundry; telephone and mail-ordered items such as flowers, magazines, and phonograph records; and the personal services of physicians, dentists, photographers, and hospitals. These exemplify the assumption and retention of all credit functions by a primary credit service operation.

Neither are open accounts limited to the retail field; they are the principal form of credit service offered by producers and wholesalers. Whereas retailers have a greater variety of forms of credit service, wholesalers and producers offer a greater variety of terms in conjunction with the open account. All of these institutions provide credit service in relation to their sale of merchandise; each, however, plays a different role in the financing of distribution. In distribution channels including regular wholesalers, the wholesaler has customarily furnished credit service for its customers, i.e., retail merchants, who, because of their small size and remoteness, were not always acceptable credit risks to manufacturers. On the other hand, manufacturers have usually sold on credit to wholesalers and to their industrial customers. Thus the flow of credit service supplied by primary establishments extends in many directions paralleling the channels of commodity distribution, and in some instances determining them.

Although national manufacturers do not often provide credit service to their ultimate consumers, petroleum producers typify exceptions to this, providing credit service throughout the channel, even to consumers, by their system of credit cards. They thus relieve retailers of the performance of the credit function. Other manufacturers in whose distribution program credit service to their customers' customers is important, such as manufacturers of industrial or photographic equipment, have also devised plans for credit intended to facilitate the moving of goods throughout the channel, even into the hands of final consumers.

Variations of the Open Account

In order to meet market needs and obtain maximum efficiency of operation, retailers have offered several variations of the open account. One is the selective charge account offered to a specific market segment, such as the Junior Charge Account, the Student Charge Account, the Starlet Circle Charge Account, the Campus Deb Account, or the Teen-age Charge Account. Some of these are designed for young people who have finished school and work full time. More recent versions of this account are for youngsters whose spending money comes from allowances and part-time work.

The scrip account is another variation, which affords control in the administration of the credit limit. By this plan, when an account is approved for a customer he is provided with scrip in the amount of the credit limit. He spends this as he would spend cash in the store. When the allotted amount has been used and payment is made in accord with the terms of the account, additional scrip is issued.

A further variation, which really is not the use of credit, is the deposit account. R. H. Macy Company, New York City, in its early years was one of the few large department stores which did not provide credit service. Its claim of ability therefore to sell for 6 per cent less than its credit competitors was ultimately disallowed by the Federal Trade Commission as not based upon fact. Subsequently, to provide the purchase convenience demanded by some customers, Macy accepted deposits against which it would "charge" purchases made throughout the store. Upon depletion of the deposit account, or at the end of the month, the customer was billed for the withdrawals and the account replenished.

Still another variation of the open account consists of a time extension made to accommodate certain types of purchases. Clothing is sometimes sold on a 90-day or 10-payment account. Multiple payments on an open account is not instalment credit service. It is, rather, a device for accelerating partial payments on accounts which are normally not paid in full on time. They also represent an accommodation to the customer for meeting larger obligations at a slower rate than might be expected for ordinary open account purchases. Up to 6 months in time is sometimes given without charge on purchases made through the decorators' studio. Another prominent store, Neiman-Marcus, Dallas, extends open account credit service up to 5 months for "investment" purchases such as coats, suits, and luggage, and longer for china, glassware, silver, and antiques; up to 12 months on the bridal trousseau account, with a service charge made only after the seventh month; and from 6 months to 12 months for furs and jewelry.

THE REVOLVING ACCOUNT

Vendor–customer relations in the use of the open account have presented several problems over the years: inability of many cash customers of a store to qualify for its regular account service; delinquency in use of the regular open account; high credit costs resulting from low volume of purchases, multiple payments, and collection efforts; and general difficulties of administering credit limits in retail stores. Search for the solution to these problems has led to the development of revolving and optional accounts.

Following World War II, what was generally known as the "revolving" account was conceived as a combination of the open and the instalment accounts. Basically it is an open account on which repeated purchases may be made up to a determined limit, and on which predetermined partial payments are made monthly along with a service charge. Originally the market for such credit service was thought to be customers whose income did not warrant the confidence required by the regular account. Part-time employees, teachers, clerks, and office employees constituted a large part of such a market. The amount which the customer could pay each month having been ascertained in conference with him, the limit to the account was set as the product of the monthly payment multiplied by the number of months in the store's plan. For example, if the customer could pay $10 a month on the account, his limit or open-to-buy would be $60 with a store having a 6-month plan, $120 on a 12-month plan, and $180 on an 18-month plan. The service charge computed on the basis of the balance outstanding at the beginning of any month was initially 1 per cent per month, later generally increased by most stores to 1.5 per cent per month.

Revolving account plans have generally been operated as exempt from usury laws because they are not concerned with the lending of money, and from the regulation of instalment sales because no mortgage is taken on goods sold on this account. Nevertheless, the fact that service charges amount to from 12 to

18 per cent per annum has raised questions concerning their legal status.[2] Consequently, most states have enacted laws of the type first passed by New York State and Kansas beginning in 1958. The New York law permitted a maximum service charge of 1.5 per cent per month on the first $500 of outstanding indebtedness and 1 per cent per month on any excess. A flat alternative charge not exceeding 70 cents per month was permitted. All other charges were prohibited, except for insurance and attorney's fees not exceeding 20 per cent of the monthly statements of the account.[3]

An alternative version of the revolving account service charge is illustrated in the law passed in Ohio in 1959. It reads as follows:

A retail seller or holder under a revolving budget agreement may charge, collect, and receive a finance charge or service charge, or both, however described, but the aggregate of such charges, however described, shall not exceed the sum obtained by applying to the unpaid balance, including therein any arrearages of finance and service charges, at the beginning or end of each period:

(1) A base finance charge at a rate not exceeding fifty cents per fifty dollars per month;

(2) A service charge at a rate of not more than fifty cents per fifty dollars per month for the first four fifty dollar units of such unpaid balance;

(3) An additional service charge at a rate of not more than twenty-five cents per fifty dollars per month for the next four fifty dollar units of such unpaid balance.

On unpaid balances less than, nor not in multiples of, fifty dollars per month, said charges shall be computed proportionately.

A minimum charge of $1 per month might be made. Thus on balances up to $200, an effectual rate of approximately 2 per cent per month was permitted. The rate declined on larger balances. These rates, however, are permissive rates and, in practice, competition has generally kept the rates at a 1.5 per cent per month maximum.

Table 12–1 illustrates the use of the revolving account and the computation of charge thereon by the simple monthly rate.

[2] For a summary of vendor credit regulation, see Barbara A. Curran, *Trends in Consumer Credit Legislation* (Chicago: University of Chicago Press, 1965), pp. 83–124.

[3] Floyd E. Britton and Charles C. Ulrich, "The Illinois Retail Instalment Sales Act—Historical Background and Comparative Legislation," *Northwestern University Law Review*, LIII, No. 175 (May–June, 1958).

It may be seen from this that the effectual rate is 18 per cent per annum only when the monthly rate is applicable to the *average* balance outstanding. Inasmuch as it is actually applied to the *beginning of month* balance instead, the true rate is dependent upon the timing of purchases and payments. If purchases are made early in a month and payments late, the end of month balance does not coincide with an average balance, and charges and rates would therefore be relatively low. If the relationship of payments and charges is reversed, the opposite is the case.

Variation in Revolving Accounts

Revolving accounts, as originally conceived, did not correct all the problems presented by the regular open account. Confinement of the revolving account to its predetermined limit was still difficult, particularly during seasons of peak purchasing. Customers sometimes held both types of accounts, using the revolving as an overflow for the regular account, and reducing that on which a charge was made while letting the "free" credit account run. Moreover, duplication of records and files was found to be costly, and even with the charges made, the revolving account did not compensate for all expenses when a fair accounting of costs was performed. A study previously quoted revealed that in representative department stores income from revolving accounts amounted on the average to $11.82 per year, against operating costs therefor of $13.64, leaving a net deficit of $1.82.[4]

Further adaptation of the revolving account was made in what has become known as the Optional Account. This plan provides the customer the option of using open account service free of charge if payment is made in accord with regular 30-day terms, or of making extended payments according to an agreement with the charge applicable to revolving accounts. Such a plan evolved gradually and out of necessity. When it was found that revolving accounts exceeded their limit, it was first required that one-third of the excess be paid in three following months, along with the regular payment and charges. Customers' willingness to make increased payments matched vendors' desire for increased purchases, and the optional plan was made to be practically "limit-

---

[4] Victor H. Brown, "Customer Credit Costs in Department Stores," *The Credit World,* February, 1965, pp. 7–8.

Table 12–1. Illustration of Computation of Revolving
Account Service Charge
(1.5% per month)

	Beginning of Month Balance	Purchases	Payments	Service Charge
First month	0			
1		10.00		
		20.00		
		20.00		
			10.00	
30				0
Second month	40.00			
1		15.00		
		30.00		
			10.00	
30				.60
Third month	75.60			
1				
			20.00	
30				1.13
Fourth month	56.73			

less," with monthly payments scaled to a percentage of the bal-ance outstanding, plus charges, if the extended option was taken. There are competitive differences in the exact terms offered on this plan, as evidenced by the following schedule for Wards and Sears.

WARDS		SEARS	
If unpaid balance is	Monthly payment is	If unpaid balance is	Monthly payment is
Up to $100.00	$ 5	Under $10.00	Balance
$100.01– 120.00	6	10.01– 100.00	$10
120.01– 140.00	7	100.01– 150.00	15
140.01– 160.00	8	150.01– 200.00	20
160.01– 180.00	9	200.01– 250.00	25
180.01– 200.00	10	250.01– 300.00	30
280.01– 300.00	15	300.01– 350.00	35
400.01– 420.00	21	Over–$350.00	1/10 of
980.01–1000.00	50		account balance

One survey made of the effects of the optional account plan reported stores as having the following experiences: [5]

Average sales increased from $6.00 to $10.50.

Bad debt loss increased only .03 of one percent over the previous year.

Credit sales increased 20 per cent during the first year, and Accounts Receivable increased 25 per cent.

Collection turnover fluctuates from 26 to 28 per cent, or a four month pay off on a six month plan.

Collections averaged between 38 and 40 per cent.

Many former habitual delinquent 30-day customers now pay their accounts in full each month to eliminate the service charge.

A customer who understands the service charge seldom objects to having it added to his account.

Customers buy more on an Optional Account.

The number of active accounts has trebled in two years time—60 per cent of these represent new accounts opened and 40 per cent transferred from our previous regular account category.

INSTALMENT CREDIT

The third form of credit service provided by vendors acting in the role of primary suppliers is that of instalment credit. This form is characterized by single rather than continuous credit

5 Dean Ashby, "The Advantages of Extended Terms for Charge Accounts," *The Credit World*, September, 1960, p. 6.

transactions, by use of a mortgage or conditional sale contract, by multiple payments, and by a charge for the credit service. Whereas revolving and regular accounts are used mainly for the sale of soft goods, instalment credit is related more to consumer durable goods, particularly automobiles.

Instalment credit is a form of credit service offered by both primary and auxiliary suppliers of credit service. The importance of vendors in the credit structure for this kind of service is indicated by available debt data. In 1965, total instalment receivables outstanding were $60.8 billion. Only 11 per cent of this was held by vendors, the remainder having been shifted to other credit specialists. Of the $7 billion retained by vendors, $0.4 billion resulted from the sale of automobiles and $6.6 billion from other consumer durable goods. By contrast, $25.1 billion of automobile credit was shifted by vendors and $8.4 billion of debt on other purchases. Of the non-automobile credit held by vendors, department stores hold $3.7 billion; furniture stores, $1.1 billion; appliance outlets, $0.3 billion; and other stores, $1.5 billion. Thus is shown something of the credit structure of vendors who perform the credit functions in connection with the sale of consumer goods.

Of all forms of retail credit, instalment credit has been the most controversial. It particularly has been regarded as a dynamic influence in the economy. It, too, has been an area of wide diversity of charges and terms and has been specifically regulated by legislation in 30 states. As such legislation pertains to the activity of instalment selling, by vendors and credit specialists alike, consideration of it in this chapter is appropriate.

Regulations of this form of credit are generally known as instalment sales laws.[6] Among the states there is a variety of legal provisions, but they generally pertain to the following subjects:

LICENSING AND EXAMINATION.   Six of 30 states require a license of retail instalment sellers, 21 of sales finance companies, 5 of retail instalment sellers who carry their own paper, and 7 of neither instalment seller nor sales finance companies. Examinations of licensees vary.

---

[6] Summaries of such legislation are published from time to time. See "A Summary of State Instalment Sales Laws—1959," *Time Sales Financing*, September, 1959, pp. 3–32; M. R. Neifeld, *Rate Sections in Collateral Statutes*, Beneficial Finance System, Third Ed., 1960; and Curran, *op. cit.*

CONTRACT REQUIREMENTS. With variations, most statutes require (1) written, signed, and delivered contracts; (2) disclosure of cash price, down payment, cost of insurance and other services, unpaid balance, time–price differential or finance charge, total contract indebtedness, and number and dates of payment; and (3) prohibition of specified practices.

INSURANCE. Recognition is generally given the right of instalment sellers to require insurance covering the chattels sold.

PREPAYMENT AND REBATES. Most states give the instalment buyer the right to prepay his contract and to secure a refund. Amounts vary, but the Rule of 78ths or the "sum of the digits" method is widely adopted.

COLLECTIONS; REPOSSESSIONS. Almost all of the 30 states permit collection of default or delinquency charges. Some states allow attorney's fees of 15 per cent of amount delinquent, plus court costs. Rights of both parties are usually specified concerning repossession.

EXTENSIONS—REFINANCING. Charges for extension or rescheduling of contracts are specified.

PENALTIES. All of the statutes carry penalties for their violation.

PERMITTED CHARGES. Although the time–price differential has long been regarded a subject for bargaining, 27 of the 30 states designated limits on this differential or charge. Most states establish classes of contracts (i.e., type of merchandise, age of automobile) and they have fixed limits for each class of contract. A few states have fixed as limits an amount equal to 1 per cent of the original unpaid balance of the contract, multiplied by the number of months the contract is to run, with a minimum charge of $15 to $25. Some charges are a composite, as in Ohio: a base charge of $8 per $100 per year on the principal contract balance plus "a service charge of 50 cents per month on the first $50 unit, or fraction thereof, of the principal balance, for each month of the term of the contract; and an additional service charge of 25 cents per month for each of the next five $50 units, or fraction thereof, of the principal balance for each month of the term of the contract." Some states do not control rates but require that current rates be filed with state authorities.

True Rate Computation

Inasmuch as the statutes of many states provide for an instalment credit charge which is based upon the original outstanding balance, reduction of that balance by instalment payments effects a true rate which is considerably higher. While this fact may be appreciated by those using such credit service, derivation of true rates requires careful consideration of several factors.

First, determination of the base to which the charge is applied. Instalment sales involve several variables, which are sometimes mentioned in legislation as a requirement of disclosure so that customers may be informed of the intricacies of this somewhat complex calculation. They are as follows:

1. Cash price
2. Down payment, either in money or goods
3. Unpaid balance (1) − (2) = (3)
4. Cost of insurance required
5. Principal balance (3) + (4) = (5)
6. Amount of the finance charge
7. Time balance (5) + (6) = (7)

The finance charge, in other words, is applied to the sum of values represented by the product and other services purchased. It is the total of these plus the finance charge, however, which is divided by the number of contract payments to determine the amount of each.

Second, the declining balance outstanding. Even when charges are specified by statute, they are not always expressed even as a simple rate, much less as a true rate. The Ohio law cited, for example, requires application of several rates for the determination of one simple rate, and inasmuch as that rate produces a dollar charge over the life of the contract, the true rate determination requires use of the formula previously explained:

$$R = \frac{r\ (2n)}{n + 1}$$

To illustrate these two considerations in terms of the Ohio provision, assume a principal balance of $1,000, with the time balance repayable in 18 monthly payments. The computation would be made as follows.

Basic charge $8 × 10 ($100 units) × 1½ years =
                      $80 × 1½   = $120.00
Service charge   50¢ × 1 × 18 months   =   9.00
                      25¢ × 5 (units) × 18 months   =   22.50
Total charge $151.50

$151.50 : $1000 = 15% nominal rate, for 18 months
15% : 18 months = X% : 12 months
         X = 10% nominal rate for 12 months

$$R = \frac{10\,(2 \times 18)}{18 + 1} = \frac{360}{19} = 18.9\% \text{ actual annual rate}$$

Management of Instalment Credit

Experience has led to the statement of certain generalizations which are widely accepted in management of this form of credit.

1. Instalment credit service, like all forms, should be extended on the basis of customers' ability to pay, notwithstanding the value which is inherent—and mortgageable—in the goods so sold. This basis of creditworthiness is fundamental to the sale of services and soft goods on instalment terms, and it has increasing application even to the sale of durables.
2. Instalment credit service, from the creditors' standpoint, has a cost-based value which cannot be computed merely in terms of the interest rate value of the money involved. Account acquisition, maintenance, and collection costs also must be considered in determining the charge to be made for this form of credit service.
3. Disclosure of credit terms and other contract provisions should be made in fulfillment of creditors' ethical obligation to customers.
4. Payments should be matched with income. Monthly intervals are most common, but where income is more or less frequent, adjustments should be made accordingly.
5. When approval of credit is based to a large extent upon the repossession value of the goods in question, the balance outstanding at any time should be less than the value of the goods. To achieve this, down payments should equal initial depreciation of the goods as they pass to the customer, or equal the amount of the gross margin on which the vendor is operating.

SUMMARY

The vendor is one of the various parties who contribute to the supplying of credit service in the distribution of products. If he elects to do so, he may perform in its entirety the credit operation, assuming responsibility for the performance of all of the inherent credit functions. In that case, along with the merchandise which he is selling, he will usually offer credit service in one of three forms: regular charge account, revolving or optional account, or on instalment terms. This election involves a top-level management decision. If, on the other hand, management is unable or unwilling to assume these responsibilities, they may be shifted to other credit specialists, as explained in Chapters 14 through 16.

DISCUSSION QUESTIONS

1. Contrast the credit offerings of a retailer and a wholesaler or manufacturer with respect to the following: forms of credit service, terms, charges, innovations, debtor–creditor relationships.

2. Considering the objectives for which retail vendors provide credit service, do the innovations in open accounts and the development of the revolving account represent changes in objectives or changes in means of satisfying former objectives?

3. Appraise the merits and demerits of the optional account in contrast to the revolving account, and appraise the applicability of this form of credit to mercantile business.

4. Compare regular, revolving, and instalment accounts with respect to vendors' credit costs and credit charges to customers.

5. Explain the environmental circumstances and the managerial practices which have led to legal controls for vendor credit service.

6. (a) What is the credit service charge for the first month on a revolving account which amounted to $400 at the beginning of the month? Compute in terms of a selected state law. (b) Assuming that the vendor operated on a 10-month revolving plan, what would be the total charge paid in 10 months if one-tenth of the limit (say $400) were paid each month. Determine whether the service charge should be paid in addition to the principal payment or added to the balance to be paid along with the principal. (c) What is the annual rate of the charge collected during the first month? During the 10 months?

7. An automobile is financed on the following terms: original price, $3,200; down payment, $640; insurance, $60; credit life insurance, $10; 36 months to repay the total contract. Compute the following, using the maximum legal rate in a selected state: (a) Cash price, (b) Down payment, (c) Unpaid balance, (d) Added charges, (e)

Principal balance, (f) Finance charge, (g) Time balance, (h) Nominal rate of finance charge, (i) Nominal annual rate, and (j) Actual annual rate.

8. A vendor offers the following instalment terms on a purchase amounting to $1,800—36 monthly payments of $63.75. What is the actual rate of charge for the credit service used?

13

Primary Credit Service Establishments: Lenders

Entirely different and apart from the group of vendor credit service suppliers discussed in the preceding chapter is another: lenders. Lenders are among the oldest of credit institutions, their business being specifically the sale of cash credit service rather than the sale of merchandise through credit. They have in the past normally performed all of the credit functions, for the possession of capital was a prerequisite to lending, in addition to having acumen to appraise creditworthiness and willingness to assume credit risk. Lenders have often been, and are still regarded to be, simply financiers, although they are in fact suppliers of credit service, and suppliers of differentiated services to a segmented market. They differ from credit vendors in authorization, operation, relation to customers, and in public control.[1]

Because of the long history of lending, many attitudes toward credit have been derived from lending practices. Foremost is the notion that the amount of the money represented in a credit transaction is the total value in the credit service performed. This idea evolved before lending was a business, even when

[1] For a summary of legislation regulating lender credit, see Barbara A. Curran, *Trends in Consumer Credit Legislation* (Chicago: University of Chicago Press, 1965), pp. 15–83.

money was denied earning power because it was thought to be non-productive. Lenders' use of the dominance they have held in the credit relationship has stereotyped them as shrews, powerful, conservative, sometimes profiteering. Lending institutions, however, have also been recognized as the heart of the credit economy. By their keen business sense and competitive skill lenders have made nice distinctions between market segments bidding for credit service. As new types of lenders have evolved, the entire field of credit serving has profited from their promotion of credit service, their examples of service differentiation, their operation within an income–cost margin, and their impersonalization of what has long been a very personal creditor–customer relationship.

The importance of lending and lenders has grown in our economy faster than many of the indexes of economic growth, for lenders are serving new social circumstances. A market economy has great need for loan credit; the complexity of the exchange economy accentuates this need. Disequilibrium of income and expenditure, of ideas and capital, of purchase opportunities and available sales credit, of immediate need and long-run credit-worthiness has stimulated the market for loan services. It has brought forth many lenders serving the commercial and the consumer markets.

Lenders constitute a distinct part of the credit structure. They are separate credit operations, in business for the purpose of providing and selling credit service. They generally employ the promissory note, in a variety of forms, rather than the open account. Their terms call for both single and multiple payments. A charge is made for their credit service. Most of them operate under the sanction of a legal license or charter. They perform mainly as primary suppliers of credit service, although they also at times undertake to perform credit functions shifted by others. They also in turn sometimes shift some of their functions to other suppliers of credit service.

The assortment of lenders is wide; those discussed in this chapter are chosen because of their contribution to the financing of markets and marketing through the supplying of credit service. The following are discussed: commercial banks, industrial banks and loan companies, personal finance companies, credit unions, and pawnshops.

COMMERCIAL BANKS

A basic institution in our credit system is the commercial bank. So termed because of its original service mainly to commercial borrowers, this bank today is also an important supplier of credit service to consumers.

The commercial bank represents a chartered creation of the state and federal governments, a lending institution providing a wide variety of services to assorted markets. To business borrowers, they make commercial or working capital loans for less than one year, intermediate loans for from 1 to 5 years, and long-term loans for up to 20 years.

In such relationships they generally serve as primary suppliers of credit service, performing all of the credit functions and lending for all types of purposes. They also act as auxiliary suppliers, taking over mainly the financing functions of other credit service suppliers, financing receivables of department stores, sales finance companies, commercial finance companies, and others. They also perform multiple credit functions for other creditors: some national banks act as factors for manufacturers and wholesalers; others provide charge account services for retail stores. Commercial banks likewise serve ultimate consumers through their consumer loan departments, and they engage in sales financing as well as in lending.

Commercial banks have traditionally operated at the conservative end of the credit risk spectrum. As trustees for depositors, banks have chosen, as their segment of the market for loan service, customers who constitute the least risk. Being dominant in their market relationship, banks have been able to select the more reputable, promising, and larger prospects. This has left many potential customers for credit service either to look to other lenders or to find credit service through other channels, as retailers have often been obliged to rely upon suppliers of trade credit rather than upon bank loans. This sense of the service which they could or should perform delayed the lending by commercial banks to personal consumers. Seeing themselves as "wholesalers," rather than "retailers" of money, commercial banks long confined their lending to business customers. Eventually recognizing the growing potential of the consumer loan market, in the 1930's they began to extend service to such customers. There, too, however, they tended to accept the better customers, leaving others to be served by other credit institutions. Unwillingness and inability of banks to serve all classes of risks have been strong influences upon the development of the credit structure.

An important determinant of the service which the commercial bank can render, and the market it can serve, is the rate of charge it may make for its loans. Banks are subject to the legal interest rate specified by states, which is most often 6 to 8 per cent. The legal rate, however, is neither always the quoted rate nor the actual rate. Market conditions generally produce a negotiated rate less than the legal rate dependent upon the quality of the risk, size of the loan, security offered, costs of funds for the bank, and competition. And banking practices often produce true rates higher than quoted rates. Both discount terms and the requirement that portions of loans be left on deposit in the bank produce a difference between the quoted and actual rates. Instalment repayment of loans the charges for which have been based upon the original indebtedness also nearly doubles the quoted rate. Finally, charges differ from simple legal rates when other types of charges are made, such as those for personal check credit accounts and for sales financing.

The commercial bank is also distinguished from other credit institutions in the sources of its funds and in the manner of its lending. Like non-banking companies, it derives capital from the sale of common and preferred stock and from debenture notes. It obtains funds from time, savings, and checking account deposits. Moreover, "funds" are made available through the provision of the Federal Reserve System for lending normally about five times the amount of vault cash and deposits placed by the member bank with the Reserve Bank. Thus not only are funds supplied by several means, but they also are made available at costs differing from those of some other lending institutions.

Still another feature of the commercial bank which differentiates it from competitors is its privilege of lending by creating or by adding to demand deposits. Whereas other lenders issue cash, commercial banks may lend by establishing a checking account for the customer. This serves several purposes. It provides for a continuing relationship with the debtor, for such loan accounts are not always fully withdrawn, and they provide a contact for easy repayment and extension of the original loan. Second, it provides a basis for the requirement of a compensating balance in the loan account. Third, it furnishes a means of opening a line of credit for a customer without charge until drafts are actually drawn and the loan activated. This last feature has been particularly important in some of the consumer loan plans which banks have devised.

An illustration of the latter type of account is furnished by that of the First National City Bank of New York. Their Revolving Check Credit Plan provides for a minimum credit line of $120 and a maximum line of $5,000. Monthly payments are one-twelfth of the credit used. If the customer does not avail himself of his line, he makes no payment and there is no charge. Interest of 0.98 per cent monthly is charged on the average of the daily unpaid balance, and life insurance charge is 6 cents per month on the same average amount in use. The charge is the equivalent of the statutory maximum permissible discount charge under the New York Banking Law of 6 per cent per annum, or an effective rate of 11.76 per cent.[2]

Whereas before 1930 commercial banks made only two types of loans—co-maker and collateral—their service to both the commercial and consumer markets has been continually broadened. The newer services to business include monthly payment business loans, made particularly to small businesses, and the factoring of sales, both in domestic and international trade. They have also increased their service to retailers by buying instalment paper held by sellers and finance companies, and by instituting in cooperation with retailers charge account systems for those who could not provide such service for themselves.[3]

One of the most notable developments in commercial banking in recent years, however, has been the evolution of the concept of retail banking.[4] This has represented a change of bankers' viewpoint from regarding business borrowers as their sole or principal market. Acceptance of the role of supplier of credit service to the consumer has been gradual, but it has been encouraged by the success which banks enjoyed in this activity. In serving consumers, banks have not only been more accom-

---

[2] F. H. Diefenbacher, "Citybank Ready-Credit," *The Credit World*, January, 1960, p. 18.

[3] See the section "Charge Account Services" in Chapter 14.

[4] For an exposition of this concept, see John Reilley, "A Panorama of Retail Banking," *The Credit World*, January, 1964, p. 9.

modating in their instalment loans and financing, but they have innovated new types of accounts, other bank services, convenience of branch locations and banking hours, building appearance and layout, and management–customer attitudes.

The position of the commercial bank in the market for consumer credit service is shown in the loan statistics. In 1930, commercial banks held about 24 per cent of all consumer instalment debt outstanding and about 35 per cent of such debt held by financial institutions.[5] By 1965, their share of the total instalment debt increased to 41 per cent and their share of that held by financial institutions to 47 per cent.

More than two-thirds (68 per cent) of the consumer debt held by banks represents the financing of sales; the remainder, cash loans to personal borrowers. In the financing of sales, automobile purchases are the most voluminous, 54 per cent of the instalment debt held by banks being acquired for this purpose. Of that, however, approximately two-thirds is obtained by purchasing paper from other financiers of automobile sales; one-third from their own direct activity in this line of financing. This illustrates the twofold function of banks in the credit system: in one instance they finance consumers' purchases through performing the *entire credit function* for the vendor; in the other they finance sales by performing the *capital investment function* shifted to them by sales finance companies. In both instances the bank acts as an auxiliary supplier of credit service, but in each it has a different market relationship.

Fourteen per cent of the banks' instalment debt is acquired through financing purchases of consumer goods other than automobiles. Personal loan and repair and modernization loans provide 22 and 9 per cent, respectively, of their total instalment holdings.

INDUSTRIAL BANKS

During the first quarter of this century the needs of commercial borrowers were being fairly well met through the services of commercial banks, but the growing need of consumers for loans had not yet been well accommodated. In that market condition several types of personal loan services began to emerge and take form.

One of them was a type of lending known by several names

---

[5] *Federal Reserve Bulletin,* July, 1965, pp. 1008–09.

but which is widely recognized as industrial banking. More important than the name was the idea in lending which it represented. On the one hand were the circumstances of the existing loan market: the need of individuals for small loans, the requirement that lending charges be confined to the legal interest rate, and the tendency of existing legal lenders to eschew personal loans as unprofitable and undesirable. On the other hand were some new technical conceptions of loan management, borrowed from European experience. Adaptation of the latter to the conditions of the American market produced the new lending institution.

The innovations in loan management were several fold. First, to avoid guilt of usury when charges were based upon lump payment of a loan but payment was actually made in instalments, payments were received into a separate account of the borrower until equal to the sum of his indebtedness, which was then paid in full in one payment. Thus the customer was a debtor on the loan but a creditor on the deposit until both positions were canceled simultaneously. Although interest was usually paid on the deposit account in avoidance of the appearance of usury, receipt of instalment payments effectually halved the original balance outstanding and doubled the actual rate of charge collected. As this scheme of lending was pioneered by Arthur J. Morris, the institution was originally known as the Morris Plan.

A second innovation was that the loans were made available not for commercial and industrial uses but to industrial employees. Thus the institution became known also as "industrial loan companies" and as "industrial banks" or "Morris Plan Banks." The term "Morris Plan" is even incorporated in some federal and state legislation but some states do not permit use of the term "Bank" in the corporate title, nor the designation of savings accounts as "deposits," thereby preventing eligibility of the institution for membership in the Federal Deposit Insurance Corporation. Notwithstanding the multiplicity of terminology, all of such institutions exist to serve the consumer market for loans.

A third innovation was in the making of unsecured, co-maker loans. Morris used a copyright note signed not only by the borrower but also by two or more other persons whom the borrower could get to assume responsibility for the debt in case of his own default. Character, not property or security, was the principal recommendation for credit, on the part of both the borrower and his co-makers.

Serving personal needs through the techniques of the deposit account and the co-maker assurance, industrial banks came to serve a distinct segment of the market for consumer loans. Although operating under the same legal rate as commercial banks, their management was market oriented in a way different from that of commercial bankers. They were permitted by industrial banking laws to make some charges not available to commercial banks, such as service fees, commissions, and other charges in addition to interest. Most common are investigation fees, amounting to 1 or 2 per cent of the principal; delinquency fees, amounting to 5 per cent of the delinquent instalment; and commissions on the sale of credit life insurance. Thus nominal charges of 6 per cent interest plus 2 per cent fees for other purposes would provide the lender an effectual rate of approximately 15 per cent per annum on instalment loans. Generally, such lenders may lend up to $5,000.

The market segment for this institution, therefore, consists of borrowers who are (1) employed, (2) have friends or relatives willing to co-sign their notes, (3) willing to have their borrowing known to such parties, (4) willing to pay charges ranging from 15 to 20 per cent per annum, and (5) desirous of borrowing sums up to about $5,000.

Time and changing circumstances have altered the initial conception of the Morris Plan of Industrial Banking, however. There are nearly 200 Morris Plan companies and some 500 banks are affiliated with the American Industrial Bankers' Association, but an estimated 125 institutions have converted to state and national bank status. Many of those remaining have diversified their service appreciably from their initial operation. Diversification has, in fact, influenced conversion, for as commercial banks engaged increasingly in consumer loans, industrial bankers wished to expand into the commercial loan field, and to do so they became commercial banks legally.

Lenders continuing as industrial banks have also altered their operations. In addition to co-maker loans they make secured or collateral loans, particularly with automobiles used as security, they discount contracts for the purchase of other consumer durable goods, they purchase instalment paper acquired by vendors, and they engage in real estate financing. Moreover, they act as primary suppliers of credit service to businesses and professional people and as auxiliary suppliers to retailers, wholesalers, and manufacturers whose receivables they either buy or finance.

Reliable statistics for this industry are sparse, but one study [6] made for the year 1957 shows the following facts:

1. Average loan made: $795
2. Operating expense: volume of loans made = 4.72%
3. Operating income: assets = 9.77%
4. Bad debts: loan volume = 0.22%
5. Net profit: volume = 1.61%
6. Net profit: assets = 1.83%

CONSUMER FINANCE COMPANIES

Prior to 1925, loan requirements of a vast portion of the consumer market were still unserved. Commercial banks still abstained from making personal loans, and Morris Plan institutions, serving industrial employees, supplied but one segment of the market. The consumer finance company, also known as the personal finance company and small-loan company, was another lending institution to emerge at that time.

The consumer finance company was the product of scientific research of the market for consumer loans. One of the obvious social and economic ills of the early part of this century was the plight of the personal borrower. Forced by economic necessity to borrow, repressed by social attitudes against borrowing, and dependent mainly upon illegal lenders, consumers were at the mercy of cruel forces of supply and demand. This fact was recognized by students of the situation working under the sponsorship of the Russell Sage Foundation, founded in 1907. They found that the absence of legitimate lenders, caused by inability to make small loans profitably under existing usury rates, had created a vast illegal business, which repressive legislation abetted rather than removed. The Foundation recommended enactment of laws exempting from usury violation specified charges for loans, made in compliance with strict requirements of the authorized lenders. Massachusetts pioneered in small-loan legislation with an enactment in 1911. Following similar actions by four other states, in 1917 the Uniform Small Loan Law was enacted by Illinois, Indiana, Maine, New Hampshire, and Utah.

Laws patterned after the model law stated the charges lenders were privileged to make, and their corresponding obligations as

[6] M. R. Neifeld, *Neifeld's Manual on Consumer Credit* (Easton, Pa.: Mack Publishing Co., 1961), pp. 384–85.

set forth in the requirements. Lenders were required to obtain a license, renewable annually for a fee; to submit to annual examination by an agency of the state; to possess a minimum capitalization at the outset; to refrain from false, misleading, or deceptive advertising; and to state charges or rates of charge fully and clearly. Some states required proof that an additional loan office would be to the "convenience and advantage" of the public where operation of it was intended. Originally, loan ceilings of $300 were set, and rates of 3.5 per cent per month were made on the outstanding balance.

The control purpose of the model law was not uniformly achieved: not all states passed such laws, and those which did deviated from the model in interpreting their own needs. As late as 1959, ten states, mostly in the South, still lacked strict control over small cash loans to consumers; some had no rate laws except the usury law, and some had loose regulations. By 1965, Arkansas alone remained without legislation authorizing the making of consumer instalment loans.[7]

Legislative Trends

In years following the first widespread adoption of the consumer instalment loan laws, changes gradually occurred,[8] reflecting both environmental conditions and changing concepts of loan management.

Loan Ceilings.   One important change occurred relative to the size of loans permitted under the law. The original intent was to provide for making "small loans"; therefore, a limit of $300 was originally recommended and adopted. The value of $300 decreased over the years, however, and beginning in the late 1920's, and particularly since the late 1930's, lenders and borrowers pressed for the increase of this limit. Today, ceilings of $2,000 and more are common, as shown in Fig. 13–1. In 1963 the average loan made throughout the industry was $524, the average account outstanding was $447.

The loan limit is an important factor: it is a determinant of the

[7] *1965 Finance Facts Yearbook* (Washington, D.C.: National Consumer Finance Association, 1965), p. 2.

[8] Lyle S. Woodcock, "Trends in Consumer Legislation," *Consumer Finance News*, February, 1962, p. 3; and DeWitt J. Paul, "Legislative Trends Affecting the Consumer Finance Industry," an address before the Pennsylvania State University Consumer Finance Summer Institute, June 18, 1958.

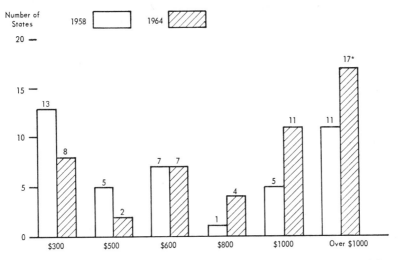

*An additional 18 states permit loans of over $1,000 by finance companies under other laws for a total of 35 states.

Fig. 13–1.   Loan ceilings under consumer finance laws, 1958 and 1964. (Source: *1965 Finance Facts Yearbook.* Washington, D.C.: National Consumer Finance Association, 1965, p. 58.)

market segment which the lending institution can serve. Borrowers patronizing small-loan companies for modest sums are turned to other sources for larger loans. Even when creditworthy, small borrowers have not always qualified for loans from commercial banks or industrial loan companies. Moreover, low loan limitations turn borrowers from one small-loan company to another when the limit of loans in one is reached.   Such multiple indebtedness works to the disadvantage of all, increasing risk and costs.   Consequently, increasing loan limits made personal finance companies more competitive and more useful to borrowers.

Rates and Rate Statements.   As the purpose of small-loan laws was to give small borrowers rate protection as well as loan availability, changes in loan ceilings were attended by changes in rates.

Initially, loan rates were almost uniformly set at 3.5 per cent per month, an all-inclusive rate calculated on the monthly *balance outstanding.*   This type of rate, constituting an effectual rate of 42 per cent per annum, prevailed during the first years of small-loan laws, until the late 1920's.

With agitation to increase loan limits in the late 1920's and 1930's, the concept of a graduated or aggregate loan rate was introduced. This gave recognition to the fact that (1) loans of increasing size are made on a declining scale of cost per dollar of loan, (2) rates on loans beyond a certain limit should approach the usury rate, or at least the rates sanctioned for lenders of larger sums, and (3) control of rates had more social justification than had the limitation of loans. A typical graduated rate structure was as follows:

> 3 per cent per month on loans of $1–$150
> 2 per cent per month on the portion of loans from $151–$300
> ⅔ of 1 per cent per month (legal contract rate of 8 per cent per annum) on the portion of loans from $301–$1000.

Loans were generally not made for less than $25, and in the larger loans it was assumed that the portion to which higher rates were applied was liquidated last. In 1962, 34 states had laws with such graduated rates.

After 1950, a trend developed away from the all-inclusive simple rate of interest applicable to unpaid balances. So long as the simple graduated rate was charged, it was widely, and often unfavorably, compared with other interest charges where the cost of money was the predominant factor. Familiarity with sales financing, however, and with the time–price differential, had shown that a rate allied to the balance *outstanding* was neither necessarily equitable nor profitable. Preference grew for a rate expressed as a number of dollars per sums loaned, a computation based on the *initial* balance and stated as an *add-on* thereto. Consequently, the state which had the rate structure cited above (Ohio) in 1961 rephrased its rate as an add-on computed on the original balance as follows:

> $16 per $100 per year on loans from $1–$500
> 9 per $100 per year on portion of loans from $501–$1000
> 7 per $100 per year on portion of loans from $1001–$2000

Apart from the nature of the charge made, the manner of expressing it has also changed. Statement of the charge has implications for both lenders and borrowers: the former desire terms which are compensatory and easy to administer; the latter, terms which are convenient and easy to understand. In early years, charges based upon the outstanding balance were added to an equal division of original principal due at each payment period, each payment thereby being different. This created uncertainty and dissatisfaction with customers. Equalization of payments was then undertaken by adding to a variable charge a variable principal payment so that all payments were identical. Equalization was also achieved by precomputing interest for all scheduled payments and adding the total to the original indebtedness, producing a grand total divided by the number of payments to yield equal payments. This is also the method employed in the add-on method of computation. Obviously, charges stated by these various methods do not always coincide with either costs or earnings, and adjustments are made, as by the Rule of the 78ths, when necessary.

Insurance. As a protection to the borrowers and as a part of the security for the loan, insurance has gained increased recognition in small-loan laws. Until the 1930's, limited use was made of insurance for this purpose. Its use expanded during the 1940's and became an accepted part of the consumer loan contract in the 1950's.

Dual Business. Regulations have also defined the areas of credit service in which small-loan companies might operate. Loans being their principal business, they have generally been restricted to that business, but increasingly diversification has found expression in loan company operations and in legislation regulating them. Small-loan laws are now written to permit licensees to engage in other forms of credit service, such as buying sales finance contracts, purchasing bulk allotments of open or instalment accounts, financing leases, providing insurance, etc. This diversification by small-loan companies is analogous to that engaged in by commercial and industrial banks.

Engagement in diversified business, however, has raised questions concerning both the business and the social justification of diverse rate structures for different forms of consumer credit, and interest in a uniform code or rate law has grown. In 1951, Missouri brought all lending agencies, including banks and small-loan companies, under a common rate structure. Their charges must be stated either as $15 per hundred or as 2.218 per cent per month on the unpaid balance—two methods of statement producing the same gross income. Personal finance and sales finance companies now sometimes belong to the same trade associations.

And the concept of a time–price differential has in a few instances been repudiated in favor of a rate charge applicable to several types of credit business. Unification of charges seems consistent with an accurate appraisal of the essential functions and costs involved in all forms of credit service.

Regulation. Regulation of most forms of consumer credit has been left to the states, but faults in state laws have produced threats of federal regulation. Such proposals as the Douglas Bill pertain to consumer lending, as well as to other forms of consumer credit, requiring advance statement of charges both in dollars and percentage per annum. While not impossible, compliance with such a requirement is no more simple for lenders than for vendors. Nor is it more necessary, except that the diversity of state laws defeats somewhat the purpose of consumer protection and the provision of needed services.

Market Characteristics

Throughout the years, personal finance research has attempted to identify characteristics of its market. With diversification practiced by most lenders, distinctions between market segments for types of lenders have become blurred. Distinctions between types of lending services required, however, remain. These, too, may be obscured in the trend toward rate simplification and code uniformity, but service differentiation will continue where supply and demand differences exist. Consequently, studies of composition of the market for personal finance services have continuing significance. There is meaning, therefore, in the following occupational classification of consumer finance customers: [9]

Skilled and semiskilled workers	58.77%
Office and other non-manual skills	7.06
Managers, superintendents, foremen, farm managers, and in business for selves	5.24
Salesmen and saleswomen	5.59
School teachers	.80
Unskilled and domestic workers	11.16
Professional and semi-professional	1.82
Persons with independent incomes	1.26
Protective services, members of the Armed Services, and other service workers	7.61
Occupations not reported and miscellaneous	.69

[9] Findings of a survey of 1,800 consumer finance offices, reported by the National Consumer Finance Association, Washington, D.C.

Related to the occupational market classification and a further indication of the nature of the market segment supplied by consumer finance companies are the uses made of small loans during a span of years, as shown in Table 13–1.

Table 13–1. Distribution of the Number of Loans Extended
by Purpose, Selected Years, 1948–63
(in per cent)

Purpose	1948	1950	1954	1958	1960	1963
To consolidate existing debt	27.8	30.2	33.7	39.5	40.0	48.0
Travel, vacation, education expense	7.8	7.4	8.4	9.3	10.0	8.0
Automobile purchase or repair	2.9	4.5	4.7	5.5	7.0	11.0
Home furnishings and appliances	3.3	5.1	5.2	4.7	8.0	3.0
Household repairs	8.3	7.3	6.8	5.1	4.0	3.0
All other purposes	49.9	45.4	41.4	35.9	31.0	27.0
Total	100.0	100.0	100.0	100.0	100.0	100.0

SOURCE: *1965 Finance Facts Yearbook* (Washington: National Consumer Finance Association), 1965, p. 51.

From this it is evident that the market for instalment loans overlaps the market for sales finance service. On the other hand, the increasing use of loans for the consolidation of debts has no parallel outside the cash loan field.

Competitive Position

The position of finance companies among all suppliers of consumer cash loan is indicated by Table 13–2. Since 1957, all types of lenders shown have increased their volume of business, but not all at the same rate. Consumer finance companies today carry about 13 per cent of the debt outstanding from consumer loans. This is a decrease from 16 per cent held in 1957 and from about 41 per cent held in both 1940 and 1950. The preponderance of their earlier position was due to the tardiness of commercial banks in cultivating consumer loan business and to the slow early growth of credit unions. Reversing their earlier strategy, commercial banks have continued in the share of market position which they had established by 1957, i.e., about 65 per cent of the loans held. Credit unions have appreciably bettered their position, increasing from 12 to 17 per cent of the market, equaling consumer finance companies in volume in 1959 and

Table 13–2. Distribution of Outstanding Debt on Loans Made by Consumer Lending Institutions, 1957–65 (billions of dollars)

Year	Commercial Banks		Consumer Finance Companies		Credit Unions		Others		Total	
	Dollars	Per Cent	Dollars	Per Cent	Dollars	Per Cent	Dollars	Per Cent	Dollars	Per Cent
1957	$12.8	65.6	$3.1	16.0	$2.4	12.3	$1.2	6.1	$19.5	100.
1958	12.8	64.3	3.1	15.6	2.7	13.6	1.3	6.5	19.9	100.
1959	15.2	65.6	3.3	14.2	3.3	14.2	1.4	6.0	23.2	100.
1960	16.7	64.8	3.7	14.3	3.9	15.1	1.5	5.8	25.8	100.
1961	17.0	63.9	3.8	14.3	4.3	16.2	1.5	5.6	26.6	100.
1962	19.0	64.2	4.1	13.9	4.9	16.6	1.6	5.4	29.6	100.
1963	21.6	64.6	4.6	13.8	5.6	16.8	1.6	4.8	33.4	100.
1964	23.9	64.2	5.1	13.7	6.5	17.5	1.7	4.6	37.8	100.
1965	28.0	65.3	5.6	13.0	7.9	17.5	1.8	4.2	42.9	100.

SOURCE: *Federal Reserve Bulletin*, July, 1965, p. 1008.

surpassing them ever since. Further reasons for their growth will be discussed in the subsequent section dealing with credit unions. While competitive position is affected by promotional strategy, it is influenced too by other internal and external circumstances. Externally, improved creditworthiness qualifying consumers for personal loans in the eyes of commercial bankers, conversion of industrial banks to commercial bank status, and diversification into cash lending by sales finance and mortgage finance companies affect the relative position of consumer finance companies. Internally, the character and cost of their operations also affect their competitive strength.

Comparisons with other financial institutions reveal some characteristics of finance company operations. The composition of their financial structure, for example, as compared with that of sales finance companies, is shown in Table 13–3. Both com-

Table 13–3. Percentage Distribution of Sources of Funds for Consumer and Sales Finance Companies, 1963

Balance Sheet Item	Consumer Finance Companies	Sales Finance Companies
Notes payable to bank	16.5%	16.7%
Commercial paper and other short-term debt	7.9	28.8
Deposit liabilities and thrift certificates (short-term)	2.3	0.7
Long-term debt (excluding subordinate debentures)	36.7	22.4
Subordinated debentures and notes	9.7	11.9
Other liabilities	4.8	7.0
Capital and surplus	22.4	12.5
Total	100.0%	100.0%

Source: *1965 Finance Facts Yearbook* (Washington: National Consumer Finance Association), 1965, p. 60.

panies are private non-bank organizations, and thus in contrast to both commercial banks, which obtain most of their funds from demand and time deposits, and from credit unions which obtain their funds almost wholly from the sale of shares to members. It is apparent from Table 13–3 that consumer finance companies rely upon long-term debt and capital financing, whereas sales finance companies rely upon short-term debt, subordinated debentures, and notes. These facts suggest that consumer finance companies act to a greater extent in the performance of all of the credit functions involved in lending, but that sales finance companies shift a greater portion of the financing function to other credit specialists.

Consumer Loans Abroad

A point worth reiterating is that the emergence of consumer lending services depends upon entrepreneurs perceiving simultaneously an existing demand for them and the technical means of supplying this demand. The coincidence of these influences has been slow to occur in other countries, mainly because of the lack of knowledge of how to manage consumer loans. Inability to retain control in the debtor–creditor relationship has been cited as a prime reason for the slow growth of lending to consumers elsewhere. Such lending had developed even more slowly than instalment sales financing, for the latter has grown with the belief that control rested in durability of goods, repossession possibilities, and tangibility. Social attitudes have also deterred the development of lending, as customers have thought of debt as improvidence, and public administrators have thought of loan charges only as interest. Where clearer rationality concerning the buying and selling of consumer loan service has prevailed, functional and structural developments have tended to parallel those in our own country.

In Europe, Holland is one of the more advanced countries in official acceptance of personal loans.[10] The Dutch have fashioned legislation similar to our Uniform Small Loan Law. Finance companies are licensed and permitted to make a realistic charge. In Belgium and Italy there is no such legislation. In England, restrictions are placed upon business solicitation and promotional practices by finance companies. Loans made by joint stock banks are generally restricted to depositors, and security is required. In West Germany, bankers have led in consumer loans, and the development of consumer finance companies has followed. In general, the situation throughout Europe in personal loans today corresponds to conditions prevailing in the United States in 1911, when social workers and business leaders began to seek solutions to the unsupplied need for cash loans. Finance conditions else-

---

[10] M. R. Neifeld, "Personal Loans in Europe," *Consumer Finance News*, September 1964, p. 11.

where in the world are equally undeveloped, and equally dependent upon factors which here or anywhere stimulate the development of this form of business, this form of service to society.

CREDIT UNIONS

As part of the structure of consumer lending organizations, the credit union has importance as one of the more rapidly growing and most controversial agencies.

Basically, the credit union is a type of consumers' cooperative. As such, it must be viewed in the context of its democratic, capitalistic environment.

The idea of self-help in consumer lending is attributed to Victor Aime Huber, who expounded the theory of cooperative credit in the early 1800's and to Friedrich Raiffeisen, who started a credit society in southern Germany in 1849.[11] From there it was introduced into Canada in 1900 and into the United States in 1909, when the first credit union in this country was formed in New Hampshire. Subsequently, laws providing for chartering credit unions were passed in 44 states, and in 1934 the United States Federal Credit Union Act was passed under which credit unions could be formed and operated even in states without their own enabling legislation.

Conditions existing at the turn of the century nurtured the growth of such cooperative financing institutions. As previously described, personal loan needs were not met by legitimate lenders at that time, and not only lending but savings lagged. The credit union was intended to remedy both deficiencies, holding savings of members and lending these funds to members in need. Its members are individuals united by a "common bond," such as employment by a common company, membership in an organization, or residential proximity. Membership is gained by paying an entrance fee of 25 cents and by purchasing one or more "shares," usually in $5 units. Dividends ranging usually from 4 to 5 per cent of shares held are paid annually, but voting power —in true cooperative fashion—is apportioned one vote per shareholder rather than one vote per share. Distributable earnings in excess of operating costs, share dividends, and reserve requirements may be distributed to borrowers in proportion to payments

[11] *International Credit Union Yearbook, 1965* (Madison, Wis.: CUNA International, 1965), p. 44.

made by them on funds borrowed. Thus the essentially democratic and non-profit character of the credit union is exemplified.

The growth of the credit union, however, has been regarded by some as the anomaly of a poverty-oriented institution in an increasingly affluent society, as a non-profit competitor in a profit-motivated system, as a political democracy in a capitalistic economy, and as a fraternity with progressively loosened common bonds. Consumer cooperatives have flourished in conditions of poverty, where necessity was joined to parsimony, sacrifice, and self-help. So it was at the beginning of this century, and so it was again during the depression of the 1930's, when federal government encouragement was given to cooperatives in general and to credit unions in particular. Again, in the United States in the 1960's, the credit union idea was infused into the War on Poverty and into the foreign policy of rendering, through the Agency for International Development, self-help aid to developing nations. Stimulation and encouragement of people to meet their own needs is a natural function of governmental agencies in the social process. The extent to which it is carried, however, depends on other factors.

Concurrently with the development of credit unions, other types of consumer credit facilities evolved in the United States. Among lenders were the consumer finance companies, industrial banks, and commercial banks; among others, the sales finance companies. In all those cases the impelling interest of the organizers and managers differ from credit unions. Shareholders' interest in return on investment is presumed to be minimal; motivation for saving through purchase of shares is humanitarian as well as mercenary. However, inasmuch as dividends generally range from 4 to 5 per cent of deposits, return to owners is comparable to that received from deposits in commercial banks and in savings and loan associations. With the rise of a variety of private, profit credit institutions, credit unions have experienced the kind of competition which private enterprise has always furnished cooperatives in our economy. Until the 1950's they fared badly, comparatively; since then their position has improved.

The vitality of credit unions in recent years has raised questions concerning their place in the entire credit structure. Representing stimulated self-help in poverty conditions or in the absence of private initiative, they served a purpose; but in a com-

petitive, capitalistic economy they might be expected eventually
to compete on grounds common to other credit service establishments. This they do not do, for several reasons. First, they are
exempt from federal and state taxes, inasmuch as that portion
of their operating surplus which they refund to customers—borrowers—has not legally been regarded as profit. Thus the fact
that they remit about 10 per cent of charges collected places
them, by reasons of taxation, in a preferential market position.
Second, operating costs of credit unions are less than those of
private enterprises. Managers of the larger unions are full-time
employees, but many other functions are subsidized by the organization to which the credit unions are attached. Space, light,
heat, collection through salary check-off plans, and part-time
credit union employees are often furnished free of charge by the
business or social organization whose employees or members
constitute the membership and clientele of the union. Costs of
performing the credit operational functions, in other words, are
not borne equally by private and cooperative lending enterprises.
Third, the cost of funds for lending, obtained through deposits
bearing a 5 per cent dividend, are also less than costs of funds
invested in and loaned to private organizations, whose earnings
are subject to taxation. Bona fide business operations have always suffered the incursions of semibusiness competitors, but the
advantage afforded credit unions by both government and business subsidization have made them a formidable contender in the
credit field. Although loan ceilings vary, $750 is the maximum
loan provided by the Federal Credit Union Act and by many
states.

The expansion ambitions of credit union organizers have not
been unlike those of other businessmen, but the urge to expand
has led to some reappraisal of credit unions. Originally, their
membership was made up of individuals whose common bond
was their similar financial plight as members of a closely identi-
fiable group. Recently, the "group" has broadened, and the
"common bond" for participation in a credit union has been
weakened. Whereas formerly membership consisted of individuals working, interacting, lending to each other, recently mere
association with an organization, however remote from each other
the individuals might be, has qualified one for membership in a
credit union. Even residence in an area has been regarded as
basis for affiliation with other residents in the area in the estab-

lishment of a credit union. Thus the nucleus of self-helpers has yielded to an amorphous mass of savers and borrowers who may not know each other and who collectively approximate the general market of money suppliers and money users in capitalistic enterprise.

Thus the credit union *as an institution* takes an expanding role in the structure of credit establishments; the credit union *as an idea*, however, provokes new resistances in the interplay of business forces. Growth of capitalistic small lending agencies has caused acceptance by borrowers, control by government, emulation by competitors. Growth of credit unions has caused acceptance by borrowers, support by government, resistance by competitors. This resistance has arisen from the ideological conflict which the credit union represents, rather than from the competition it affords. A non-profit institution in a capitalistic economy, a tax-exempt institution in a democratic society, a government-encouraged institution in a free-enterprise system, a quasi-social undertaking of a business function, the credit union has cut across several roots of our traditional business system. Turbulence has developed, therefore, around the taxability of earnings and the extent to which volunteer self-help and common bond characterize credit union membership. Basic trends in our social development, rather than mere vested business interests, will have most influence in reconciling these divergences.[12]

Measurements of Credit Union Activity

The importance of credit union activity in our credit structure and in our economy is measured by several criteria. As it is a function in which people associate for meeting mutual needs, the numbers of unions and their members give some idea of the prominence of this lending institution. In 1964 there were 47,097 credit unions throughout the world with 25,700,421 members.[13] Of these, 21,876 unions (divided almost equally between state- and federal-chartered unions) with 15.6 million members were in the United States, and 4,671 unions with 3.4 million members were in Canada. Union members comprised 8 per cent of the United States population and 17.7 per cent of the Canadian

12 See "Credit Unions and a Tax Loophole," *Times Sales Financing*, March–April, 1963, p. 3, and "Tax Equality and Credit Unions," *The Industrial Banker & Time Sales Financing*, May, 1965, p. 5.
13 *International Credit Union Yearbook, 1965*, p. 1.

population, with increases in both numbers and percentages occurring annually. Other countries with large numbers of credit unions include India, West Germany, and France.

Membership in credit unions is drawn from a wide assortment of classes of people, and their relative prominence is not the same in all countries. Table 13–4 indicates the composition of membership in three area classifications.

Table 13–4. Percentage Distribution of Credit Unions by Classification, 1964

	United States	Canada	Elsewhere
Associational: church, co-op, labor union, fraternal	17.6%	13.17%	14.26%
Occupational: agriculture, forestry, fisheries, mining, contract construction	.94	.62	1.55
Manufacturing: food, textile mill, lumber and wood, paper, and rubber, fabricated metal products, leather, stone, glass and clay, printing, publishing, petroleum, refining, primary metal industries, machinery and transportation equipment	34.74	15.25	9.69
Transportation, communication, electric, gas, and sanitary services	9.53	3.36	3.63
Wholesale, retail, finance, insurance, and real estate services	10.74	2.86	6.32
Educational services	7.05	1.00	1.83
Federal government	7.40	2.86	2.42
State, country, and local government	7.50	2.25	4.45
Residential	4.04	58.63	55.85
Total	100.00	100.00	100.00

SOURCE: *International Credit Union Yearbook, 1965*, p. 7.

Total assets of credit unions in the United States rose to $9.34 billion in 1964, although one-third has assets less than $50,000, two-thirds less than $200,000, and fewer than 10 per cent has assets exceeding $1 million.

Although credit unions and their membership are dispersed worldwide, heavy concentration of their activity in collecting savings and making loans lies in the United States. Savings of members held by credit unions amounted to $11 billion throughout the world, but $8.2 billion were in the United States. Of worldwide outstanding loans amounting to $8.8 billion, $7 billion also were in the United States. Within the United States, however, both the savings and the loan activities of credit unions were small relative to other major financial institutions, as is shown by Table 13–5.

Table 13–5. Distribution of Personal Savings and of Instalment Loans, by Holders, United States, 1964

Savings		Loans	
Postal savings	0.2%	Consumer finance companies	8.6%
Credit unions	3.2	Credit unions	10.9
Mutual savings banks	17.6	Total retail outlets	12.5
Savings and loans associations	35.9	Sales finance companies	24.9
Commercial banks	43.1	Commercial banks	40.3
		Other financial institutions	2.8
	100.0%		100.0%

SOURCE: *International Credit Yearbook, 1965,* pp. 10, 11.

Holding 10.9 per cent of all instalment debt outstanding in 1964 and 12.4 per cent of that held by financial institutions (excluding retail outlets), credit unions have steadily increased their position relative to both, as shown in Table 13–6.

About 50 per cent of the U.S. credit union members are

Table 13–6. Outstanding Loans Held by Credit Unions, as a Percentage of Total Instalment Debt and of Debt Held by Financial Institutions, 1939–65

	Per Cent of Instalment Debt	Per Cent of Instalment Debt Held by Financial Institutions
1939	2.1	4.3
1941	3.2	4.4
1945	4.1	5.6
1957	7.1	8.3
1958	7.9	9.2
1959	8.3	9.4
1960	9.1	10.3
1961	10.0	11.1
1962	10.2	11.7
1963	10.5	12.0
1964	10.9	12.4
1965	11.3	12.7

SOURCE: Computed from data in *Federal Reserve Bulletin,* selected years.

borrowers. One-third of the money loaned is for automobile purchases. The primary security for loans is character of the borrower, although larger loans ordinarily require additional security, such as a chattel mortgage or co-signer. While laws vary concerning loan limits, many credit unions can lend up to $750 on the member's signature alone. Although loans are made on real estate, credit unions hold only 1/30 of 1 per cent of the mortgages on 1–4 family homes. Earnings of credit unions are derived from charges on loans, which cannot exceed 1 per cent per month on the outstanding balance. Out of this are paid all administrative and operating expenses, dividends on deposits, and refund to borrowers. About 20 per cent of the U.S. credit unions paid such refunds, the most common refund rate being 10 per cent.

PAWNBROKERS

As a part of the credit structure, pawnbrokers make a contribution to consumer borrowers which is distorted by popular image of them. They are legitimate lenders, serving the market for loans generally of small size and short duration, a market whose creditworthiness is based primarily upon the value of a pawn given as security. Their image as lenders bordering loan sharks derives from their history, their clientele, their operations, and their rates of charge.

Historically, pawnbrokers antedate all other types of legalized lenders in this country. Their origins, in fact, extend backward into the roots of the Western civilization, for temples, churches, states, and private entrepreneurs have all performed the function of making small personal loans.[14] Loans were made on the basis of objects of value deposited at the Greek, Egyptian, and Assyrian temples of the pagan gods. In church-dominated states of western Europe, the church performed pawnbroking; in others, the autonomous states chartered private lending agents. Pawnshops became both numerous and sizable in England in the eighteenth century, and regulations were enacted relating to charges and operations. The role of pawnbrokers has not been confined to the West, however, and throughout the world one finds operations of this type.

[14] M. R. Neifeld, *Neifeld's Manual on Consumer Credit* (Easton, Pa.: Mack Publishing Co., 1962), pp. 411–14.

In the United States, pawnbrokers emerged in a milieu comprised of loan sharks and remedial loan associations. Loan sharks represented a natural response to the growing need for cash loans, compelled by the increasing exigencies of the exchange economy. Remedial loan associations began as semiphilanthropic efforts to counteract illegal lending. Sometimes taking pledges, sometimes taking chattel mortgages on household goods, remedials were a hybrid of lender types, charging more than early credit unions but far less than loan sharks. As other types of lenders appeared in response to new legislation after 1915, philanthropic services diminished, but pawnbrokers continued to serve a distinct market. Their legitimacy has been established by state laws prescribing their rates and their practices. They are also subject to local ordinances relating to police regulation of businesses in channels in which stolen goods tend to enter the market.

The clientele of pawnbrokers has also contributed to their image of marginal operators. Generally, although not always, borrowers from pawnbrokers are of the low-income class, with some personal property but no real estate, with tight budgets scaled to short income periods. On the other hand, borrowers are sometimes of more affluent status who seek temporary liquidation of personal belongings. Today there is less stigma attached to borrowing from pawnbrokers than formerly, because then the distinction between legal and illegal lending was not so clearly drawn.

The market for pawnbrokers' services has several characteristics: need for small sums of money, typically $10 to $25; desire for privacy and anonymity in borrowing; dependence upon value in the pawn rather than upon character and capacity for creditworthiness; and indifference to the percentage rate of the loan charge. This is a distinct segment of the market for credit services and should not be regarded merely as a poor-risk section of some other market. Although money lending is the principal function of pawnbrokers, it is not the only service for which they are used. The service of storing goods pledged for the loan takes on a value of its own in the eyes of some clients. Safe vaults for jewelry and properly conditioned facilities for furs and other seasonal clothing attract some individuals who regard a small loan as an inexpensive means of acquiring otherwise unavailable storage services.

The practice of pawnbrokers, whereby lending is combined with merchandising operations, cheap goods with better, and new products with used, also deepens the image of an atypical operator. It is claimed that 95 per cent [15] of the pawned articles are redeemed, the other 5 per cent being disposed of at either retail or wholesale. To pledge stock, pawnbrokers often add other merchandise. Unmarketable products they dispose of by selling at auction or through dealers' exchanges to other outlets. The loan advanced bears no relation to consumer price of the good, but rather to what the broker can realize in a quick sale to consumers or to other dealers. As much as 80 per cent of this amount may be loaned.

Pawned merchandise is held for the duration of the arranged loan. Thereafter, if unclaimed following notification of the borrower, the goods may be sold at auction, the pawnbroker himself bidding if he wishes to resell the merchandise. Either renewal or payment of the loan will prevent disposal of the goods. As loans from this source are arranged with respect to the time involved, they are customarily single-payment loans, not instalment.

In their operations pawnbrokers are also obligated to comply with police regulations for reporting merchandise taken in. The daily compliance with this demand is part of the business of pawnbroking. So too is the annual inspection by state finance authorities.

Rates of charge made by pawnbrokers vary from state to state, but in general they exceed those of other legalized small-loan suppliers. This difference is due primarily to the size of the loans made, rather than to the low-risk quality of the borrowers, for the security of the pledge virtually removes the risk element. Capital must be provided and an appropriate place of business maintained. Rates reflect the relation of these functions to the volume of business and the size of individual transactions.

The Ohio law relating to pawnbrokers, for example, authorizes charges of 5 per cent per month on loans up to and including $25, or 3 per cent per month on portions of loans in excess of $25. In addition to such rates of interest, the licensee may make a total charge for the storage of pledged articles held as security for the loan, a sum not exceeding 25 cents per month, and for the storage of cumbersome articles such as furs, clothing, trunks, or motorcycles, a sum not exceeding 50 cents per month. The effectual

[15] *Ibid.*, p. 418.

rate on these terms amounts to more than 60 per cent per annum on loans of $25 or less, a rate justifiable only in terms of the small scale on which the loan service is provided.

Similarly, New York permits a charge which is graduated with respect to both amount and duration of loans. Loans of less than $100 may bear a charge of 3 per cent per month during the first six months and 2 per cent per month for each month thereafter. Loans exceeding $100 bear during the first half-year 2 per cent per month and 1 per cent per month for additional months.

DISCUSSION QUESTIONS

1. Which of the lending institutions engage in both primary and auxiliary credit services?
2. Relate the operations of commercial banks shown in Table 9, to the concept of the primary and auxiliary credit services.
3. Illustrate with experiences of commercial banks the principle of diversification in credit service offerings. Relate this trend in commercial banks to changing environmental conditions.
4. Contrast consumer lending agencies with respect to the time of their initial development, the incentives which encouraged their growth, public image, and social control.
5. Compare the credit service offerings of industrial banks, personal finance companies, and credit unions and determine to what extent they are competitive institutions.
6. Prepare a case for the proposition that legal loan rates should be simplified and their differences reduced.
7. Appraise the environmental and managerial factors which have produced the trends shown in Table 21.
8. Appraise consumer loan rate differences in terms of costs incurred by institutions to which they apply.
9. Compare the consumer cooperative movement in the United States with the growth of credit unions. What factors have affected each?
10. A consumer borrows from a consumer finance company $1,200 which, along with charges is paid off in 15 months. What is the amount of the charge and the true rate of charge?
11. Assume that a loan of $400 is made from each of the following institutions: (a) the personal loan department of a commercial bank, (b) a consumer loan company, (c) a credit union, and (d) a pawnshop. Compute the charge for each as authorized in a given

state, calculated on the basis of a 15-month repayment. State the charges in dollars and in percentages.

12. A travel loan may be obtained from a commercial bank under the following terms: amount to be borrowed, $300; 18 months to pay; charge, $4.25 per annum discount per $100 face amount of loan. What is the actual annual rate charged?

14

Full-Function Auxiliary
Credit Establishments

Performance of the credit functions is a normal activity of vendors
and lenders whose products and services are sought on credit.
Identification of the credit functions and segregation of them from
other business activities, however, have stimulated the invention
of specialists to whom credit functions may be shifted. Some of
these specialists perform for vendors the entire array of credit
functions, acting fully as their credit department. Others perform for vendors, lenders, and even for other credit specialists
some but not all of the functions. This chapter is concerned with
the former group, the full-function credit service auxiliaries.
Chapters 15 and 16 deal with the others.

Included as full-function specialists are factors, charge account
banks and companies, sales finance companies, and credit card
companies.

FACTORS

To understand factoring, distinction is made between factoring and factors. Factoring is a type of credit service; factors are
establishments whose principal business is factoring. Factors
sometimes perform credit services other than factoring; on the
other hand, some factoring is done by establishments other than

factors. Thus the function and the functionary are distinguished. Factoring is that type of credit service whereby *all* credit functions are shifted by a vendor to a credit specialist. The specialist assumes responsibility for investing funds in receivables resulting from the vendors' sales, for bearing *all* credit risk without recourse, and for performing the routine of the credit operation, including initial approval of creditworthiness and final collection of debts. Variations of this service, whereby not all functions are performed, are regarded as "types" of factoring, but, strictly speaking, they are types of service other than factoring offered by factors.

History

Modern factoring is the product of an interesting historical development. Until relatively recently, factors were usually engaged also in selling, acting as a type of commissioned selling agent or functional middleman. Evidence of factors as distributors is found as early as ancient Babylon. They were present in early Roman civilization. During the seventeenth and eighteenth centuries, they were instrumental in the trade between England and the American colonies, where they financed and sold corn, wool, and textile products.[1] Acting primarily as selling agents, for an additional fee they assumed responsibility for the payment of accounts.[2] As assumption of credit financing and risk bearing became more prominent in their activities in this country, during the decade prior to World War I, factors began to abandon their selling activities. Today, virtually all factors have ceased to engage in the selling function. The financing of open accounts[3] receivable, however, has come about since the beginning of this century.

Because of the early activity of textile selling agents in financing, factoring was for many years most closely associated with that industry. The tendency of New England or foreign mills to deal through representatives located in New York City resulted in some of the largest factoring organizations being established

[1] Herbert R. Silverman, "Factoring as a Financing Device," *Harvard Business Review*, September, 1949, p. 596.

[2] H. Felix Pereira, "Factoring: New Help in Foreign Markets," *Credit and Financial Management*, December, 1963, p. 12.

[3] See Theodore H. Silbert, "Financing and Factoring Accounts Receivable," *Harvard Business Review*, January–February, 1952, p. 47.

there. The applicability of the principles of factoring to other industries, however, has in recent years led to use of this credit service by manufacturers and wholesalers of other industries: shoes, furniture, equipment, electrical appliances, wearing apparel and dry goods, paint, paper, and toys.

Suppliers of factoring service include both non-bank and banking organizations. Among the commercial establishments are some engaged primarily in factoring who are known as "old-line" factors. Among the largest of them are Commercial Factors Corporation, William Iselin Company, Inc., Textile Banking Company, Inc., United Factors Corporation, and Meinhard Greeff and Company. Others who engage in factoring but also in open accounts receivable financing include Walter E. Heller & Company, James Talcott, Inc., Standard Factors Corporation, and A. J. Armstrong Company, Inc. The structure of this industry is such that factors are sometimes acquired as subsidiaries of even larger financing firms. C.I.T. Financial Corporation and Commercial Credit Company are two which embrace some of the largest factors, thus providing specialized credit service within a diversified service structure.

Factoring by banks is of even more recent development. The Trust Company of Georgia was first to enter the field, in 1939.[4] The First National Bank of Boston began to factor accounts in 1945, and the Bank of America also subsequently provided this service. In 1965, the First National City Bank of New York bought Hubshman Factors Corporation. A 1963 ruling by the Comptroller of the Currency held factoring to be a legitimate business for national banks, and this decision gave impetus to additional banks expressing interest in the activity. Through factoring, banks hope to diversify their service to clients. Factoring, however, is an activity which some commercial firms have found more difficult and less profitable to perform than they had expected.

Another development in factoring for both banks and non-banking firms has been the extension of factoring into international business. Import purchases have long been factored, the financing firm offering its credit to the foreign seller. With the development of export sales, foreign operations, and multinational firms, factoring houses have turned to factoring exports, as well as foreign and international sales of overseas subsidiaries and

4 "Big Banks Dip into Factoring," *Business Week*, May 22, 1965, p. 58.

affiliates. The service of factoring to importing is illustrated by use which Japanese exporters have made of this credit service. Unfamiliar with creditworthiness of U.S. customers, credit checking procedures, and credit terminology in English; constrained by Oriental courtesy from declining uncreditworthy customers; and curbed by governmental restrictions on credit extensions to independent sales organizations in this country, Japanese exporters have found factoring by U.S. firms a relief from credit functions which they preferred to shift rather than perform.[5]

With internationalization of many American businesses, factoring firms have also internationalized their activities to serve their domestic clients. Thus by export sales factoring, exporters have shifted to factors functions which formerly by letters of credit they had shifted to domestic and foreign banks.[6] Willingness of factors to participate in supplying credit service for international sales has been increased by the availability, since 1962, of export credit insurance through the Foreign Credit Insurance Association. The First National Bank of Boston was the first bank in the country to offer non-recourse export financing, and James Talcott, Inc., was one of the first of the old-line factors to inaugurate such a program.

Another move in international factoring was made in 1961 when the First National Bank of Boston helped start International Factors, Ltd., in London.[7] Those two organizations in turn created International Factors A.G., a Swiss holding company, parent of the London company and of international companies in West Germany, France, Sweden, Switzerland, Ireland, Belgium, the Netherlands, Denmark, South Africa, Israel, and Australia. Typically, the Swiss parent owns 50 per cent of each company and local banking interests own the rest; local banks also own stock in the holding company. The biggest volume of business of this network of factoring firms is in traditional, non-recourse factoring, although some companies do recourse factoring in domestic business. Overseas factoring—both domestic and international—in 1965 exceeded $300 million,[8] of which 75 per cent was split between West Germany and Britain and the rest scattered throughout the world.

[5] Irwin Naitove, "International Factoring: Where the Twain Do Meet," *Credit and Financial Management,* January, 1965, p. 20.

[6] David G. Mitch, "Export Factoring Assayed," *The Christian Science Monitor,* January 7, 1964.

[7] "U.S. Factoring Leaps Atlantic," *Business Week,* January 30, 1965, p. 86.

[8] *Ibid.*

The total volume of sales factored in the United States in 1965 approximated $7 billion. Seventy-five per cent of this was still in the traditional areas of textiles and clothing, whereas until 1946 more than 90 per cent of factoring business was confined to those lines.[9]

Operational Procedure in Factoring

As true factoring is a distinct credit service, the segment of the market for which it is useful, the price at which it is offered, and the competition which it meets are determined by the operational processes involved.[10] To begin with, factoring is available only in commercial, not retail, transactions. It represents a continuing contractual relationship between the factor and the vendor, who agrees to factor all his sales throughout the contract period. The vendor maintains no credit department or operation of his own; he shifts this work in its entirety to the factor. The vendor thus discharges himself of all responsibilities for investing funds in accounts receivable, for bearing the risk inherent in credit selling, or for investigating, processing, and collecting accounts. While factoring eliminates the need for a credit manager in the vendor's organization, it does not relieve general management from its responsibilities relating to credit terms, policy, and agreements.

The service of factoring is often referred to as "the buying of a vendor's accounts." It were better described as the buying of his *invoices*, for strictly speaking the vendor himself never possesses accounts under a factoring arrangement. The customers are his, so are the orders, but no account receivable exists until an order is approved by the factor. Approval of a credit transaction on orders submitted to the factor follows the normal course of investigation and appraisal of creditworthiness. To make credit decisions expeditiously, the factor maintains a staff supplied with current information services and resources. In doing this work the factor not only approves individual sales, but he may establish a line of credit for his client's customer. He may even furnish an advanced credit opinion prior to the placing of an

[9] Gerrit J. Popma, "A Behind-the-Scenes Look at Factoring," *Credit and Financial Management*, May, 1963, p. 31.

[10] For a detailed study of factoring, see Clyde William Phelps, *The Role of Factoring in Modern Business Finance* (Baltimore: Commercial Credit Company, 1956).

order in the case that specialized manufacturing must be under-taken.

Upon approval of creditworthiness, the vendor makes ship-ment and notifies the customer that payment of invoice should be made to the named factor. This practice is known as factoring "with notification," and it is a feature distinguishing this service from some other forms of receivables financing. Notification in-dicates that, in addition to having made the investigation, the factor assumes responsibility for following up the account, for receiving payments, and for making collection efforts if they are necessary. Simultaneously with shipment, a copy of the invoice is sent to the factor "without recourse." Thus is shifted to the factor the bearing of credit risk.

Upon receipt of the invoice, the factor stands ready to advance to the vendor 100 per cent of the value of the invoice, less factor-ing charges. If the vendor is in need of finances, he may draw immediately upon an account to which the sum of the factored sales is credited. Thus the vendor has achieved the effect of selling for cash, although his customer has been able to buy on credit.

All subsequent handling of the account is the responsibility of the factor. It is up to him to make collections, grant exten-sions, and pursue whatever legal course may be necessary to ob-tain payment.

New Factoring Services. Keeping pace with the growing and changing market for their services, factors have in recent years modified some features of their business.

NON-NOTIFICATION FACTORING. One alteration has been in the traditional notification of the vendor's customer that the ac-count has been factored and that payment should be made to the factor and not to the vendor. The desire of potential clients to use the service of factoring, but their reluctance to announce that they are doing so, has led factors to accede to the request that "notification" be not required when a shipment is invoiced. Re-ceipt of payment and possibly collection effort are reserved by the vendor, although all other functions are shifted. The vendor then receives payment in trust for the factor, and prompt re-mittance is made to him. This new service of the factor is a con-cession to the expansion of business into fields whose sales are traditionally unfactored.

THE "FACTORING MATURITY PLAN." Although the rendering of financial assistance is one of the principal services of the modern factor, some clients need assistance with the credit analysis and in bearing risk more than they need financial aid. Consequently, the account available to the vendor upon the placing of his invoice with the factor may not be drawn upon. If it should stand untouched for the full duration of the credit period, the vendor and not the factor would have performed the financing function, and no charge would be made by the factor for that service. In fact, should the vendor not withdraw his credit with the factor until *after* the maturity date of the invoice, the factor would be his debtor and would pay per diem interest at the usual rate on the sum involved.

The advantage of this service to the factor's client is that it serves as insurance against loss on his accounts. Risk, investigation, and collections are shifted to the factor; the function of financing is retained. The client is thereby guaranteed 100 per cent return on his accounts, less the service charge made by the factor. An alternative to this form of assurance is the purchase of credit insurance. Such insurance, however, does not provide as complete coverage and is costly. That factoring is not more generally used primarily for its insurance features is due to several facts. Not all companies or industries are equally acceptable to the factors. Moreover, the loss of control over the credit operation and direct contact with customers on credit matters may be more important to a vendor than the risks to which he is exposed. Furthermore, if the risks involved in an operation are small, the vendor may be indifferent to shifting them to either an insurance company or a factor.[11]

THE "DROP SHIPMENT FACTORING PLAN." Drop shipping is the practice of a distributor buying in his own name merchandise which he requests to be shipped directly from the producer to his customer. Often a small operator, the drop shipper does not always enjoy a credit standing with his resources. His service, however, supplies a real distributive need, and factors furnish him stature by virtually factoring the manufacturer's dropped shipment at the request of the drop shipper. The factor pays for the manufacturer's shipment at the request of the drop shipper. The factor pays the manufacturer the cash value of the invoice

[11] Theodore H. Silbert, "Financing and Factoring Accounts Receivable," *Harvard Business Review,* January–February, 1952, p. 47.

upon receipt of evidence of shipment. He remits to the drop shipper the difference between his sales price and the factored invoice. He assumes the credit risk and collection responsibility.[12]

Non-Factoring Functions. As factors have dropped their selling function, they have added other services not normally a part of their business. They have undertaken to finance their client's purchases as well as their sales. This financing function might be undertaken by any of several institutions. The factor's interest in his client, however, makes him a natural financial resource to whom to turn. His funds are loaned sometimes for the financing of inventories, as when a seasonal interval occurs between purchase and sale or as when a long process or period of production is necessary before raw materials can be processed and sold. He also renders clients an advisory service. The factor may assist in planning the financial budget, in styling merchandise, in marketing research, in planning production, in estimating sales, or in determining the best terms of sales to be used.

The Charge for Factoring

As factors provide many combinations of services, their schedule of charges is also variable. Factors' charges consist of two components: an interest rate and a service charge. An interest charge, slightly higher than prevailing bank rates, compensates the factor for the credit financing function. This is commonly 6 per cent per annum, applied to the advance made by the factor to his client, computed for the term of the credit period. For example, a vendor selling on terms of net 30 days would pay 0.5 per cent of the invoiced amount if he drew from the factor invoiced credit at the time of sale. If, not needing the money immediately, he delayed its withdrawal 15 days, interest would amount to 0.25 per cent of the sum involved. The rate is applied to a daily adjusted balance of indebtedness of the vendor to the factor. The exact interest rate charged by the factor varies with changes in the time-loan rate which banks charge for loans to factors.

A service charge is the second part of the factors' compensation. This is a flat charge ranging generally from 1 to 2 per cent of the volume of sales factored. It is not expressed in terms of a time period; rather, it is a direct rate of commission for the fac-

[12] *Ibid.*

toring services performed. It is a negotiated rate providing the factor compensation for performance of the credit operation and for assumption of the credit risk. The exact amount charged for this service is dependent upon the volume of sales factored, the number of customer accounts carried, the number and size of orders factored, the nature of the credit risks inherent in the industry or the business of the factor's client, the familiarity of the factor with credit conditions of the industry of the vendor, and the nature and number of services for which the factor is engaged.

To illustrate the charges of the factor, assume that sales amounting to $1.2 million during a year are factored, and that an interest rate of 6 per cent per annum and a service charge of 1.5 per cent are made. Monthly sales are $100,000. If the vendor withdraws his credit for this amount upon presentation of the invoices to the factor, his financing charge at 6 per cent would be $500 per month (0.5% × $100,000), or $6,000 per year ($500 × 12). This portion of the charge conceivably could be less if the vendor used the maturity plan of factoring. The service charge for factoring sales for a year would be $18,000 (1.5 × $1,200,000). This too could be decreased or increased depending upon the services which the factor provided the vendor. The annual factoring charge in this case would be $24,000 ($6,000 + $18,000), subject to variations one way or another.

Management's Decision To Factor

The decision to factor its sales is one which may face a vendor either at the time when business is begun or subsequently. For many businesses which have begun to use the services of the factor in recent years, it has been a decision to abandon their regular credit operation and to shift the credit functions to the factoring specialist. In making this decision, several circumstances would have to be considered:

1. The availability of factoring service. Factors have operated traditionally in certain industries. They have recently expanded into other fields. Their familiarity or unfamiliarity with the problems in a particular line of business may affect their willingness to undertake the credit operations in that field. The availability of their services to a client may also be affected by the nature of the business which he could provide them.
2. The functions needed to be performed—whether all would be shifted or whether some would be retained by the vendor.

3. The cost of factoring as compared with the cost of maintaining one's own credit.
4. The impression which factoring of sales would give to a vendor's customers.

Although factoring has found wider acceptance in many kinds of industries, in any of them there are circumstances where factoring may not be advantageous: [13]

1. Businesses selling principally on cash, C.B.D., or C.O.D. terms
2. Contract manufacturers where the credit risk is secured
3. Firms selling on very short terms, except where unusual credit risks are involved
4. Firms whose entire output is sold to one or a few companies
5. Firms with regular volume less than $250,000 annually
6. Firms whose financial condition or management is unsound

SALES FINANCING

The shifting of all credit functions to auxiliary specialists has been more common in wholesale trades than in retailing. In the latter, closeness of the buyer–seller relationship, subordination of regard for credit to selling, and independence of merchants in their credit activities kept credit functions combined with merchandising functions. Changes in business, however, have effected some separation of these and have evolved three types of full-function credit auxiliaries in retailing. The contributing changes have been the growing importance of expensive durable consumer goods, the impersonalization of creditworthiness and of credit management, greater mobility of the market population, and increased regard for both the costs and the earning potential in the rendering of credit service. The three institutions which these trends have produced are the sales finance company, the charge account services, and the credit card plans.

Sales finance companies have arisen as an institution to which vendors shift all credit functions in connection with the sale of the more expensive, durable consumer goods. Sales finance companies engage primarily in the financing of instalment sales, or in sales financing, which may be defined as follows: the providing of instalment credit service by other than the vendor, on the basis of an endorsed, mortgage-secured note accepted from buyers of durable goods, in either wholesale or retail transactions. Sales finance companies are non-vendor, non-bank, private credit spe-

[13] Phelps, *op. cit.*, p. 17.

cialists performing all of the credit functions for vendors. Sales finance companies sometimes engage in other forms of financing and even in lending. At the same time, not all sales financing is done by sales finance companies but also by vendors and other types of credit specialists.

This type of full-function credit auxiliary is found primarily in the distribution of automobiles and household appliances. Both are commodities bought on instalment terms; both are high priced. For these reasons both pose problems of financing for distributors and dealers as well as for consumers. Because no existing credit specialists met the need for this particular type of credit service as the market for it appeared, sales finance companies developed representing a new combination of relationships among vendors, buyers, and credit specialists.

Sales financing is distinguished from the service of other credit specialists. Whereas factoring represents the shifting of credit operations of vendors selling on open account in wholesale trades, and charge account services represent the shifting of credit operations of vendors selling on open account in retail trades, sales financing represents the shifting of credit operations of vendors selling on instalment terms in both wholesale and retail trades.

Procedure in Sales Financing

Sales financing, like other forms of credit specialization, is distinguished by the procedure and relationships which it involves. The parties to this service are the buyer, the vendor, and the sales financing organization. As in straight instalment selling, transactions are consummated between the vendor and his customer. In straight instalment selling, however, credit functions are performed by the vendor, who determines his terms, investigates the creditworthiness, assumes the risk, and finances his own receivables. In sales financing, the credit specialists perform these functions by "accepting" the instalment contracts made between the vendor and his customer. It may appear from this statement that sales financing is the same as the financing of merchants' accounts receivable, whereby their existing accounts are assigned, pledged, or sold to a finance company. This is not the case, and on a fine distinction at this point rests an essential feature of sales financing. The sale of a vendor depending upon sales financing assistance is not consummated until assurance is given by the sales finance company that the credit of the buyer, represented by the mortgage and instalment contract, will be taken over or "accepted" by the credit specialists. Thus when the sales finance company accepts the credit instrument, it bears not only the signature of the buyer but the endorsement of the vendor and is transferred by the vendor, sometimes "with recourse," sometimes "without recourse."

The sales finance company in this process of approving credit states the terms of its relationship with both the vendor and the buyer. After making an investigation, if the buyer is found to be creditworthy, he is notified of the acceptance of the credit and a schedule of payments is agreed upon, including charges to be paid the credit agency. Simultaneously, there is credited or advanced to the vendor that portion of the contract balance represented by the cash price of the sale. Understanding is also reached concerning the recourse which the financing agency has against the vendor in case the buyer defaults his contract and concerning the disposal of repossessed merchandise.

As the contract runs its course, the sales finance company assumes responsibility for billing, receiving payments, and making collections. Thus by the use of sales financing the vendor is able to shift to the credit specialist the work of account acquisition, maintenance, and follow-up and the financing of receivables. In those areas of the country where contracts are accepted without recourse, the vendor relieves himself also of the bearing of credit risk.

Charge for Sales Financing

Unlike factors and charge account services, sales finance companies collect their charge wholly from buyers; vendors, whose sales they finance, pay nothing for this service. The rate of charge is that which may be charged on any instalment sales contracts. Of the states having instalment sales legislation, most have some designated limits on the finance charge of the "time–price differential." In the remaining states, including those which have no special instalment sales legislation, the time–sale price is generally approved by judicial decision. Further details of instalment credit charges have been discussed in a preceding chapter in connection with the regulation of instalment selling.

Floor-Plan Financing

The procedure and charges described above relate particularly to the manner in which a dealer shifts his credit operation to a sales finance company in selling to ultimate consumers. A similar service is rendered by sales finance companies in the distribution of the same goods from manufacturers to their distributors and dealers. Although manufacturers in this way shift their entire credit operation to sales finance companies, this finances both the vendor's sales and the distributor's purchases or inventory. Because of the nature of the manufacturer–distributor relationship, the credit operation and risk functions are subordinated to the financing function. On the other hand, it should not be overlooked that in performing this service, sales finance companies are rendering for manufacturers the identical service of a credit operation which they perform for dealers selling to ultimate consumers.

Although automobile manufacturers sometimes extend 15–30 days credit to dealers, they will not as a rule release cars from their plants until they receive cash or check payment, or until a sales finance company has executed an agreement in favor of the manufacturer to pay for the cars delivered to the dealer. The manufacturer thus shifts entirely his credit operation. Such financing of the sale, or the purchase, of a shipment is preliminary to the process of floor-plan financing. Upon the arrival of the goods, the buyer may either continue with the same sales finance company a floor-plan financing arrangement, or he may secure financing for his inventories from other sources. With whomsoever the arrangement is made, the dealer executes a promissory note and a chattel mortgage as security for his credit. This relationship is intended to continue until the dealer sells the automobile or other product so financed, at which time the car is released from trust by the dealer's mailing to the sales finance company a check for the balance owing on that unit. The sale, of course, may, like the purchase, be financed by a sales finance company. If the same company handles both transactions, it involves mainly a bookkeeping transaction wherein the obligation of the customer cancels the debt of the dealer to the finance company. Any difference in the amount, reflecting the dealer's gross margin, may be paid to him by the finance company as a cash settlement.

The charge for floor-plan financing consists of two types of payments. One is a flat charge applied to each vehicle financed to cover the cost of account acquisition, insurance, etc. The flat charge varies from a fixed sum per unit sold to a small per cent of the value financed ranging from $1.50 to several dollars per transaction. The second charge is an interest charge to cover the cost of capital actually borrowed. This is governed by the rate of interest which the sales finance company pays in order to obtain its own funds, ranging from 4 to 6 per cent.[14]

Other Services of Sales Finance Companies

Although the financing of retail sales, and of wholesale purchases of distributors and dealers, of products sold on the instalment plan is the principal function of sales finance companies, it is not their sole function. In addition, many of them engage directly or indirectly in a wide variety of financing activities. One is the financing of dealers' accounts receivable, through purchase or loans made thereon, with full, limited, or no recourse to the dealers. Another is the making of capital loans to businesses for the purchase of buildings and facilities. Direct loans are also made to individual consumers, through either subsidiary industrial banks or personal loan companies or under license obtained by the sales finance company branch offices. Through subsidiaries, sales finance companies also engage in factoring, as through the Textile Banking Company, Inc., of New York, a subsidiary of Commercial Credit Company. Still another service is the providing of insurance through subsidiaries, usually in connection with the articles sold on the instalment plan and financed by the finance companies.

Sales Financing Contrasted with Factoring

A credit manager may never be faced with making a choice between using the services of a sales finance company and those of a factor, because in general they serve two different markets for credit service. Nevertheless, the characteristics of each may be accentuated by a comparison of the two. The following are the principal points upon which they may be contrasted.

[14] Albert G. Sweetser, *Floor-Plan Financing by Sales-Finance Companies* (Newton Highlands, Mass.: Albert G. Sweetser, 1957), pp. 567–91.

Sales Financing	Factoring
1. Serve mainly the ultimate consumer although to some extent industrial users and distributors.	1. Serve exclusively the wholesale trade.
2. Mortgage taken as a security.	2. No security taken.
3. No contractual relationship with the vendor.	3. Contractual relationship with vendor.
4. Credit service for instalment sales contracts.	4. Credit service for open account sales.
5. Instalment contracts "accepted" generally with recourse.	5. Accounts taken without recourse to the seller.
6. Vendor does not determine by which sales finance company the transaction is financed.	6. Continuing contractual relationship providing for factoring of all of vendor's sales with the particular factoring concern.
7. Sales finance company "accepts" vendors' contracts or accounts.	7. Factor takes over approved credit invoices.
8. Buyer pays for the credit service.	8. Vendor pays for the credit service.
9. Operating mainly in automobile and appliance lines.	9. Operating mainly in lines of textiles, articles of apparel and upholstery made of synthetic fibers and plastics, shoes, furniture, equipment, and appliances.
10. Credit charge based upon time-price differential expressed as an "add-on charge."	10. Credit charge consists of interest plus a service charge.
11. Regulation by state instalment sales laws.	11. No regulation except legal interest rate provisions.
12. Sales finance companies are sometimes subsidiaries of the manufacturing concerns whose distribution they facilitate.	12. Unassociated with manufacturers or with the principals whom they serve.
13. They lend to vendors for other purposes.	13. They lend to vendors for other purposes.
14. They advise dealers on financial matters.	14. Source of information and counsel to vendors.

Evolution of the Sales Finance Company

The conception of the sales finance company was a case of necessity mothering invention. The need grew from the increasing production of and market for expensive durable goods, and from the fact that existing credit agencies did not provide a service required for the distribution of these goods. Commercial banks and other financing organizations did not provide a service whereby businesses could be supplied with the additional working capital needed to carry inventories and to sell durable goods on an instalment plan. Commercial banks were purchasing drafts acquired by vendors in international transactions, but they would not accept vendors' accounts receivable or their customers' notes accepted in domestic trade. Neither were factors prepared to render such a service.

The supplying of this unfulfilled need began during the first decade of the twentieth century with the formation of several financing organizations employing a new technique. One was the Mercantile Credit Company, incorporated by Arthur R. Jones and John L. Little, whose need for working capital grew out of their instalment selling of the *Encyclopedia Americana*.[15] At the same time, in 1908, Henry Ittleson formed a company which later became C.I.T. Financial Corporation, one of the present three largest sales finance companies. This organization bought open accounts of manufacturers and jobbers on the non-notification plan and purchased their draft receivables. In 1912, Alexander E. Duncan founded the Commercial Credit Company, the second of the "Big Three" sales finance companies, which as early as 1916 began the purchase of automobile time paper. The third of the "Big Three," the General Motors Acceptance Corporation, was incorporated in 1919.

The principal purpose of those early sales finance companies was to assume the credit financing function of manufacturers and distributors. It was not primarily to facilitate the distribution of products, particularly automobiles, from manufacturers to consumers. This latter purpose evolved during subsequent years. During the decade 1920–1930 both the offices and the assets of sales finance companies increased at a rapid rate, as they helped

15 Phelps, *The Role of the Sales Finance Companies in The American Economy* (Baltimore: Commercial Credit Company, 1952), pp. 49–78.

provide markets for automobiles, radios, refrigerators, home appliances, and many other time- and labor-saving devices. That was an era of the improvement of such products and the lowering of their prices, made possible by the increased scale of their manufacture and the realization of attendant economies of production. The depression years of the 1930's were a period of consolidation of the gains which sales finance companies had made. Less efficient companies were eliminated, and improved methods were introduced.

During the 1930's two significant changes in their practices occurred. One was the introduction in 1935 by GMAC of a "6 per cent plan" of financing. By this announcement of their financing charge, two results were accomplished: consumers were given a rate which they could understand and in which they had confidence; and something of a standard was set forth to which competitive rates tended to gravitate. Unfortunately, this confidence of many consumers was misplaced, for this was not the "6 per cent interest" which they seemed to regard as a fair and common charge for the use of money. It was a rate on a declining principal. The Federal Trade Commission ultimately required discontinuance of the practice which gave the impression that this was an *actual* rate of 6 per cent. A second development of this period related to the practice of automobile manufacturers' subsidiary sales finance companies of pressuring dealers to use only the factory-preferred or -controlled finance company. Out of this grew in 1938 indictments of General Motors, Ford, and Chrysler and their associated finance companies for restraint of trade. Consent decrees were signed by Ford and Chrysler, and they agreed not to participate in auto financing. General Motors, on the other hand, engaged in a prolonged fight, losing the criminal suit pertaining to putting pressure on dealers, but late in the 1940's winning the civil suit that sought to compel it to divest itself of GMAC. Ford thereafter obtained a release from its consent decree and in 1959 prepared again to enter into the sales financing business.

During World War II, sales financing was beset by the loss of business resulting from the cessation of production of automobiles and many other durable goods. The number of branch offices was drastically cut, and the businesses remaining undertook to diversify their activities by the introduction of personal loan departments or subsidiaries and by the purchase of manufacturing plants. Following the war, the recovery of sales financing corresponded to that of the consumer durable goods industries and the branches and the volume of financing soon reached unprecedented size.

CHARGE ACCOUNT SERVICES

Retailers' credit functions are not performed by factors, and only those arising from instalment sales are shiftable to sales finance companies. Performance of the functions involved in retail open accounts, therefore, fell to retail merchants themselves, until the development of two other credit specialists: charge account service organizations and universal credit card companies. Both perform the full credit work of their merchant clients. As full-function auxiliary suppliers of credit service, both resemble factors, although each has unique features in its relationships with merchants and with consumers.

Evolution of Charge Account Services

The idea for specialization in charge account service grew from the inability of many retailers to provide such service for themselves, at a time when a market for such service was clearly at hand. Selling on open accounts has generally been associated with larger retail stores, their volume of business being sufficient to support a credit department operation—to engage credit analysts, to obtain capital, and to bear credit risk. Smaller single-line and specialty stores, however, have often avoided selling on credit because of technical and financial disadvantages. In this environment was conceived the idea of specialists to perform for such stores the credit functions which they lacked.

The history of this credit specialization has been brief. It did not begin until the late 1940's, but its potentiality was quickly recognized and by 1951 it had gained national attention. Commercial banks were the first to engage in this service, showing more initiative to innovate in this business than they had in making consumer loans or in financing instalment sales. In 1958, two of the country's largest banks, the Bank of America and The Chase Manhattan Bank, instituted programs of charge account service. Having access to funds at a low cost, already engaged in commercial and consumer credit activities, and envisioning earnings from rates higher than those on conventional loans, commercial banks in many cities launched what was known as Charge Account Bank plans. According to the Charge Account Bankers Association, in 1960 its 123 members operated in 29 states, and a third of the country's 100 largest banks offered central charge service.[16]

Expectations of the banks were not fully realized; in fact, two-thirds of the charge plans started by banks failed. As banks withdrew from the field, non-bank operators tended to take their place. In 1962, The Chase Manhattan bank sold its program to a private individual who thereafter called it Uni-Serv. Other banks also yielded to entrepreneurs who consolidated and enlarged the programs. Yet some banks continued, most notable of which are the Bank of America, the Marine Midland banks in upstate New York, the Atlanta's Citizens & Southern National Bank, and the Bank of Hawaii. With experience giving better assurance of success, in 1965 three more banks announced retail credit card plans, including the Melon National Bank & Trust Company of Pittsburgh. Some banks offer account holders loan privileges as well as purchase privileges. As size seems an element in the success of all these plans, the charge account service which initially was a local offering has taken on more of the characteristics of the universal credit card services.

Operational Procedure

Initiative in the development of charge account service falls to the specialist rather than to merchants. It is they who organize the participating vendors, acquire capital, and promote use of the service by consumers.

The credit specialist selects the area in which he would operate and then interests merchants in shifting to him the credit functions which they perform, or rather which they are unable to perform. The merchants may be large or small, but large department stores have not generally participated in such programs, for they already have operations large enough to minimize the advantages of cooperation. On the other hand, neither is there good potentiality among retailers whose cash business would be

[16]"New Look in Consumer Credit," *Dun's Review and Modern Industry*, August, 1960, p. 49.

merely shifted to credit business, whose customers would not find credit purchasing beneficial, or whose business would provide a flood of small-sales transactions which would be expensive to authorize and administer. The most likely prospects for this service are small- and medium-size retailers and service establishments whose market stands to be increased by selling on credit, but whose operations are too small to achieve efficient and economical credit operation. Among the trades in which charge account services have found satisfactory clients are the following: appliances, auto accessories and repairs, building materials, dentists, doctors, drug stores, florists, furriers, grocery stores, hotels, music shops, photographers, restaurants, shoe stores, typewriter shops, and variety stores.

When willing participants are found, a contractual agreement is made setting forth the responsibilities of each. Some merchants are required to make an initial deposit as evidence of good faith, refundable after a period of time or upon attainment of a determined volume of business. Others pay a flat sign-up fee and a nominal annual rental for each imprinter. Merchants may provide a direct mail list periodically. They also agree to display the charge account service company's name and symbol in their advertising. To encourage volume business, a schedule of discounts or rebates to the merchants is offered when volume of business placed with the specialist reaches stated levels.

Consumers desiring to use charge account service makes application for it at the service company's headquarters or branch, and also at participating stores. It is not expected that merchants engage to any extent in interviewing the applicant, and certainly not in investigation of his creditworthiness. That is a function shifted to and performed by the specialist in the usual manner, through reporting services, interviews, references, and the like. Notification that an account has been opened for the consumer is accompanied by a customer credit card to be used for identification in purchasing at member stores.

At the time of sale, the merchant fills out a charge slip and calls the service company for authorization of the sale. Authorization responsibility may be given to salespeople for small transactions; others are referred. Merchants daily submit to the company sales slips of all credit transactions. Matching funds, less the service charge, are then added to the merchant's account.

All account records of customers are maintained by the company, showing purchases, payments, and adjustments. Such account files are the basis for further authorization of sales. Monthly statements issued to customers are a consolidated statement showing purchases made at each of the merchants participating in the plan. Payments are made to the service company, which assumes responsibility for collecting on delinquency.

Charges

The basic charge for this type of service is paid by the merchant whose functions are shifted. The retail customer pays nothing for the service rendered him, provided he pays his account in full within 30 days of billing. Otherwise, 20 or 25 per cent falls due immediately, and a charge of 1 or 1.5 per cent per month on the outstanding balance will be made. Thus from the customer's standpoint, the plan is similar to the optional charge account plan offered by many vendors.

The charge for loans made to holders of bank-sponsored accounts is illustrated by terms on the BankAmericard. For cash advances, there is an extra 4 per cent service charge when the money is drawn. If the cardholder receives $100 in cash, his bill reads $104. There is no further charge if the money is paid back within 25 days; if not, the charge is the same as that levied on purchases of goods from retail stores, i.e., 1.5 per cent per month.

The charge made of merchants is a flat per cent of the value of sales financed, commonly 6 per cent, deducted from the value of the sales slips deposited daily. Some companies charge 5 per cent of sales for 30-day accounts and 6 per cent of sales for revolving credit accounts. Recognizing that costs of performing this service vary with the volume and type of business involved, a graduated schedule of refunds is offered to merchants whose business attains a certain volume, measured either or both by the size of the average transaction and the number of sales slips involved. Discounts vary also for different types of business: 3 per cent for clothing; 4 per cent for hotels and restaurants; 5 per cent for service stations, food, liquor and drugstores. The discounts announced by one of the large banks for its charge plan are as follows:

AVERAGE TRANSACTION REFUND

Average transaction	Original service charge	Allowable refund	Effective charge
Under $5.00	6%	None	6%
$5.00–$7.49	6	½%	5½
$7.50–$9.99	6	1	5
$10.00–$14.99	6	1½	4½
$15.00–$24.99	6	2	4
$25.00–$34.99	6	2½	3½
$35.00–$49.99	6	3	3
$50.00 and over	6	Rates upon application	Rates upon application

VOLUME REFUND

	Net number of sales slips	Refund per slip
First	1,000	No refund
Next	9,000	1¢ per sales slip
Next	10,000	1½¢ per sales slip
Over	20,000	2¢ per sales slip

Appraisal

The basis of the success attained by this kind of credit service is the advantage it holds for all concerned. Merchants purchasing the service avoid the performance of functions for which they may be less well prepared, and they increase their business by selling to customers who presumably otherwise would not make cash purchases. Merchants have experienced not only increase in number of customers but increase in average transaction. One study showed the average charge for merchants affiliated with a bank plan to range from $10.25 to $13.35, in contrast to the average gross sales in department stores ranging from $4.55 to $5.80 during a comparable period. Consumers benefit from having credit service for purchases where it would not otherwise be available, and they can pay for all purchases through one consolidated billing. Suppliers of such credit service enjoy a lucrative business. Banks with charge account services receive other patronage from both merchants and consumers using the plan.

In essence, charge account services represent the application of familiar principles to another type of business situation. Its similarity to factoring and to sales financing is apparent in the assumption of functions by specialists who command access to funds for carrying receivables. The economies of large-scale operation are also apparent in each. Moreover, each illustrates the divisibility and shiftability of all of the credit functions. Most of these features are also present in the credit card plans.

The form taken by charge account services, however, may have several variations. As explained, both banking and non-banking organizations are capable of providing such service. It can also be offered either by profit or cooperative enterprises. The latter have taken the form of community central charge plans, wherein merchants attempt collectively and jointly to provide charge account service common to them all. The relative merits of the respective plans on several points are shown in Fig. 14-1.

UNIVERSAL CREDIT CARD COMPANIES

A fourth type of specialist performing all credit functions for vendors is the universal credit card company. Serving retail stores and service establishments nationally and internationally, this supplier of credit service has extended the application of credit management and at the same time facilitated the development of new markets for credit service.

Distinguishing Characteristics

Because it represents the shift of all credit functions, the universal credit card operation is similar to charge account services, sales financing, and factoring. However, important and distinguishing differences exist in the service rendered and in the operations performed.

Universal credit card service is typified by the operations of three companies: American Express Company, Diners' Club, and Carte Blanche. Vendors for whom they provide credit service are primarily in the field of travel and entertainment, whereas charge account services are related mainly to retail merchandising. Both, however, invade the other's domain; the card services serve also men's wear stores, gift shops, gasoline stations, and car rental agencies, and account services have participants among hotels, restaurants, and transportation agencies. Vendor affiliation is determined primarily by the character of the consumer market which companies serve. The card services have catered to men in business roles, with high incomes, and to whom convenience

CHARGE CREDIT SYSTEMS

Summary of the Advantages & Disadvantages to the Merchant

Plan Numbers

		1	2	3	4	5
		Merchant Owner	Bank Charge Accounts	Community Central Charge	Credit Purchase Cards	Factor
ADVANTAGES						
Increased Sales		Yes	Yes	Yes	Yes	Yes
Customer Purchase Record		Yes	No	No	No	Yes
Increased Store Traffic	{ Due to Paying on Account etc.	Yes	No	No	No	Yes
Monthly Reminder of Store with Mdse, Inserts, etc.		Yes	No	No	No	Yes
More Customer Loyalty		Yes	No	No	No	Yes
DISADVANTAGES						
Requires Additional Permanent Capital (Without which could get into trouble)	⌈ For Accounts Receivable	Yes	No	No	No	No
	⌊ For Office Equipment & Increased Inventory	Yes	No	No	No	Yes
Normal Interest Charge on Borrowed Capital		Yes	No	No	No	No
High Interest Charge on Borrowed Capital		No	Yes	Yes	Yes	Yes
Additional Operating Expenses	⌈ Due to Additional Office Help, Supplies, Postage, etc.	Yes	No	No	No	Yes
	⌊ Due to Credit Reports, Collections, Bad Debt Charge Off.	Yes	No	No	No	Yes
Requires Store Owner's Time & Effort		Yes	No	No	No	Yes

Fig. 14–1. Charge credit systems. (Source: Gerald D. Grosner, "How To Set Up a Credit System," *Men's Wear*, January 22, 1960, p. 58.)

is a prime consideration. A survey of Carte Blanche, owned by Hilton Credit Corporation, card holders showed one-half with incomes exceeding $20,000 and two-thirds over $12,000 annually. By contrast, the market for charge account services is families in low-income brackets, to whom extended credit purchasing power rather than mere convenience is a prime consideration. Reflecting these differences in their markets, card services charge customer members an annual fee but account services do not.

Both charge vendors a percentage of sales handled and account services charge customers on balances not paid within 30 days.

Historical Development

The history of universal credit card services has been one of struggle for survival, for even the most successful have parried with failure as they sought the best combinations of merchants, customers, risks, charges, records, and operating policies. Of numerous entrants into the field, only three continue as evidence that there is a scale on which such service can be offered profitably to the existing market.

The Diners' Club, founded in 1950, was the first to be established. Within six months it had 200 restaurant and club affiliates in New York, Chicago, Boston, Philadelphia, Miami, and Los Angeles, and 22,000 customer members paying annual dues of $3. At the end of another year these numbers had been increased to 500 and 70,000, respectively.[17] As operations continued to expand, branch offices were opened throughout the United States, as well as in Canada, Europe, Havana, Rio de Janeiro, and Tokyo.

Among the early imitators and competitors of the Diners' Club were several whose rise and fall disclosed increasingly the essential bases upon which success in this type of operation would probably be achieved. National Credit Card, Inc., founded in 1951, was an example of extremely rapid growth in participants but not in business, and at the time of its collapse in 1954 it had twice the number of card holders and four times more participating vendors than the Diners' Club, but only half the billings.[18] Status membership was the customer appeal exploited by some clubs, such as Go Europe n' Sign and the Who's-Who Credit Club of New York, but useful service, not just status, is necessary. Companies with nationwide operations simulated the universal cards with their own extended coverage cards. Among them were oil companies, the Bell Telephone System, travel agencies, airlines, auto rental companies, hotels, motels, nightclubs, and restaurants. Although affording broad credit privileges, they do not provide the diversity of purchase opportunities which the functional specialist offers.

[17] John Lineham, "Diners' Club," *Barrons,* January 9, 1956, p. 15.
[18] Frank Breese, "There Are Many Headaches and Problems in Running National Credit Card Setup," *National Petroleum News,* June 10, 1953, pp. 27–28.

The formidable contenders for the type of business which the Diners' Club developed were the American Express Credit Card and Hilton's Carte Blanche, both launched in the fall of 1958. Both differed from the Diners' Club in that they were the product of organizations already large; therefore they had access to sources of capital which the predecessor had not had. The three companies simultaneously sought to increase their membership, for volume business was essential to survival.

In its expansion program, the Diners' Club grew by merging with other similar smaller companies. Duplication of membership on several card lists, however, made this process less fruitful than might have been expected. It also employed advertising, publicity, and mailing campaigns. American Express, beginning with worldwide operations and reputation, appealed through advertising mainly for businessmen membership. Carte Blanche had immediate access to the more than one million credit card holders of Hilton Hotels. Efforts were made to solicit membership among foreigners, women, non-travelers, and marginal risks, but most of these efforts yielded only modest membership additions.

Expansion also required inclusion of additional vendor participants. The objective was universality, a goal sought by diversification of participants and by better identification of them to customer members. The Diners' Club followed a theory that customer membership attracts vendor participation; American Express followed the reverse, that a good list of vendors attracts customer membership. Hilton encompassed not only hotels but Socony Mobil Oil Company and some airlines, using somewhat radical vendor service innovation methods.

Operations

In their operations, the card companies act as credit specialists for participating merchants. Like other full-function auxiliary specialists, they perform the routine operations, soliciting and investigating credit customers, providing them with identification, and making collections. The credit card company does not have the same control of authorization of sales that charge account companies have, and thus they are exposed to considerable risk. Risk is taken without recourse, however, as a major part of the operation. Funds are also supplied by the specialists for the carrying of accounts, advances being made to vendors upon sales, monthly, semimonthly, or immediately.

Because of the advantages provided both vendors and customers through this operation, charges for universal card service are made of both. Merchants are charged from 4 to 7 per cent of the sales made on credit. The percentage varies with the type of merchandise sold and with the negotiations between the parties. The amount of this charge has fluctuated from time to time as both parties have sought earnestly to determine the point at which they can afford to enter into this type of credit relationship. The charge made of customer members ranges from $5 to $10, payable upon affiliation, and annually. This income, which provides at times one-third of total revenue, is often used for building and maintaining customer membership.

Appraisal

As a full-function credit auxiliary, universal card companies perform in a dual capacity. On the one hand, they concentrate credit activities into a large-scale operation, relieving numerous small vendors who would not or could not perform them themselves. On the other hand, while providing credit service *for* vendors, they provide it *to* a unique segment of the market for credit service: the itinerant, affluent purchaser who buys in a regional, national, or international, rather than merely in a local, market, and to whom the establishment of creditworthiness, the availability of credit service, and the convenience of central billing have value. Although billings of universal companies are in millions of dollars, they still constitute a small percentage of total credit business.

By reason of the peculiarities of their business, card companies have also unique operating problems. One relates to recruitment of customer members. Standards higher than usual have been established, as minimum income of $7,500 and minimum age of 25 years have been set by some companies. Another concerns delinquency and the misuse of lost and stolen cards. Although liability of card holders has been upheld, the legal responsibility of the customer member and not the card company has not been fully established. Another arises from the far-flung scale of the operations. Computers have been used to minimize the time and paper work that would otherwise be involved.

In view of the advantages inherent in the performance of one's own credit functions, it is unlikely that full-function specialists will completely supplant traditional credit operations. However, the advantages of shifting functions in their entirety are increasingly recognized throughout industry, and the expectation of wider adoption of the universal card system should not be considered entirely visionary.[19]

DISCUSSION QUESTIONS

1. Compare the practice of shifting credit functions with that of shifting other functions of business.

2. It has been thought that factoring is evidence of financial weakness of the firm which factors its sales. Is this a warranted conclusion? Why?

3. As a non-bank financial institution, factors enjoy what advantages compared with commercial banks?

4. Trace the adaptation of factors to changing business opportunities in their environment.

5. Assume that a factor charges 1.5 per cent of sales factored plus a charge of 6 per cent per annum for funds advanced. What would it cost a vendor selling on terms of 2/10, net 30 to factor a month's sales of $100,000? A year's sales of $1,000,000? What would be the annual rate of charge as a per cent of sales factored?

6. Diagram the relations of a sales finance company to a manufacturer, a dealer, and a consumer when the same finance company provides the credit service for both the wholesale and the retail transactions.

7. Compare and contrast factoring with charge account credit plans. With universal credit card plans.

8. Given a choice of purchasing under a vendor's revolving charge plan or a specialist's charge account plan, which would you choose for economy? Under what circumstances might your answer differ?

9. Illustrate the overlapping nature of services rendered consumers by commercial banks' check credit plans, charge account plans, vendors' charge accounts, and credit card plans.

10. To what circumstances and attitudes in our society do you attribute the growing extension of services of the full-function auxiliary credit establishments?

[19] An extensive study of the development and operation of universal credit card companies was made by Charles Geyer Megowen and submitted as an unpublished thesis for the Master of Business Administration degree at The Ohio State University, in 1965.

15

Limited-Function Auxiliary Credit Establishments

The structure of credit establishments includes primary and auxiliary operations, the latter comprising both full-function and limited-function specialists. Auxiliary specialists facilitate vendors and lenders, performing credit services which they would otherwise have to perform. Some vendors shift all of their credit responsibilities; more shift some but not all functions. There exist, therefore, an assortment of specialists performing services supporting and augmenting the credit operations of others. The service of some such specialists is limited to supplying funds for carrying receivables; that of others, to the performance of some part of the routine of the credit operation such as supplying information for the credit appraisal, determining creditworthiness, or collecting accounts; that of still others, to the bearing of risks inherent in credit service. Credit specialists assisting others through the performance of less than all of their credit functions are the limited-function auxiliary establishments of the credit structure. Those concerned with finance and operational functions are discussed in this chapter; those with risk, in the next.

FINANCING RECEIVABLES

The financing of receivables is inseparable from credit service, and the funds required must be supplied either by the vendor or

224

lender holding receivables or by someone else. Some vendors shift this function along with all others to specialists described in the preceding chapter. Others obtain through equity and debt sources capital for the financing of receivables before those receivables exist. Still others, after receivables are acquired, seek financial assistance in carrying them to the expiration of the credit period. This last quest for capital leads to the shifting of credit financing to specialists and is the process of accounts receivable financing. Peculiar to this process, and differentiating it from factoring, is the fact that the receivables exist *before* the financing of them is shifted, and the shift of financing does not shift the credit risk.

The need for financial assistance in the performance of credit service exists throughout the business world in general and the credit structure in particular. Capital being probably the most scarce factor in the production of credit service, the deficiency is felt not only by credit vendors and lenders but also by specialists in the credit structure. Although credit card companies and factors assume the financing of vendors' receivables, even they in turn seek financing for carrying the receivables of others which they have taken over. Thus the market for receivables financing is broad and diversified.

Suppliers of credit financing service are also diverse. They include many types of organizations with funds to invest in a fairly secure commercial paper, but a few of these are most prominent, among which are the commercial bank and, as a nonbank type, the commercial finance company.

Commercial Banks

Commercial banks act as both primary and auxiliary suppliers of credit service. They lend to borrowers for other than credit purposes, and they lend to borrowers in support of their credit functions. It is this latter business with which we are here concerned, a business which may arise from either wholesale or retail credit transactions.

The relationship between commercial banks and commercial borrowers who shift the financing function of their own credit service is usually a discontinuous one, established when need for such financing arises, as to accommodate seasonal peaks. Loans of this type involve only the bank and the vendor in the creditor–

debtor relationship. The vendor's customer–debtors are not involved, for his accounts serve only as security for a loan as would any other asset he could offer. The vendor's customers are not notified, either at the time of sale or at the time of financing, that their accounts have been placed, pledged, assigned, or hypothecated as basis for a commercial loan. Payments are made by customers to the vendor–creditor, who receives them in trust for the bank. Delinquencies, defaults, collections, and losses are primarily the concern of the vendor, for loans made on this basis are not only without notification but also without risk—with recourse. Inasmuch as loans or advances made on the basis of receivables are less than the face value of the accounts pledged, the bank enjoys a margin of safety against shrinkage of their value.

The position of the bank in such financing is that of a preferred creditor. It is not the intention or expectation of the bank to take over the accounts financed, for it does not assume the operational routine of the credit vendor. They are interested in a return on their investment, not in a service charge. Loans of this kind are made to retailers on instalment, revolving, and even open accounts, to producers and wholesalers on open accounts, and to lenders on loan accounts. The rate of charge for such service is the going commercial rate, negotiable in terms of conditions of the particular market. Although this financing is a function of commercial banks, it is also performed by non-bank establishments.

Commercial Finance Companies

While the bank process described is the financing of accounts receivable, the term "accounts receivable financing" particularly identifies a process of financing open book accounts owed to sellers *by business firms,* a function characteristic of commercial finance companies. The difference between the service of banks and that of commercial finance companies, however, is not confined to the retail or wholesale status of the accounts financed. Other important conceptual, behavioral, and operational differences characterize this type of auxiliary credit service and this type of institution.[1]

---

[1] An extensive exposition of this credit function may be found in Clyde William Phelps, *Accounts Receivable Financing as a Method of Business Finance* (Baltimore: Commercial Credit Company, 1957).

Receivables Financed. The "receivables" financed by this process, as set forth in terms of the contract, are not only open account receivables and invoices arising on such accounts, but also notes, acceptances, drafts, contracts, and choses in action. Not included are instalment purchase contracts, thus differentiating this credit service from that of sales finance companies. Moreover, this service is available only for the financing of trade accounts, those of a vendor selling to other business organizations. It is not, as is charge account banking, a means for shifting or financing retailers' consumer accounts.

Purchase of Receivables. Whereas banks *lend* on receivables assigned as security for a loan, commercial financing of receivables involves the *purchase* of accounts, under conditions set forth in the contract.

Receivables so financed are accounts already existing on the vendor's books, accounts which he has approved and accepted. In this form of financing, the routine functions of the credit operation are not shifted. The decision to accept a customer's credit remains the responsibility of the vendor. Thus this service is distinguished from factoring, sales financing, and charge account banking, in all of which the investigation function is shifted to the credit specialist.

Vendors may sell their accounts either periodically or continually, depending upon their need. In the first case, a group or all of existing accounts may be sold at one time; otherwise, as orders are approved for credit and filled, an invoice of the account is sent to the commercial company for purchase. This procedure goes on continually. It is important that in both instances the accounts sold are live accounts and not tag-end receivables being disposed of for liquidation or collection purposes.

With Recourse; Without Notification. Although the transfer of receivables constitutes a "sale" of that asset, it is usually a condition of that sale that any eventual loss on it will be borne by the vendor. There are exceptions, but this is the general rule. A contrast is thus made with factors and charge account banks, both of whom accept receivables without recourse. This they are willing to do, because they initially approve the customers' creditworthiness. In sales financing, as in accounts receivable financing, loss usually, but not always, reverts to the vendor.

Care is usually taken that no indication be given buyers that accounts are being financed by other than the vendor. In factoring this is not the case; notification is usual. In commercial financing, because of unfamiliarity of the trade and sometimes because of the discontinuous nature of receivables financing, payment is received by the vendor who, with an endorsement "Payable to any bank or banker," avoids having the finance company's signature appear on customers' checks turned over to it.

Partial Advance. Whereas in factoring, sales financing, and charge account banking, the vendor is supplied with 100 per cent of the value of accounts surrendered, less service charges, users of commercial financing service receive from only 70 to 95 per cent of the gross value of their accounts. The amount of the advance varies and is determined in any case by "the credit rating of the underlying trade debtors, the hazards of the borrowers' line of business, the past collection experience and debt record, the selling terms, the selling costs, the number of accounts sold, and the profit margin." [2]

Interest Rate Charged. Unlike other credit services already considered, only a rate of interest is charged for accounts receivable financing. There is no additional service charge. The charge is paid by the vendor and consists of a per diem rate applied to the gross receivables purchased. In other words, a determined rate is applied to an outstanding balance each day.

The fact that services, risks, and volume of business vary in all credit operations, giving rise to a flexible structure of rates charged, has no exception in accounts receivable financing. These factors, however, are reflected indirectly rather than directly in the rate charged a client by the commercial finance company. The variable conditions inherent in a particular credit operation determine the per cent advance which is made on the accounts; this per cent of advance, in turn, is the basis of the interest rate charged. A commercial finance company endeavors to employ a rate which, in terms of its average advances outstanding, will provide for its operating costs and profit. In the larger finance companies, an annual rate of 10 or 11 per cent on the amount of cash advanced accomplishes this. Smaller companies and those obliged to serve less preferential vendors may require as high as an 18 or 20 per cent rate.

[2] Raymond Rogers, "Factors, Bank Financing of Accounts Receivable, Commercial Paper," in Herbert V. Prochnow (ed.), *American Financial Institutions* (Englewood Cliffs, N.J.: Prentice-Hall, Inc., 1951), p. 212.

In any particular commercial finance company, approximately the same effective annual rate is charged all its customers. Only the per diem rates vary, depending upon the percentage of advance received. Phelps explains that

for customers contracting for cash advances of 75, 80, and 85 per cent, the financing institution establishes per diem rates of charge on average daily outstanding gross receivables of $\frac{1}{49}$ of 1 per cent, $\frac{1}{46}$ of 1 per cent, and $\frac{1}{43}$ of 1 per cent, respectively. The result is that the financing institution obtains a yield at the rate of ten per cent per annum (from 9.92 to 10.14 per cent, to be exact) in each case from the application of these different per diem rates. And its customers, regardless of the cash advances they contract to receive—ranging from 70 to 90 per cent, or even 95 per cent in some cases—pay virtually the same ten per cent rate per annum on the cash they obtain.[3]

Continuing Contract with Vendor. Although the sale of accounts receivable to a commercial finance company may be a one-shot proposition, it is usually—as it always is with factoring and charge account banking—a contractual relation between the vendor and the finance company which sets forth the details of the terms.

Security. In commercial accounts receivable financing the finance company has no particular security, but only recourse. Sales financing, by contrast, provides the mortgage on the goods financed as security for the finance company.

Other Services. Whereas it is common for factors to work closely with their clients in the planning of financial budgets, providing space for storage and display, etc., it is not so common for commercial finance companies to engage in these activities.

Regulation. Commercial finance companies are not restrained in the charge they make for their services, as sales finance companies must comply with the provisions of instalment selling legislation.

Procedure in Accounts Receivable Financing

Once a contractual arrangement is made between the commercial finance company and a vendor, upon receipt of an order the vendor passes upon the credit involved, makes shipment, and sends to the finance company a copy of the invoice and evidence of shipment. Immediately an advance, in the agreed per cent

[3] Phelps, *op. cit.*, p. 39.

of the value of the account, is sent to the vendor. There is *no maturity date for this financing,* but it stands until the account is paid by the vendor. Upon receipt of payment from his customer, the vendor relays payment to the financing institution. Thus his own obligation is cleared, and he receives additionally from the finance company a check for the difference between the value of the account financed and the advance which was initially made. Because accounts placed with the finance company are self-liquidating, furnishing their own means of repayment, there is effectually no limit to the amount of accounts which may be financed, and therefore to the amount of credit service which the vendor may furnish his own customers, except the limit of risk which he is willing to take in approving his customers' credit.

Supplementary Services

Commercial finance companies also undertake other forms of financing and lending. In addition to accounts receivable financing, they make inventory loans, mortgage and equipment loans, and unsecured loans. They are thus in a position to provide credit service not only in connection with the sales of a business organization but also for their purchases.

History and Development

Like sales financing, commercial financing began in the early years of this century, and in fact both practices were initiated by the same companies. The growth of open account financing was slow until World War II, while instalment sales financing grew apace with the rise of durable goods industries. However, the success which commercial finance companies had up to that time not only provided them a firm base for later growth, but was also an inducement during the depression years to commercial banks to explore means by which they could engage in this business. During World War II, impetus was given the growth of this type of financing by the Assignment of Claims Act, passed by Congress in 1940, aiding small- and medium-size producers holding government contracts. This act permitted for the first time assignment of claims against the government growing out of such contracts, to institutions engaged in financing or commercial banking activities.[4] Since the end of the war, the growth of commercial

4 *Ibid.,* p. 61.

open accounts financing has been rapid. This has been due in part to the unprecedented need for working capital, resulting from business expansion and creeping inflation. It has been due also to an increasing understanding of the role which receivables financing does and can play in our business system. Greater use is being made of all forms of credit today, both in consumer and mercantile credit, and the more extensive use of accounts receivable financing is part of this development.[5]

FACILITATING OPERATIONAL SERVICES

The operational processes in credit management, like financing and risk bearing, can be shifted to functional specialists, in whole or in part. As credit appraisal, authorization, and collection are the heart of credit business, however, these activities are often reserved even when creditors shift other functions. Nevertheless, operational activities are shifted under three circumstances: when all credit functions are shifted, as to factors and charge account services; when all or part of the operation is shifted along with the risk, as in maturity financing by factors; and when only portions of the operational activities are shifted alone, as in the purchase of credit information and collection assistance. In the supplying of facilitating operational services, several specialists have evolved which are now important parts of the credit structure.

Credit Information Services

The gathering of information from which creditworthiness can be appraised is one of the operational functions most generally shifted. It need not be, however, and a large part of this activity is performed by creditors in their own credit departments through direct exchange with other creditors, from references, and from credit applicants themselves. This process of assembling infor-

---

[5] Developments in the shifting of the financing function in credit service are discussed in the following articles: "Bridging the Gap," *The Industrial Banker & Time Sales Financing*, April, 1965, p. 7; Phillip I. Blumberg, "Interim Financing: Money Break For Business," *Credit and Financial Management*, January, 1965, p. 28; Herbert Pechman, "Instant Cash for Your Company," *Credit and Financial Management*, July, 1964, p. 14; Joseph E. O'Grady, "Bank Participation: New Dimension in Commercial Financing," *Credit and Financial Management*, September, 1963, p. 12; David H. Zimmerman, "The Case for Bank Financing of Hospital Accounts," *The Credit World*, February, 1964, p. 19.

mation poses problems for which creditors are not always adequately staffed or technically competent. Moreover, it involves excessive time and costs when performed on a small scale, repetitively, by every creditor. Consequently, while part of this function is retained in the investigation process of creditors, much of it is shifted to specialists.

Credit information specialists include credit *agencies* and credit *bureaus*. In practical usage, the terms are not always mutually exclusive, but the distinction implied is one of ownership of the service. Credit agencies are usually privately owned, profit enterprises; credit bureaus are usually jointly owned by cooperating users of their services. Prominent among agencies are Dun & Bradstreet, Inc., National Credit Office, Inc., Retail Credit Company of Atlanta, Georgia, and Lyon Furniture Mercantile Agency. Bureaus are typified by firms affiliated with the National Retail Merchants Association; Associated Credit Bureaus of America, Inc.; and National Association of Credit Management, Credit Interchange Service and Foreign Credit Interchange Bureau.

As users of information service seek information concerning widely different types of customers, they constitute a segmented market for suppliers of information. Information sought by retailers pertains to an entirely different group of credit applicants than that sought by manufacturers and wholesalers. Specialists have arisen to serve both markets. Vendors and lenders serving the wholesale or commercial trades patronize bureaus and agencies such as Dun & Bradstreet, Inc., and the bureaus of the National Association of Credit Management. Retailers patronize their own set of suppliers. Although Dun & Bradstreet provides some service on both levels, such diversification of services is uncommon.

Information specialists are also structured on the basis of the trades and areas which they serve. This, too, is determined mainly by the needs of their markets. Dun & Bradstreet alone attempts to furnish information concerning all manufacturing, commercial, and service establishments throughout the United States, and it also has extensive facilities in many other countries. Generally, national firms confine themselves to a restricted line of products. Lyon, for example, serves creditors of retailers, manufacturers, jobbers, and wholesalers in the following trades: furniture, interior decoration, major home appliances, carpet, some wood products, and funeral supplies and services. National Credit Office, Inc., supplies information for creditors of business buyers of metals and metal products; paint, ink, rubber, and leather; men's and women's apparel; textiles; household goods; and commercial paper. The Retail Credit Company's services are used by petroleum companies with national credit cards, insurance companies, and retail organizations with store chains throughout the country. Line or product specialization also characterizes agencies and bureaus supplying a local clientele, such as jewelers, lumber dealers, physicians and dentists, or consumer lending agencies. The scale of the specialists' operations is determined by the nature of information required, by the scope of the client's market, and by the financial and technical ability of the information specialist to perform.

Further distinction among information suppliers is made in terms of their services. Some, like Dun & Bradstreet, offer a full and diversified assortment of services; others provide only a few. The following are some of the services more commonly provided by this portion of the credit structure.

Credit Reports. The heart of the information service is the credit report, which conveys, to the degree intended, the evidence upon which debtor–creditor interaction is to be based. Reports differ in degree of completeness. Some are given orally; most are in writing. However complete, the report contains the kind of information which the user is presumed to need. In their most complete form, reports contain personal information concerning the subject—personnel and organization; current activity and operation, as well as history, background, and development; financial condition, representing both values and capacity to perform; ledger experience, or relations of the subject to other creditors.

Such information, in part or in full, may be expanded according to the nature of the reports prepared by an information supplier. Mercantile credit agencies usually present a report containing all of these types of information. The amount of detail depends upon the complexity of the subject, and reports for manufacturers and large commercial firms usually are more elaborate than those for the average retailer. Mercantile credit bureaus' reports consist wholly of ledger or trade experience. Reports prepared by both agencies and bureaus concerning retail customers are alike and give a full coverage of the subject.

Sample reports are shown in Chapter 21, where the interpretation of them for credit analysis is discussed.

As reports present a description of conditions at a point in time, their usefulness is subject to the extent to which they anticipate or record change. Trends may be incorporated in the content of the report, and periodic reports may be issued supplementally as need occurs.

Information assembly is a process in which the credit specialist is presumed to excel. His sources include creditors of the subject, his customers and competitors, the subject himself, official public records, and unofficial news reports. From these sources data are gathered by personal interviewers, mail, and phone contact. Sources are recontacted with sufficient frequency to keep the information current. As such reports are prepared for many types of users, costs of search which would be excessive for any one creditor are apportioned over a volume of business which justifies the existence of the specialist.

Credit Ratings.   Credit ratings are a digest of salient features of credit reports. Ratings are presented in conjunction with reports and are not offered alone without reports. Ratings are symbolic forms of communication, and suppliers of information have attempted to convey by one, two, or three symbols the maximum information. Few specialists prepare ratings.

In general, credit ratings disclose customers' paying habits and their financial strength. Dun & Bradstreet, instead of showing only paying habits, attempts to condense all factors bearing upon the subject's paying ability and to give a composite credit appraisal in its rating. Lyon uses three instead of two symbols, giving additional information and instructions to the user. The few retail agencies which prepare ratings attempt mainly to indicate paying habits, or degree of satisfaction of creditors with the subject.

Ratings are published in books made available to subscribers of the credit service. Such books may include names of subjects throughout the country, although state and regional editions are also prepared for the use of local vendors and of salesmen covering sectional territories. Revision of ratings books is done bimonthly by Dun & Bradstreet and less often by others.

Special Reports.   The depth of investigation desired by some creditors exceeds that provided in the standard credit report, and to meet this need special reports are written both by general agencies such as Dun & Bradstreet and by more specialized agencies such as Bishop's Service, Inc., and Proudfoot Reports, both of New York. Specialized reports are the result of especially conducted research concerning a firm's operations or its personnel. By representing an undisclosed client, the information specialist may obtain information which a normal creditor could not. Moreover, he maintains a continuity of research which would be uneconomical for most creditors.

Other Services. Reports and ratings in various forms are the principal service supplied by credit information specialists, a service substituted for performance of the function by creditors themselves. Like other specialists, those supplying credit information have also undertaken to provide additional services, among which are recommendation service, collection service, debt adjustments, and various kinds of credit and marketing research. The distribution of these services among the leading mercantile and retail information specialists is indicated in Table 15–1.

Credit Decision Service

One of the prerogatives of credit management is to decide whether a customer's credit should be accepted. Unless this responsibility is shifted along with all other functions, it is one of the last to be separated from vendors' credit operations. Although credit information, adjustment, and collection services may be bought, responsibility for deciding upon creditworthiness is generally retained. When they are shifted, even then only a few specialists perform the credit decision service, and they operate in a highly restricted field.

As furnished by the Credit Clearing House division of Dun & Bradstreet, Inc., and by Credit Exchange, Inc., this service is variously referred to as "credit checking," "credit clearing," "credit advisory service," and "credit recommendation." It consists of the passing of credit judgment on *specific purchase orders* submitted for approval. Thus it is a combined credit approval and credit purchase authorization service. It is available only to vendors in the apparel trades.

History. As functional specialization in the credit structure goes, credit advisory service is not new. Its antecedents are

Table 15-1. Services Provided by Credit Information Specialists

Services	Dun & Bradstreet, Inc.	National Credit Office	Credit Exchange, Inc.	Lyon Furniture Mercantile	Proudfoot Reports	National Association of Credit Management	Retail Credit Bureaus and Agencies
Complete reports	Yes	Yes		Yes			Yes
Specialized reports	Yes				Yes	Yes	
Ratings	Yes	Yes	Yes	Yes	Yes	Some	Some
Financial statements	Yes		Yes	Yes			
Weekly supplements	Yes		Yes	Yes			
Interchange meetings			Yes				
Collections	Yes	Yes	Yes	Yes	Yes	Yes	Yes
Adjustments	Yes					Yes	Yes
Research	Yes					Yes	Yes

traced to the Credit Clearing House, an independent local supplier of credit information, organized in St. Paul, Minnesota, in
1888. Advice on credit orders was first offered about 1912, and
demand for the service caused it to expand rapidly. By 1924, the
supplier combined the advisory and risk functions, guaranteeing
vendors against loss from bad debts due to faulty judgment in
the credit approval. This guarantee was discontinued after two
years. At the same time, in 1921, the Credit Exchange, Inc., was
founded to render information service to the apparel trades, and
they also came to provide advisory service. Subsequently, Dun
& Bradstreet also offered this service, and in 1942 it absorbed
through merger the Credit Clearing House and continued its
operations.

Both companies serve vendors selling to retailers and jobbers
in the apparel trades, including men's and boys' wear, women's
and misses' apparel, infants' and children's clothing, accessories,
dry goods, notions, novelties, and leather goods. Although the
service is provided principally through offices located in the 25
leading apparel centers, it is also available through their communication networks in the more extended offices of the companies.

Bases of Decision Service. The bases upon which vendors make
credit decisions are the same as those of decision specialists, but
the bases upon which advisory service is given differ from the
credit information which they usually supply. Advisory service
is based upon the specialist's knowledge of customers' buying
habits. From information assembled in the course of their investigations, they construct for each buyer in the apparel trades
a model of anticipated buying behavior, including the likely
amount of purchases and their dispersion. This model reflects
both past and prospective buying, gauged from internal and external circumstances of the vendor. Deviations from the pre-
dicted pattern of purchasing are cause for warning and reconsideration of a request for credit service. Excessive buying, erratic
buying, or buying from an uncommon number of sources and locations may signal uncreditworthiness and are watched. Such
evidences of caution are not limited to apparel trades but pertain
also to others. The fact that this service is given only in such
limited area is due not to any peculiarity of apparel risks but to
management conditions in the apparel industry. Often the scale
of operations is so small, the technical competence so unqualified,

that individual credit management is unfeasible. Thus has arisen a market for credit advisory service.

Recommendation Reports.   As in all credit approval and authorization, decisions may or may not be a clear "yes" or "no" conclusion. Consequently credit recommendations reflect several degrees of advice. Being asked in effect, "Should this particular order from X be accepted?" advisors have the following general responses:

"You may be advised to ship the order."
"You may be advised to ship if you can afford to wait for payment."
"You may be advised to ship part of the order."
"For reasons indicated, individual judgment is suggested."
"You are advised not to make shipment."

Dun & Bradstreet, Inc., does not give a "not recommended" verdict; Credit Exchange, Inc., does. Behind such caution is the recognition that ultimately the credit decision must rest also upon factors other than the information in possession of the information agency. Vendors' credit policies, competition, information about customers known to vendors, and the like may dictate other than a negative recommendation. In positive recommendations, it is presumed that the information and interests of the vendor and the decision specialist coincide.

Collection Service

In every credit operation, provision must be made for receiving funds due. Some are received within the period of the credit terms; others are received later but with no great difficulty; still others are received with much difficulty and only after skillful collection effort is brought to bear upon the debtor. Most creditors who perform other operational functions are prepared to handle receipt of funds in the first two ways. Few, however, are in a position to carry collection effort to its ultimate end. Rather they are inclined to shift this function to specialists who, by reason of superior skill and their impartial position, attempt to collect for them. Such specialists, or collection agencies, constitute part of the credit structure.

Use of collection agencies, however, involves more than a mere progression of force in the collection effort. A point of "no return" may be reached in one's own efforts with no intention to go further by shifting the collection function. Such creditors eschew introducing another party to the trade relationship or letting a difficult relationship be handled outside the firm. On the other hand, as collection agencies are not necessarily the last step in collection effort, use of them should be made with some foreknowledge of other steps to which a shift of this function could lead, i.e., collection by attorneys or suit in court.

Debtor Conditions for Collectors. Not every debtor in the normal course of business is a potential subject for special collection activity. Most debtors present attitudes and circumstances which can be coped with by the creditor himself. The circumstances warranting collection effort differ from these, and the seriously delinquent debtor usually has the following traits:

Habitually slow pay

Financially immature

Irresponsible as to employment, and usually equally irresponsible as to family obligations

Unavoidably involved in debt, and incapable of handling his own problem

Skips, who run away from debt

Deliberate credit criminals

Chisellers, who hope to, and do, reduce just debts by way of frivolous and constant complaints

Hardship cases [6]

Most such debtors should not have been judged creditworthy in the first place, and better credit granting would result in fewer extreme collection cases. Credit business being what it is, the problem is to deal with such cases when they are discovered, and that is when they are delinquent. After normal commercial collection efforts have been made, creditors are interested in salvaging what they can of their investment and they turn to collection specialists for assistance.

Collection Specialists. Collection agencies are specialists whose stock in trade is knowledge of how to locate and deal with delinquent debtors having attitudes described above. They are independent entrepreneurs providing special service comparable to other limited-function credit auxiliaries. Their services are used by all types of creditors—wholesale and retail vendors, lenders,

[6] *The Creditors Collection Guide* (Minneapolis, Minn.: The American Collectors Association, Inc., 1963), p. 19.

professionals, and by other credit establishments, such as factors and credit card companies, to whom the credit functions of others have been shifted.

The Directory of the American Collectors Association lists some 2,300 independent collection agencies serving more than 9,000 communities in the United States, Canada, Mexico, Puerto Rico, Virgin Islands, Sweden, Liechtenstein, the Near East, Guam, the Philippines, and Australia. These agents serve primarily local creditors, 80 per cent of their business originating in this way. The remainder of their business originates at a distance and involves a process of forwarding through a network of cooperating agencies developed by the Association. Each month more than 300,000 accounts, representing in excess of $17 million per month, are forwarded among the members.

Individuals willing to take over the processing of delinquent accounts for a fee have probably existed as long as credit business. The establishment of this service as a bona fide business activity, however, has occurred mainly during the past quarter of a century, resulting largely from the efforts of the American Collectors Association, organized in 1939. Prior to that time, as early as 1917, organized groups of collectors operating on the Pacific Coast had integrated their activities, but with the development of the ACA, groups in all states have been integrated and a vast network of these service establishments formed.

Modern collection agencies perform a service which is unpopular in the eyes of some debtors, but their greatest handicap has been a public image derived from the operations of collection agencies of former days. Before credit service became simply another business functions, loan sharks and collectors were commonly appraised to be much alike. Early unethical operators in both fields have been succeeded by legitimate, respectable, and efficient agencies. Collection agencies today are a necessary part of our credit structure, and their relations with debtors are no less courteous because they are a third party to a transaction, or their creditors' interests, and no less mutual because of a creditor's desperation. Progressive collectors in their client relations even assist credit managers in improving their performance, knowing that with our society's behavior toward credit there will inevitably be collection problems beyond the competence and facilities of creditors.

Agency Operations. A study of agency operations made of a sample of its membership by the American Collectors Association gives some evidence of the operation of this segment of the credit structure. In size, agencies ranged from 1 to 41 employees, but 50 per cent employed fewer than 4 persons. Only 5 per cent of the agencies surveyed reported having more than 22 employees.

Agency business for the country as a whole was classified as follows: wholesale, 2.8 per cent; professional, 47.7 per cent; retail, 48.7 per cent; and repossession, 0.8 per cent. Larger agencies do 6.5 per cent of their business in collecting for wholesale trades and 9.9 per cent in repossessions; they do correspondingly less in collecting for professional creditors, whose business falls more to smaller agencies. Seventy-nine per cent of new business is derived from local creditors; 21 per cent is forwarded. Twenty-five per cent of the business of the larger agencies is forwarded.

Commission rates charged by collectors vary depending upon whether business is wholesale, retail, and forwarded. A typical rate schedule is as follows:

Retail Accounts	Wholesale Accounts
33⅓% net	20% on first $750
	15% on next $750
	13% in excess of $1,500
	$20 minimum commission on accounts between $40 and $100
	50% on accounts of $40 or less

When retail accounts are forwarded to another agency for out-of-town collection, or to an attorney, the gross charge is 50%, of which two-thirds goes to the forwardee and one-third to the forwarder. On forwarded commercial accounts, charges to creditors are as stated, but forwardees receive 15 per cent on the first $750 and 10 per cent on the excess of $750.

DISCUSSION QUESTIONS

1. Under what circumstances are loans by commercial banks a primary credit service, and under what circumstances an auxiliary credit service?
2. Distinguish the markets served by commercial banks and by commercial finance companies in their lending on the security of receivables.

3. If a commercial finance company charges $\frac{1}{46}$ of 1 per cent per day on the face value of accounts of which 80 per cent has been advanced, and a factor charges 6 per cent per annum on funds advanced plus a 2 per cent service charge, which is the more expensive service to buy? Cite both rates.

4. Both factors and commercial finance companies offer a range of rates. Why? What factors underlie their rate differences?

5. To what establishments in other business structures do credit information agencies correspond?

6. Relatively few of the credit operational functions are shiftable separately. Why is this so?

7. Upon what kind of model of creditworthiness is the credit advisory service based? In what ways might the credit specialist's model differ from that of a vendor?

8. What is the special service provided by collection agencies?

16

Credit Risk Specialists

Among the limited-function auxiliaries supplying credit service are those bearing credit risk shifted by others. Risk is inseparable from every credit operation, and if it is not borne by the creditor it may be shifted to others in one of three ways. It may be shifted to other units in the distributive channel. Manufacturers, for example, unable or unwilling to assume the risks inherent in selling to numerous, small, poorly financed, remotely located retailers may select a wholesaler channel, passing the credit functions to a middleman. It may be shifted to credit specialists performing also other credit functions, such as factors and charge account services. It may be shifted to insurance companies and other institutions engaging primarily in credit risk bearing. However, in no case can all the risk in a credit transaction be shifted entirely through insurance. Furthermore, the shifting of credit risk is not the only means of risk management, as was shown in Chapter 7.

Credit risk specialists, like others, have arisen in response to a variety of needs which identify distinctly segmented markets for this service. One is the market of vendors selling to commercial accounts, not to ultimate consumers. Commercial credit insurance is available for this need. Another is the market of retailers and others financing the sale of durable goods on instalment terms. Credit life insurance permits the shifting of some of the credit risk in this type of business. No risk insurance is available, however, for non-instalment retail business. Still another is the market for exporters confronting not only commercial risks in foreign markets but also political and war risks in international relations. Export credit insurance is available for the shifting of these risks to private and public agencies.[1]

COMMERCIAL CREDIT INSURANCE

The insurance service through which risks inherent in the credit transactions of manufacturers, wholesalers, factors, and some service organizations are shiftable is known as commercial credit insurance. It is provided only for wholesale credit transactions and covers only the abnormal credit losses of the insured. Although more than 40 companies write credit risk insurance, two companies are the principal insurers: American Credit Indemnity Company of New York and London Guarantee and Accident Company, Ltd.[2]

The Credit Risk Contract

Terms of the relations through which credit risk is shifted from a vendor to the insurance company are spelled out in their contract, or insurance policy. Both suppliers offer a fairly uniform contract, but variations are introduced to meet the particular needs of any customer. In general, the policy specifies the amounts and types of risk which are shiftable, procedures for the acceptance and recovery of risks, and charges.

Causes of Loss. Insurable credit loss is that which results from insolvency, which for insurance purposes results from conditions itemized in the insurance policy:

---

[1] All these forms of credit insurance should be distinguished from what is known as "accounts receivable insurance," which insures the loss of collections due to fire or other perils which destroy the records of a firm.

[2] Expositions of credit insurance are found in the following publications: J. L. McCauley, Credit Insurance: Its History and Functions (Baltimore: American Credit Indemnity Company of New York, 1959); Clyde William Phelps, Commercial Credit Insurance as a Management Tool (Baltimore: Commercial Credit Company, 1961); John A. Churella, An Evaluation of Credit Insurance and Its Effects on Business Management (Baltimore: American Credit Indemnity Company of New York, 1958); Joseph T. Trapp, Credit Insurance a Factor in Bank Lending (Baltimore: American Credit Indemnity Company of New York, 1953); John H. Magee and David L. Bickelhaupt, General Insurance (Homewood, Ill.: Richard D. Irwin, Inc., 1964), pp. 541–48.

1. A debtor shall have absconded.
2. A sole debtor shall have died.
3. A sole debtor shall have been judged insane.
4. A receiver shall have been appointed for a debtor.
5. A debtor shall have transferred or sold his stock in trade in bulk.
6. A writ of attachment or execution shall have been levied on a debtor's stock in trade and said stock sold thereunder, or an execution returned unsatisfied.
7. A debtor shall have made a general offer of compromise to his creditors for less than his indebtedness.
8. There shall have been a recording of or taking possession under a chattel mortgage given by a debtor on his stock in trade.
9. A debtor's business shall have been assigned to or taken over by a committee, appointed by a majority in number and amount of his creditors.
10. There shall have been a recording of or taking possession under an assignment or a deed of trust made by a debtor for the benefit of his creditors.
11. A voluntary or involuntary proceeding shall have been instituted to adjudge a debtor bankrupt.
12. A proceeding for the relief of a debtor shall have been instituted in a court of bankruptcy.

Insolvency for any of these reasons constitutes a legal or effectual loss in the eyes of the insurer and requires the insured to file notification and claim of loss. The debt may subsequently be collected, but in terms of the contract effectual loss (insolvency) and actual loss (uncollectibility) are different stages in the processing of shifted credit risk.

Coinsurance. Claims of loss passed by a creditor to the insurer are subject to qualification. Filed claims are first reducible by an amount of coinsurance which the insured is required to bear. Depending upon circumstances and agreement, coinsurance ranges from 10 to 20 per cent of the net loss. Risk involved is the principal determinant, although terms are subject to negotiation.

As in other types of insurance, the coinsurance requirement fixes upon vendors a continuing interest in caution in their credit management. It reduces the possibility of unselective credit approval and of excessively liberal credit policies, and it reduces recovery to an approximation of the cost of goods, rather than sales value including profit.

Primary Loss.   In addition to coinsurance, normal loss is also uninsurable, unshiftable. This loss, called "primary loss," is assumed to be certain, and certain loss is uninsurable; to be insurable, risk must be uncertain.

Primary loss is expressed in the policy as a percentage of sales, but in no case is it less than a stated number of dollars. It is determined from a study of the insured's previous experience or from the insurer's knowledge of credit risks in that industry. The insured's losses over a recent three-year period of normal business are considered a sufficient basis. The specified amount of primary loss is excluded from the responsibility of the risk specialist and remains with the vendor. In computation of insurance benefits, primary loss is deducted from net claims filed less coinsurance.

The primary loss tables of the American Credit Indemnity Company are based upon three factors: the field of business of the insured, the insured's annual volume of sales, and the extent of coverage provided by the policy. For loss purposes, distinction is made between vendors selling mainly to manufacturers and jobbers and those selling mainly to retailers. Also, firms with larger sales volume, and therefore usually with the more efficient credit departments, merit relatively lower primary-loss percentages. Primary loss is less for businesses whose accounts are all well rated. It is less too for those whose consistent credit experience has been favorable. On the other hand, primary-loss deduction may arbitrarily be increased, with a corresponding reduction in premium.

Coverage.   Coverage is the amount of risk which the insurer accepts for any specific account or group of accounts. Basically, a limit is set for accounts according to the rating given them by Dun & Bradstreet, Inc., or by some other rating agency. As such blanket limitation may not coincide with a vendor's needs, variations are possible through policy endorsements. Limits may be increased for any of the rating groups; coverage may be restricted to only the better-rated accounts; or specific coverage limits may be set for individual accounts within any rated group.

Coverage of individual higher-grade risks is also obtainable on a variable scale whereby the amount owing by each debtor is reported to the insurer at the end of each month, and the premium is then calculated only on the actual coverage used. This service, known as "available coverage," is the least expensive form of coverage, for all the service purchased is completely used.

Policy Amount. When insolvency losses qualify as claims within the requirements of coverage, coinsurance, and primary loss, an additional limitation is imposed upon credit risk shifting by the total of the coverage agreed upon. This is known as the policy amount and is the stated maximum liability of the insurer under the particular contract. As the total coverage needed varies among creditors with the volume of their business, their normal loss, and the number and size of their accounts, the policy amount may vary for different creditors and according to the amount of protection desired by any one of them.

Claims and Collection. When insolvency of a debtor is evident, claim for the loss must be made with the insurer, who thereby assumes responsibility for collecting from the debtor and for reimbursing the creditor. Generally, the insured is required to file receivables covered by the policy before they are more than three months past due. Final statement of claims must be submitted not later than one month after termination of the policy, and payment must be made within two months after receipt of the final statement.

During the period following filing of claims, the insurer proceeds with usual commercial and legal collection means. If collection is effected within 10 days of filing and without the services of an attorney, no charge is made for collecting and receipts are remitted to the insured. Collections made thereafter are subject to charges of 15 per cent on the first $750 and 10 per cent on amounts in excess of that. Higher rates are charged if the services of an attorney are used.

When debts are collected after the insured has been reimbursed for insurable loss, the percentage of the loss deducted for coinsurance is also remitted to the insured, and the insurance company retains the remainder.

Types of Policies. As creditors' needs vary, an assortment of policies is provided to graduate the shifted risk. The most commonly used policy is one which covers, on the basis of the mercantile agency rating, all accounts with all types of ratings. Coinsurance varies, with 10 per cent applicable to the better-rated accounts and 20 per cent to other ratings. A variation of this is a policy which provides a single limit of coverage to all debtors. No reference is made to ratings. Coinsurance is also uniform, a flat 25 per cent. A second variation is a policy which permits the insured to handle his own collection efforts. A third variation is a policy which insures only losses on sales and shipments made during the policy term, and not those already on the books when the policy is taken out. A fourth variation is a policy which excludes coinsurance; its premium is, of course, correspondingly higher.

History and Operation

The history of commercial credit insurance is a record of faltering attempts to provide each service from 1869 until 1892 and of continuous availability of such insurance in the United States since that time.

The writing of credit insurance began in England in 1869 with the London Guarantee and Accident Company, Ltd., which in 1892 established a branch in the United States. In 1893, after several previous unsuccessful attempts, the American Credit Indemnity Company of New York was organized. Both have operated continuously since then.

The following are some of the dates important in the development of credit insurance, marking social and business trends which have made possible the form in which this service is currently offered. Legislation authorizing the incorporation of companies to write such insurance was first enacted in New York in 1885. With the passage of the National Bankruptcy Act of 1898, the credit insurance policy was liberalized to include a much broader definition of insolvency.[3] As early as 1907, attempts were made to analyze credit risks for the purpose of distinguishing between insurable and uninsurable risks. In 1918, a manual of rates and coverages based on actuarial tables was devised. In 1923, both the American and the London companies introduced policies designed to insure selected debtors by name, rather than merely to provide coverage based on mercantile agency ratings as had been the practice. In 1936, the American Credit Indemnity Company was acquired by the Commercial Credit Company of Baltimore, and additional forms of coverage were developed.

[3] McCauley, *op. cit.*, p. 5.

The extent and nature of the activities of these two firms is indicated in data furnished by them which is summarized in Table 16–1. It is apparent that, over the five years shown, an

Table 16–1. Combined Credit Experience, American Credit Indemnity Company of New York and London Guarantee and Accident Company, Ltd., 1960–64

	Manufacturers		Jobbers (Wholesalers)	
Year	Gross Direct Premiums Written less Return Premiums	Gross Direct Losses Paid less Salvage	Gross Direct Premiums Written less Return Premiums	Gross Direct Losses Paid less Salvage
1960	$6,878,809	$1,415,468	$3,427,995	$ 734,117
1961	7,047,475	4,326,868	3,207,024	1,477,800
1962	6,997,596	2,857,191	3,173,940	1,113,601
1963	6,948,436	3,206,001	3,024,945	1,344,628
1964	6,605,594	1,298,447	2,926,692	604,286
Average	$6,895,580	$2,620,797	$3,152,119	$1,054,886

SOURCE: American Credit Indemnity Company of New York, 1965.

average of 37.5 per cent of premiums collected from manufacturers was paid out for losses, and 33.3 per cent of premiums collected from wholesalers. Premiums collected remained quite stable during the period, but claims and losses paid fluctuated widely, ranging from 20 per cent of both manufacturers' and wholesalers' premiums in 1960 and 1964 to 61 and 47 per cent, respectively, in 1961.

Credit insurance was written by the companies for 21 lines of business during the period 1960–1964, the principal users being (1) *manufacturers* of textile and related products; apparel and other finished products made from fabrics and similar materials; lumber and wood products (except furniture); leather and leather products; primary metal industries; fabricated metal products (except machinery and transportation equipment), and electrical machinery, equipment, and supplies, and (2) *wholesalers* of textile and related products, and of lumber and wood products (except furniture).

The erratic nature of credit risk is evidenced by the patterns of payments shown in detailed data provided by the companies. First, losses paid exceeded premiums paid by manufacturers of five industries in given years. Three of these occurred in 1961, when producers of lumber and wood products, furniture and fixtures, and leather and leather products were especially hit by credit losses. On the other hand, in eight instances the salvage of claims previously placed exceeded payments of losses made during a year to manufacturers of an industry. Thus it is apparent that credit loss varies from industry to industry and is not a universal or uniform experience. Second, losses of manufacturers and of wholesalers in the same line of business do not necessarily coincide during any one year. The credit stability of the customers of each seems dependent upon different factors. Third, in years following high loss payment in an industry, premiums collected seem to increase. This is due both to readjustments of premium rates to reflect changed risk conditions and to increased receptivity of members of the industry to credit insurance.

Appraisal

Commercial credit insurance, like other credit services, is not equally useful to all credit managers. As its value lies in contingencies which it is hoped will never occur, positive measures of the value of this service are difficult to find. Claims of the insurer, based upon its wide experience, must be considered along with appraisals of the insured, based upon their individual experiences.

The following claims are made for commercial credit insurance by insurers: [4]

1. It offers stability to an existing market and in the expansion of credit lines to good customers.
2. It guarantees that portion of working capital represented by insured accounts receivable.
3. It provides a basis for extending credit; it backs the credit executive's judgment and provides him with a yardstick on which to rely when approving credits.
4. It creates harmony between the credit and sales departments by creating a proper balance between sales and bad debts.
5. It establishes an automatic system of credit approval by permitting the sales force to operate almost independently of the credit department; thus it makes for greater efficiency.
6. It provides an endorsement of the debtor's promise to pay, by creating a real instead of a questionable value for receivables.

[4] McCauley, op. cit., pp. 28, 29.

Such advantages, and others, are claimed also by objective appraisers of credit insurance.[5] Claimed advantages are the maintaining and increasing of sales volume, improvement of borrowing power and credit standing, increase of capital turnover and decrease of expenses, and assistance to general administration and credit executives.

On the other hand, neither credit managers nor analysts of the subject are without reservations concerning the benefits of credit insurance. Neither experience nor beliefs concerning it commend it universally, even as other credit services must be bought with consideration of gain and costs. Two studies made with the cooperation of the credit insurance companies during the 1950's disclosed aspects of their operations and their market which have continuing credibility.[6]

The Greene study indicated that credit insurance underwriters appeared to take a restrictive view, writing into policies deductibles much higher than the average rate of bad debt losses in most lines of business over a period of years. Protection, therefore, seemed limited. Evidently for this and other reasons, credit insurance has failed to obtain widespread support of industry in the United States. Sixty per cent of the premiums were collected from five states and Canada, and over 50 per cent of the insurance written was in the textiles and heavy machinery industries. Three-fourths of all premiums were collected from firms with sales less than $3 million annually. From 1910 to 1955, less than 30 per cent of premiums collected were paid out for losses, and profits of the insurers were above average.[7] Moreover, the lapse rate on policies was high, especially during the early years—between 12 and 14 per cent of policies written lapse after the first year,[8] and only 30 per cent of the premiums collected are on policies outstanding 10 years or more.[9] Although similarity in the need for insuring the receivables and other assets is argued, credit risk, because of lack of adequate empirical evidence con-

[5] Phelps, op. cit.

[6] These studies are two unpublished doctoral dissertations written at The Ohio State University: Mark Richard Greene, An Analysis of Credit Insurance, 1955; James Gordon Sheehan, Credit Insurance from the Policyholder's Point of View, 1955.

[7] Greene, op. cit., pp. 322–29.

[8] Data furnished by the American Credit Indemnity Company also indicate an attrition rate of about 12 per cent per year.

[9] Greene, op. cit., pp. 101, 102.

cerning this risk, was not regarded as an ideal subject for insurance.

The Sheehan study, made at the same time but from a different point of view, reflected attitudes of credit managers—users and non-users of credit insurance—toward this kind of risk protection. Essentially his findings were expressed as follows:

Sixty-eight per cent of those who have used credit insurance or are still using it do not believe, according to evidence presented, that it has, for their firms, advantages claimed by proponents. By nearly three to one they did not believe that it backs their judgment as credit executives. The majority did not believe that credit insurance promotes efficiency in organization and management, did not agree that credit insurance helps create and maintain a more harmonious relationship between the credit and sales departments.[10]

Divergencies between two viewpoints concerning the merits of commercial credit insurance are largely resolvable through an understanding of the nature of the business considering credit insurance and measurement of benefits in terms of the costs. In principle, the idea of shifting selected amounts or types of credit risk has merit, although by the multiplicity of accounts carried risk may be averaged or self-insured. However plausible the idea, credit insurance must be considered in terms of the exclusions written into the policy and the costs of the remaining protection. These are factors subject to negotiation and to determination within the framework of one's own operation.

CONSUMER CREDIT INSURANCE

Commercial credit insurance provides for the shifting of credit risk only in transactions where the buyer is a business establishment. It does not cover credit risk in retail sales or in loans to consumers. The shiftability of credit risk, however, is no more feasible in wholesale than in retail transactions, and the need for it has led to the development of specialists bearing the risk of consumer credit.

Unlike commercial credit insurance, which insures a *vendor's asset*, i.e., receivables, through policies written individually to cover customers' general insolvency, consumer credit insurance insures a *buyer's liability* through individual or group policies written to cover non-payment due only to a customer's death or

[10] Sheehan, *op. cit.*, p. 210.

disability. Such insurance in both instances provides for the shifting of the credit risk function which otherwise would be borne by vendors and lenders. Suppliers of such credit service constitute part of the credit structure.

History

The insurance of consumer credit risk has developed along with the growth of consumer instalment credit, particularly instalment sales credit. Its origin is attributed to Arthur J. Morris, founder of the Morris Plan Bank.[11] Risks inherent in consumer loans were reduced by his company through requiring the payment guarantee of a cosigner. That means of risk reduction through dispersion was often too personal, and therefore unpopular. He then conceived a plan whereby the outstanding balance of a loan at the time of the borrower's death would be paid by an insurance company. As existing insurance companies were cool to the idea, Morris in 1917 incorporated the Morris Plan Insurance Society, dedicated to the proposition that "No man's debts should live after him." In 1923 another company, later called the Old Republic Life Insurance Company, was organized and flourished in the writing of consumer credit insurance on an individual contract basis.

The writing of consumer credit life insurance on a group basis was fostered by three incidents. In 1928, The Prudential Insurance Company issued a policy to the National City Bank of New York covering the Bank's unsecured personal loans, guaranteeing completion of loan repayments outstanding at a debtor's death. In 1935, the Credit Union National Association organized under Wisconsin statutes the CUNA Mutual Insurance Society, which has devoted itself exclusively to insuring credit union members. In 1941, Prudential underwrote for General Motors Acceptance Corporation a group policy covering the indebtedness of all of its customers. In 1957, this contract covered 3,286,578 customers for indebtedness amounting to $2.9 billion.[12] In the 1960's, 85 per cent of all credit life insurance written was on group policies.[13]

The most rapid growth of consumer credit insurance occurred

11 Daniel P. Kedzie, *Consumer Credit Insurance* (Homewood, Ill.: Richard D. Irwin, Inc., 1957), p. 18.
12 *Ibid.*, p. 22.
13 *Life Insurance Fact Book*, 1964 (New York: Institute of Life Insurance, 1964), p. 32.

after 1945, resulting within 10 years in a 4,000 per cent increase, or in the insurance of 41 per cent of consumer debt outstanding. Such growth was the result of several factors: the increase of durable goods and instalment selling following the war, favorable word-of-mouth publicity given this insurance by users, the increased number of insurers, and the extension given the consumer market by creating creditworthiness where it was lacking without insurance of repayment.

Availability

Insurance of consumer credit is available in several forms designed to meet the needs of creditors and their debtor customers. It is written either as debtor life insurance or as accident and health insurance. The former insures the life of a borrower of money or purchaser of goods in connection with a specific loan or credit transaction; the latter in a similar situation insures against loss of time resulting from accident or sickness.

This insurance is available also either in ordinary or in group policies. Ordinary, or individual, policies are written for specific individuals and specific transactions; these, too, are of two types. One, level-term life insurance, is sold mainly in conjunction with loans of the non-instalment variety and provides throughout the contract insured repayment of the *original* balance of the indebtedness. The other, decreasing-term life insurance, by far the more common, provides insurance in force equaling the *remaining* indebtedness outstanding on instalment loan or sales contracts. The cost of the former is about twice the cost of the latter. Similarly, ordinary accident and health insurance is written in two types of policies. One, the Elimination Plan, employing the "deductible principle," provides for no payments during the beginning of the disability period, ranging from 3 to 30 days. The other, the Retroactive Plan, after delaying payments for an initial waiting period, makes payment on behalf of the debtor for the entire period of disability retroactively.

Group consumer credit insurance, written to cover all debtors of the creditor, relates primarily to protection in the case of death and not for disability. Payment under such a policy is made to the creditor as the beneficiary and master policyholder, up to the amount of the remaining balance. Premiums are paid by the creditor, although generally passed on to his customer.

The rate for ordinary consumer credit life insurance is usually $1 per year per $100 of initial indebtedness, payable in one payment at the time the loan or sale is made. Thus the premium due is determined by both the amount of the debt and its expected duration, computed at the given rate. For example, a $200 indebtedness would have a premium of $2 for one year; a $100 indebtedness would have the same premium for 2 years. Group life policies generally carry a lower rate. In 1965, for example, the GMAC group policy with Prudential stipulated a charge of only $0.375 per $100 of debt per annum. Ordinary consumer credit accident and health insurance rates vary with the number of days eliminated in the waiting period, but typically they are, with a 14-day waiting period, $1.50 per $100 of debt on the Elimination Plan and $2.20 on the Retroactive Plan.

Markets for the Service

Although debtors may pay for credit life insurance, creditors are really the market for this type of insurance, for it is they who shift their credit risk. Consequently, the market consists of various types of lenders and vendors eligible for this service. Eligibility consists largely of their catering to types of debtors whose degree of risk falls within the range of what it is the intention of the insurance company to insure. Lenders with questionable reputation and clientele are often unacceptable to the credit life insurance companies. Among those who are, are credit unions, commercial banks, and personal loan companies. Sales finance companies also constitute a market for this credit risk service, as do some retail outlets. Department stores, mail order houses, and furniture, appliance, and automobile dealers all shift risks involved in their consumer credit operations. Although originally this service was confined to contracts in the sale of consumer durable goods, increasingly it is being extended to cover transactions on revolving and optional accounts, on which both hard and soft goods are sold.

Appraisal

Although the concept of consumer credit insurance is widely accepted in principle, problems have been experienced in the administration of this service. Finance companies have sometimes formed captive insurance companies which they wholly owned, and which were intended to constitute a source of additional income by providing insurance in connection with their own sales or loans. They and others have been guilty of selling excessive insurance, pyramiding coverage and charges beyond actual indebtedness in the process of debt consolidation, overcharging legal rates, failing to give evidence of insurance, failing to pay claims, and coercing debtors to buy credit life insurance and/or to buy it from specified insurers. Another type of problem lies in creditors acting as agents for insurance companies and collecting a commission in this role.

These abuses have been recognized by the National Association of Insurance Commissioners, through its Credit Life and Credit Accident and Health Insurance Subcommittee, which has also worked toward the elimination of them. States have enacted legislation dealing with undesirable practices, and the Federal Trade Commission and the Comptroller of the Currency also have issued regulations. The heterogeneity of efforts and actions, however, leaves something to be desired in the future.

EXPORT CREDIT INSURANCE

The normal risk in credit transactions is multiplied in international business, for the causes of non-payment are increased by commercial and cultural differences in the buyer–seller relationship and by factors in the international environment for which there is no parallel in domestic trade. There are the usual perils of insolvency, delay of payment for lack of working capital and dissatisfaction with the goods, refusal to accept the shipment upon its arrival, and cancellation of an order during the production process. In international trade, such commercial risks involve uncommon costs and difficulties because of distances and time, unfamiliar legal systems, language and culture obstacles, and national biases. Beyond those risks, however, are still others growing out of political and war situations, as when goods are expropriated by a foreign government, import authorization is revoked, currencies are devaluated, purchase of foreign exchange prohibited, or goods destroyed through combat or revolution. Businessmen are able to cope somewhat with even extraordinary commercial risks and willing to venture into international trade, but their inability to cope with situations created by governments has led to the development of export credit insurance.

As insurance for export credit risks has been inspired by circumstances beyond individual control, so has it also served interests beyond those of the individual commercial parties involved. Stimulation of export trade is a national as well as a personal objective, for sales beget purchasing power, and an export trade surplus serves in the international balance of payments to counteract national deficits incurred through military expenditures, foreign aid grants, and in other ways. By assisting in providing export credit insurance, governments have been able to achieve other fiscal objectives.

Credit terms, always a factor in the competitive offering of vendors, are especially important in international business, where competitive advantage often rests with companies in countries to whom export credit insurance is available. Germany, the Netherlands, France, and Great Britain have supplied a variety of types of export credit insurance prior to its availability in the United States. And such insurance is currently in force in 20 countries [14] of the free world as represented by the "Berne Union."

History in the United States

While most plans of export credit insurance have come into existence since World War II, its antecedents originated years earlier.[15] In 1919, the American Manufacturers Foreign Credit Insurance Exchange was formed, a cooperative organization managed by American Foreign Credit Underwriters. On the basis of combined ledger experience of members, ratings were determined, and members could submit *individual* credit transactions for insurance. Risks covered included insolvency and uncollectibility at law. Risks not covered included mere failure to pay, trade disputes, refusal to accept delivery, catastrophes, or exchange restrictions. This insurance was discontinued in 1932. Two years later, the Export Credit Indemnity Exchange offered insurance to subscribers offering *every* export shipment made on credit terms. Coverage was extended to 75 per cent of the value of approved transactions. Operations of this company were restricted from 1942 to 1944. In 1956, a British insurance corpora-

[14] Australia, Austria, Belgium, Canada, Denmark, Finland, France, West Germany, India, Israel, Italy, the Netherlands, Norway, Pakistan, South Africa, Spain, Sweden, Switzerland, the United Kingdom, and the United States.

[15] Ronald L. Kramer, *International Marketing* (Cincinnati, Ohio: South-Western Publishing Co., Inc., 1959), pp. 520–32.

tion offered export credit insurance to American exporters of consumer goods on terms up to 6 months; individual shipments could be insured up to 85 per cent of invoice value, but no political risks were covered. Similar coverage was offered by the Continental Casualty Company of Chicago after 1958, who also insured risks on capital goods sales up to 2 years. In 1954, the Export-Import Bank of Washington, D.C., began a program of export credit financing *without recourse* up to 60 per cent of specific or revolving credits. In 1960, the Export-Import Bank extended its insurance to cover political risks.

It was not until 1962, however, that an effective program of export credit insurance was available providing the protection exporters needed and which placed them in a position competitive with vendors from other countries. This program was offered cooperatively by the Export-Import Bank and the Foreign Credit Insurance Association (FCIA), a group of 74 insurers. The Bank took the political risk and the private underwriters the commercial risk.

The Policy

The export credit insurance policy is written to cover short-term (up to 180 days) and medium-term (181 days to 5 years) credits; commercial and/or political risks; case-by-case, repetitive, or whole turnover sales; and coverage up to 85 per cent of commercial risks and 95 per cent of political risks.

Shippers on short-term credit have been the most numerous users of this insurance. From its inception in 1962 until 1965, 2,000 short-term policies totaling $1 billion were issued, in contrast to 700 medium-term totaling $35 million. Either comprehensive coverage, including political risks, or political risk coverage alone may be obtained for either short- or medium-term credits. When short-term insurance is used, the entire exports, or a reasonable spread of risks, must be insured to give the insurers a basis of experience; in medium-term policies, while the whole turnover *may* be insured, insurance may also be bought for individual transactions or for the repetitive sales for individual buyers. Underwriters insure 90 per cent of the commercial risk on all policies covering this risk. The government insures 85 to 95 per cent of all political risks, depending upon the comprehensiveness of the policy and the length of the credits.

In addition to the insurance program available to exporters, medium-term guarantees are offered by the Export-Import Bank to commercial banks financing exporters on a non-recourse basis. This is designed to encourage bank financing of exports and to facilitate the sale of export paper to commercial banks, factors, and other institutions. The Eximbank guarantees political risks for early maturities and both commercial and political risks for later maturities. Coverage is provided either case by case or on a revolving line of credit to one buyer. However, neither guarantees nor insurance provide coverage when a dispute exists between buyer and seller, or when an exporter fails to live up to his contractual obligations. Moreover, the FCIA insures sales only in U.S. dollars.

After some experience with the original policy terms, certain extensions to coverage were added in 1965. They provided for insurance of political risks for a considerably larger amount than the commercial risks insured in some cases; for conditional coverage of the risk of non-acceptance of goods by the foreign buyer, for increase of coverage on commercial risk from 85 to 90 per cent on both short- and medium-term policies, and for payment of 4.5 per cent interest to financing institutions during protracted default periods on non-recourse financing which they have provided.[16]

Charges for Insurance

The cost of export credit insurance is expressed as a percentage of the gross invoice value insured, but the rate is determined in terms of the risks apparent in the environment of the buyer. Factors such as economic conditions, balance of payments, foreign exchange holdings, fiscal and budgetary policy, and political trends are taken into consideration in rate determination.

On the basis of these considerations, the countries of the world are classified. "A" markets, with the highest rating, include such as the European countries and Japan; "B," such as Mexico; "C," most of Latin America; and "D," such as Argentina, Brazil, and Egypt. Rates vary according to the risks of the different areas. At a time when the charge of 1.66 per cent was made on sales to "D" market customers, 0.36 per cent was charged on sales to "A" market buyers.

[16] "FCIA Broadens Its Coverage," *Business Abroad and Export Trade*, June 14, 1965, p. 24.

Indicative of the variation in charges for this service found in different countries, the following comparisons were made on policies issued for shipments to "D" and "A" areas: [17]

	"D" areas	"A" areas
Canada	2.00%	1.10%
United States	1.66	0.36
Germany	1.50	1.50
France	1.30	0.90
United Kingdom	1.24	0.25

Rates vary also according to the time and manner in which the policy is written. A flat premium of 0.75 per cent of invoice is charged for the preshipment risk and 1.5 per cent of the invoice amount for postshipment risk up to six months credit. An additional charge of 0.1 per cent of the invoice amount for each month in excess of six is also made. Although there are exceptions, rates in the United States generally fall in the range of 0.25 per cent to about 2.5 per cent of the invoices offered for insurance.

Appraisal

Newness of experience with insurance of export credits has caused some reluctance to use it on the part of exporters and some readjustment of their offering on the part of insurers. It is estimated [18] that even in the United Kingdom, where export credit insurance has reached its highest acceptance, probably no more than half of all eligible exports (excluding from exports some short-term credits and sales guaranteed in other ways) are insured. In 1962–1963, 23 per cent of the total exports from the United States were covered by insurance contracts. The proportion of total exports insured in other countries is as follows: Switzerland, 10.5 per cent; Denmark, 7.9 per cent; West Germany, 7 to 8 per cent; France, 7.6 per cent; United States, 6 per cent; the Netherlands, 5.8 per cent.[19]

In the United States part of this reticence to insure derives from insurers' insistence on insuring the whole turnover rather than selected risks. It has been due also to delays in approving or disapproving applications, to indifference of banks toward ex-

[17] Greene, "Export Credit Insurance—Its Role in Expanding World Trade," *The Journal of Risk and Insurance*, June, 1965, p. 182.
[18] *Ibid.*, p. 184.
[19] *Ibid.*, p. 183.

port credit insurance, and to lack of marketing effort in the sale of the insurance. On the other hand, insurers have found that most claims have arisen from commercial risk conditions, particularly from protracted default of debtors. Moreover, exporters needs have not exactly coincided with provisions of export insurance as originally conceived, and insurers have not always been able to render the service desired. This has led to reconception and revision of policies.

On the whole, availability of export credit insurance has made possible the shifting of another type of credit risk to specialists. Utilization of it is a question for management decision, a question to be decided on the basis of cost and service factors, in terms of which the shifting of all credit functions is determined.

DISCUSSION QUESTIONS

1. What are the markets for suppliers of commercial credit insurance, credit life insurance, and export credit insurance?
2. Contrast the causes of credit loss covered by each of these three forms of credit insurance.
3. What are the limitations to the types and amounts of credit risk which may be shifted under each of these relationships?
4. Under what circumstances is commercial credit insurance most advantageous?
5. Appraise the proposition that the insuring of receivables is like the insuring of a firm's other assets.
6. Contrast commercial and consumer credit insurance from the standpoints of market, causes of loss, payer of the service charge, coverage, and beneficiary.
7. What role has the government played in regulating any aspects of credit insurance? What role has it played in helping to provide it? Account for its participation in one field and not in others.
8. What reservations might an exporter have about using export credit insurance? What alternative forms of protection from credit loss are available to an exporter who does not avail himself of export credit insurance?
9. Is the governmental guarantee of American private foreign investment a form of credit insurance? Why?

17

Credit Systems

In the previous pages and chapters attention has been given to the characteristics and operations of various components of the credit structure, the integrated and segregated, the non-specialized and specialized operations among which the credit processes are functionally divided and performed. Separate consideration of each operation, however, is insufficient to convey the full picture of credit in our business relations, in our economy, or in our society in general. Further attention must be given the interactions of these structural elements and their interaction with the entire distributive system. In other words, the systems or sets of relationships among participants in the credit processes must be recognized, for their myriad forms are the alternatives subject to managerial decision. Credit operations do not exist as isolated enterprises, nor merely as competitors in an industry or like kinds, but rather as units of operation related forward, backward, laterally, and obliquely in the systems or channels of credit, through which flow the elements of information, promises, payments, finances, risk, authority, initiative, and responsibility.

The traditional view of relationships in credit performance has been that of clusters of services attached to production and distribution enterprises. Thus certain credit service organizations have been related to mercantile creditors—manufacturers and wholesalers—and others to retailers. Little attention has been given to the continuity of processes and services throughout the series of relationships linked by credit. As in contemporary studies of distribution the distributive channel in its entirety is regarded as a unit, with common and correlated objectives and facilities, so the subsystems of credit relationships among pairs of participants collectively comprise composite systems with pervasive goals, problems, and processes.

Several examples illustrate this. First, in the distribution of automobiles a common objective of the distributive channel components is to move the high-investment product through and into the hands of buyers and sellers with a minimum involvement of personal funds. The need not only for financing but for continuity of financing throughout the distributive process has led to the conception of a single type of credit service at two distributive levels: floor-plan financing from manufacturers to dealers, and sales financing from dealers to consumers. Second, the need for adequate promotional use of credit in the retail sale of camera equipment has led manufacturers of that product to devise and furnish to dealers plans of credit service for consumers with whom the manufacturers have no direct contact. Third, in the distributive channels it is known that merchants are less able to pay for their inventory purchases before they have had a reasonable time to dispose of that inventory or turn it to some profitable use. Consequently, manufacturers' net credit periods to wholesale customers, and in turn theirs to their customers, are somewhat related to the customers' own sale and credit terms. In these three incidents the interrelatedness of credit operations is evident. Other examples could be given illustrating the systemic rather than the insular character of the credit structure.

While it is true that credit is usually allied to distribution and is a promotional element in distributive processes, credit service is an economic product itself, having its own markets, production specialists, and channels of distribution. As this is more generally appreciated, improvements should occur in credit granting, in the conception of new credit services allied to economic and social change, in the integration of credit legislation and credit practices, in credit ethics, and in the making of decisions concerning credit by creditors and debtors alike.

To clarify and emphasize the concept of credit systems or channels, the idea can be presented diagrammatically. Let the following symbols represent the principal types of participants in the credit processes.

Primary Credit Service Establishments

Vendors:

Producers = P   i.e.,   P

Wholesalers = W

Retailers = R

Lenders: L

Consumers: C

Primary Establishments Shifting Credit Functions   W

i.e.,

Auxiliary Credit Service Establishments

Full-function: F

Limited-function: L   i.e.,   L

Additional numerical identification may be given specific credit specialists in the various categories:

Full-function	Limited-function
Mercantile credit	Mercantile credit
1. Factor	10. Commercial banks
2. Sales Finance Company	11. Commercial finance companies
Retail credit	12. Credit information
2. Sales Finance Company	13. Credit checking
3. Charge Account Service	14. Collection service
4. Credit Card Plan	15. Credit insurance
	16. Export credit insurance
	Retail credit
	10. Commercial banks
	17. Credit information
	18. Credit life insurance

The functions performed by the various specialists may also be identified:

$$F_i = \text{Financing function}$$
$$R_i = \text{Credit risk function}$$
$$O_p = \text{Credit operational function}$$

One of the simplest credit systems is that represented by the neighborhood retailer who sells to his known customers repeatedly on a credit basis. Their relationship may be represented as follows:

R F_i R_i O_p C

It is here represented that the retailer is a primary credit service operator, furnishing credit service to his customers, performing all of the functions and shifting none. This is a complete credit system, and no recourse is made to external specialists.

Another retailer may delegate the work of supplying credit service to such specialists as charge account companies, credit card services, or sales finance companies. Thus all functions may be shifted to a full-function auxiliary, in which case the system would appear a little differently:

In this case a charge account bank or company undertakes to perform all of the functions, collecting information upon which credit approval is made, investing its own funds, bearing risk, making collection. Similar depiction could be made of the service of a factor to a manufacturer. The designation in the circle would then be F-1.

It would be unlikely that either a factor or a charge account company would perform all functions if it operated on a large scale. Either may have recourse to banks or other financial organizations for funds invested in receivables, thus shifting the financing function while retaining the others. Such an action would bring another party into the credit system:

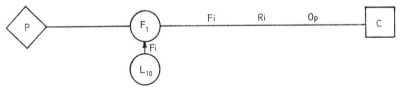

As the full-function specialist continues to supply some of his own financing, and as the newly introduced limited-function specialist has no interaction with the customer, no connection is made between L-10 and C.

In longer channels of distribution, the distributive system and the credit system may or may not coincide. For many goods distributed in the so-called regular wholesale channel, involving manufacturer–wholesaler–retailer–consumer relationships, the two systems may be identical (see next page).

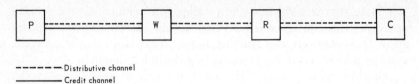

------ Distributive channel
———— Credit channel

In such distribution each vendor performs his own credit functions, moving title with the receipt of the credit promise to pay. Choice of distributive channel, however, is not always the determinant of credit relationships. To the contrary, demands for credit service sometimes dictate the distributive channel used. Retailers generally need financing for their inventories, and this investment is often obtained from mercantile creditors. Unwillingness or inability of manufacturers, for various reasons, to provide such credit service may leave them no choice but to avoid such customers or to sell through a distributor who will provide the credit service. Regular wholesalers and selling agents are two who have justified a position in distributive channels partly on the basis of the credit services they can render customers of manufacturers whose products they handle. Thus in effect a producer aiming at a retail market may shift his credit functions to a wholesaler, represented as follows:

Differences between the two systems arise more often from the engagement of credit specialists who have nothing to do with the sale and distribution of products. The combinatons of each are numerous, for many factors of sellers and buyers, creditors and debtors, lead to alternative courses of action. Sellers may use several channels to reach different market segments or to exploit the services of various specialists. Different sellers in similar circumstances may employ dissimilar distributive channels because of differences in managerial philosophy and competence. Likewise in the structuring of credit systems, both circumstances and managerial judgment are influential, and those in management who are responsible for achieving the credit objectives may deal in systems of which the planners of distribution are uninformed and unconcerned. Sellers may use different credit systems for different parts of their business. Department stores, for example, may perform all credit functions for holders of regular open accounts but resort to financing assistance from others for instalment credit. Manufacturers may carry their mercantile accounts with dealers but establish a credit subsidiary for handling consumer credit business; they may carry commercial credit insurance on some accounts and not on others and use export credit insurance for foreign credits. Thus the complexity of credit systems increases with knowledge of alternatives and with the development of credit services intended to meet special needs of creditors.

The following is a diagram of a rather elaborate credit system extending from manufacturer to consumer, wherein different types of specialization available on three distributive levels are employed.

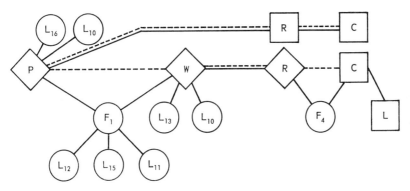

In this organization, a producer is shown selling through two distributive channels: directly to retail distributors overseas and to wholesalers in the domestic trade. In his foreign dealings, he has subscribed for export credit insurance, thus shifting that risk, and has discounted his trade draft with a commercial bank, shifting to it the financing function. The producer presumably has gathered his own information upon which the credit sale was based and will bear whatever portion of the risk is uninsured. On his domestic business the producer divorces himself completely from the credit functions, turning them over to a factor. Invoices factored are without recourse and with notification, so that he is responsible for collecting directly from the wholesale buyer. The factor, however, subscribes to the information services of a credit bureau, pledges some of his receivables with a commercial finance company, and insures his receivables with one of the companies providing commercial credit insurance. The wholesaler in the distributive channel, if the product handled is apparel, might request of a credit advisory specialist a decision on whether to accept a particular order. He may then sell the account to a bank. The retailer, at the end of the distributive channel, creates another credit system by affiliating with a credit card company, whose cards he honors in his sales. That specialist presumably might perform all of the functions involved in serving the ultimate customer.

Credit systems are the arenas in which free enterprise develops diversification, innovation, and competition in the providing of credit services. Credit establishments may participate in many different credit and distributive systems. They compete among themselves for advantage in producing service and a profit. They exert different pressures upon users of their service because of their dominance in the system. They are more or less progressive depending upon their leadership and initiative, their cooperation with others in the system, and their ability to manage the factors in their own operations efficiently. Credit systems, more so than individual credit operations, invoke the regulation imposed by government. They reflect the joint contribution of economic and other social forces in modeling a means of meeting the individual and collective needs for credit service.

DISCUSSION QUESTIONS

1. Distinguish between credit systems and credit structure.
2. Distinguish between credit systems, distributive systems, and financial systems.
3. Explain the concepts of channels and flows as they are applicable to the analysis of credit behavior.
4. Explain the idea that a vendor's credit objectives may extend beyond the scope of his immediate credit transaction.
5. Interpret the interaction which occurs in a credit system from the standpoints of who initiates interaction, loyalty in relationships, authority to determine credit terms, dominance of power, and mutuality of interests.
6. Experimentally diagram several elaborate credit systems and appraise them from the standpoint of realism and feasibility.
7. What historical evidence of flexibility in credit systems may be found?

V

INTERNAL
ORGANIZATION
FOR CREDIT OPERATION

18

Organization for Credit Management

Organization is to an individual credit establishment what credit establishments are to the credit system as a whole: an integration of specialized components cooperating for the performance of functions necessary for the supplying of credit service. Both organization and credit structure are determined by activity, rather than vice versa. Both are subject to managerial determination and their variety expresses intelligent but different ways of solving problems. Both represent means of achieving managerial objectives related to effectiveness and efficiency. Both, even in their diversity, are related to principles which pervade the logic by which they are determined. Credit establishments are the structural components of credit systems; organization is the structural form of the individual credit operation.

Organization is the sets of relationships and their interaction patterns by which the processes in supplying credit service are performed. Organization is both formal and informal, the former being the determined relationships, the latter those evolved through interaction and not necessarily set forth in charts and plans. Individuals in business processes never perform alone. Individually they may do work for which they alone are responsible, but in the collective business undertaking the individual acts *in relation to* other individuals, because of them, and in consideration of them. The objective of organization is to devise such relationships and patterns of behavior that the work at hand will be performed expeditiously.

Although credit organizations differ among manufacturers, wholesalers, retailers, and consumer and commercial lending agencies, all credit organizations have characteristics in common. The similarity of the work to be done in all effects a uniformity of credit organizational structures. The differing circumstances under which the credit operation is carried out, however, produce the diversity of organizational structures actually found. It is as important to recognize the common elements in organization as to discern the modifications in basic organizational structure which circumstances produce.

Regardless of the nature of a specific credit operation, several inherent and common tasks must be performed. First, promotion of credit service: credit service must be sold, whether for its own sake or in conjunction with the sale of merchandise. Second, credit approval: credit risks must be investigated, applications approved or rejected, and customer contacts maintained. Third, authorization: use of credit must be authorized in specific transactions, and records of this use filed. Fourth, records maintenance: accounts receivable records must be maintained and preserved; bills must be issued and, where necessary, adjusted. Fifth, collections: payments must be received during the credit period, and thereafter collections carried out. Organization consists, however, not only of relationships involved in physical work flows but also of those involved in the creation of policies, plans, and image. These are the functions which organizations are created to perform.

Management of the credit processes requires organization comprising relationships of a threefold character: those of credit manager with personnel within the credit group, who are responsible for operational routines; those with peers and superiors outside the credit group but within the larger framework of the enterprise; and those with individuals outside the enterprise in positions related to the credit service. The interaction of credit managers with persons in each of these categories is the subject of organization with which this chapter is concerned.

CREDIT TASKS AND RELATIONSHIPS

There are a wide variety of types of credit organizations. Their differences are not entirely arbitrary. They reflect managerial competence to form an adequate organization, but they also indicate the diverse needs requiring organizational forms for achieving the credit objectives under different circumstances. The principal determinants of credit organization are (1) the task assigned to the credit function, or the role expected of it in the entire business, and (2) the relationships deemed essential for the accomplishment of the assigned task. Differences in types of business, in managerial philosophy, and in management efficiency produce a variety of organizations based upon these two basic influences.

The task assigned to credit reflects the contribution which credit is expected to make to the business; this expectation in turn determines the personal involvement which must occur to accomplish the task. Some companies assign to credit a routine or perfunctory task. Emphasis is given to duties performed by the credit work group and to relationships within that group, between credit personnel and their supervisor, and between credit personnel and customers whom they directly contact. In other companies, credit is assigned a role of facilitating the performance of other functions, such as selling. In that position, the credit manager or supervisor interacts with his peers within and without the firm, including finance, sales, and personnel managers, and with credit managers of other companies. In still other firms, credit is assigned the responsibility for contributing to the fulfillment of over-all company objectives. In that responsibility, credit managers interact more with management on higher levels of responsibility. Thus the role which credit is expected to play in the business is an important determinant of organization for credit management, for it prescribes the other individuals with whom the credit manager interacts and therefore the relationships which constitute organization structure. These relations of function to interaction systems are indicated in Table 18–1.

More than prescribing mere relationships, management's concept of credit's role in the enterprise determines also the dominance, initiative, cooperation, and leadership likely to be found in the relationships of the credit manager. As credit management has evolved, the position of credit manager has been subordinated to those in charge of finances, sales, and personnel. In the sales department, credit and sales managers have interacted sometimes with conflict, sometimes with cooperation. The predominant authority given one or the other position also defines the organization for credit. Similarly, the authority given credit

Table 18–1. Credit Manager Relations Associated with Credit Management Functions

Credit Manager Performing	Interacts with					
	Top Management	Finance Management	Sales Management	Personnel Management	Peers	Customers
Role of credit in the overall business	X	X				
Credit decision process	X	X	X	X	X	X
Credit operational routine			X	X		X

managers for initiating, recommending, or influencing changes in the financial aspects of their work also determines the organizational structure and patterns for credit. Many patterns of interaction are developed, some formally and some informally. An illustration of a possible pattern of relationships is shown in Fig. 18–1.

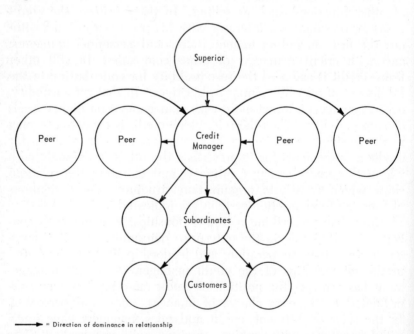

——▶ = Direction of dominance in relationship

Fig. 18–1. An illustration of patterns of dominance in credit relationships.

LINE, FUNCTIONAL, AND STAFF RELATIONSHIPS

Patterns of relationships in organizational structure are commonly designated as line, functional, and staff types of organization. It is within these frameworks that most credit organizations are set up. A line organization is that in which authority extends directly to immediately subordinate positions and indirectly to successively subordinated levels; in which authority embodies power to act or to command action; and in which an individual, in whatever position, is responsible to a single superior. A functional organization is that in which lines of authority are not only vertical but oblique, to the end that a position may be responsible to two or more superiors, in contrast to one as in the line organization. The multiple responsibility of the functional organization usually uses to good advantage functional specialists whose contributions to the whole organization complement those of a regular line organization. Finally, a staff position is one which carries responsibility but not authority, at least not authority to command action. The responsibility of a staff position may be to advise, to gather facts, to analyze, to research, or to recommend.

Examples of the three types of organizations are shown in Fig. 18–2. The first is illustrative of a line organization. It represents an organization which may be found in an enterprise devoted to the performance of credit service, such as a bank or loan company. The divisions of a bank, for example, may represent the organizations for commercial credit and for personal credit. Each would be responsible for the complete performance of all of the credit functions related to it. Thus under each may be found a credit approval department and a collection department, each comprising its own personnel, responsible to the division manager alone, and independent of any other activity within the general organization. Within another lending establishment such as loan company, divisions may represent geographic divisions, the branches, branch offices each comprising personnel capable of performing the entire credit work.

This form of organization has the advantage of single accountability, simplicity, and the fact that additional units on any level can be created without disturbing the organization as a whole. On the other hand, it represents duplication of effort, inasmuch as some functions are performed repeatedly in each

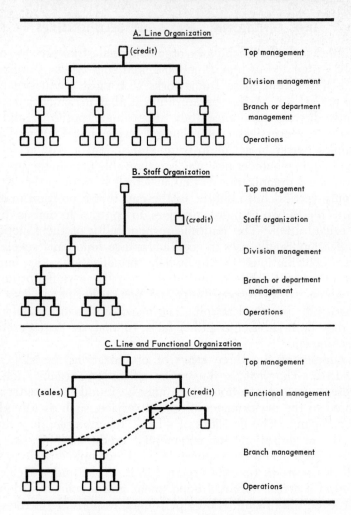

Fig. 18–2. Credit department organizations.

organizational unit. It does not use to best advantage functional specialists.

In the second part of Fig. 18–2, to a line organization is added a staff, which is related to the general organizational structure only by a line of responsibility to positions on a higher level. Such a staff unit might occur on any level of the line organization. It is rare for a credit department to occupy such staff position, being merely advisor, if one regards the approving of credit to be a line function. If, on the other hand, the work of a credit department were to analyze risks and simply to make recommendations to others who make the final credit decisions, then such a department would be in approximately a staff position. Likewise, a credit department advising and assisting top management in the formulation of credit policies is acting in a staff capacity.

The third part of Fig. 18–2 represents the credit department —a line organization in itself—in a functional or supervisory relation to other operational units of the business. This typifies the relation of the credit department to the organizational structure in most vending establishments, wherein the credit department approves credit and makes collections for each of the departmental, product, territorial, or other general divisions of the organization. Although the relationship of the credit department to the various branches or other departments is advisory, as the credit department exercises greater initiative in discovering and building up potential credit sales customers, its line of authority in selling may approximate the character of a straight-line organization.

This question of the distinction between functional and line performance involves more than simply a study of relationships. It relates deeply to the basic conception of the role of the credit department. At one time credit was regarded as a non-productive activity, at least in comparison to selling. Subsequently, it was deemed "sales-supporting" and elevated a little in its appraisal. There is a growing tendency to view the providing of credit service as directly contributory to sales and other corporate objectives and thus to attribute to it a share of the production. Authority to command action in direct line with the income and producing activity of the business has been one of the characteristics of its line organization. Another, as illustrated by the sales department, has been the direct relationship with customers through which salesmen exercise initiative in building business. In a passive capacity, the credit department lacks this characteristic, but as one who seeks out credit customers, builds their creditworthiness, arranges terms on which trade can be carried on, and adapts the product of his credit service to the demands of discernible market segments, the credit manager is as truly a line functionary as others. This view, however, remains to be proven in the experiences of any firm, and mere designation of line or functional position is of little significance in itself.

ORGANIZATIONAL POSITION OF THE CREDIT DEPARTMENT

In organizing for credit management the first question logically to be considered is the position of the credit department within the entire business structure. This is a question of top-management policy and business philosophy rather than one of the efficiency of detailed credit operations. The routine of credit granting may be carried on in the same manner regardless of the location of the credit department. The total contribution of the credit operation to the business, however, is not likely to be unaffected by the department's position.

Historically, the credit department has generally held one of three positions: subordinate to the general finance function; subordinate to the sales function; in an independent status. So long as credit granting was considered to be a function of finance, the departmental credit organization was commonly located under the general supervision of the treasurer or comptroller. As the sales potentiality of credit selling became recognized, the credit department was more frequently placed under the jurisdiction of the sales manager. Later, as the technical activities of the credit operation increased in scope and importance, reasons were found for divorcing the credit department from either of the other two and giving it an independent status. This for many years has been regarded as ideal and in the best interests of the business as a whole.

While arguments may be advanced for locating the credit department in any one of these positions, the reasoning behind the arguments is most important to consider. Today it is increasingly recognized that credit is but one—although a very important one—factor in the over-all management mix. Management must combine in different proportions the factors which are essential to a successful business undertaking: money, material, personnel, sales effort, credit service, space, time, etc. No two business managers combine all of these in the same proportions. One may emphasize sales effort; another, credit terms. One may emphasize low absolute costs; another may take a higher calculated risk in anticipation of correspondingly higher returns. Thus the objective held for the credit operation determines its relation to other management functions and, in turn, the position of the credit department in the general credit organizational structure. Additional factors bearing upon this are the following: the need to establish channels upward and downward, from the credit department to any other division of the business; the need to establish a system of checks and balances between the credit operation and the general financial organization; and the need to integrate credit operations with departmental and top policy formation.

Treasurer's Department

Much may be said in support of placing the credit department in the financial section of a business structure. There it is almost always found in retail store organizations, and often in mercantile organizations. In retail establishments, of course, there is scarcely an alternative because of the nature of traditional merchandising organization. It is argued that a credit operation is basically a financing operation; it involves the handling of non-merchandise dollar values, and some of the principal measures of its control relate to the amount and cost of investment in receivables and the return earned thereon. Moreover, the treasurer, in control of general financial matters, is in the best position to anticipate the financial needs of the credit department and to arrange for financing its variable needs.

Because credit management is much more than merely a financing function, there are dangers in its being placed entirely within the treasurer's department, where for the most part it is treated as a staff function. The usual conservatism of traditional money managers restricts the promotional use of credit. The importance of the calculated risk may be overlooked in face of the fact that a risk is being assumed.

Sales Department

To place a credit department under the sales manager is to emphasize the promotional character of the credit operation. A position titled Manager of Credit Sales has sometimes been created in the sales department, as a means of attracting customers to the business through offering credit service. When it is realized that sales can be increased by working with potential credit customers to increase their creditworthiness, there is justification for this point of view in organization. Little is gained today by taking a passive point of view toward a credit operation.

To place the credit department in the sales department, however, is to expose it to the danger of promoting credit for the sake of credit volume rather than for the sake of profitability. When imbued with an urgency to sell on credit, salesmen acquire orders to their own detriment and that of the customer. Over-zealous sales managers, not always temperamentally compatible with the calm judgment required in credit appraisal, overlook negative evidences which should be heeded.

Independent Status

Disadvantages of placing the credit department under either the treasurer or the sales manager have been avoided by giving it an independent status. Whether this action is good or bad depends upon the nature of that independence. Too often it has meant that the credit department was independent not only of the other operations mentioned but also of top management cognizance. Independence has sometimes meant that while the credit manager could recommend policy to his superiors, he had no active role in policy formation and was responsible for carrying out whatever policy was determined. In such a position, a credit department is at a great disadvantage, for it has only responsibility without authority. Credit management then becomes mainly a technical operation, unintegrated with the business as a whole.

The remedy for ineffectual independence is found in the increasing regard for credit as an essential part of the management mix, the responsibility for which extends to the highest level of management. The integration of credit with activities in every related department is the integration which must be achieved. In technical respects, the credit department needs independence and freedom to act in accord with its best technical judgment. But the credit manager himself must be cognizant of the relation of credit to other functions and of its potential contribution to them and to the general business objective. The proper position of the credit department in over-all organization is not merely a question of spotting a location. Rather, it is a matter of orienting it in the perspective of all departments and individuals with which it is related, and of confirming this orientation with the necessary lines of communication, authority, and responsibility.

CREDIT DEPARTMENT ORGANIZATION

The objectives of management govern its organizations. Thus the position of the credit department in the general business organization is determined by the objectives of management for the credit operation. As shown, placement of the credit department under the treasurer, sales manager, or an executive officer in an independent status reflects what is expected of the credit department. Similarly, organization within the credit department reflects the objectives of the credit department itself. It expresses a concept of the best means of accomplishing both the departmental and executive goals in credit operation.

In general, the activities which occur in the credit department, and for which organization must be provided, fall into two general classes. One group includes all those activities by which the credit department is brought into direct contact with the credit customer. The functions in this part of the credit work are regarded as line functions or activities. They include the following:

1. Promoting credit sales
2. Appraising creditworthiness
3. Estimating lines of credit
4. Authorizing charge-take credit transactions
5. Approving customers' orders
6. Billing
7. Receiving payments
8. Bill adjustment
9. Collecting
10. Customer contacts
11. Improving customer creditworthiness

The second group of activities are those which are advisory or mainly of service to the department in performing its work. These are the staff functions of the credit department. Among them are the following:

1. Filing
2. Records maintenance
3. Hiring and training
4. Credit market research
5. Appraisal of business conditions
6. Analysis of controls

7. Interdepartmental and intercompany liaison
8. Cooperation in industry association activities
9. Legal activities

The activities of the credit department may be organized in different ways. One arrangement of them is shown in Fig. 18–3, which distinguishes between staff and line functions and groups the latter as pertaining to credit sales, authorization, records and accounts, and collection and payment. Thus are segregated the distinctly different types of work performed in the credit department: the first including all of the contacts between the credit department and the credit customer, the second including the mechanical or impersonal contacts with the customer at the time of sales, the third including the paper work and records of the department, and the fourth relating to all of the payments received from the customer.

There are endless variations of the division and combination of the activities performed within the credit department. Few companies will be so fully organized with staff assistants as is shown in Fig. 18–3. Instead, the credit department will generally avail itself of the services of other staff offices in the general organization. The general personnel office usually employs people for the credit department. The legal department handles credit problems of a legal nature, as well as those for other departments. Market and economic research is carried on by the general research office, and records analysis is performed by the credit manager or one of his assistants.

The line activities shown in Fig. 18–3, although they are standard and inherent in all credit operations, may be differently grouped, designated, and emphasized in particular business situations. The organization plan shown is approximately that used by a large department store. A commercial bank in its personal loan department classifies its activities as interviewing, record keeping, receiving, collecting, and promoting. Similar functions could be enumerated for personal loan companies, mercantile credit departments, and other types of credit agencies.

So long as a credit operation remains small, simple, and centralized, functional specialists generally operate as components of a straight-line plan. With the development of a business along product or territorial lines of organization, however, a more complex organization for credit management results. In such cases,

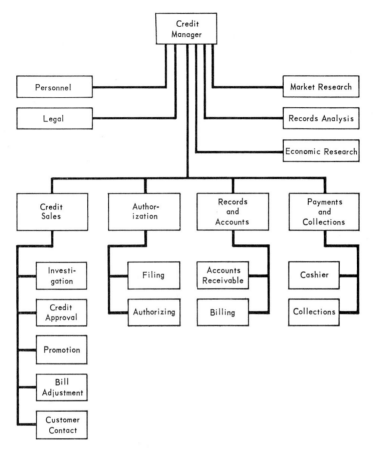

Fig. 18–3. Organizations of subfunctions in the credit department.

one development is the decentralization of the credit work among the various branches or operating units, illustrated in Fig. 18–4. Virtual autonomy is given each of the branch credit managers, who are responsible for the performance of all credit activities in their area of operation. A general credit manager may coordinate their activities and represent the credit operation on a higher level. This plan is appropriate particularly when the divisional units themselves are relatively self-contained and autonomous.

When branches are not given the responsibility for the credit operation, but when it is retained in the central office, an organization plan somewhat like that shown in Fig. 18–5 may occur. The functions are then specialized at headquarters, and the in-

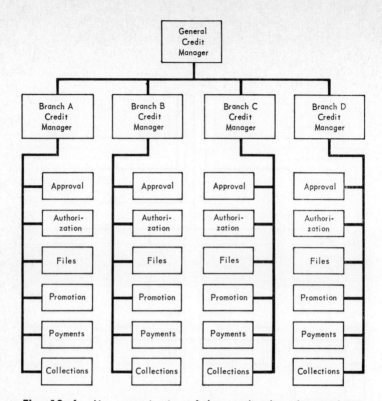

Fig. 18–4. Line organization of decentralized credit operation.

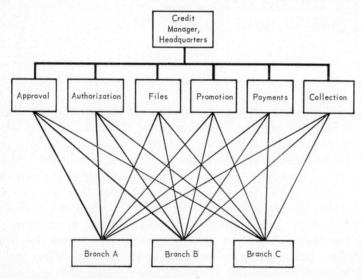

Fig. 18–5. Functional organization of centralized credit operation in decentralized organization structure.

dividual responsible for each maintains contact with his corespondent in the branch, who may be the branch manager, sales manager, or even a nominal credit manager. Such a system provides the advantages of specialization to branches whose volume of credit business is insufficient to warrant such an organization on the branch level.

Still another degree of credit department development is that in which a functionalized organization is maintained both at the central office and in the branches, as shown in Fig. 18–6. Such is the situation sometimes found in a bank which maintains a number of local branches. It may also occur in a wholesale or retail establishment in which sales are made both at a central location and at branch locations. With possible staff units omitted,

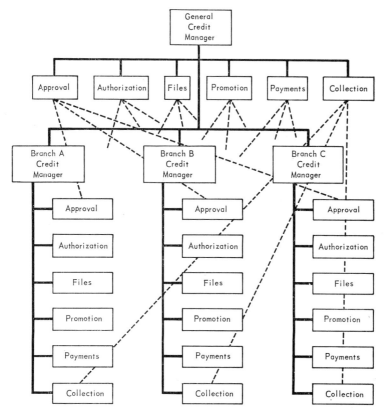

Fig. 18–6. Line and functional organization of decentralized credit management.

a line type of branch credit operation is augmented by a functional central organization whose components act in an advisory capacity to the branch personnel. The operating units of the central office level may also perform additional functions, as in approving credit applicants of such a size or character not entrusted to the branch credit granting personnel, or in promoting the credit service of the entire organization or in handling exceptional collection problems.

FACTORS AFFECTING CREDIT ORGANIZATION

Differences among credit departments result from a number of factors, including the line of business, the level of production or distribution, and the legal form of the business. The most significant influences upon credit organization, however, are the following:

Size of Credit Service Organization

The volume of business done on credit may in a particular operation alone affect the nature of organization for credit management. Credit volume will be so small, or so sporadic, as to require no organization. The corner drugstore or neighborhood grocery store, whose credit business is a service of convenience, has no credit organization. Decisions to accept credit fall usually to the proprietor or manager; few activities are performed, and no specialization is needed. Growth of credit business, however, usually imposes the need for handling a greater volume of credit business and for performing additional functions. When this occurs, the addition of personnel or the division of responsibilities evolves a credit organization.

Credit Functions Undertaken

To the extent that major credit functions are shifted to specialists outside the organization, the need for internal credit organization is reduced. For example, textile manufacturers who factor their sales, or garment manufacturers relying upon the credit judgment of Dun & Bradstreet Credit Clearing Service, have little if any credit organization. Likewise, vendors who engage in no extensive investigation and who keep a minimum of records also have little need for organization. Vendors who contract for charge account banking service or who cooperate with credit card companies also undertake a minimal performance and therefore need only a corresponding organization. On the other hand, banks, consumer lending agencies, and all kinds of distributors who assume complete responsibility for a credit operation must develop organizations commensurate with this undertaking.

Nature of Credit Service

Lenders' organizations for credit management usually differ from those of vendors. The whole business structure of a lender is built around the credit operation. Therefore, such functions as research, personnel management, and promotion may be more closely related to the organization for credit granting than in a vending establishment where these functions are related to merchandising rather than to credit. Organizational demands differ also depending upon whether instalment or regular account service is offered.

General Business Organizational Structure

The credit department organization may be determined primarily less by the credit work to be done than by the existing organizational structure in which it must fit. Many business organizations have been shaped by strong management personalities and through no other cause. Credit service sometimes too has started as a stepchild under a person with other primary interests. Under those conditions, the credit operation may grow to illogical proportions. In other cases, because preference may be held for one form of organization, the credit department may be required to fit in. This may determine whether credit is developed as a line or staff function, or whether it is organized along commodity or territorial lines.

Types of Customers

Credit operators who cater to but one type of customer generally have a simpler organization than those whose clients fall into several classes. Commercial banks, whose clients are engaged in real estate, commerce, and household consumption, provide different organizational units to serve each type of customer. Finance companies which engage in both personal and sales financing also usually segregate these activities in different departments. Department stores handle their contract sales to industrial buyers apart from their normal consumer credit business.

Number and Size of Accounts

To process and to service the hundreds and thousands of accounts which a department store may have, each account small and used frequently, impose different demands upon an organizational structure than do the few hundred large accounts of a manufacturer doing a comparable volume of business. Not only must the organization of the former involve a greater number of records, more transactions, and more people interviewing, investigating, and authorizing, but it may involve also different levels of responsibility in the assumption of the credit risk. Most of the transactions in the department store may be routine authorizations. More of the manufacturer's credit decisions are unique and must be handled individually. Thus not only the number but the caliber of the personnel in the organizational structure is affected.

Complexity of Decision and Credit Risk

The complexity of a credit decision is not always in proportion to the size of the account or the amount involved. The creditworthiness of business customers is sometimes made complex by the difficulty of determining the outlook of the business with respect to the credit in question. Complicated financial structures make for difficulty in risk analysis. The unsnarling of a customer's debt situation may offer a challenge to the credit manager. In a credit operation where there is wide range of risks and complexities, an organizational hierarchy may have to be provided for assigning different risk situations to different levels of management.

Location of Credit Operation Units

Some credit operations are performed at widely scattered places. Branch sales establishments, subsidiary organizations, mail order selling, and the traveling customer with the credit card, all represent instances posing organizational questions of where and how the credit functions should be performed. There is no one rule to be applied, no one organization plan which is always best, but the credit department structure under such circumstances will differ from that in an operation performed at one place.

Relative Importance of Credit Subfunctions

The relative simplicity of manufacturers' and wholesalers' credit departments is due in part to the fact that authorization is performed differently than in a department store. In the latter, with charge-take transactions predominating, prompt authorization from the sales floor or from the credit department is extremely important. In the mercantile establishment, orders received by mail or from salesmen may be processed without the pressure of a waiting customer. In the one case, organization must provide for an extensive authorizing staff; in the other, little if any department personnel need be provided for performing this function. Similarly, the relative importance of collection activities varies in different businesses. Gasoline companies and others selling on credit cards, as well as some retail store chains, must provide for the assembly of credit sales slips and develop a far-flung collection organization. The organizational requirements for performing this function are simplified when the sales operation is performed in a single place.

Related Objectives

Organization for credit management is sometimes regarded as a means for the development of managerial talent. The credit department of sales branches, therefore, is sometimes made an autonomous organization, responsibility and authority being surrendered by the general credit manager except for control purposes, as a means of developing the initiative and acumen needed in branch offices. By contrast, in closely held family businesses, or where opportunities for internal advancement are slight, organizations may be designed not to develop talent but to minimize costs and risks.

Organization plans which illustrate these influences are shown in Figs. 18–7 to 18–10.

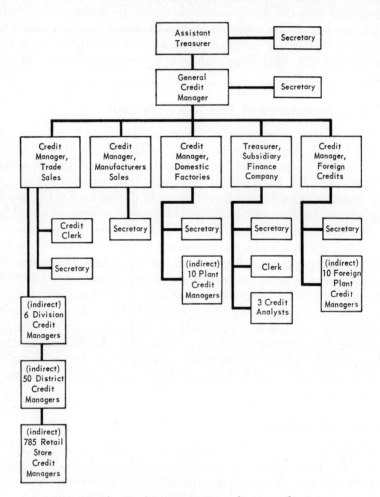

Fig. 18–7. Credit organization of a manufacturer.

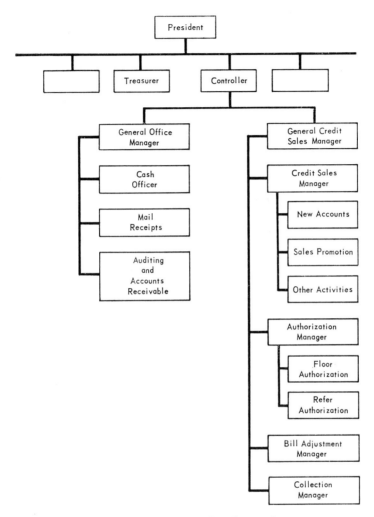

Fig. 18–8. Credit organization of a large department store.

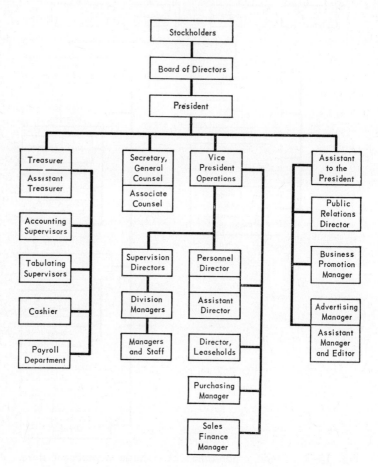

Fig. 18–9. Organization of a consumer finance company.

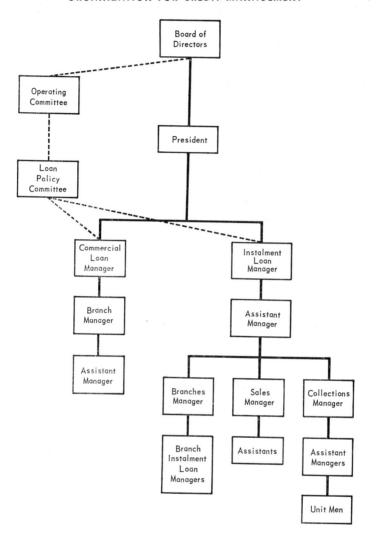

Fig. 18–10. Credit organization of a commercial bank.

DISCUSSION QUESTIONS

1. To what extent is credit organization determined by each of the following: the nature of the credit processes, other aspects of organizational structure, nature of markets, technical credit facilities?

2. In what ways has the evolution of the position of the credit operation in the over-all organization been influenced by such concepts as marketing, management by objective, integrated management, group behavior?

3. What organizational means may be used to implement the idea that credit service is a productive function of any business?

4. Contrast the organizational plans which might be based upon traditional line-function concepts and those based on concepts of role and group behavior.

5. When it is recognized that there are credit objectives held by management on several levels of responsibility, what effect has this on organization of the credit function? Illustrate by diagrams.

6. What factors cause the credit organization of a department store to differ from that of a manufacturer? Of a manufacturer from that of a manufacturer integrated with distributive branches?

7. Draw up a list of characteristics which every credit organization should have.

19

The Credit Manager

The quality of a credit operation and the efficiency of an organization for credit depend largely upon the caliber of the credit management. This responsibility is often attributed to the credit *manager*, per se, for that position is regarded as the embodiment of the credit performance. Thus much interest is shown in the definition of the credit manager's duties and in the selection and training of individuals for that position.

It is already apparent, however, that a distinction must be made between "credit management" and "credit managers," insofar as the latter term designates a specific individual or a specific position of credit management. In its larger dimensions, credit management is a function shared by many persons in a business organization, including some outside the formal organization for credit operation. Finance, sales, and general managers all share responsibility for credit decisions and for integration of the credit processes into the over-all corporate objectives and activities. They are specifically responsible for decisions concerning forms of credit service to be offered, credit terms, risk acceptability levels, sources and uses of funds invested in receivables, and for standards by which the entire credit operation is judged. These are duties not often assigned to the credit *manager*, yet they require of other executives no less competence in important aspects of credit management than do the more technical responsibilities of the credit manager himself. It is essential, therefore, that in considering qualifications for work in credit that the requirements of all levels of administration be included.

Preparation for executive responsibility for credit decisions is a process which managers undergo gradually and continually, usually more or less informally. It is no credit to business management to say that although the credit function has been included in the business it has been neglected and misunderstood by many officials outside the immediate area of credit activity. Social and economic changes which have propelled credit to the fore in business have likewise impelled better integration of this function into over-all company plans and procedures. This has required education of general managers, as well as of finance and sales managers, in basic and changing aspects of credit. This education has been achieved in different ways: through inclusion in executive development programs of broad credit subjects; through advancement into higher management positions of individuals experienced in credit management; and through the establishment within the area of credit management of higher levels of responsibility, with credit managers having accessibility to top management and responsibility for the formulation of top credit policy.

Evolution of the Credit Manager

When the responsibility of others than the credit manager for successful credit management is recognized, attention must be given primarily to the requirements of credit managers, for on the management team, if not responsible for policy determination, they are usually responsible for policy implementation. The position of credit manager is one which is the culmination of proven competence in the many credit processes. It is also one which is a point of departure for higher administrative assignments.

Like the whole field of credit, however, the role of the credit manager has evolved throughout the years. His transition has been from the position of a low-level technician to that of broad management responsibility. In both retailing and wholesaling, early credit managers were essentially bookkeepers, traditionally characterized by green eyeshades, black vests, and drawn faces. Little more than record keeping was expected or required of early credit managers, whose decisions were made on the most conservative evidences of creditworthiness, if indeed it was the prerogative of the credit manager to make the credit approval decision. Called the "credit man," he was primarily responsible for authorizing, billing, and collecting.

With the increase of credit business and the development of credit departments, responsibility of the credit man increased in interaction with other credit personnel, as well as with customers. Association among credit managers for the exchange of information and ledger experience brought about another type of contact and interaction, extending his domain outside the particular business firm. Although supervision occupied a great portion of his time, and although augmentation of sales volume was expected of him, he still was not accepted into the management team for decision making, even with regard to credit policies. If emergence from bookkeeper to supervisor and department head elevated the credit manager's status, it did not place him on a par with production and sales managers, in measure of production, creativity, compensation, or esteem. As credit man, the head of the credit function continued in a passive, circumscribed position.

A third stage in this evolution is that in which the head of the credit function became known as "credit manager." The national association of men and women responsible for this work on the wholesale level also changed its name from National Association of Credit Men to National Association of Credit Management. The implications were clear: the occupation was gaining professional status, a higher level of expectation was attained, and the potentialities of credit in the business were more fully appreciated. More than change of function was involved, however; change of image accompanied it, and management was wont to represent its credit authority as an outgoing, counseling, advisory type of service agent. The name of "credit manager" itself gradually seemed inadequate, and names such as "financial manager," "customer finance manager," "manager of credit sales," and "director of credit sales" were offered in substitution.

The new image and status of the credit manager reflected the larger role which credit really occupies in business. In addition to being clerical and supervisory, specialized management of credit is sales supporting and sales creating, policy building, and income producing. No longer simply a recording and financing function, it is part of the production process of the firm, and the talent brought to bear upon the utilization of resources for credit business must match that engaged in other departments. Scientific management, automation, and social responsibility are as applicable to credit operation as to other phases of the business.

Profile of the Credit Manager

The seasoned credit manager is an emergent phenomenon, a product of the corporate and industrial environment in which he works and develops. He becomes so through the blending of characteristics he possesses in coming to this work and of demands which are made upon him in the position. Unlike salesmen who were formerly thought to be "born and not made," credit managers develop in competence and professional status on the job, and personnel policies have taken this into consideration. Consequently, it has long been accepted that individuals with certain given personal and educational attributes qualified for this work and could be trained for it. Just what these attributes are has been determined hypothetically, more recently by scientific study.

In an attempt to compare credit managers with other executives in their business and to determine qualifications for credit management, Sears studied their management group.[1] Identifying and defining the characteristics of management, they found credit managers in their organization to have the following traits:

"Mental Ability: problem-solving ability, linguistic ability, and overall ability."

Credit managers ranked well above the average executive level in all classifications.

"Personal traits: sociability, insight, optimism, emotional stability, general activity, social leadership, dominance, self-confidence, composure, objectiveness, agreeableness, tolerance."

Credit managers appeared to be well-balanced, rating higher than the executive level.

"Motivation: analytical, economic, aesthetic, social, political, and religious characteristics."

The typical credit manager prefers to work on concrete problems; he does not take a highly analytical approach or think strictly on a theoretical level. He is not an aesthetic person. He has a clear sense of social responsibility.

[1] Frank Ross, "What Have You Done To Justify a Place on the Top Management Team in Your Store," *Credit World*, April, 1963, pp. 10, 11.

"Vocation: mechanical, computational, scientific, persuasive, artistic, literary, and musical aptitudes."

   The credit manager is a highly persuasive man. His interests lie along lines of computation and semiscientific, but not purely scientific, matters.

Such a profile is illuminating, but it is not necessarily descriptive of credit managers in manufacturing and wholesale establishments, nor of all types of retail credit managers. The Credit Research Foundation of the National Association of Credit Management has also profiled credit managers in cooperation with Edward K. Strong of Stanford University, and have gained inclusion of a career category of "credit manager" among the profiles of the Strong Vocational Interest Test.[2] It is hoped that in this way more scientific selection of credit personnel can be achieved.

   The Credit Research Foundation also sponsored a study published in 1953 detailing credit management duties and setting forth the qualifications which they required.[3] Inasmuch as it was a study of mercantile credit managers, and presumably valid today, it furnished a meaningful supplement to the study of retail credit management made by Sears.

LEVELS OF CREDIT MANAGEMENT

The study analyzed credit management as occurring on six different levels of the credit organization or department. The positions were identified as follows:

Position 1: Over-All Credit Management and Administration. This position is the highest in the credit organization and reports to the Chief Executive or Corporate Officer. Its own title is usually General Credit Manager, or Credit Manager.

   The objective of this position is to formulate credit policies and practices and to administer all credit operations in a manner that will increase distribution and sales volume, contribute to profit and customer stability, and provide for the protection and turnover of capital invested in accounts receivable.

   The responsibilities of this position include conduct of research and analysis; formulation and management of policies, proce-

---

   [2] "New Directions in Credit Management," *Credit and Financial Management*, April, 1964, p. 34.
   [3] *Analysis and Evaluation of Credit Management Functions* (New York: Credit Research Foundation, Inc., 1953), pp. 10–41, 155–243. This study is reproduced in part in *Credit Management Handbook* (2d ed.; Homewood, Ill.: Richard D. Irwin, Inc., 1965), pp. 87–96.

dures, and practices; staffing, training, and maintenance of an organization; direction of credit extension and collection; formulation and application of controls; maintenance of internal and external relationships. This position carries unlimited authority.

Position specifications for this position include both educational and experience requirements. College education or its equivalent is necessary, particularly in business administration, accounting, and credit principles. Eight to ten years of progressive and balanced experience in credit management are also requisite. Moreover, such a position demands a high degree of professional interest, loyalty, enterprise, and personal effectiveness, which characterize all high-level management positions.

Position 2: General Assistant for Over-All Credit Organization. This position is similar to that previously described, except that it applies to heads of smaller credit organizations—but not necessarily to smaller companies. It also reports to the Chief Executive, Corporate Officer, or General Manager.

The objective of this position is to assist in the formulation of policies and to interpret them in the planning, organizing, and controlling of the departmental activities.

The duties and activities correspond closely to those of position 1, but they may include more of the recurring research and analysis, deal with internal operating policies and procedures, and participate in credit operations involving exceptional cases. In maintaining internal relations, the workings of the credit department are coordinated with those of the sales, finance, legal, customer service, and personnel departments. External relationships, too, are maintained with major credit customers, credit and collection services, financial institutions, the trade, the profession, and with other creditors.

Position specifications for this position include a college education or its equivalent, with emphasis upon credit principles and practices, accounting, and financial statement analysis. Knowledge of commercial law, banking, and economics is also expected. Credit experience of from five to seven years should include credit research and analysis, management and administrative responsibility, and a successful diversity of internal and external relationships.

Position 3: Responsibility for the First Major Organizational Breakdown Below Position 2. As a designated part of the credit organization, this level may represent responsibility for a branch, affiliate, or subsidiary; a territorial division; a product division; a type of customer; etc.

Its objective is to direct the credit activities of the unit in accord with the general credit policies of the company. Its responsibility for research is confined more to industry trends and developments. Recommendations may be made for adaptation of the company policies and procedures to the areas of its responsibility. Management responsibility includes periodic review of all activities, appointment of lower-level personnel, employee training, counseling, and supervision. Its operational responsibility includes direction and control of all credits within a designated sphere of operations, general direction of collection efforts, and periodic review and analysis of operating reports submitted by subordinates. Relations are maintained with all interested internal departments and externally with customers and relevant organizations.

Specifications for this position include also a college education or its equivalent, with emphasis on subjects related to credit management, plus five to six years of experience in the full assortment of credit activities.

Position 4: Responsibility for a Subdivision of a Major Part of the Credit Organization Represented by Position 3. This is a position on the line supervisor level, with responsibility for direct supervision of line operations. Its research responsibility consists mainly of keeping up to date by reading materials provided by the credit organization. It may participate in surveys as directed. It interprets standards by which lines of credit are set. It analyzes work loads, assigns duties, counsels individuals, trains subordinates, supervises the granting of credit, devotes attention to questionable accounts, supervises collection activity, maintains internal relations through referring and conferring on problems, and maintains working relationships with external organizations necessary for the performance of its duties.

Specifications for this position include high school graduation plus two years of college training in business subjects and experience of from three to four years in credit investigation and analysis and collection of receivables.

Position 5: Staff Position Providing Special and Technical Service, Advice, and Assistance to Credit Executives and Line Supervisors.

This position reports to position 1 and has little or no responsibility for customer accounts. It is responsible for the investigation, analysis, interpretation of current and trend information covering economic, legal, and related matters; market and business conditions; and statistical analyses. It has responsibility and authority to make observations and to conduct studies on those aspects of credit operations which pertain to its responsibilities.

Specifications for this position include a college degree in business organization, with special emphasis upon economics, finance, accounting, statistics, marketing, credit, management, and research methods. Three to four years experience in credit and in research are expected.

Position 6: Line Position Concerned Primarily with Credit and Collection Transactions. It reports either to position 3 or 4. It is responsible for keeping informed on new developments through reading bulletins and publications and through contact with members of the credit associations. It has no direct management responsibility, no direct subordinates, but exercises functional supervision over credit, collection, and clerical personnel assigned to its accounts. It analyzes credit information, approves or rejects accounts, sets temporary limits on new accounts, ages accounts, assists customers in working out satisfactory programs of payment, and supervises collection correspondence.

Specifications for this position include a high school education plus courses in fundamentals of credit analysis and operation. Two or three years of experience should include familiarity with credit information sources, analysis of financial statements, preparation of credit reports, etc.

The foregoing organization structure, as is clearly evident, pertains to a large credit operation. Its descriptions relate primarily to a credit operation in a large industrial or commercial establishment. The principles involved, however, are equally applicable, with modifications, to other kinds of businesses offering credit service.

TRAINING FOR CREDIT MANAGEMENT

It is evident from the position specifications stated that one pursuing a career in credit needs certain training, not only preparatory to employment but continuing throughout his professional development. Some educational facilities, such as colleges, provide theoretical and practical courses which qualify one to work in a variety of credit organizations. Additional training is needed, however, in the policies and procedures of the specific types of credit organizations, and this is gained through more-specialized training programs. These include on-the-job training, orientation training, formal training, informal training, and outside educational activities.[4]

On-the-Job Training

One form of training found at several management levels is that provided through working in a variety of positions. Experience is the teacher; the individual learns by doing. This trial-and-error method of teaching is in some ways costly and time consuming, but it takes the place of more formally organized programs, which may be unfeasible in small operations or where a very few individuals are in the process of being trained. Moreover, such training acquaints one with practices of the past but provides little insight into their weaknesses or to the administrative policies which govern the practices.

Orientation Training

The deficiencies of on-the-job training are sometimes corrected by a program of explanations designed to inform an employee of the basic policies, procedure, persons, and relationships in the business. Thus is conveyed a better mental picture of the credit work as a whole, and the trainee is given insight into not only what is done but why it is done. To accomplish this, although company manuals are sometimes used, personal communication is preferable, for it permits an exchange of ideas rather than merely a one-way flow of thought.

Formal Training

On-the-job and orientation training are sometimes organized into extended formal training programs which include a planned course of study. Such programs are most useful where the num-

[4] For an extended discussion of training for credit management, see *Credit Management Handbook*, a publication of the National Association of Credit Management (2d ed.; Homewood, Ill.: Richard D. Irwin, Inc., 1965), pp. 98–130.

ber of credit personnel is large and where over a period of time personnel turnover is large enough to warrant regular repetition of this form of instruction. It also is useful when the credit organization embraces several management levels and when the work is functionally specialized.

Informal Training

A less formal, although not unplanned, program of training consists of a series of conferences, lectures, or discussion sessions. Topics of timely interest may be programmed. Problems facing the credit department may be analyzed. The results of individual research and experiences may be shared. Recommended readings may be assigned as preparation for the session. Tours of other credit facilities and operation may be conducted. Such efforts are most effective when they are planned and integrated into the general operation.

Supplementary Educational Opportunities

Apart from the training opportunities provided by a business organization, there are others from which its employees may benefit. They include the monthly meetings of credit groups at which speakers are presented; industry-wide conferences, clinics, workshops, or seminars, in which the facets of a subject may be explored by a variety of speakers; correspondence courses on the college level; and executive development programs.

The program for professional education sponsored by the National Institute of Credit and the Credit Research Foundation, both organizations of the National Association of Credit Management, illustrates the accomplishments of one group along this line. Working through its chapters in principal cities of the United States, the Institute cooperates with local colleges and universities in a program of correspondence courses and classes leading to two award certificates. The Associate Award program covers courses in credit and financial fundamentals, including general or business economics, introductory or basic accounting, credit and collection principles, advanced credit, and business correspondence. A minimum of 14 semester hours is required in this work. The Fellow Award program is a continuation of the Associate Award program and is designed as preparation for the more advanced phases of credit and collection activity and for managerial and supervisory responsibilities. Sixteen semester hours of work are required in the following areas: law of contracts and agency, law of business transactions or negotiable papers, public speaking, salesmanship or marketing, credit management problems, financial statement analysis, applied general or business psychology, and techniques of management. Four to 6 additional semester hours of elected courses must also be taken. Following completion of this work, the student must pass a comprehensive examination given by the National Institute of Credit in order to receive his award.

For the development of credit personnel on the executive level, the Credit Research Foundation has sponsored annually at Dartmouth College and at Stanford University two-week programs held in a three-year sequence. Attended by credit executives, this Graduate School of Credit and Financial Management provides education in subjects other than detailed credit operation, which the students are presumed already to know. Courses and seminars offered pertain to credit policy, financial management, executive development, and the like. Study projects continue throughout the year, and at the termination of the training an acceptable thesis must be presented. It leads to the granting of the Executive Award, the highest bestowed by the credit profession.

The Foundation also sponsors Credit Management Workshops at which are brought together credit and financial executives for intensive three-day work sessions, in which they exchange ideas and share experiences. The workshops, informal in nature, are held in different parts of the country and are devoted to a variety of subjects.

Still other programs are offered. The National Credit Office in New York City offers a correspondence course in credit fundamentals. The American Management Association also sponsors workshop meetings devoted to discussion of credit. These meetings are held throughout the country. Dun & Bradstreet, Inc., too, provides a correspondence course in credit and financial analysis.

DISCUSSION QUESTIONS

1. Under what circumstances may "credit management" be synonymous with "credit managers"? Under which may it not?

2. If the role of the credit manager is determined by the objectives and means for which he is responsible, how would you define or delimit the position of the credit manager?

3. Assuming his competence at his assigned work, what program would you prescribe for a credit manager to advance his progress in the firm?

4. It is sometimes said of salesmen that they are "born and not made." Would this be true of credit managers?

5. What differences of characteristics and qualifications would there be for mercantile, retail, and loan credit managers?

6. What justification is there for credit courses in a university, a business school, a trade school, a high school?

VI

THE MANAGEMENT OF CREDIT BUSINESS

20

Profiling and Appraising Creditworthiness

Appraisal of the creditworthiness of credit applicants is a focal process in the entire credit operation, for every approval of credit by lender or vendor involves the decision: Has the applicant credibility, and in what measure? So important has this consideration loomed in credit granting that it has often been regarded as the primary, if not the sole, function in credit management, and management skill has been honed to cut between acceptability and unacceptability in qualifications. Credit evaluation is of course not the whole of credit management, and so to regard it drops this business activity to a routine, semiclerical level. It is nevertheless a vital function, for in credit appraising are manifested corporate credit policies, departmental routines, and interaction patterns of credit managers with customers, subordinates, superiors, and peers.

Appraisal of creditworthiness, however, is not simply a succession of decisions of "yes" and "no" in an area of obviously favorable and unfavorable determinants. In the first place, appraisal requires initial determination of the criteria of creditworthiness for the particular business involved. A profile of creditworthiness becomes a model against which individual applicants are measured. The succession of decisions occurs only after general standards of creditworthiness have been established.

Moreover, appraisal is not unqualified; there are degrees of acceptability leading to different types of action, different debtor–creditor relationships, and to recognition that some types of creditworthiness make larger contributions to profit than others. Furthermore, the evidences and determinants of creditworthiness are not self-evident; they are often obscure and suggestive, and the very searching out of adequate evidence is part of the task of credit appraisal.

As a credit management process, risk or creditworthiness analysis consists of four activities. First, search for evidence of creditworthiness: Evidence is found in the behavior and in circumstances of the credit applicant. It is sought in observation of the applicant himself, in opinions and experiences of others relating to him, and in a variety of documents which reveal something of his creditworthiness. Second, the sorting and evaluating of evidence: The professional credit analyst develops a logical frame of reference whereby his observations become classified according to useful concepts—the "C's" of credit. He must appraise the quality of evidence. Third, interpretation of the meaning of the evidence: The meaning of evidence is dependent upon the point of view from which it is regarded. The evidence gathered must be interpreted for its relevance to credit policy. Fourth, the judging of creditworthiness: The meaning of evidence must be interpreted for the specific case at hand in terms of acceptance or rejection and with respect to amount and terms.

The significance of credit appraisal must be recognized as extending far beyond the effects it has upon the single credit transaction or the individual creditor. Laxity or severity in credit appraisal swells or shrinks the volume of business and the magnitude of debt outstanding. Concern has been expressed that standards for appraisal have been eroded by continued prosperity, "easy credit" terms, and demand for "instant credit." Losses have not supported these fears of credit deterioration, but bankruptcies, defaults, and indifference to credit obligations do show the effects of credit appraisal and credit policies.

Credit appraisal is specifically the effort made to determine *at the time of credit approval* the probability of repayment. Nonpayment results from circumstances both existing at the time credit is extended and arising thereafter. In credit appraisal an attempt is made to evaluate present circumstances and to project their type and trend into the future. Credit appraisal does not include re-evaluation of a risk after acceptance. That involves similar considerations, information, and sources, but is another process of credit management. Credit appraisal relates primarily to the initial credit evaluation.

Criteria of Creditworthiness

One of the early significant contributions to credit thought was the conception of the criteria of the credit risk. Even before 1920, credit practitioners and writers viewed creditworthiness not as a single qualification but rather as a combination of characteristics which warranted confidence in a person's promise to pay later for values received. These attributes found alliterative expression in what became known as the "C's" of credit: Character, Capacity, and Capital. To these three were added during later years three others: Collateral, Conditions, and Country.

These terms epitomize factors which contribute to creditworthiness, upon which it is based, and in terms of which it is analyzed. These are the hues of creditworthiness which credit managers examine and which credit applicants hope to exemplify. They are technical concepts. Their meaning in credit language are as follows:

Character: Those mental qualities and action of a debtor which impel him to pay his debts; that sense of obligation to fulfill the payment promise; sometimes summarized as "willingness to pay"

Capacity: Those means and faculties which provide the funds with which payment is made; resources possessed or incoming; the "ability to pay"

Capital: Those possessions or equities from which payment might be expected when Character and Capacity become lacking; that from which payment may be taken under duress, if necessary

Collateral: Special forms of Capital which are usually negotiable or readily represented by conveyance of claim or title; specific security offered for credibility of the credit promise

Conditions: Those circumstances external to and usually beyond the control of debtors which nevertheless affect their paying behavior

Country: Those conditions of foreign and international character, reflecting cultural and political circumstances, which may further qualify creditworthiness as determined by the other factors

Each of these factors has relevance to both personal and business creditworthiness.

Character. The credit character of an *individual* consists of such qualities as responsibility, integrity, honesty, punctuality, and consistency. Whatever combines to motivate a debtor to make payment constitutes his principal qualification for creditors' confidence. Character activates self-government in credit relationships and produces cooperation rather than conflict, debtor initiative rather than resistance. With character, debtors are conscientious, organized, balanced, foresighted, and sensitive to the limit of their ability to discharge debt.

Recognizing these characteristics, credit analysts seek evidence of them in the experience of credit applicants. As indicated in Table 20–1, there are numerous evidences by which credit character may be identified.

Table 20–1.   Elements of Credit Character

	Evidence	
Elements	Personal	Business
Responsibility	Past paying record	Character of principal officers
Integrity	Stability of residence	Past paying record
Honesty	Nature of employment	Bankruptcies
Punctuality	Marital status	Policy for taking discounts on purchases
Consistency	Social class	chases
	Public service	Routines for handling bills
	Opinions of others	

Past paying behavior is one of the best indications of willingness to pay. Those who consistently pay in accord with their credit terms are manifestly willing. On the other hand, default is no assurance of unwillingness, for the best intentions "gang aft a-gley." An erratic paying record may evidence carelessness, indifference, or neglect, all of which smirch credit character.

Stability of residence and employment is another evidence of credit character. The individual who continues to live or work in the same location is more likely to express acceptable credit traits than one who is itinerant or shifting. Continuity in an environment indicates a probability of conformity to the mores of some group, whether it be a neighborhood or a company, and acceptance and approbation are strong motivations in groups, whether high or low in the social scale. A group may be low-risk quality in other respects, but so long as its members maintain residential and occupational stability, this is a favorable factor, for it suggests discipline and conformity to group standards and expectations, without which responsibility for debt would be even less. Deviation from group behavior expressed in excessive itinerancy often accompanies debt irresponsibility. Therefore, persistent brevity of tenancy or employment is taken to be symptomatic of deficiency of credit character and cause for discounting creditworthiness.

The nature of one's employment also hints at his credit character inasmuch as some positions require traits developed by discipline and self-management, which are essential in creditworthiness, while others are filled by loose mental qualities, which constitute no credit recommendation. Positions of responsibility, trust, professional certification, and mental and physical skill generally engage people with qualities which make for better credit risk. This is due largely to the personal development, through training and experience, which they entail, as well as to the continuity, integration, and group references which they involve. On the other hand, positions requiring minimal performance, which might be met by anyone, embrace more of the poorer risks. Of course, there are fraudulent bank cashiers and honest bartenders, and employment indexes serve only as a starting point from which other analyses are suggested.

Credit character may vary with the marital status of an individual, but the significance of this factor changes throughout the life cycle. Unless responsibility is learned through upbringing, debt behavior of young adults in their early years of employment may be undisciplined, their wants stimulated, their earning prospects good, but their budget experience meager. At that stage, through the early years of the 20's, being married compels development of credit character if one assumes the responsibilities of marriage. In later years, the mere fact of marriage may be less significant, for the stability and responsibility which it represents earlier may have been established. At any stage, however, the breaking up of a marriage may alter debt responsibility. Separations and divorces result in repudiation of debts incurred by a spouse and in announcements of no further responsibility for another's purchases. Like other criteria, marital status is suggestive rather than definitive of credit character.

Willingness to pay is related also to the social class of debtors.

Status in the social structure is determined by age, education, family, income, religion, race, political affiliation, membership in organizations, and the like. Relations with groups affect credit character through the attitudes toward debt which they engender. Paradoxically, high social status often accompanies lower credit character than lesser positions, for indifference and carelessness often characterize the social elite and pseudosophisticates. On the other hand, in middle social classes, particularly in suburban circles, debt is somewhat of a status symbol, a symbol of conformity, and busyness with debt management produces credit character. Nationality groups afford a particularly interesting study of character, for they embody imported attitudes. Abhorrence of debt evokes in some immigrants extreme caution in the use of credit and meticulous care in meeting obligations. In others, unprecedented opportunity to use credit available in a new environment excites purchasing beyond their economic qualifications.

When credit character is equated with age groups, it is apparent that the period of one's upbringing affects his attitudes. People who have experienced the depression of the 1930's and economic adversity consider debt more seriously than those who have never experienced such a condition. But people educated with economic philosophies of deficit spending, debt accumulation, and an ever expanding economy sometimes think such theories applicable to private as well as to public economics. This accounts for some of the attitudes of "the younger generation."

What occupation may not reveal about credit character other activities of an individual sometimes do, particularly his participation in public or social service. Activity with welfare, cultural, educational, political, religious, and recreational groups, while it may not produce credit character, evidences conspicuous involvement, which is generally compatible with debt responsibility. Lack of such activity is not derogatory, but evidence of it corroborates other impressions.

Many miscellaneous and sometimes minor factors are taken into consideration in this evaluation process. One of them is the opinions of others. Reputation is not synonymous with character, and certainly not with credit character, but reputation is sometimes a clue to attitudes and behavior. Another is one's bankruptcy record. Bankruptcy is a legitimate recourse, but some individuals' attitude toward this means of debt settlement may caution other creditors against further involvement with them. Still another evidence is the order and cleanliness of one's person and household. A disorderly person often lacks consideration of others. Automobile sales financists have found that some of the most abused cars are repossessed from the worst credit risks. Accordingly, making residence calls preliminary to some credit transactions has been deemed advisable.

Numerous other evidences of credit character may be found, and it is part of creative credit management to discover the proper evidence in any particular case. Not that more and more evidence is sought; single observations, if sufficiently revealing, may suffice for reaching a decision. Such outstanding characteristics, however, are not always easily found; usually, decisions must be based upon the collective significance of a number of factors rather than upon one. Thus emerges the difference between decisive judgment based upon the quality of one criterion and indecisive judgment based upon the sum of several factors. For assistance in the latter type, which actually constitutes the majority of cases, credit managers attempt to devise formulas and scoring systems for evaluating creditworthiness.

Credit character is a criterion of creditworthiness of *businesses* also. It has the same meaning: Is the business firm responsible, willing to pay its debts and to pay them as agreed?

When the business is dominated by one or a few individuals, their credit character may determine the credit character of the business, and semipersonal analyses may be made. In larger organizations, personal characteristics become subordinate to policies and systems of behavior which determine the prospects of payment. Inasmuch as business firms are dependent upon lines of mercantile and bank credit, maintenance of credit standing is of prime importance. The taking of cash discounts is important. Therefore, sheer carelessness or negligence is inconceivable, and lack of creditworthiness is more attributable to deficiencies and inefficiencies and to the more extreme attitudes leading to nonpayment. Evidence of likely willingness to pay may be found in the established paying behavior, in bankruptcy and fire records, and in the financial policies of the company. It is found, too, in the business systems and routines of the debtor.

Capacity. In contrast to credit character, credit capacity relates to the ability of a debtor to pay. It is a quality of creditworthiness in both personal and business subjects.

As ability to buy and to pay in a continuing existence is dependent primarily upon continually incoming purchasing power, earnings and the ability to sustain and increase them are of major importance in credit capacity. Availability of income for additional debt, however, depends also upon two other factors: short-run availability modified by existing debt, by existing claims upon income; long-run availability conditioned by the spending pattern of the debtor.

In *personal* creditworthiness, credit capacity is equated almost entirely with earnings, i.e., income and other cash receipts, for few people resort to permanent savings for consumption except under unusual circumstances of unemployment, disability, emergency, or retirement. On the other hand, short-term savings are a fund which must be considered as part of one's capacity, for flows of income and outgo are not always synchronized, and reservoirs of savings are evidence of capacity for certain types of purchases and debt.

Information concerning earnings alone, however, is insufficient basis for determining personal credit capacity. Factors underlying earnings must be considered. Earnings are a reflection of one's ability and capacity to earn, and this is affected by a number of mental and physical circumstances, as shown in Table 20–2: the type of employment in which one is engaged, occupational position and opportunity for advancement, skills at the command of the subject, extent and type of education, physical stature and mental and physical health, industriousness, continuity of employment, and attitudes toward work. Although some credit analysts content themselves with a knowledge of income, more careful analysis, especially of marginal risks, may require consideration of these more basic conditions.

Debt-paying power of *business* risks is derived from their sales, gross profit, or net profit. All payments are made from receipts from sales, and therefore knowledge of volume and trends of sales is essential. Disbursement of income, however, is related to different components of sales, particularly the portions representing cost of goods sold and gross margin. Therefore, information concerning profits is as essential as that concerning total income.

Table 20–2.   Elements of Credit Capacity

Elements	Evidence Personal	Evidence Business
Income	Salary and other in-	Sales volume
Earning capacity	come	Profit margin
Existing debt	Type of employment	Nature and size of business
Spending pattern	Education and skills	Location
	Health and vitality	Franchises and lines carried
	Stability of employ- ment	Modernity and appearance of es- tablishment
	Attitudes toward work	Management and technical com-
	Indebtedness	petence
	Marital status and size	Business interruptions
	of family	Short- and long-term indebtedness
	Level of living	Operating expenses
	Reference groups	

As in personal situations, business income is dependent upon many factors: the nature, size, and age of the business; the distributive level of its operation; the importance of research and development in the industry; competition; types of customers; and stability of the industry. Additional internal evidences of credit capacity are the location, lines, appearance, services, and personnel of the business.

Income is not the sole criterion of credit capacity, however, either for the individual or for the business risk. Ability to pay out of income is modified by existing claims against that income. Persons with instalment debt may have consigned future disposable income and have no creditworthiness left. Others with liens, mortgages, or contingent liabilities also may lack capacity for additional obligations, even though their income is impressive. Similarly, business capacity suggested by sales may be reduced by short- and long-term debt—by tax claims, liens, accounts and notes payable, bonds, and payment claims on invested capital.

Credit capacity is also influenced by established spending patterns of individuals and businesses. Regardless of debt, individuals whose expenditure patterns are set by large-family demands, by conspicuous emulation of others, or by traditions may be less qualified for credit than others with identical incomes but with small families, modest tastes, and less prescribed consumption practices. The specific nature of the spending pattern and its significance must be interpreted in each case. In businesses, similar influences exist. High costs for materials, labor, services, or capital reduce capacity for other or additional commitments. Other evidences of this limitation are found in the extent of automation, the labor contracts of a company, the composition of its capital structure, tax rates, and costs of services.

Capital. Capital, as viewed in the appraisal of creditworthiness, represents a residual or cushion of equities available for the payment of a debt if other means of payment fail. In extreme situations, unpaid creditors may seize the assets of debtors. They normally do not expect to; they do not want to. Profit lies in the making of completed sales, not in replevin or attachment. Nevertheless, it is to such equities that creditors look on some occasions. (See Table 20–3.)

Table 20–3. Elements of Credit Capital

	Evidence	
Elements	Personal	Business
Assets	Tangle and intangible assets	Tangible and intangible property
Equity	Mortgages and liens	Equity interests
	Legal exemptions	Preferred creditors
		Net worth
		Liquidation values
		Costs of seizure

The average *personal* debtor has little capital. What he possesses falls in one of three categories: the item bought; chattels, including personal property and money; and equity in real estate. Individuals do not as a rule prepare formal statements of their assets or equities. They may be unable to estimate the value of certain things which they possess. Furthermore, a creditor may be estopped from claiming any of their assets by the law of limitations. To avoid having to make recourse to personal capital, an increasing number of creditors are turning to credit life insurance as a means of settling a debt, rather than looking to settlement by seizure.

Almost without exception, *businesses* use physical assets in their operation. Their equity in these assets constitutes the capital in which a creditor is interested in credit risk analysis. Normally, such equity is shown in the net worth section of a balance sheet. There are two weaknesses, however, in regarding that as a meaningful evidence of capital. First, if seizure is contemplated, one must consider the value of the assets in liquidation. Unless the book value is understated, it is unlikely that in a sale the assets would have the value shown. Second, if total liquidation is not to be effected but only seizure of particular pieces of property, it must be determined whether the assets are such that they could be divided, or that they are in a condition to be taken as in the right of replevin.

Collateral. Creditworthiness is sometimes adjudged in terms of collateral, which is a special form of asset pledged for security in a credit transaction. Although it is a form of capital, it differs from credit capital in that the latter is an ultimate recourse; collateral is simply a type of security for credit.

Lenders and sales financists commonly look to collateral in their transactions, taking securities, negotiable instruments, postdated checks, and chattel and real estate mortgages as pledges.

Conditions. The fifth of the credit "C's" is conditions. However competent and creditworthy a subject may be, he operates in a business and social environment not entirely of his making. He moves with the currents of general conditions, at times to his advantage, sometimes to his adversity. The credit manager, therefore, must acquaint himself with the conditions surrounding his subjects. These vary. Increasingly it appears that cyclical patterns differ among industries. Instead of fluctuating in unison, troughs and peaks are staggered, with the over-all effect of moderate, general cyclical fluctuations. The pattern of one industry is not necessarily the pattern of another. Particular environments must be understood. Unionization and strikes differ among industries; resources and markets tend toward depletion; the rise of competition, new products, and diversification leave debtors stranded high and dry.

Country. With the growing importance of international trade, credit appraisal must include analysis of the international and foreign cultural circumstances affecting creditworthiness. These collectively are designated by the term "country."

Apart from the usual qualifications for credit, international private credit transactions involve other risks stemming from the social and political character of the country. Different societies have different concepts of debt responsibility, different legal and judicial systems, different commercial instruments and business practices. Moreover, national governments pursuing supra-commercial interests alter exchange rates, cancel import privileges, expropriate inventories and properties, or block the conversion of funds into foreign currencies. Furthermore, international credit transactions, by reason of the distance, time, and border crossing involved, pose problems of price terms, insurance claims, and customs duties for credit managers which have no parallel in domestic business. Many of these circumstances are covered in provisions of export credit insurance, but the credit analyst who is informed of them is best able to appraise the specific and general qualifications of his risks.

Relative Factor Importance.   In the analysis of creditworthiness, qualitative factors are considered, but efforts are continually being made to refine analysis along quantitative lines through assignment of weights and values to qualities. Progress in this direction is being made, but such research is relatively new. With developments in quantification, automation, and computerization, new approaches to credit analysis are likely to be taken. Meanwhile, conclusions as to the relative importance of factors in creditworthiness continue to be reached by logical means.

By process of elimination, it can be said that capital is the least important of the three basic qualifications. This conclusion is based upon the fact that in a business world teeming with credit transactions, creditors do not expect to obtain payment through attachment, replevin, or liquidation of the debtor's assets. Continuity of relationship is expected, with whatever additional assurance or security capital and collateral can provide.

Between character and capacity, the latter is more important if the former can be taken for granted, if it can be assumed that "most people are honest." Most appraisals are made on this basis. On the other hand, if nothing is taken for granted, character is of prime importance, for persons with integrity are less likely to get into ill-advised debt, or, being in debt, they make conscientious efforts to extricate themselves. Ultimate collection from such a person is more assured than from one possessing capacity but who lacks the motivation to pay.

An analyst must be aware of his own presuppositions and vary his emphases to meet each individual case. Even then, conclusions concerning creditworthiness differ. Unequal competence among analysts produces different appraisals. This is the result of differing abilities to perceive and synthesize the evidence at hand. Differences in evidence observed produces the same effect. Lacking complete evidence, or having fragmentary evidence different from another analyst, one may imagine creditworthiness where it does not actually exist. Another cause of different interpretations is the risk policy of the analyst. If acceptance standards are low, risks with marginal character or capacity may be accepted; if high, they are not. Finally, differences in credit analysis are attributable to calculated risk policies themselves, whereby analyses are not carried beyond a point because of the costs, time, and effort which would be required in doing so.

Occupational Groups and Credit Risk

It is evident from the aforestated principles that there is a range of creditworthiness and that certain types of risks are better than others. The validity of this is demonstrated for both personal and business credit risks by several studies made over a long period which ranked occupational groups on the basis of delinquencies and credit appraisals.[1]

In studies of personal risks, as shown in Table 20–4, the best risks are generally found in the executive and professional groups, including business executives, accountants and auditors, retail store managers, chain store managers, physicians, surgeons, dentists, engineers, and military officers. The second most preferable group includes people in operational positions, including clerks, skilled factory workers, retail salespeople, nurses, and travelling salesmen. Also in this group are school teachers, public officials, clergymen, lawyers, and judges. A third group includes tradesmen and craftsmen, such as carpenters, guards, watchmen, truck and bus drivers, printers, machinists, and mechanics. A fourth group, lowest in the range of credit ratings, consists of unskilled workers, laborers, section hands, domestic servants, barbers, musicians, and farm laborers.

In explaining credit standing as equated with defaults reported by credit bureaus and stores, Hancock said

Stability of income is a more tangible characteristic of the better rated occupations. . . . A large income does not seem to indicate general credit

---

[1] Dwight A. Stewart, *Factors Affecting Credit Ratings of Consumers in Franklin County, Ohio,* Research Monograph No. 30 (Columbus, Ohio: The Ohio State University, Bureau of Business Research, 1942); P. D. Converse, "The Occupational Credit Pattern," *Opinion and Comment,* August 12, 1941, pp. 1–9; Robert S. Hancock, "Occupation and Credit Risk," *The Credit World,* April, 1953, pp. 4 ff.

Table 20-4. Relative Standings of Various Occupational Groups— 1936, 1941, and 1951

Occupation	1951	1941	1936
Business executives	1	1	7
Accountants and auditors	2	—	6
Retail managers (independent)	3	7	—
Chain store managers	4	3	—
Physicians, surgeons, dentists	5	12 and 14	5
Engineers (chemical, civil, etc.)	6	9	10
General farmers (owners)	7	10	—
Army and navy officers	8	2	8
Office workers (clerks and stenographers)	9	5	4
College professors and instructors	10	—	1
Railroad clerks	11	—	—
Skilled factory workers	12	4	—
Post office employees	13	15	17
Railroad workers (trainmen)	14	6	—
Hotel and restaurant managers	15	—	—
Other schoolteachers	16	11	3
Clergymen	17	18	28
Nurses	18	16	15
Public officials	19	—	22
Retail sales people	20	13	19
Printers	21	—	31
Lawyers and judges	22	21	2
Traveling salesmen	23	17	39
Plumbers	24	24	28
Policemen and firemen	25	20	27
Carpenters	26	25	—
Guards and watchmen	27	—	32
General farmers (tenants)	28	28	—
Truck and bus drivers	29	—	64
Soldiers and sailors (enlisted)	30	35	—
Unskilled factory workers	31	26	60
Janitors	32	27	62
Section hands	33	22	—
Plasterers	34	34	—
Barbers	35	33	58
Coal miners	36	31	—
Common laborers	37	29	—
Bartenders	38	36	—
Musicians	39	39	—
Domestic servants	40	30	—
Painters	41	37	—
Farm laborers	42	38	—

SOURCE: 1951 and 1941—Robert S. Hancock, "Occupation and Credit Risk," *The Credit World*, April, 1953, p. 6; 1936—Dwight A. Stewart, *Factors Affecting Credit Ratings of Consumers in Franklin County, Ohio* (Columbus, Ohio: Bureau of Business Research, The Ohio State University, Research Monograph No. 30), 1942, pp. 24, 25.

acceptability when stability of incomes of army and navy officers, office workers, schoolteachers, post office employees, and so on are compared with the equivalent but irregular incomes of lawyers, traveling salesmen, general farmers, plasterers, coal miners, musicians, and similar groups.[2]

Credit standing of occupational groups is a function of both amount and regularity of income; therefore, changes in economic conditions alter the comparative position of different groups. This is evident in the three studies cited. At different times there is consistency in the ranking of some categories but changes in others. The credit position of educators was comparatively better when general incomes were low, because then the incomes of educators were relatively high and fairly stable. Business executives occupied the foremost positions in all but the depression years. Unionized groups also occupied improved positions in the later years.

Efforts have also been made to classify business firms according to risk. This has been done in connection with the setting of credit insurance rates. Some years ago, risk was equated with the producer of merchandise sold.[3] In terms of bad-debt records, the following grouping was made of industries according to the Standard Industrial Classification, ranging from the supposedly least risky, in Group I, to the most risky, in Group V.

I. Advertising, steel, carpet manufacturers, coal mines, glass manufacturers, lumber, barrels, coffee, foundry products, industrial machinery and woven labels.

II. Cotton yarn, candy and confectionery, cereals, manufacturers of girdles, printing, leather tanners, hardware and enamelware.

III. Baby carriages, linoleum jobbers, bedding, concrete products, fertilizers, furniture, scrap iron, scales and balances, trunks and bags, store and office fixtures and office furniture.

IV. Boys' clothing, leaf tobacco, clocks, knit goods, millinery, radio and television supplies, work clothing, notions and silk.

V. Beer, women's shoes, costume jewelry, furs, gold, silver and platinum refiners, precious metals, straw hats and junk.

Since 1959, the American Credit Indemnity Company has classified risk on the basis of the type of account to which merchandise is *sold*, rather than on the basis of the type of *producer* of the merchandise. As customers, retailers constitute greater risk than

[2] Hancock, *op. cit.*, p. 5.
[3] Joseph T. Trapp, *Credit Insurance a Factor in Bank Lending* (Baltimore: American Credit Indemnity Company of New York, 1953), p. 20.

do manufacturers and wholesalers. Two classes of risks, therefore, are identified: Class 1, when the sales volume is 50 per cent or more to debtors who are manufacturers or wholesalers; Class 2, when more than 50 per cent of the sales volume is to debtors who are retailers. Mail order houses, department stores, and chain stores, possessing capital of $125,000 or more are regarded as wholesalers.

Credit Scoring Systems

Personal judgment in credit appraisal has always been regarded as indispensable. Yet because of the inevitable similarity of many applications, routine classification can often replace much of the personal evaluative work. Such saving of effort has become increasingly important, as the number of applications has increased and as mechanical and electronic means of recording and analyzing data have been devised. Consequently, much attention has been given to development of systems for the scoring of applicants and the evaluation of their creditworthiness.

These systems consist of procedures which (1) select principal criteria of creditworthiness, (2) convert them into numerical quantities and standards, and (3) compare individual scores with those standards. Computation of standards requires determination of statistical evidence of significance in the measurable difference between acceptable and unacceptable creditworthiness, and determination of statistical significance in the difference between specific scores and standard measures.

Although analysis of creditworthiness is logically made along lines heretofore explained, credit analysts from their experience are inclined to select specific criteria which they deem most important. Even among experts the number selected differs, but one list of credit factors, in relative order of importance, proposed by a management advisory firm was as follows:

1. Type of neighborhood
2. Time at address
3. Occupation
4. Time at job
5. Telephone
6. Bank account
7. Marital status
8. Number of dependents
9. Amount of income
10. Living status

11. Source of additional income
12. Department store reference
13. Company region
14. Amount of additional income
15. Finance company reference
16. Time at previous job
17. Number of rooms
18. Jeweler reference
19. Type of merchandise
20. Total indebtedness
21. Down payment
22. Type of store
23. Time at previous address
24. Length of terms
25. Furniture store reference
26. Automobile
27. Total number of references
28. Other business references

In terms of any list of criteria, credit applicants can be arrayed from those best on all points to those worst on all points. Between such extremes fall others who combine an assortment of good and bad qualities. To array all such cases requires assignment of values and/or weights to the qualitative factors so that numerical expressions may be found. Each criterion may be given a uniform value which is added if the quality represented is evidenced. Hypothetically, a perfect score by the above-listed points would total 28. To accentuate value differences on certain points, a range of values for each quality may be assigned. For example, values on time at address and marital status might be as follows:

Time at address		*Marital status*	
0	0–6 months	1	Single male
1	7 months to 1 year	3	Single female
2	1–2 years	4	Married
4	2–5 years	0	Divorced or separated
6	5 years or more	2	Widow

Still another means of scaling values and accentuating the significance of difference is to assign both values and weights. A formula may thus be developed in the form of a mathematical equation as follows: [4]

---

[4] Joel Zelnich, "Theoretical Process for Automating a Credit Evaluation System," *The Credit World*, September, 1964, p. 9.

Score = (Weight of Characteristic 1) × (Value of Characteristic 1)
+ (Weight of Characteristic 2) × (Value of Characteristic 2)
+ (Weight of Characteristic n) × (Value of Characteristic n)

Assume, for example, that the values and weights of three characteristics are:

	Value	Weight
Number of dependents	4	2.00
Assets (dollars)	200	.03
Monthly income (dollars)	500	.04

The score for such a risk would be:

$$(2) \times (4) + (200) \times (.03) \text{ * } (500) \times (.04) = 34$$

Similar scores could be computed for a sample array of risks ranging from good to bad. By application of statistical tests of significance of difference, the meaning or import of spread in the scores can be determined.

From such analyses a variety of studies may be made, but a common objective is to determine the probability of payment in terms of a rating score. In each score category may fall both good and bad accounts, giving evidence that the scored factors do not fully account for creditworthiness or lack thereof, and do not take into consideration circumstances which changed *after* the risk is initially appraised and rated. If the criteria and scoring are sound, high-score categories should have a higher percentage of good risks and a small percentage of bad risks. The results of one such study made by a finance company are as follows: [5]

Credit score	No. bad	No. good	Total	Probability of going bad	
200–300 pts.	5	1	6	83%	(5/6)
301–400	10	10	20	50	(10/20)
401–500	13	25	38	34	(13/38)
501–600	24	115	139	17	(24/139)
601–700	19	140	159	12	(19/159)
701–800	19	260	279	7	(19/279)
801–900	6	200	206	3	(6/206)
Over 900	4	240	244	2	(4/244)

[5] Richard J. Zaegel, "A Point Rating System for Evaluating Customers," *The Credit World*, October, 1963, p. 11.

Against such scales and such information, it is hoped that each subsequently scored application can be appraised more easily and more surely. While such scoring may be done manually, the information may also be computerized, so that subsequent additional information will yield immediate revision of credit rating.

The uses of credit scoring systems recognized by one student of the subject [6] are as follows:

1. A minimum score limit can be set, below which applicants are either rejected or referred to a higher level of management for approval.
2. Score limits may be set above which credit interviewers of lesser experience and authority can extend a temporary line of credit.
3. Upper limits may be set above which credit is automatically approved without further analysis or investigation.
4. The expiration date of credit identification cards can be made sooner for customers having lower scores.
5. Scores may be used to determine the necessary amount of credit bureau information to purchase, or further investigation to be carried on.
6. Scoring systems may be used in training new credit evaluators.
7. Cut-off points on the score scale can be changed by management to meet current needs.
8. Score systems can be used to facilitate credit approving in branch operations.

DISCUSSION QUESTIONS

1. Distinguish between the criteria of creditworthiness, the elements of creditworthiness, evidence of creditworthiness, and sources of such evidence.
2. Define the criteria of creditworthiness in your own words, making certain that when taken together they furnish complete assurance of credibility.
3. Under what circumstances is there a direct or an inverse relationship between social implications of character and credit character?
4. Interpret the formative influences upon character shown in the analysis of social attitudes and circumstances made in Chapter 2.
5. Is the technical competence of a credit manager to be judged more by his understanding of the elements of creditworthiness, by his

[6] James H. Myers, "Numerical Scoring Systems for Retail Credit Evaluation," *The Credit World*, April, 1963, pp. 5–8.

ability to specify and interpret evidence of creditworthiness, or his familiarity with sources of this evidence?

6. What relationship is there between elements of country as a criterion of creditworthiness and the types and extent of credit insurance provided by the Export-Import Bank?

7. Do the rankings shown in Table 32 confirm or destroy popular stereotypes of good credit risks, or bad? Are such stereotypes a function of the times?

8. What contribution does the computer make to credit risk analysis and credit management?

9. Explain the statistical measure of significance of difference, as it applies to analysis of credit risks.

21

Credit Ratings and Reports

Evidence of creditworthiness upon which approval is based is obtained from numerous sources. Some come directly from applicants through applications and interviews. Others come from a variety of sources which supply information about the applicants. Some of those are specialized credit information agencies which make a business of such reporting service. Others are possessed of credit information by reason of their other business functions but nevertheless furnish valuable evidence for justification of creditors' confidence in a risk. This chapter is concerned with the ratings and reports supplied by credit specialists; other types of information are discussed subsequently.

CREDIT RATINGS

Ratings are symbolic references to evidence of creditworthiness, capsulations of a broader array of information usually included in credit reports, along with which, when ratings are prepared, they are usually available. In preparation, ratings follow the compilation of reports, for ratings condense their information. In use, reference is usually made to ratings prior to study of reports, for their concise evidence may either support a decision or suggest the need for additional evidence. When available, ratings are presented to subscribers in book form, in which ratings for all subjects covered are listed. They are available for both business and personal credit subjects; for the former primarily through the credit reference service of Dun & Bradstreet, Inc., and for the latter through a small number of organizations supplying rating information on a local scale.

Business Credit Ratings and Reference Information

In the field of business reference and rating information, the Dun & Bradstreet Reference Book is a model by which this type of service may be understood. Claimed to be the largest regularly published book in the world, it contains listings of nearly 3,000,000 business concerns in the United States and Canada. Published six times a year, it lists manufacturers, wholesalers, retailers, and other types of businesses buying regularly on credit terms, and it reflects business changes reported in the previous 60 days. In addition to the complete book (the United States and Canada edition), each revision is also available in an edition covering the United States alone and in a number of sectional editions, each including a combination of several states. The January and July revisions are also published as State Sales Guides— separate books for each of the fifty States, the nine Canadian Provinces, and several of the largest cities in the United States.

The organization of the Reference Book is alphabetical, by states, cities, and subjects rated. As background information for credit approval, a number of facts of an environmental nature are supplied. As shown in Fig. 21–1, from the Reference Book one may learn names of banks in the locality of the subject, the corporate status of his business, its headquarters and branch locations, the town population, county name, and code number of the Dun & Bradstreet reporting office. Such information assists in contacting banks with whom the subject is likely to have an established line of credit, in judging his market and his competition, in appraising the extent of his operations.

Specific information concerning each listed subject is shown on the line devoted to the name. Each type of information is intended to facilitate credit appraisal of the subject and to assist study and research of the Reference Book for other sales and credit purposes.

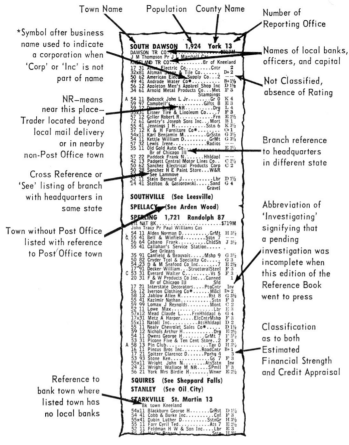

All names used in this illustration are fictitious

Fig. 21–1. Dun & Bradstreet Reference Book symbols and what they mean.

A typical line of the Reference Book is as follows:

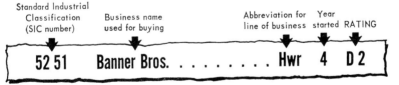

The Standard Industrial Classification Code Number, adopted in the 1957 SIC Manual, classifies subjects and makes for easy identification of types of businesses, compilation of mailing lists, and comparison of business subjects. The Code is divided into nine principal sections:

	First two digits
Agriculture, forestry, and fisheries	01–09
Mining	10–14
Contract construction	15–17
Manufacturing industries	19–39
Transportations, communications, and other public utilities	41–49
Wholesale trade	50–51
Retail trade	52–59
Finance and real estate	60–65
Services	70–89

By the second two digits further refinement of the industrial classification is shown, as is illustrated by the following partial list:

CONSTRUCTION

15 11 GENERAL BUILDING CONTRACTORS

16 11 HIGHWAY AND STREET CONSTRUCTION (except Elevated Highways)

16 21 HEAVY CONSTRUCTION (except Highway and Street Construction)

WHOLESALE

50 32 DRY GOODS (general line)
50 33 PIECE GOODS
50 34 NOTIONS AND OTHER DRY GOODS
50 39 FOOTWEAR
50 42 GROCERIES (general line)
50 44 COFFEE, TEA, AND SPICES
50 45 CONFECTIONERY
50 47 MEATS AND PROVISIONS
50 55 FRESH FRUITS AND VEGETABLES

RETAIL

53 11 DEPARTMENT STORES
53 21 MAIL-ORDER HOUSES,

GENERAL MERCHANDISE

53 31 VARIETY STORES
53 92 DRY GOODS AND GENERAL MERCHANDISE STORES
53 93 GENERAL STORES
54 12 GROCERY STORES, WITHOUT FRESH MEAT
54 13 GROCERY STORES, WITH FRESH MEAT
54 22 MEAT MARKETS
54 23 FISH (Sea Food) MARKETS
54 41 CANDY, NUT, AND CONFECTIONERY STORES

SERVICES

70 11 YEAR-ROUND HOTELS
70 12 SEASONAL HOTELS
72 11 POWER LAUNDRIES WITH OR WITHOUT CLEANING AND DYEING FACILITIES
72 13 LINEN SUPPLY WITH OR WITHOUT LAUNDRY FACILITIES
72 21 CLEANING AND DYEING PLANTS (except Rug Cleaning)

Following the industrial classification, the name of the business which is used in its buying is given. This is customarily referred to as the "trade style" of the company.

Next is provided an abbreviation of the line of business of the company listed. The following used for manufacturers illustrates the longer list which appears in the front of the Reference Book:

Acc	Accessories	Fert	Fertilizer
Advg	Advertising		
Agri	Agriculture(al)	Gds	Goods
Appl(s)	Appliance(s)	Groc	Groceries
Bak(s)	Bakery(ies)	Hdwre	Hardware
Btlr	Bottler(s)		
Botlg	Bottling	Kntwr	Knitwear
Bldr(s)	Builder(s)		
Cast	Casting(s)	Mgt	Management
Chem(s)	Chemical(s)	Mkt	Marketing
Clng	Cleaning	Ppr	Paper
Clo	Clothing	Plbg	Plumbing
Conf	Confectionery	Prod	Produce
Constr	Construction		
Contr	Contractor	Spptgds	Sporting Goods
Distr	Distributor(s)	Tv	Television
		Undwr	Underwear
Elec	Electric		
Eng	Engine	Whl	Wholesale(rs)

Next in the line of symbols may be shown a number, just left of the rating, indicating the year the business started or the year in which it came under present control. Such information is shown for starts or changes occurring during the past ten years. For example, the number "4" indicates 1964. As creditworthiness is affected by changes of administration, as well as by the newness of a business, this information has definite significance.

To the left of the Standard Industrial Classification number may also be one of two letters: "A" or "C." "A" indicates that the name has been added to the Reference Book in this edition; it did not appear in the preceding edition 60 days before. Knowledge of additions can be used in directing sales—and credit sales—effort. "C" indicates a change in the rating of the business, a change which has taken place during the past 60 days. As this change may be either upward or downward, credit managers find this a useful guide to changes in creditworthiness which otherwise might not come to their attention promptly. Inasmuch as both the "A" and the "C" designations appear in only one issue of the Reference Book, managers who purchase less than the six editions a year may miss some of this information in the editions which they do not receive.

| A 52 41 | | C 52 51 |

All of these types of information are useful, but the main reason for the Reference Book is the publications of ratings. In the rating symbols are conveyed the succinct, essential information concerning creditworthiness, as reflected in financial condition, paying habit, and other credit qualifications of the subject. By a scalar key to ratings, graduation of credit risk is expressed, as interpreted by the agency providing the ratings. Some agency ratings consist of two symbols, some of three, but apart from this difference they have similar meaning and use.

Ratings prepared by Dun & Bradstreet, Inc., contain two symbols: a letter and a number (see Fig. 21–2). The letter represents "estimated financial strength"; the number, "composite credit appraisal." By financial strength is meant the net worth or capital of the subject, and it is presented in 16 categories ranging from under $1,000 to over $1,000,000. It has long been a presumption of the agency that creditworthiness is related to size of the subject company.

The "composite credit appraisal" is represented by numerical symbols classified as "High," "Good," "Fair," and "Limited." The meaning of these terms is as follows:

High: Payment by discounting; prospects unquestionable
Good: Generally prompt payment; prospects favorable
Fair: Payment sometimes slow; prospects satisfactory if longer collections are acceptable
Limited: Payment slow; outlook questionable; risk appreciable

In arriving at such a credit appraisal for a subject, agency analysts take into consideration a number of factors which suggest the future likelihood of the subject's meeting his credit obligations. Paying habit as reflected in past performance is important, but also included are such factors as adequacy and liquidity of working capital, competitive strength, management competence,

KEY TO RATINGS

ESTIMATED FINANCIAL STRENGTH			COMPOSITE CREDIT APPRAISAL			
			HIGH	GOOD	FAIR	LIMITED
AA	Over	$1,000,000	A1	1	1½	2
A+	Over	750,000	A1	1	1½	2
A	500,000	to 750,000	A1	1	1½	2
B+	300,000	to 500,000	1	1½	2	2½
B	200,000	to 300,000	1	1½	2	2½
C+	125,000	to 200,000	1	1½	2	2½
C	75,000	to 125,000	1½	2	2½	3
D+	50,000	to 75,000	1½	2	2½	3
D	35,000	to 50.000	1½	2	2½	3
E	20,000	to 35.000	2	2½	3	3½
F	10,000	to 20,000	2½	3	3½	4
G	5,000	to 10,000	3	3½	4	4½
H	3,000	to 5,000	3	3½	4	4½
J	2,000	to 3,000	3	3½	4	4½
K	1,000	to 2,000	3	3½	4	4½
L	Up to	1,000	3½	4	4½	5

CLASSIFICATION AS TO BOTH
ESTIMATED FINANCIAL STRENGTH AND CREDIT APPRAISAL

FINANCIAL STRENGTH BRACKET

EXPLANATION

1	$125,000 to	$1,000,000 and Over
2	20,000	to 125,000
3	2,000	to 20,000
4	Up to	2,000

When only the numeral (1, 2, 3, or 4) appears, it is an indication that the estimated financial strength, while not definitely classified, is presumed to be within the range of the ($) figures in the corresponding bracket and that a condition is believed to exist which warrants credit in keeping with that assumption.

NOT CLASSIFIED OR ABSENCE OF RATING

The absence of a rating, expressed by the dash (—), or by two hyphens (- -), is not to be construed as unfavorable but signifies circumstances difficult to classify within condensed rating symbols and should suggest to the subscriber the advisability of obtaining additional information.

SEE REFERENCE BOOK FOR EXPLANATION OF ABSENCE OF A LISTING AND ADDITIONAL SYMBOLS USED IN REFERENCE BOOK

Dun & Bradstreet, Inc.
Offices in Principal Cities of the United States

Fig. 21–2. Dun & Bradstreet key to ratings.

local conditions, trends of the business, etc. Together these provide a "composite credit appraisal."

Additional information also is conveyed by several other symbols designating both financial strength and credit appraisal but not representing them separately. When numerals only ("1," "2," "3," or "4") appear, a presumed size of capital is stated and a belief that conditions exist which "warrant credit in keeping with that assumption." When less evidence is possessed by the agency, or when circumstances are difficult to classify, an absence of rating is expressed by the dash (−). This is not a sign of unfavorable circumstances. Omission of rating is also indicated by two stars (**), which are a reminder to look to another designated town or other name for the rating, inasmuch as the name starred is a branch or a secondary name of the subject. Still another symbol is (inv), which signifies that a pending investigation was incomplete when the Reference Book went to press. In each of these circumstances, use of information in the report is recommended.

A contrasting set of rating symbols is provided in the *Lyon Red Book*, published by the Lyon Furniture Mercantile Agency. It differs visibly in that it presents three symbols, instead of two as in the Dun & Bradstreet rating. The contents of the symbolization, however, are essentially the same, inasmuch as by the three are shown estimated financial worth, pay ratings based upon a majority of reports, and special credit conditions based on general information. No effort is made to synthesize factors into a composite rating, but by these various symbols are shown much that is condensed into the composite appraisal, as well as shown in other symbols in the Dun & Bradstreet Reference Book. Although the Red Book provides for three symbols, three are seldom used, leaving usually information concerning only capital and paying habit. The complete Lyon credit key is shown in Fig. 21–3.

The use of credit ratings is not confined to mercantile credit. Although there are not many agencies preparing rating or reference books in consumer credit, there are a few. Among them are The Credit Bureau of Lincoln, Nebraska, which has published the *Blue Book* of credit ratings since 1889; the Merchants Retail Credit Association of Dallas, Texas, which has published the *Red Book* of ratings since 1897; and the Credit Bureau of Minneapolis, which has published its *Yellow Book* credit guide since

Form 93

LYON RED BOOK — CREDIT KEY

CAPITAL RATINGS Estimated Financial Worth	PAY RATINGS Based on suppliers' reports
A...............$1,000,000 or over B .... 500,000 to $1,000,000 C .... 300,000 to 500,000 D .... 200,000 to 300,000 E .... 100,000 to 200,000 G .... 75,000 to 100,000 H .... 50,000 to 75,000 J .... 40,000 to 50,000 K .... 30,000 to 40,000 L .... 20,000 to 30,000 M .... 15,000 to 20,000 N .... 10,000 to 15,000 O .... 7,000 to 10,000 Q .... 5,000 to 7,000 R .... 3,000 to 5,000 S .... 2,000 to 3,000 T .... 1,000 to 2,000 U .... 500 to 1,000 V .... 100 to 500 Z - No financial basis for credit reported.	1—Discount. 2—Prompt. 3—Medium. 4—Variable, prompt to slow. 5—Slow. 6—Very slow. 7—C. O. D. or C. B. D. 8—Pay rating not established, but information favorable. 9—Claims to buy always for cash.

INDEFINITE RATINGS

F —Estimated financial responsibility not definitely determined, presumed high.

P —Estimated financial responsibility not definitely determined, presumed moderate.

W—Estimated financial responsibility not definitely determined, presumed small.

Y —Estimated financial responsibility not definitely determined, presumed very limited.

The omission of a rating is not unfavorable, but indicates that sufficient information is not at hand on which to base rating.

SPECIAL CONDITIONS

12—Business recently commenced.
13—Inquire for report.|
21—Buys small, usually pays cash.
23—Sells on commission.
24—Name listed for convenience only.
29—Rating undetermined.
31—Financial statement declined, or repeatedly requested and not received.

SYMBOL INTERPRETATION

● or 12 — Business recently commenced.
✦ or 116—New statement recently received.
▲—Indicates information of unusual importance.
⊖—Sells on installment plan.
(?)—Sells from residence, office or catalogue.

CREDIT GRANTORS—NOTE

No system of ratings can ALWAYS convey an accurate summarization of existing conditions. Book ratings reflect conditions believed to exist when assigned, and are based upon information obtained from financial statements, from the trade, special reporters, correspondents, financial institutions and other sources deemed reliable, but the correctness thereof is in no way guaranteed.

Conditions are constantly changing, and changes as made are shown in the "LYON Weekly Supplement and Report", and in Lyon Credit Reports.

Should any error, or inaccuracy in rating be noted, it should be reported only to the Agency, in order that correction may be made.

Inquire for Detailed Credit Report on all NEW ACCOUNTS, and make inquiry at least once a year on old accounts or when change in rating is indicated in the "LYON Weekly Supplement and Report".

Fig. 21–3. Lyon Furniture Mercantile Agency *Red Book* credit key.

1915. Each gives ratings for personal credit subjects, although also included are some individuals in a professional capacity or in a proprietorship business activity. As ratings change, new books are published regularly several times a year.

The keys to the ratings offered by two agencies are shown in Tables 21–1 and 21–2. Ratings given by the Lincoln bureau in-

Table 22–1. *Blue Book* (Lincoln, Neb.) Key to Ratings

Open Accounts	Symbol	Instalment Accounts
Prompt—account paid in 30 days	P	
	A	Account, either secured or unsecured, on which instalment payments are made regularly as agreed
Limited exerience or new customer	L	Limited experience or new customer
Good—account paid in 60 to 90 days	G	Payments 15 to 30 days after due date
Account paid in 90 days to 6 months	S	Payments 30 to 60 days after due date
Account paid in 6 months or longer	R	Payments over 90 days after due date
Call Credit Bureau for information that needs explanation	F	Call Credit Bureau for information that needs explanation

dicate the number of creditors reporting different kinds of information. Typical ratings found in the *Blue Book* are as follows:

11P2G　　PA4G2S　　2A　　2P2AG5S　　2P2A

On the other hand, the Dallas association provides only one rating symbol which is a sort of composite appraisal, as indicated in their key. Typical ratings found in the *Red Book* are as follows:

4　　3S　　8B　　3SX　　V*　　1

Use of Ratings. Considering that ratings are a symbolic digest of credit reports, which in turn present various evidences of creditworthiness, ratings, both in mercantile and consumer credit appraisal, are most useful when summary generalizations concerning a subject are needed. Ratings often serve as a starting point for credit appraisal. If their evidence is conclusive, either favorably or unfavorably, reference to the rating may be the extent of the investigation. Otherwise, they may lead to the additional use of reports and other information sources. Ratings also give

Table 22–2. Red Book (Dallas) Key to Ratings

Symbol	
1	Reported good for amounts in excess of $1,000 at several places for personal accounts on thirty days' time and estimated worth over $50,000 and perfectly good for all contracts.
2	Reported good for $400 to $1,000 at several places for personal accounts on thirty days' time and estimated worth over $20,000 and perfectly good for all contracts.
3	Reported good for $100 to $400 at several places for personal accounts on thirty days' time; have a good income and have always taken care of their personal accounts.
4	Reported good for $50 to $100 at several places for personal accounts on thirty days' time; have moderate income and well regarded for their accounts.
5	Reported good for $25 to $50 at several places for personal accounts on thirty days' time; usually financial worth limited but well regarded for their accounts.
8B	Only find where the party has been sold on credit with a guarantee of lien attached.
K	This party has requested that nothing be charged to him without written order bearing his signature.
M	Indicates that the party is a member of this Agency. If in doubt about credit, telephone for a report.
ML	This usually refers to a woman who has married. A report should be secured on the husband.
S	Does not always pay the original purchase in full and sometimes carries a balance.
V	This indicates that we do not have a complete record on this party, only known in a limited way, but favorable. Ask for additional reference if amount wanted is large, or send party to our office to furnish us the desired information upon which to base a rating.
X	Indicates that party has one or more disputed accounts.
*	Rating is based on information from towns where the individual lived before coming to Dallas.

an impartial specialist's opinion. Report writers select what in their judgment is the most representative rating; this decision is sometimes reached after conference concerning the matter. Ratings provide an easy means of checking changes in listings and creditworthiness without resort to more detailed information. Moreover, so long as one has access to a rating or reference book through subscription to an information service, use of ratings may eliminate the costs of credit reports. On the basis of the information they contain, decisions may be made to accept or reject a credit application, to make a provisional or temporary commitment, to identify an account for follow-up observation or collection action, to promote or curtail credit sales to the subject, or to set what seems to be an appropriate credit limit.

CREDIT REPORTS

The heart of credit information exchange is the credit report. It is a communication of composite information, gathered from numerous sources, and comprising a variety of facts. As such, it is a synopsis of risk characteristics, and it suggests a pattern for risk analysis.

Although credit reports take varied forms, in both quality and content they are quite uniform. This is determined in part by the universal needs of users of reports, and in part by the coordinative efforts of those who prepare the reports. Uniformity in retail credit reports is achieved through the Associated Credit Bureaus of America, Inc., and in mercantile credit reports by the Credit Interchange Bureaus of the National Association of Credit Management. It is also through these associations that interbureau exchange of credit information is facilitated.

Differences among credit reports reflect primarily differing needs for credit information. Some reports are presented orally, by phone; usually, however, they are in writing and are delivered or mailed to the user. Some are basic reports, containing information covering months or years; others are periodic reports conveying timely information concerning change in creditworthiness. Some reports are brief and simple; others, because of the complexity of the subject, are lengthy and analytical. Some are prepared upon special request; others are prepared as a routine matter and duplicated for multiple use. Some report all aspects of creditworthiness; others contain only trade or ledger information. Some report only facts; others make a credit recommendation.

General Mercantile Reports

One type of report is prepared for business subjects. The general reports of this group are designed to convey a complete picture of the credit risk and to need supplementing only as the individual credit manager should deem advisable in his situation. The contents of such reports generally include the following types of information:

1. *Historical or Background Information:* Sometimes called ante-

cedent or personnel information, this relates the origin and development of the subject, and officers and executives and their personal and official qualifications.

2. *Operations:* Nature of the business, growth, competitive position, location, facilities and premises, policies.

3. *Current Information:* This analytical portion of the report relates recent developments, problems, policy and personnel changes, working capital position.

4. *Banking:* The name of the bank with which the subject deals.

5. *Financial Information:* Financial statements, both balance sheets and operating statements, to the extent that they are available, may be presented. Recent as well as current statements may be given for comparative purposes, and an analytical interpretation may be made for the larger and more complex subjects.

6. *Trade Experience:* Information drawn from ledgers of other creditors, showing extent of line of credit, current and past due indebtedness, and manner of payment. This information is usually uninterpreted.

7. *Credit Suggestion:* In mercantile reports, several types of credit recommendations are made. In Dun & Bradstreet Credit Advisory Reports, recommendations are made for acceptance of specific orders, and the National Credit Office in its reports suggests a line of credit that seems consistent with the reported situation. Almost all reports summarize the general creditworthiness.

8. *Credit Rating:* The agencies which prepare ratings and reference books in their reports give their ratings as a capsule condensation of the information provided.

In the following pages several sample reports of information agencies are given to illustrate their contents and analysis. The first is a simple report prepared by Dun & Bradstreet (Fig. 21–4). The second is a more analytical report prepared by Lyon Furniture Mercantile Agency (Fig. 21–5).

Mercantile Trade Reports

In contrast to the general reports, those prepared by the Credit Interchange Bureaus on business subjects include only ledger or trade information. These relate the experiences of creditors with the subject, as reported by them to their credit bureaus, which, in turn, through the bureau interchange system, assemble the information for a final report. An example of such a report is furnished in Fig. 21–6.

Dun & Bradstreet Report

RATING
UNCHANGED

SIC	NAME & ADDRESS		STARTED	RATING
34 61	803-4520	CD 13 APR 21 19-- N	1947	D 1½
	ARNOLD METAL PRODUCTS CO	METAL STAMPINGS		
	ARNOLD, SAMUEL B., OWNER			

	53 MAIN STREET	TRADE	DISC-PPT
	SOUTH DAWSON MICH	SALES	$177,250
		WORTH	$42,961
		EMPLS	8
		Tel 215-000-0000	

SUMMARY   SALES ARE INCREASING THROUGH SUB-CONTRACT WORK AND PROFITS ARE BEING EARNED AND RETAINED. A SATISFACTORY FINANCIAL CONDITION IS MAINTAINED.

TRADE

HC	OWE	P DUE	TERMS	Apr 1 19--	SOLD
3000	1500		2-10-30	Disc	Over 3 yrs
2500	1000		2-10-30	Disc	Over 3 yrs
2000	500		1-10-30	Disc	Old account
1000			30	Ppt	Over 3 yrs to 3-6-
500	500		30	1st sale	

FINANCE   Statement Dec 31 19--

Cash	$ 4,870	Accts Pay	$ 6,121
Accts Rec	15,472	Notes Pay Curr	2,400
Mdse	14,619	Accruals	3,583
Total Current	34,961	Total Current	12,104
Fixed Assets	22,840	Notes Pay Def	5,000
Other Assets	2,264	NET WORTH	42,961
Total Assets	60,065	Total	60,065

Net sales 19-- $177,250; Gross profit $47,821; net profit over and above drawings of the owner $4,204. Inventory valued at lower of cost or market. Reserve for doubtful accounts $1,508. Reserve for depreciation $6,912. Fire insurance merchandise $15,000; fixed assets $20,000. Annual rent $3,000, lease expires January 1 19--.
Signed Apr 21 19-- ARNOLD METAL PRODUCTS CO by Samuel B. Arnold, Owner
Johnson Singer, CPA, South Dawson
-----0-----
Sales increased last year due to increased sub-contract work and this trend is reported continuing. Arnold bought new equipment in September at a cost of $8,000 financed by a bank loan secured by a lien on the equipment payable $200 per month. With increased capacity he has been able to handle a larger volume.
On April 21 19-- Arnold stated that for the first two months of this year volume was $32,075 and operations continue to be profitable. Collections are made promptly and operations are adequately financed.
Medium to high four figure balances are maintained at a local depository where an equipment loan is outstanding and being retired as agreed.

OPERATION   Manufactures light metal stampings for industrial concerns and also does some work on a sub-contract basis for aircraft manufacturers. Terms are 30 days net. Owner is active and has five production, two office employees, and one salesman. LOCATION: Rents a one-story cinder block building with 5,000 square feet of floor space located in an industrial section. Premises are orderly.

HISTORY   The trade style was registered by the owner January 10, 1947 and is used for general business purposes.
Arnold, born 1908, married, was graduated with a B.S. degree in Mechanical Engineering from Lehigh University in 1931. Employed 1931-1940 by Industrial Machine Corporation, Detroit, and from 1940-46 as production engineer by Aerial Motors, Inc., Detroit. He started this business in 1947 with $7,500 derived from savings.
4-21 (803 PRA)

Fig. 21-4. Dun & Bradstreet credit report.

Form 20   1-64

LYON CREDIT REPORT

This report compiled from our records is sent to you confidentially, for your exclusive use, in accordance with the terms of your contract.
The Lyon Furniture Mercantile Agency shall not be liable for any loss or injury consequent upon its negligence or that of its agents, in obtaining, compiling
or communicating this information; and said Agency does not guarantee correctness of same.

(SAMPLE REPORT - NAMES & ADDRESS FICTITIOUS)

DOE, JOHN CORPORATION   FC & Apl O   NEW YORK.........N.Y. 10016
                                                    629 West 34th Street

Morris Doe, Pres.-Age 50, Md.
Frank Blank, Treas.-Age 47, Md.
John Smith, Secy.-Age 49, Sgle.

Directors: The officers

REV:(mf;31) September 1, 1965

ANTECEDENTS
             Incorporated under New York State laws March 15, 1939, continuing the
business of the former John Doe Furniture Co., which had conducted business at this
same address as a partnership between Morris Doe and Frank Blank.

             Morris Doe is a son of the late John Doe who started in the furniture
business February 6, 1900 as John Doe Furniture Co., at 1600 Dodge Street, New York,
N.Y. John Doe died May 5, 1955, at which time a partnership was formed between his son,
Morris Doe, and Frank Blank, a son-in-law, as John Doe Furniture Co., to continue the business
which at that time moved to 629 West 34th Street. Morris Doe had been assisting his father
in the conduct of this business, working part-time, while attending school and after graduating,
giving his full time to the business. Frank Blank had been employed by the late John Doe
for about 10 years.

             The partnership between Frank Blank and Morris Doe continued until
December 1, 1938, when they executed an assignment for the benefit of creditors. On December
5, 1938, an involuntary petition in bankruptcy was filed against them and at the Trustee's
sale in bankruptcy, the assets were purchased by the present corporation, the unsecured
creditors of the partnership receiving a first and final dividend of 50% on November 28, 1939.
The partners received their discharge from bankruptcy January 12, 1940.

             Control of this corporation is divided equally between Morris Doe, Frank Blank
and John Smith. John Smith joined with Morris Doe and Frank Blank in forming this corporation
to acquire the assets at the sale in bankruptcy, previous to which time he had been employed
for about eight years as a furniture buyer by the New York Department Store, New York, N. Y.

             On December 16, 1944, a fire which occurred here as a result of the faulty
operation of an oil burner, caused damage to stock of about $10,000 with insurance adjustment
being received in that amount.

Fig. 21–5. Lyon Furniture Mercantile Agency credit report.

Form 20   1-54

LYON CREDIT REPORT

This report compiled from our records is sent to you confidentially, for your exclusive use, in accordance with the terms of your contract.
The Lyon Furniture Mercantile Agency shall not be liable for any loss or injury consequent upon its negligence or that of its agents, in obtaining, compiling or communicating this information; and said Agency does not guarantee correctness of same.

DOE, JOHN CORPORATION   -2-   NEW YORK......N.Y.

September 1, 1965

GENERAL INFORMATION

    Principals of corporation experienced and attentive, although the President and Treasurer have been identified in the past with an unsuccessful venture.

    Company occupies a three story building which it owns in a good shopping center, each floor having about 10,000 sq. ft. of display space, the basement being used for warehouse and storage purposes.

    Corporation carries a complete line of home furnishings and has a good sized electrical appliance department handling only major appliances. Deals in medium to low priced lines, with about 90% of sales made on the installment payment plan. Company has enjoyed a fairly good sales volume during the past few years. However, there appears to have been some falling off in volume during the past several months, with prospects at this time for a continuance of previous satisfactory sales volume appearing not favorable, local conditions of strikes resulting in unemployment of some weeks having curtailed sales volume in general.

FINANCIAL INFORMATION

    Company has an authorized capital of $300,000 in preferred stock, divided into 3,000 shares with a par value of $100 each. The paid-in capital is $150,000, $50,000 each having been contributed by the three principals.

COMPARATIVE SUMMARIZED STATEMENTS

DATE	ASSETS	LIABILITIES	RESERVES	NET WORTH	SALES
Dec. 31, 1961	261,724	101,827	2,428	157,468	–
Dec. 31, 1962	317,062	122,674	7,260	187,127	220,647
Dec. 31, 1963	370,085	138,864	14,537	216,683	250,128
Dec. 31, 1964	384,117	147,824	17,027	219,266	270,877
June 30, 1965	371,780	138,473	18,236	215,070	125,608

    The following statement, received by mail, showing condition from books and physical inventory of June 30, 1965:-

ASSETS:
Current Assets:
Cash on hand & in bank   5,096.28
Accounts Rec., install.   220,174.05
Merchandise Inventory   50,649.00
    Total Current Assets   275,919.33

Fixed Assets:
Real Estate   75,000.00
Furn., Fixt., & signs   15,427.18
Delivery Equipment   4,908.76
    Total Fixed Assets   95,335.94

Fig. 21–5. *Continued.*

Form 20   1-64

LYON CREDIT REPORT

This report compiled from our records is sent to you confidentially, for your exclusive use, in accordance with the terms of your contract.
The Lyon Furniture Mercantile Agency shall not be liable for any loss or injury consequent upon its negligence or that of its agents, in obtaining, compiling or communicating this information; and said Agency does not guarantee correctness of same.

DOE, JOHN CORPORATION   -3-   NEW YORK.........N.Y.

September 1, 1965

FINANCIAL INFORMATION

Deferred charges:
Prepaid Insurance & Interest   524.51

         TOTAL ASSETS   371,780.78

LIABILITIES & CAPITAL:

CURRENT LIABILITIES:

Accounts Payable	89,452.02	
Notes Pay.-Bank, secured by endorsement		
of Pres. & Treas.	15,000.00	
Taxes Pay., Federal & State	1,521.87	
Total Current Liabilities		105,973.89
Fixed Liabilities:		
Real Estate mortgage		32,500.00
Reserve for Depreciation of Fixed Assets:		18,236.20
		156,710.09
Capital:		
100 shares preferred stock		150,000.00
Surplus		65,070.69
TOTAL LIABILITIES & CAPITAL		371,780.78

Sales for six months ending June 30, 1963, $125,608. Insurance on merchandise, $45,000.
Insurance on building, $60,000.

                (SIGNED) JOHN DOE CORPORATION
                  BY   FRANK BLANK, Treasurer

ANALYSIS

          Summarized statements show net worth has been steadily increasing from
1961 to 1964, but for the six months ending June 30, 1965, there has been some reduction in net
worth.

          Comparison of current statement with that of December 31, 1964, shows a
reduction in cash of about $47,500, accounts receivable have increased about $25,000, and
inventory has increased about $10,000. Accounts payable have increased about $28,000. Bank
indebtedness has increased about $5,000 while taxes have been reduced by about $2,400, and
an item of about $40,000 previously shown owing to officers no longer appears in the statement,
Frank Blank stating upon interview that this had been paid to officers which also explained a
good part of the reduction in cash position.

Fig. 21–5. *Continued.*

Form 20

1-64

LYON CREDIT REPORT

This report compiled from our records is sent to you confidentially, for your exclusive use, in accordance with the terms of your contract.
The Lyon Furniture Mercantile Agency shall not be liable for any loss or injury consequent upon its negligence or that of its agents, in obtaining, compiling or communicating this information; and said Agency does not guarantee correctness of same.

DOE, JOHN CORPORATION   -4-   NEW YORK........N.Y.

September 1, 1965

ANALYSIS (CONTD.)

Current statement shows a liquid ratio of about .57 to 1., and a current ratio of 1.05 to 1., both of which are well below accepted standard. Sales compared with receivables indicates average collection period of about 313 days which is slower than accepted standard, indicating that some of the accounts are becoming old on the books. Inventory compared with sales indicates a fairly satisfactory turnover of about 2.4 times a year.

While the current and liquid positions are below accepted standard, the net worth ratio, which is about 1.4 to 1., is satisfactory and there is indicated some margin of ratable worth placed at slightly better than $60,000, after allowing for adjustments and depreciation.

BANK INFORMATION

Satisfactory account maintained for several years. Balances previously averaging in moderate five figures, but at present average in moderate four to high four figures. Accommodations extended in high four to low five figures, secured by endorsements of principals and cared for as agreed.

TRADE INVESTIGATION

NATIONAL INTERCHANGE OF TRADE EXPERIENCE
March 25, 1965-Results-18 Houses Reporting

PAYMENTS	OWING	PAST DUE
1-Discount	125.	-
2-Discount	-	-
3-Discount	77.	-
4-Medium	340.	-
5-Medium	260.	-
6-Medium	180.	180.
7-Medium	410.	-
8-Medium	-	-
9-Medium	100.	-
10-Slow	600.	320.
11-Slow	390.	175.
12-Slow	740.	650.
13-Slow	367.	367.
14-Slow	239	140.
15-Very Slow	842.	842.
16-Very Slow	726.	560.
17-Very Slow	163.	163.
18-Very Slow	639.	160.
Totals	6198.	3557.

Fig. 21–5. Continued.

Form 20   1-64

LYON CREDIT REPORT

This report compiled from our records is sent to you confidentially, for your exclusive use, in accordance with the terms of your contract.
The Lyon Furniture Mercantile Agency shall not be liable for any loss or injury consequent upon its negligence or that of its agents, in obtaining, compiling or communicating this information; and said Agency does not guarantee correctness of same.

DOE, JOHN CORPORATION   -5-   NEW YORK.........N.Y.

September 1, 1965

TRADE INVESTIGATION
          Inquiry of August 16, 1965:

Manner of Payments	Now Owing	Past Due	No. Days Slow	High Credit	Date Last Sale
1-Medium	125.	-	-	400.	8/65
2-Medium	680.	110.	-	725.	8/65
3-Slow	319.	284.	30	667.	8/65
4-Slow	723.	416.	30	981.	8/65
5-Slow	1,276.	962.	30-60	1,519.	7/65
6-Slow	693.	487.	60	724.	7/65
7-Very Slow	981.	876.	90	1,263.	7/65
8-Very Slow	1,547.	1,029.	90	1,849.	6/65
9-Very Slow	820.	820.	180	1,057.	5/65
10-Very Slow	716.	616.	120	716.	5/65

COLLECTION RECORD

Mar. 7, 1965 - Claim (H-35782) for $420.50 placed with High Point Office for inv. 11/6/64. Collected by Agency 4/1/65.

Apr. 22, 1965 - Claim (C-48581) for $232.60 placed with Chicago Office for goods sold 1/65. Collected by Agency 4/26/65.

June 15, 1965 - Claim (H-36784) for $195.80 placed with High Point Office for inv. 2/6/65. Collected by Agency 7/7/65.

June 16, 1965 - Claim (H-36787) for $527.00 placed with High Point Office for inv. 1/5/65. Collected by Agency 7/8/65.

June 30, 1965 - Claim (N-57602) for $947.18 placed with New York Office for goods sold Dec. through March 1965. Collected by Agency 7/26/65.

SUMMARY
          PRINCIPALS EXPERIENCED AND ATTENTIVE, HOWEVER, PRESIDENT AND TREASURER HAVE BEEN IDENTIFIED IN THE PAST WITH UNSUCCESSFUL VENTURE. CURRENT STATEMENT SHOWS SUB-STANDARD WORKING POSITION, ALTHOUGH SOME RATABLE NET WORTH IS INDICATED. TRADE PAYMENTS DURING THE PAST FEW MONTHS HAVE BECOME SLOW WITH SOME CLAIMS APPEARING FOR COLLECTION.

N: Rate 13-H-5-116   (s.i.)

Fig. 21–5. Continued.

FORM 7

NATIONAL ASSOCIATION of CREDIT MANAGEMENT
Credit Interchange Report

OFFICES IN PRINCIPAL CITIES

October 20, 1965

The accuracy of this Report is not guaranteed. Its contents are gathered in good faith from members and sent to you by this Bureau without liability for negligence in procuring, collecting, communicating or failing to communicate the information so gathered.

BUSINESS CLASSIFICATION	HOW LONG SOLD	DATE OF LAST SALE	HIGHEST RECENT CREDIT	NOW OWING INCLUDING NOTES	PAST DUE	TERMS OF SALE	PAYING RECORD DISC.	PAYS WHEN DUE	DAYS SLOW	COMMENTS
*DAYTON										
38-907-19										
38-3-929-10										
*492										
285 Elec	yrs	9-65	3700	3700	10	2-10px	x			DISPUTE ON 10.
218 Elec	yrs	11-64	17			2-10pxN30		x		
176 Plbg	yrs	7-65	51			2-10-30		x		
115 Gls	1 sl	8-65	7			1-10-30		x		
199 Hdwe	10-60	9-65	37,950	37,950		2-10-30	x			
150 Elec	yrs	5-65	250			CD10px	x			
492 Elec	1 mo	9-65	7000	5200		N10SPEC		x		
*COLUMBUS										
*C141 Gls	1 yr	11-64	200			1-15-30			60+	
C226 Elec	yrs	curr	5000	4736	1700	2-10N30			30-120	
CINCINNATI										
14-1006-412										
108 Elec	yrs	10-65	31,000	20,000	6000			x	60+	DISPUTE OVER UNPAID ITEMS
*MEMPHIS										
15-1008-209										
444 Ppr	yrs	12-64	4990			DATING			30-90	
*CHICAGO										
3-929-10										
E6 Conf	6-65	6-65	119			2-10-30	x			
E9 "	9-64		200			2-10N15		x		
E10 "	8-64	8-65	394	356	356			x	92-96	DISCOUNT VIOLATOR
E76 "	8-64	4-65	68					x		
E148 "	1-63	8-65	2400	1200		2-10-30	x			3700 KEATS DR.
E251	11-62	3-65	316						30	
740		8-63	799			2-10N30			60	
742	1963	5-65	1100	97		dating			90	
743	11-64	5-64	800		97	2-10px	x			

Fig. 21–6. National Association of Credit Management credit interchange report.

As such trade reports are unanalyzed, interpretation of them is left to the user. From this type of report can be ascertained, according to the business classification column, the number and dispersion of the sources from which the subject buys on credit. The length of their dealing with him is indicative of several possible conditions, which must be further determined by other elements of the report. Long-standing relationships bespeak continuing confidence, as a rule. Recourse to new sources of merchandise may indicate desperation, if other sources appear to be closed; sagacious buying, if price or product advantages are to be gained that way; or strength, if the business is in a stage of expansion. Recency of sale, particularly from older resources, and especially if accompanied by favorable paying record, points to confidence. Absence of recent dealing may indicate closed accounts, reluctance to sell, or buyer dissatisfaction.

Information concerning the highest recent credit, by which is meant the maximum balance on the account during the past year, must be interpreted in the light of current and past-due indebtedness. A strong, growing business may extend its credit with many suppliers, and often the current debt coincides with the maximum credit extended. If this is also not accompanied by appreciable past-due debt, it may indicate strength; if it is, it may indicate weakness and inability to pay for merchandise purchases. Vendors sometimes continue to supply weak customers as the only means of obtaining payment for previous shipments.

Terms and paying record also are considered together. Terms of sale given the subject indicate the normality of vendors' relations with him. Terms usual to the trade suggest a normal expectation. On the other hand, C.O.D. and advance payment terms when not normal indicate caution on the part of other creditors. Paying record, as reported by other creditors, suggests the rate at which a new creditor might expect to be paid. Comments made by creditors give further evidence of the creditworthiness of the subject.

Reports of ledger information prepared for vendors engaged in international trade are prepared by the Foreign Credit Interchange Bureau (Fig. 21–7) and are adapted to terms of sale and manners of payment characteristic of that type of business. Interpretation of such reports is made along lines of those used in domestic business.

FOREIGN CREDIT INTERCHANGE BUREAU
NATIONAL ASSOCIATION OF CREDIT MANAGEMENT
44 EAST 23RD STREET   NEW YORK 10. N. Y.
THIS REPORT IS STRICTLY CONFIDENTIAL AND FOR YOUR OWN INDIVIDUAL USE ONLY.
WHILE THE INFORMATION GIVEN IN THIS REPORT IS OBTAINED FROM SOURCES DEEMED RELIABLE, THE ACCURACY OF THE INFORMATION IS NOT GUARANTEED AND NO RESPONSIBILITY IS TO ATTACH TO THE BUREAU OR ANY OF ITS REPRESENTATIVES OR AGENTS.

TF

REPORT ON·

October 25, 1965

TERMS OF SALE

1. OPEN ACCOUNT PAYABLE ___ DAYS FROM DATE OF
   (a) INVOICE
   (b) FACTORY SHIPMENT
   (c) EXPORT SHIPMENT
2. OPEN ACCOUNT PAYABLE IMMEDIATELY UPON RECEIPT OF
   (a) DOCUMENTS
   (b) INVOICES
   (c) GOODS
3. ACCOUNT GUARANTEED
4. VOLUNTARY REMITTANCE WITH ORDER
5. SELL FOR CASH IN ADVANCE ONLY
6. C O D OR S/D R R, B/L ATTACHED.
7. CASH AGAINST DOCUMENTS UNDER
   (a) IRREVOCABLE L/C - CONFIRMED
   (b) IRREVOCABLE L/C - UNCONFIRMED
   (c) REVOCABLE L/C
8. AUTHORITY TO PURCHASE OR LETTER OF ADVICE.
   (a) IRREVOCABLE WITH RECOURSE
   (a) IRREVOCABLE WITHOUT RECOURSE
   (c) REVOCABLE WITH RECOURSE
   (b) REVOCABLE WITHOUT RECOURSE

9. BANK ACCEPTANCE OF BANK IN THIS COUNTRY AT. ___ DAYS
10. BANK ACCEPTANCE OF FOREIGN BANK AT. ___ DAYS.
11. DRAFT AT. ___ DAYS SIGHT D/A.
12. DRAFT AT. ___ DAYS DATE D/A.
13. DRAFT AT. ___ DAYS SIGHT D/P.
14. DRAFT AT ___ DAYS DATE D/P.
15. CLEAN DRAFT AT. ___ DAYS SIGHT.
16. CLEAN DRAFT AT. ___ DAYS DATE.
17. CONSIGNED STOCK. TERMS ?
18. CASH AGAINST SHIPPING DOCUMENTS. DOCK RECEIPT OR WAREHOUSE RECEIPT.
   (A) AT CUSTOMER'S OFFICE.
   (B) AT PAYING AGENCY OTHER THAN BANK.
   (C) AT BANK.
19. _____

MANNER OF PAYMENT

OPEN ACCOUNT
A. DISCOUNTS,
B. PAYS WHEN DUE,
C. SLOW
D. TAKES UNAUTHORIZED DISCOUNTS

GENERAL
N. ACCOUNT SETTLED BY ATTORNEY
O. ACCOUNT SETTLED BY ARBITRATION OR COMPROMISE
P. ACCOUNT STILL IN DISPUTE,

DRAFTS
H. ANTICIPATES - PAYMENT
I. ACCEPTS AND PAYS PROMPTLY
J. ACCEPTS PROMPTLY - DELAYS PAYMENT
K. DELAYS ACCEPTANCE-PAYS PROMPTLY
L. DELAYS BOTH ACCEPTANCE AND PAYMENT,
M. MAKES UNJUST CLAIMS.

WE RATE THE ACCOUNT
Q. HIGH,
R. GOOD
S. SATISFACTORY,
T. UNSATISFACTORY
U. UNDESIRABLE,

HOW LONG SOLD YEARS	TERMS OF SALE KEY NO.	TERMS OF SALE DETAILS DAYS	HIGHEST RECENT ACCOUNT, WITHIN PAST YEAR	DATE LAST DEALINGS	AMT, NOW OWING (INCLUDING OUTSTANDING DRAFTS)	AMOUNT PAST DUE	LENGTH OF TIME PAST DUE	MANNER OF PAYMENT (USE CODE)	RATING (USE CODE)	REMARKS
yrs	18	C	1454	10-65				I	R	
'63	1a	10	540	10-65				B	R	
yrs	S/D	D/P	300	8-65					S	
yrs	S/D		1006	8-65				I to y days	slow	
'58	net	90	60000	8-65	30000			I	R	
8	13	sight	4740	7-65				I	S	
yrs	L/C		14000	6-65					S	
yrs	1	30	1000	6-65				B	Q	
'61	S/D	D/A	500	5-65				I	R	
yrs	11	30	1100	4-65				I	S	

A Banking Source Advises:

The subject has maintained a satisfactory account with us
since 1952. Average balances are low to medium five figure
proportions. We have granted them the use of our credit
accommodations to medium five figures with satisfactory
results.

Fig. 21–7. National Association of Credit Management foreign credit interchange report.

Consumer Credit Reports

Consumer credit reports are prepared by many vendor-sponsored and privately owned credit bureaus and agencies throughout the country. The mutual bureaus serve mainly local clients, reporting on consumers in the vicinity and cooperating with a nationwide network in interbureau exchange of information. Dun & Bradstreet, Inc., also prepares individual reports, although this is a minor part of its business. Among the private reporting agencies, one of the most prominent is the Retail Credit Company, of Atlanta, whose credit reports are especially designed for national merchandising and service operations, such as mail order houses, petroleum companies, and finance and mortgage companies.

An example of a typical regular retail credit report is shown in Fig. 21–8. It contains essentially the same types of information which are in the mercantile reports, although adapted to the individual consumer. These include identification, employment and income relationships, character appraisal, and credit record as reported by other creditors, both merchants and lenders. The key to retail bureau reports is shown in Fig. 21–9.

Special Reports

In addition to the credit reports here discussed, special reports not solely for credit purposes but nonetheless useful for credit analysis are available. These are customized reports on individuals and business organizations, detailed studies of a subject, which are usually confidential and provide a basis upon which a variety of business decisions can be made. Two agencies preparing such reports are Proudfoot Reports, and Dun & Bradstreet, Inc., in their Key Account Service.

Credit reports are not always the sole source of credit information; neither are they the first or the last to which the credit analyst turns. Interviews, applications, and ratings are often used prior to the credit report. Financial statements, references, and consultation with others who can give light to the credit appraisal are often used along with reports. But unless information from such other sources is conclusive in itself, credit reports supply an incomparable assortment and balance of information for the credit manager.

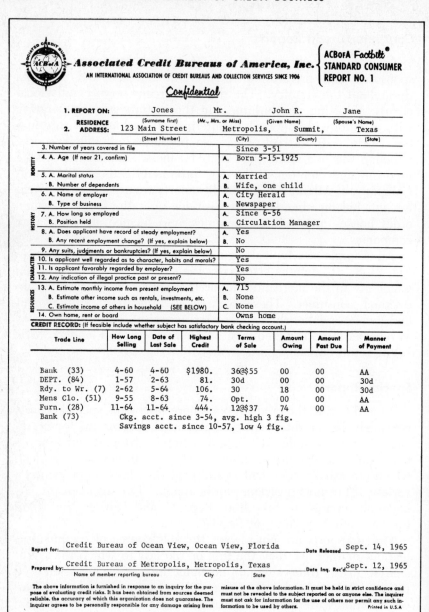

Associated Credit Bureaus of America, Inc.

AN INTERNATIONAL ASSOCIATION OF CREDIT BUREAUS AND COLLECTION SERVICES SINCE 1906

ACBofA Factbilt® STANDARD CONSUMER REPORT NO. 1

Confidential

1. REPORT ON: Jones (Surname first) Mr. (Mr., Mrs. or Miss) John R. (Given Name) Jane (Spouse's Name)

2. RESIDENCE ADDRESS: 123 Main Street (Street Number) Metropolis, (City) Summit, (County) Texas (State)

	3. Number of years covered in file	Since 3-51
IDENTITY	4. A. Age (If near 21, confirm)	A. Born 5-15-1925
	5. A. Marital status	A. Married
	B. Number of dependents	B. Wife, one child
HISTORY	6. A. Name of employer	A. City Herald
	B. Type of business	B. Newspaper
	7. A. How long so employed	A. Since 6-56
	B. Position held	B. Circulation Manager
	8. A. Does applicant have record of steady employment?	A. Yes
	B. Any recent employment change? (If yes, explain below)	B. No
	9. Any suits, judgments or bankruptcies? (If yes, explain below)	No
CHARACTER	10. Is applicant well regarded as to character, habits and morals?	Yes
	11. Is applicant favorably regarded by employer?	Yes
	12. Any indication of illegal practice past or present?	No
RESOURCES	13. A. Estimate monthly income from present employment	A. 715
	B. Estimate other income such as rentals, investments, etc.	B. None
	C. Estimate income of others in household (SEE BELOW)	C. None
	14. Own home, rent or board	Owns home

CREDIT RECORD: (If feasible include whether subject has satisfactory bank checking account.)

Trade Line	How Long Selling	Date of Last Sale	Highest Credit	Terms of Sale	Amount Owing	Amount Past Due	Manner of Payment
Bank (33)	4-60	4-60	$1980.	36@$55	00	00	AA
DEPT. (84)	1-57	2-63	81.	30d	00	00	30d
Rdy. to Wr. (7)	2-62	5-64	106.	30	18	00	30d
Mens Clo. (51)	9-55	8-63	74.	Opt.	00	00	AA
Furn. (28)	11-64	11-64	444.	12@$37	74	00	AA
Bank (73)	Ckg. acct. since 3-54, avg. high 3 fig.						
	Savings acct. since 10-57, low 4 fig.						

Report for: Credit Bureau of Ocean View, Ocean View, Florida Date Released Sept. 14, 1965

Prepared by: Credit Bureau of Metropolis, Metropolis, Texas Date Inq. Rec'd Sept. 12, 1965

Name of member reporting bureau City State

The above information is furnished in response to an inquiry for the purpose of evaluating credit risks. It has been obtained from sources deemed reliable, the accuracy of which this organization does not guarantee. The inquirer agrees to be personally responsible for any damage arising from misuse of the above information. It must be held in strict confidence and must not be revealed to the subject reported on or anyone else. The inquirer must not ask for information for the use of others nor permit any such information to be used by others.

Printed in U.S.A

Fig. 21–8. Associated Credit Bureaus of America, Inc., credit report.

A NEW LANGUAGE FOR CONSUMER CREDIT

We Agree

Credit granters and credit bureaus agree on the need for a common language—the same symbols should mean the same things throughout the consumer credit industry.

Through Research

These standardized abbreviations and terms have been developed through careful research. Representatives of major credit granting industries and credit bureau representatives consulted with each other to work out the best possible method of communicating precise information.

Let's Use Them

The new terms and abbreviations have been adopted. Now they must be put to use by everyone concerned.

It's So Simple

The new language is simple, and easy to learn. It is important that it be adopted as quickly and completely as possible.

KIND OF BUSINESS CLASSIFICATION

CODE	KIND OF BUSINESS
A	Automotive
B	Banks
C	Clothing
D	Department and Variety
F	Finance
G	Groceries
H	Home Furnishings
I	Insurance
J	Jewelry and Cameras
K	Contractors
L	Lumber, Building Material, Hardware
M	Medical and Related Health
O	Oil and National Credit Card Companies
P	Personal Services Other Than Medical
R	Real Estate and Public Accommodations
S	Sporting Goods
T	Farm and Garden Supplies
U	Utilities and Fuel
V	Government
W	Wholesale
X	Advertising
Y	Collection Services
Z	Miscellaneous

TERMS OF SALE AND USUAL MANNER OF PAYMENT

USUAL MANNER OF PAYMENT	SYMBOL
Open Account, 30 Day Account 90 Day Account = 0	
Too new to rate; approved but not used	O-0
Pays (or paid) within 30 days of billing; pays 90 day accounts as agreed	O-1
Pays (or paid) in more than 30 days, but not more than 60 days	O-2
Pays (or paid) in more than 60 days, but not more than 90 days	O-3
Pays (or paid) in more than 90 days, but not more than 120 days	O-4
Pays (or paid) in 120 days or more	O-5
Bad debt; placed for collection; suit; judgment; bankrupt; skip	O-9
Revolving or Option Account = R or RS___	
Too new to rate; approved but not used	R-0
Pays (or paid) according to the terms agreed upon	R-1
Not paying (or paid) as agreed, but not more than one payment past due	R-2
Not paying (or paid) as agreed, and two payments past due	R-3
Not paying (or paid) as agreed, and three or more payments past due	R-4
Bad debt; placed for collection; suit; judgment; bankrupt; skip	R-9
Instalment Account = I or IS___	
Too new to rate; approved but not used	I-0
Pays (or paid) according to terms agreed upon	I-1
Not paying (or paid) as agreed, but not more than one payment past due	I-2
Not paying (or paid) as agreed, and two payments past due	I-3
Not paying (or paid) as agreed, and three or more payments past due	I-4
Repossession	I-8
Bad debt; placed for collection; suit; judgment; bankrupt; skip	I-9

*Where the monthly payment is known, it should be shown as in the following examples: R$20   I$78

Fig. 21–9. Key to retail credit reports.

DISCUSSION QUESTIONS

1. Explain the compilation of the Dun & Bradstreet and Lyon ratings and compare their respective merits.
2. Explain the significance to the credit analyst of each of the symbols shown in the Dun & Bradstreet rating.
3. Explain under what circumstances and to whom credit ratings might be a useful tool of information.
4. Distinguish clearly between "composite credit appraisal" and "pay rating."
5. Compare the quality of retail ratings and mercantile ratings.
6. Appraise each type of credit report for its contribution of evidence of creditworthiness.
7. Reconstruct the reasoning which led to setting the particular credit rating given in the Dun & Bradstreet report.
8. What conclusion concerning creditworthiness do you reach from the Lyon report?
9. Explain what evidence is good and what is bad in the Credit Interchange Report.
10. In general character, are retail reports different from or similar to mercantile credit reports?

22

Financial Statement Analysis

Among the sources of credit information available to mercantile creditors, financial statements are one of the most used and most respected. They evidence all the "C's" of credit: Character, Capacity, Capital, and Conditions. Moreover, because with accepted accounting standards meaning is built into financial statements, credence can be given this information. However, because tolerances exist in financial accounting, interpretation for credit purposes requires particular analytical skills. Possessing this ability, credit managers find in financial statements an invaluable source of information.

In using financial statements, the first problem is to obtain them. They may be obtained in several ways, each with some advantages. Such information is sought by credit reporting agencies and is often included in their reports. If so available, this is a convenient means of obtaining financial information, and it may have the additional advantage of being interpreted by agency analysts. On the other hand, agencies do not always obtain statements, and their acquisition of them may not coincide with the time when they are needed by a credit manager. Consequently, other means are also employed. Direct request of statements from a customer is common, made either by the credit manager or by salesmen. This practice informs the customer of the nature of the investigation being made; it provides recent information; and it affords opportunity for discussion of conditions disclosed. As request for this information is not contributory to the sales presentation or relationship, acquisition by salesmen is a less preferred means. Statements are also obtained from reports published, furnished stockholders, and used for other purposes, but as these do not always contain information useful for credit analysis, they are not regarded as primary sources of financial information.

The needs of credit analysis prescribe the form in which statement information is sought. To facilitate reporting and interpretation, the National Association of Credit Management has approved several statement forms which are widely used by its members. One example of an approved form is shown in Fig. 22–1. Others of more complex nature are also provided. Varia-

THIS FORM APPROVED AND PUBLISHED BY THE NATIONAL ASSOCIATION OF CREDIT MANAGEMENT

Form 1B

FINANCIAL STATEMENT OF

Date_____19_____

FIRM NAME_____

Address_____City_____

At close of business on_____19___State_____Zone_____

ISSUED TO_____ {NAME OF FIRM {Requesting Statement.

[PLEASE ANSWER ALL QUESTIONS, WHEN NO FIGURES ARE INSERTED, WRITE WORD "NONE"]

ASSETS	Dollars	Cents	LIABILITIES	Dollars	Cents
Cash in Bank and on hand			Accounts Payable		
Accounts Receivable			Notes Payable — Unsecured:		
Notes and Trade Acceptances Receivable			Banks		
Merchandise Inventory (Do not include Merchandise on Consignment)			Partners or Officers		
Other Current Assets (Describe)			Other		
			Notes Payable — Secured:		
			Owing to		
			Taxes Payable or Accrued:		
			Withholding and Payroll		
			Federal and State Income		
TOTAL CURRENT ASSETS			Other		
Land and Buildings (Depreciated Value)			Accrued Payroll and Other Expense		
Machinery, Fixtures and Equipment (Depreciated Value)			Other Current } Liabilities (Describe) }		
Due from Others — Not Current (Describe)			TOTAL CURRENT LIABILITIES		
			Mortgage on Land and Buildings		
			Liens on Merchandise or Equipment		
Other Assets (Describe)			Other Liabilities (Describe)		
			TOTAL LIABILITIES		
			Net Worth {Capital $ {Surplus $		
TOTAL ASSETS			TOTAL LIABILITIES AND NET WORTH		

SUMMARY OF SURPLUS (or of NET WORTH if not Incorporated)

Surplus (or Net Worth at beginning of period) Dated_____19_____ $_____
Add — Profit for Period $_____ and Adjustments $_____ $_____
TOTAL ADDITIONS_____ $_____
Deduct—Loss for Period $_____ and Dividends (or Withdrawals, if not incorporated) $_____
TOTAL DEDUCTIONS_____ $_____

SURPLUS (or NET WORTH) in Statement Above $_____

Fig. 22–1. Financial statement form.

STATEMENT OF PROFIT AND LOSS FOR PERIOD FROM_____ TO_____

		DETAILS OF EXPENSE		
1. NET SALES _____		Salaries — Officers or Owners_____		
(Cash $ _____) (Credit $_____)		Employees_____		
2. Inventory — Beginning $_____		Rent_____		
3. Purchases $_____		Heat, Light, Other Occupancy Expense_____		
4. Total (Item 2 plus Item 3) $_____		Advertising_____		
5. Deduct Inventory — Close $_____		Interest_____		
6. COST OF SALES _____		Taxes, except Income Taxes_____		
7. GROSS PROFIT _____		Depreciation, (Fixtures, Trucks, etc.)_____		
8. Less Total Expense _____		All other Expense_____		
Other Additions and Deductions_____		**TOTAL EXPENSE** _____		
9. Profit Before Income Taxes _____				
10. Less — Income Taxes_____				
11. NET PROFIT After Taxes _____				

LIST PRINCIPAL SUPPLIERS AND BANKS

NAMES	ADDRESSES

Amount you are liable for as endorser, guarantor, surety	Latest year income tax examined_____
$_____	Date of latest physical inventory_____
Amount of merchandise held on consignment	
$_____	Date of latest audit_____
Amount of current assets pledged	Date business established_____
$_____	
Amount of Taxes past due	If premises leased state annual rental_____
$_____	Expiration date of lease_____
Monthly payment on equipment lease or conditional sale contracts	
$_____	Continued on Reverse Side ➞

DETAILS OF LAND AND BUILDINGS

DESCRIPTION & LOCATION	TITLE IN NAME OF	Cost	Accumulated Depreciation	Depreciated Cost	Assessed Value	ENCUMBRANCES	
						Amount	To Whom

INSURANCE STATEMENT

1. Do you carry fire insurance (including extended coverage) Yes_____ No_____ Total Amount $_____
2. Do you have periodic insurance appraisals and inventories to determine if coverage is adequate to prevent becoming co-insurer?
Yes_____ No_____ Date of most recent appraisal_____19_____
3. Have your liability insurance limits been reviewed recently? Yes_____ No_____ Date of most recent review_____19_____
☐ If checked, please complete form below for list and description of all insurance policies.

NAME OF INSURANCE COMPANY	POLICY NUMBER	EXPIRATION DATE	DESCRIPTION OF COVERAGE	AMOUNT OR LIMITS	SPECIAL FEATURES

Name and Address of Agent or Broker_____

This statement has been carefully read by the undersigned (both the printed and written matter), and is, to my knowledge, in all respects complete, accurate and truthful. It discloses to you the true state of my (our) financial condition on the date indicated. Since that time there has been no material unfavorable change in my (our) financial condition, and if any such change takes place I (we) will give you notice. Until such notice is given, you are to regard this as a continuing statement. The figures submitted are not estimated. They have been taken from my (our) books and physical inventory taken as on date shown.

Name of Individual or Firm_____

If Partnership, Name Partners_____

If Corporation, Name Officers_____

Signed by_____

Title_____

Fig. 22–1. Continued.

STATEMENT OF FINANCIAL CONDITION AND PHYSICAL INVENTORY OF

Name..Business...

Street and No...City...Zone No.................State.......................

AS OF (DATE)...19.......

Owner or Partners—Officers and Directors	Home Address	Title	If Director √

ASSETS	$	LIABILITIES	$
CASH IN ....Bank		ACCOUNTS PAYABLE	
ON HAND		TRADE ACCEPTANCES and NOTES PAYABLE for merchandise	
ACCOUNTS RECEIVABLE for merchandise sold and delivered to customers aged as to shipments during months of:		NOTES PAYABLE (to Banks)	
a. ....$		a. Unsecured	
b. ....$		b. Secured	
c. ....$		NOTES, LOANS or EXCHANGES (do not offset)	
d. Prior Months .....$		LOANS secured by accounts receivable	
Total $		Due to Partners or Officers (do not offset)......	
Less reserves discounts $		Due to contractors without deduction for merchandise in their possession	
doubtful $ $			
NOTES AND TRADE ACCEPTANCES RECEIVABLE for merchandise sold and		TAXES—Accrued and payable: a. Fed. & State income..$	
delivered to customers...$		b. All other ....$	
Less amount discounted.$		Reserve for Partners' Income Taxes..........	
PHYSICAL INVENTORY OF MERCHANDISE (Valued at cost or market whichever is lower)		Reserve for Taxes—On earnings since last tax closing	
Raw materials ....$		ACCRUED WAGES & EXPENSES	
In process ....$			
Finished merchandise ..$			
Sample lines ....$			
CURRENT ASSETS			
NOTES, LOANS or EXCHANGES (do not offset)		TOTAL LIABILITIES	
Cash value life insurance (do not deduct loans)		(If Not Incorporated) NET WORTH	
Investments (give details below)		(If Incorporated) CAPITAL STOCK	
Machinery, Plant, Fixtures $		Authorized Paid In	
Less depreciation .....$		Preferred $ $	
Due from partners, officers or employees......		Common $ $	
Deferred charges		SURPLUS $	
....		DEFICIT $	
TOTAL ASSETS		TOTAL LIABILITIES & CAPITAL	

DESCRIPTION OF INVESTMENTS AND REAL ESTATE	TAXES
....	Are any Federal, State or Local taxes or tax assessments in arrears? ....
....	IF NOT INCORPORATED, is the Net Worth shown on the above balance sheet subject to withdrawals for personal income
....	taxes?..................... Amount $............................

INSURANCE COVERAGE

Merchandise (Fire) $......................, Plant and Equip. (Fire) .... Use and Occupancy $....................Burglary $...................

Credit......................., Life Insurance in favor of Business $........................ Have any insurance policies been assigned, transferred

or pledged?....................If so, to whom?................

Fig. 22–2. Financial statement form.

PROFIT AND LOSS STATEMENT

FOR PERIOD FROM.........................194...... TO...........................194......

GROSS SALES .... $_____

Less returns ......$_____

Less discounts ......$_____ $_____

NET INCOME FROM SALES.............. $_____

Inventory at beginning $_____

Purchases—net ... .$_____

Labor ....$_____

Taxes on factory payroll
(Soc. Sec.& Unemp't) $_____

Factory overhead....$_____

Total ....$_____

Inventory at end....$_____

Cost of goods sold (deduct)............. $_____

GROSS PROFIT ON SALES................ $_____

Salaries of principals.$_____

Selling & shipping exps. $_____
General & Administra-
tive expenses .....$_____

Taxes (except income) $_____

Bad debts written off.$_____
Provision for doubtful
accounts ....$_____

Depreciation ....$_____ $_____

INCOME OR LOSS ON SALES........... $_____

Other income (exclude discounts earned).... $_____

Total income or loss...................... $_____

Income deductions .... $_____

NET PROFIT or LOSS..................... $_____

PROVISION for Federal & State Income Taxes $_____
NET PROFIT or LOSS to SURPLUS
(or NET WORTH)..................... $_____

STATEMENT OF SURPLUS (or NET WORTH if unincorporated)

SURPLUS (or NET WORTH) (date)............. $_____

Add: Profit for period..$_____

Adjustments ......$_____ $_____

Total................. $_____

Deduct: Loss for period.$_____

Dividends or Withdr'ls $_____

Adjustments .....$_____ $_____
SURPLUS (or NET WORTH) per
financial statement (date)................. $_____

ACCOUNTANT

Name ....

Address .... Zone No............

Is he certified?..................registered?..................or licensed?..................

Do these statements agree with your books and records and the report
of your accountant?..................Tax closing date?..................

How often does your accountant audit your books?..................

Do you retain the original detailed inventory records permanently?......

Itemize books of account.

ASSETS

During the year immediately preceding the date of signing hereof, have
you sold, pledged or assigned any of your accounts receivable or
pledged any of your merchandise or other assets as security for any
debt?..............If so, give details..................

Do the accounts receivable include any accounts for merchandise held
for or shipped to any concern in which you or any of your officers or
partners have a financial interest?..................

Do the accounts receivable include any charges for merchandise out
on memorandum or consignment, returned but not credited, or charged
but not delivered?..................

Have all bad, failed, insolvent accounts receivable been written off? ......

How much mdse. was carried over from preceding seasons? $..................

LIABILITIES

State amount of merchandise received or charged to you not included
in assets or liabilities $..................

State liability for merchandise charged to you for others and not included in this statement of financial condition $..................

State amount of all future commitments $..................

Have you any agreements with officers, employees or others based on a
percentage of sales or profits?..................

Has your concern or any of its principals given or endorsed notes or
trade acceptances for the accommodation of others, or incurred any
liability, contingent or otherwise, as guarantor or surety?..................

If so, amount $..................To whom?..................

If not incorporated, are there any notes, mortgages, judgments, etc.
for personal debts outstanding against the proprietor, or any partner,
which are not included in this statement?..................

Annual rent $..................Lease expires (date)..................

GOVERNMENT CONTRACTS — Are any of your profits subject to renegotiation?.................. If so, approximately what portion is subject
to renegotiation and for what years?..................

Has there been any decrease in your Net Worth since the date of this
statement and physical inventory by withdrawal, retirement of capital,
payment or declaration of dividends or bonuses?..................

If so, state amount $..................

If not incorporated, is there a written agreement providing for the
continuation of the business in the event of the death of any principal?..................

If incorporated, has any corporate stock been pledged?..................

TO NATIONAL CREDIT OFFICE, INC.   (READ CAREFULLY)
Two Park Ave.,
New York 16, N. Y.

I (We) hereby authorize my (our) accountants to supply such information as may be requested by you and by any business concerns to whom you send a copy of this statement, and to notify you in the event their services are discontinued.

I (We) further agree that I (We) will notify you and creditors at once if I (We) pledge or sell any of my (our) accounts receivable or pledge any of my (our) merchandise or other property. If such sale or pledge is made without the written consent of my (our) then existing creditors, I (We) agree that all sums owing to any concerns who shall have relied on this statement shall become due and payable at once irrespective of the terms of sale.

The undersigned personally has read the foregoing statement carefully, both printed and written parts, and personally knows and warrants that the foregoing figures and answers are true and accurate in every respect. The undersigned hereby orders it mailed to you with the intention that it shall be relied upon in the extension of credit or insurance by such concerns, including factors or agents, who may subscribe to your service now or hereafter.

Dated at..............this..........day of..................19......
Signed in the presence of: ....
                                                   (Name of Corporation, Partnership or Individual)

Name   ....   By..

Address ....
                                                   (Signature of Officers or Partners)   (Title)

Fig. 22–2. Continued.

tions of these are made by credit managers in the effort to collect the specific evidence upon which they can base a decision concerning creditworthiness. One such variation is shown in Fig. 22–2, a form used by the National Credit Office.

Theory of Financial Statement Analysis

The use of financial statement analysis is relatively new in the methodology of business research. James G. Cannon is credited with making the first comparative analysis of balance sheets about 1900, when he posted successive balance sheets in parallel vertical columns as a means of observing change in the items.[1] A few years later, this method of analysis was advocated for use in banks, although only selected statement items were subjected to comparison. By 1923, all items in the balance sheet were subject to comparative analysis, and since then this method of credit investigation has been widely employed.

The idea that creditworthiness is revealed by financial statements is based upon the fact that financial structure has direct bearing upon debt paying ability. Financial condition reflects management decisions concerning the sources and uses of funds, and these decisions determine commitments and obligations and consequent freedom and capacity to act in credit relationships. Balance and proportion in financial structure indicate the adequacy of facilities and funds for the performance of the intended tasks. The needs of a company determine its use of resources; and the patterns of assets, liabilities, capital, and expenditures reflect the vitality, profitability, control, and *creditworthiness* of the enterprise. As institutional structures evolve for the performance of varied inter-establishment processes, so financial structures evolve for the performance of intra-establishment processes.

The usefulness of statement analysis for determination of credit capacity cannot be overemphasized, but this is not the extent of its usefulness. It reveals also evidence of capital, or the net worth of the business. It also reveals character of the subject and the conditions in which he operates. Evidence of integrity, ethics, and attitude toward debt is found in the business, finance, and accounting practices related to financial statements.

[1] Roy A. Foulke, *Practical Financial Statement Analysis* (5th ed.; New York: McGraw-Hill Book Co., Inc., 1961), p. 446.

Use of financial statements in credit analysis is based upon two presumptions. One is that statement figures represent conditions of an enterprise which affect creditworthiness and that these conditions can be ascertained by internal analysis, by study of the trends, proportions, and relations between items and groups of items in the statements. The other is that creditworthiness is relative as well as absolute, a condition that can be appraised by comparison of one company's balance sheet with another or with accepted standards.

The first expresses the idea that creditworthiness lies within the financial conditions of a subject. Both static and dynamic, absolute and relative analyses are used to determine this. As financial statements depict condition at a point of time, mere observation of reported values furnishes some meaning to a credit analyst. A variation of this is the comparison of the absolute values reported in successive statements, as, for example, the increase or diminution of cash, inventory, debt, etc., in successive years. When relative or ratio analysis is made of statement items, evidence of balance and proportions is sought. While such analysis may be made without reference to external standards, such standards, however, usually are employed.

The second presumption is that standards exist with which a subject's individual statement may be compared. Such standards do exist, of several types, reflecting different concepts of what is meaningful in financial condition. The following are some of the more commonly used standards of statement analysis.[2]

Composite Statements. One of the earliest-used bases for comparison of statement information was the composite statement. It is a non-real balance sheet made by averaging items from statements from a number of firms in a given industry or line of business. Such statements are prepared by the National Credit Office, Inc., for producers and distributors in such highly defined groups of the apparel line as manufacturers of woolen and worsted men's suits, manufacturers of women's cotton dresses, and manufacturers of knit outer wear. These statements are presented either as the averaged dollar values of the individual statement items or on a percentage basis. When the latter is used, all statements in the composite balance sheet are computed as a *percentage of working capital* (current assets minus current liabilities), and all

[2] Edward W. Knaus, *Composite and Pattern Statements* (New York: National Association of Credit Management, Credit Research Foundation, Inc., 1952).

operating statement items are computed as a percentage of *net sales*. Working capital is used rather than some other base, because it is regarded as less variable and therefore a more sensitive indicator of changes in other statement items. The Research Department of National Credit Office regards working capital as the most satisfactory denominator by which to preserve internal balance sheet relationships when comparing identical items on separate balance sheets.[3] Like all measures of central tendency or averages, composite statements, however, furnish only mean measures; they give no evidence of the range of component items or of the relation of individual statements to size and other characteristics of the businesses which they represent.

Pattern Statement. Refinements in the composite statement intended to reduce its disadvantages are found in what are known as pattern statements, also prepared by National Credit Office, Inc. Thereby firms whose statements are combined in the composite statements are first classified so as to facilitate the comparison of individual statements. Statements of firms in an industry are grouped according to the following characteristics:

1. Net worth
2. Rate of working capital turnover
3. Price ranges (low, medium, better)
4. Location (New York City and out of town) and price range
5. Form of business (incorporated and non-incorporated)
6. Gross profit as per cent of sales

When the statements have been grouped on each basis, composite or average figures for each item, or the percentage relation of each item to working capital or net sales, are presented, depending upon whether it is an item in the balance sheet or in the operating statement. Each of these six factors is relevant to creditworthiness, and by observing the patterns or relationships common to other firms in an industry, one is in a better position to appraise the creditworthiness of any single firm whose financial statement is a subject of analysis.

Robert Morris Associates Studies. Another standard for statement analysis is prepared by Robert Morris Associates, a national association of bank credit managers, which prepares statement studies for about 100 lines of business in manufacturing and in

[3] *Ibid.*, p. 9.

wholesale and retail trades. Their studies are published an-nually. The distinctive feature of their studies is their classifica-tion of firms into asset-size groups in an industry, and in their conversion of all statement items into *percentages of total assets* (in balance sheet analysis) and of *net sales* (in operating state-ment analysis). The theory employed is similar to that underly-ing composite and pattern statements: that proportions are of primary importance and that proportions are most meaningful when comparison is made among firms of similar characteristics. The use of total assets rather than working capital is more or less an arbitrary difference in methodology.

Ratio Analyses. Still another variation of statement analysis presents the relation of items to not merely one base, such as total assets or working capital, but to each other. This approach has been widely expounded in both accounting and credit circles and has been most popularly expressed in the "fourteen important ratios" prepared by Dun & Bradstreet, Inc. Many financial au-thorities and credit analysts have proposed ratios which they regarded as important. Eugene S. Benjamin in his book *Practical Credit Analysis*, published in 1933, presented seven ratios for credit analysis. J. P. Stevens and Company, a textile firm, like many companies, over the years has computed financial statistics for its own customers, using generally eleven ratios.[4] The Dun & Bradstreet ratios include the following expressed in per-centages:

1. Net profit on net sales
2. Net profit on tangible net worth
3. Net profit on net working capital
4. Fixed assets to tangible net worth
5. Current debts to tangible net worth
6. Total debt to tangible net worth
7. Inventory to net working capital
8. Current debt to inventory
9. Funded debt to net working capital

The following are expressed as a number of times figure:

1. Current assets to current debt
2. Turnover of tangible net worth
3. Turnover of net working capital
4. Net sales to inventory

[4] Knaus, *op. cit.*, p. 23.

One ratio is expressed as a number of days: the average collection period. The ratios are shown with interquartile ranges, and no dollar figures are indicated. The fourteen ratios do not represent characteristics of individual statements on a composite or average basis.

The difference between the Dun & Bradstreet ratios, which are shown with interquartile ranges, and in which no dollar figures are indicated, and those prepared by others stems from the method of their derivation. From the year-end financial statements which this credit information agency obtains, a sampling of corporations is made. Each of the fourteen ratios is computed for every concern sampled, and the ratios are punched on data processing cards and arranged into industry groups. All of the values for each ratio are arrayed and the range divided by the median, upper- and lower-quartiles. The ratios are not derived from composite statements, but from individual statements. Such ratios are computed for manufacturers, wholesaling establishments, and retailers in a number of lines of business.

Inasmuch as the Dun & Bradstreet ratios are published and readily available, they will be used to illustrate statement analysis in the remainder of this chapter.

Classification of Balance Sheet Items

Before analysis of any financial statement can be made, reasonable certainty must be gained that the values reported are truly representative of the financial condition of the company *as a credit analyst would see it.* His objective is to determine debt paying ability, and statements which may be accurate from the standpoint of an independent public accountant may inaccurately report credit information. It is therefore necessary in credit analysis to classify and evaluate each item preparatory to ratio analysis. Some factors which must be considered are discussed in the following paragraphs.[5]

Cash on Hand and in Banks. Cash on hand and in banks is a verifiable item, but the total reported cash is not always credible to a credit analyst. Reservation must be made for cash set aside and earmarked for specific purposes, cash in foreign banks and

[5] For more detailed analysis of these topics, one might refer to Foulke, *op. cit.,* Chapter iv.

possibly subject to exchange restrictions, cash representing assets of consolidated companies, and cash in closed banks. Exclusion should also be made of the portion of cash deposits required by banks as compensating balances related to the line of credit extended, and of irretrievable cash in petty cash funds and advanced for expense allowances. Conservative estimation of the cash position also deducts from unrestricted cash an amount sufficient to cover all operating expenses exclusive of merchandise invoices, for a period of one month. Consideration should be given to these items, and deductions generally made for them, before the true value of "cash" for further statement analysis can be known.

Accounts Receivable. Accounts receivable are classified as a current asset only when they represent amounts due from the sale of merchandise. They then should correspond to invoiced sales, except that in the stage of being receivables some alterations occur in their value, alterations which must be appraised in evaluating this asset in creditworthiness. If sales terms involve large discounts, it should be known whether the receivables have been listed at gross or net values. If they include both current and delinquent accounts, an age analysis would be significant. If they will not be fully collectible, a deduction for bad debts should be reserved. If some of the receivables have been pledged against a loan, reducing the quality of the residue or making a contingent liability of the borrower, some evidence of this should be shown.

Receivables due from other than customers—from officers, salesmen, and other employees; from subsidiaries; or from the purchaser of other assets of the business—are not regarded as current assets, for they cannot be expected to mature into cash in the near future, in the normal course of business.

Notes Receivable. Notes receivable are an uncommon asset in mercantile trade, but because even there it has some legitimacy the circumstances of its use must be understood. Three circumstances give rise to the use of notes: a buyer's need for longer than usual terms of the trade; the buyer's financial weakness, his credit being strengthened by the written evidence of the obligation; and the closing out of a past-due account in consideration of the stronger debt evidence of the note. Knowledge of trade practices and some familiarity with circumstances of a subject should indicate what interpretation must be given this item in credit analysis.

When it is indicated that notes receivable have been discounted with a commercial lender, it is recommended that for sound credit analysis the amount of discounted notes be added to notes receivable in current assets and that an equal amount be added to the amount owing to banks or other loan sources. Notes due from other than merchandise customers should be deducted from this current asset item.

Merchandise. Merchandise is an asset for which a value is less easily determinable, yet in credit analysis its debt paying potential must be ascertained. The value of purchased inventory may be set at cost, market, or resale price, depending upon the line of trade and individual accounting practices. A credit analyst would prefer that which is most conservative. Qualitative factors would also be considered: obsolescence, damage, shrinkage. Inventory in production should be classified as finished, in-process, and materials. Inventories of operating supplies should be distinguished from inventories which will mature into sales and are not considered current assets.

Fixed Assets. Fixed assets also are not easily appraised, but evaluation of them is less urgent for most merchandise creditors than for creditors extending long-term credits. In any case, it must be recognized that several means of expressing the value of fixed assets may be used: original cost, depreciated value, probable reproduction cost, or reappraised value. As each of these may be applicable to each type of fixed asset, this balance sheet item is at times subject to considerable study.

Miscellaneous Assets. Miscellaneous assets, such as the cash surrender value of life insurance, investments, and deferred charges and prepaid expenses, are relevant to credit analysis in that they represent an allocation of resources, constitute a type of values redeemable under certain circumstances for meeting creditors' claims, and indicate the character of the accounting which has gone into the financial statement. Not all of these will be of interest in every credit analysis, but when pertinent their specific characteristics will influence the credit decision.

Accounts Payable. Accounts payable arising from the purchase of inventories are of special importance to the credit analyst, but like accounts receivable those connected with merchandising transactions should be segregated from those related to other activities. The relevance of this liability to general debt paying capacity, however, must be interpreted in the light of circumstances. Larger companies generally have a small amount of accounts payable, for the taking of cash discounts keeps such debt low. Larger companies often resort to bank loans in order to take such discounts, thus creating loans payable in place of accounts payable. Smaller companies, on the other hand, often lack bank lines of credit which make this possible; thus accounts payable may comprise most or all of their current liabilities.

When the quality of accounts payable is questioned, an age analysis of payables discloses the portions which are current and past due. Verification of this condition may be gained from information in credit interchange reports.

Notes Payable. Notes payable arise from several types of situations, which have different meanings to the credit analyst. First, notes payable for merchandise are uncommon outside the jewelry, fur, leaf tobacco, automobile tire, and some durable goods lines of business. When otherwise given, they often represent a substitution for an unpaid account payable. Second, notes payable to banks may evidence credit strength instead of weakness, for banker appraisals are generally sound and conservative. Terms of such a loan, however, are also significant, whether personal signatures of officers were required or assets pledged as security. This information may be obtained from the lending bank. Third, notes payable to officers, directors, friends, and discount finance companies evidence creditworthiness when the advance represents an accommodation, but lack of creditworthiness when it has been obtained in lieu of borrowing through more normal commercial channels. Analysis of currency and delinquency in notes payable is also essential in segregating assets of little debt paying capacity.

Other Current Liabilities. Other current liabilities which must be taken into consideration before the financial statement can be properly interpreted include accruals, deposits, advance payments, reserves for taxes, dividends declared but not paid, reserves for contingencies against possible losses, and current maturity of a funded debt.

Long-Term Liabilities. Long-term liabilities also concern the credit analyst but these are rarely found in statements of smaller businesses. In statements of larger firms, the points of interest to creditors are when the obligation will mature for payment, the priority on earnings and assets attached to certain liabilities, and the consistency in matching assets with the respective types of liability.

Stockholders' Equity. Stockholders' equity represents the amount of funds invested at the risk of the business enterprise and is an item significant both for its relation to other types of investment and for the character of funds management—past and future—which it represents. In proprietorships and partnerships, net worth is usually a single account item. In a majority of corporate statements, it consists of common stock and retained earnings. In large corporations, it may be broken down into the following items: preferred stock, common stock, class A, B, and C stock, capital surplus, retained earnings, and undivided profits. The analyst is interested in all of these for their origins, their commitments for management, and their effects upon debt paying capacity through the scalation of claims on earnings.

RATIO ANALYSIS

Creditworthiness evidenced in financial statement ratios is found in the proportions which the components of assets, liabilities, and stockholders' equity hold to each other. Payment probability is found in the slack and tensions among the factors relating to debt paying capacity. Some of the indicators are short run, some long run; some reflect wholly controllable factors, some factors involve actions of others; some depict the maturing of present assets into debt payment, others the income yield of sales activity, the relative claims of owners and creditors, or the allocation of funds to working and fixed capital uses.

Current Assets to Current Debt

When current assets (cash, marketable securities, receivables, and merchandise inventory) are related to current debt, the probability ability to pay this debt in the near future is evidenced. This ratio, commonly called the "current ratio," has since the beginning of this century been the most popular single criterion of liquidity, and the belief long persisted that a "2 to 1" ratio of such assets and debts was clear evidence of a satisfactory condition.

Refinement of this measure, however, has evolved along two lines: first, a "2 to 1" ratio is not equally good for all businesses; and second, even such a ratio is no assurance of liquidity or quality of the assets. In their normal operations some types of business require different assets or acquire different liabilities than others. Vendors selling on credit require an investment in receivables; those selling only for cash do not. Lenders and credit service specialists carry no inventory; vendors do. Some are traditionally financed by trade credit; others, by other forms of credit and investment. The result is that the median of current ratios for department stores arrayed by Dun & Bradstreet in one year was 3.48; discount stores, 1.64; lumber yards, 4.28; wholesalers of lumber and building materials, 2.44; bakers, 1.85; and manufacturers of agricultural implements and machines, 2.42. Thus it is apparent that the current ratio in a specific analysis has to be compared with similar firms and judgment passed whether it was average or better or worse than their average. Normality implies likelihood of there being sufficient current assets to meet current obligations.

Composition of current assets is the second factor which must be interpreted relative to the current ratio. Adequacy of dollars represented by current assets is no assurance of liquidity, for the investment may be in inventory rather than in receivables and cash. On the other hand, it may be in sluggish receivables rather than in merchandise and cash. By relating the current assets, singly and in various combinations, to the current liabilities, further information can be obtained. Dun & Bradstreet, for example, reports the ratio of current debt to inventory. In one year the median of firms reporting was 57.6 per cent among retailers of men's and boys' clothing (when their current ratio was 3.13), but 103.1 among retailers of farm and garden supplies (when their current ratio was 2.47). When comparisons are made against such standards, inferences may be drawn concerning receivables and cash. Similarly, when comparisons are made of receivables and cash to current debt, this ratio being referred to as the "quick" or "acid test" ratio, inferences may be drawn concerning the inventory on hand.

Inventory Analysis

Inventory, in addition to having as one of several current assets a relationship to debt, has also meaningful relationship to sales and to net working capital.

The ratio of net sales to inventory is a turnover figure which is indicative of two important evidences to the credit analyst. First, it is an indicator of the quality of an inventory, for if in relation to sales, inventory is high, so also is the probability of obsolescence, damage, and shortage high and its salability correspondingly reduced. On the other hand, excessively high turnover rates may also signal a condition of "outs" and thin assortments which reduce the total sales potential. The former condition is the more likely of the two hazards to creditworthiness. Second, it is an indicator of profitability of the investment made in inventory. All inventories represent costs incurred through investment, maintenance, insurance, deterioration, and the like. Profit derived from the incurrence of these costs comes from the profit margin on each increment of sale. Consequently, an inventory turnover of five times, other things remaining equal, holds the potentiality of more incremental profit than sales turning the same inventory investment four times. As turnover figures cannot be taken as unquestionable credit evidence, analysts must view them from several standpoints in order to determine their best meaning.

As both inventory and sales are variables which may move in concert with each other yet unconcerted with other business conditions, some other independent, stable referent for inventory change is needed. This need is satisfied in the item of net working capital, which normally varies less than either sales or inventory. Changes in inventory value, particularly those resulting from price changes, signal changes in creditworthiness through working capital depletion rather than through changes in the relationship with sales.

Choice of the point of reference for inventory ratios is important, but equally important is the means used for determining the value of the inventory. Methods differ between merchants, whose inventories are bought as finished goods, and manufacturers, whose inventories are bought as raw materials, semiprocessed goods, and subassemblies and remain in various stages of finishing. In addition, inventory valuation may be determined by no less than six methods: first-in first-out, last-in first-out, replacement value, average cost, standard or rationalized costs, and the retail method of valuing inventory at cost or market, whichever is lower.

Accounts Receivable Analysis

The accounts receivable item is another indicator of management efficiency often used by credit analysts. Related to credit sales, the investment in receivables is a basis for judging (1) the productivity of that investment and (2) the investment cost of those sales.

Dividing the volume of net credit sales by average accounts receivable produces a number known as the accounts receivable turnover rate. It is the relation of credit volume to outstanding debt. In general, a higher turnover rate indicates that a greater volume of credit sales is being achieved with a given investment of funds. To increase turnover rate by increasing sales is preferable to decreasing receivables with constant sales, for profits of vendors of merchandise are derived from sales, not from receivables outstanding. As this is a ratio, it is not an absolute measure of the cost of investment in receivables; rather, it is a study of the productivity of that investment.

Opinions differ whether for this computation reserve for bad debts should be deducted from the value of the receivables. Not to omit them implies that an investment is made in the total amount of the receivables. There is some precedence for this method in the valuation of other assets on the balance sheet. On the other hand, to omit the reserve for bad debts implies that the normal, anticipated, preplanned debt loss is no investment but a planned expense from the outset. Although nominally shown in the balance sheet, it is in reality an expense item. The ratios of Dun & Bradstreet are computed with the reserve omitted. Some practitioners follow the other line of reasoning. So far as credit loss is concerned, the bad debt becomes an expense either way. Until it is actually written off, however, there is an interval of time during which funds actually are invested, and an accounting for the investment cost of them during that interval may furnish another basis for appraisal.

The receivables turnover rate is converted into a time period by dividing the rate into 365 days of the year. The number of days for one turnover of accounts is the length of time that average receivables are outstanding. Costs of invested funds can be computed for that time period.

Although this period is sometimes termed the "average collection period," [6] it does not really express the collectibility of the accounts nor the collection activity of the creditor. Collectibility of a subject's receivables is also shown by the rate at which receivables actually on hand are collected. This measure is derived by dividing collections during a month by receivables carried at the beginning of the month. By multiplying this ratio times the 30 days in a month, one obtains still another time measure which is also termed collection rate or the collection period. As terminology is not uniformly or consistently used, and as measures and methods of calculation in use differ subtly, credit analysts must be precise in their interpretation of receivables information in judgment of creditworthiness.

Debt to Equity

A fertile area of information concerning creditworthiness lies in the relationship between debt and owners' equity in the financing of a firm. The proportionate contributions of these two sources of funds determines a subject's flexibility to meet extraordinary conditions, the costs of the capital he uses, claims and liens against his assets, and the order in which some disbursements will be made. In particular, the analysis of debt requires distinction of three types, each of which has different meaning to credit analysts: current liabilities, total liabilities, and funded debt.

Most businesses have only short-term indebtedness, making their total obligations synonymous with current liabilities. In such cases the ratio of current liabilities to equity is an index of all of the information which the relationship of these two fund sources can convey, and it is sufficient for creditors considering extension of additional short-term credits. Access to outside sources of funds is desirable and often evidence of good money management. However, as liabilities expand, the flexibility enjoyed through recourse to creditors turns into various constraints. Having heavy current liabilities closes doors to further credit in times of need; it increases operating costs in the form of interest charges;

6 Foulke, *op. cit.*, pp. 362–69.

and it causes all types of assets to be pledged or assigned as security for the current indebtedness, thus preferring some creditors and forcing others to recognize that further credit dealings would be in terms of reappraised creditworthiness. As a general principle, the smaller the firm the lower will be the ratio of current debt to tangible net worth, although typical ratios vary widely among different lines of business, ranging on a five-year average from 77.4 for airplane parts and accessories manufacturers to 18.5 for manufacturers of lumber. Careful analysis should be made of firms with heavy current liabilities, especially when such liabilities exceed two-thirds of the equity of commercial or industrial concerns ranging from $50,000 and $250,000, or three-quarters of that of concerns in excess of $250,000.[7]

Liabilities other than those which must be paid within a year are considered separately in credit analysis. Special attention must be given to views of the management which incurred such debts and to the conditions under which they were incurred. Creditors are concerned with the terms for maturing the obligation, and especially with the payments which may fall due in the near future. Payments on long-term debts which are made within a year are, of course, regarded as current liabilities. Other things being equal, concerns with long-term debt may reasonably have a higher ratio of total liabilities to net worth, for it would be presumed that they would have a longer period of productive activity for retirement of that debt.

Fixed Assets to Owners' Equity

Creditworthiness is evidenced also by a healthy relationship between the contribution which owners have made to a business and the portion of it which they have used for fixed assets of the business. Fixed assets are to current assets what a theater and stage are to a play. "The play's the thing"! So too is the rotation of elements of working capital in the setting provided by the fixed assets. One should provide enough of the latter to achieve the desired environment for the business processes, but the less the portion of equity funds invested in this type of asset the better it is as a condition of creditworthiness.

The significance of this ratio lies in the fact that when an abnormally large portion of owners' investment is put into fixed

[7] *Ibid.*, p. 229.

assets, a relatively small portion is available for other purposes. This, in turn, imposes upon the concern heavy financing and depreciation costs, and it at the same time forces the business to rely upon outside sources for working capital financing. As has been shown before, this entails restraints and obligations without which management of the firm would be happier, and possibly more successful.

Throughout the past century there have been two opposite trends relative to the importance of fixed assets. One has been the growing importance of the buildings and facilities represented by these assets. This has been a result of industrialization, mechanization, and automation. At the same time, there has been in recent years increased renting and leasing of fixed asset facilities. By this practice managers are relieved of rigidities which ownership imposes upon them, and they are provided known charges in the place of unknown rates of deterioration, depreciation, obsolescence, and risk. Owners' investments are thereby made available for the more active, profit-producing processes of the business.

In certain cases, a credit analyst will be concerned with the manner in which the fixed assets of a subject are valued, whether by the method of cost less depreciation, market value, replacement less depreciation, or liquidation value. However computed, ratios vary widely in the various lines of business. Some manufacturers have low ratios, such as cotton goods converters (1.3) or manufacturers of men's shirts, underwear, and pajamas (6.4); others high, such as bakers (71.9) and job printers (58.0). Similarly, there is a range among wholesalers: dry goods (4.7) and petroleum products (42.3); and retailers: men's and boys' clothing (12.8) and independent groceries and meats (54.0). In any given line of business, the larger the concern the better able it is to operate with a higher ratio of fixed assets to equity, although even in firms with equity exceeding $250,000, if more than three-quarters of it is invested in fixed assets, careful attention should be given the situation.[8]

Sales Analysis

As sales are both the result of the total input of a business and the source of funds from which the obligations of the business

---

[8] *Ibid.*, pp. 296–97.

are fulfilled, measures of this activity are especially significant. Three measures of sales activity are widely used by credit analysts. One is the ratio of sales to inventory, which has already been discussed. As might be shown by relating sales to any particular asset, it shows the contribution of a specific type of investment to the output of the business, and, indirectly, to profits. In two other ratios, sales are related to owners' equity and to net working capital.

The ratio of sales to owners' equity is a measure of the activity of investment, not investment in particular assets but investment made by owners. When, relative to sales, net worth is low, in comparison to similar firms, a condition of overtrading, or over-reliance upon contributions of creditors, is suggested. Conversely, undertrading on the owners' investment is indicative of some kind of management ineffectiveness, for it indicates insufficient utilization of owners' contribution. Either condition can adversely affect creditworthiness, although remedies depend upon conditions revealed by other ratios. Overtrading is dangerous because of the leverage it gives outsiders and the restraints resulting from dependence upon outsiders; this condition is improved generally by the addition of capital, although sometimes by curtailment of sales activity. Undertrading is usually remedied by more vigorous efforts to sell.

Closely related to this ratio is that of sales to net working capital. As net working capital, being the difference between current assets and current liabilities, is directly a function of the amount of liabilities and indirectly affected by the amount of equity, it too is a measure of utilization of investment. It reflects, however, the adequacy or excessiveness of investment in fixed assets, as a complement of current assets, in terms of the owners' contribution. An above-average ratio, while showing lively sales activity, may also indicate heavy current liabilities. Thus overtrading is reflected simultaneously in the ratios of sales to both equity and net working capital.

Profit Analysis

Still another point of concern in credit analysis is the profitability of the operation. This is of importance in both the short-run and long-run vitality of the subject. Perhaps the most commonly used short-run measure is the ratio of net profit to sales; long-run, net profit to the investment of owners.

Net profit being the margin of income in excess of all obligations, it is evidence of the subject's ability to pay both his operating expenses and merchandise creditors out of sales. As net profit, however, is a source of funds which flow not only into the cash account but also into other uses, it is no evidence of liquidity of working capital. Rather, it is a symptom of an acceptable degree of management efficiency, granted that its source is normal operating procedure and not some extraordinary windfall.

When related to stockholders' equity, on the other hand, net profit is an indicator of the ability of management to use the investment to good advantage. More of long-run significance, this measure reflects the attractiveness of the firm to investors, a factor which is of more significance to some credit analysts than to others, depending upon the nature of the credit service they are providing.

Flow of Funds Analysis

Although ratio analysis of financial condition provides insights over and above mere valuation analysis, it still depicts the creditworthiness of a business in a static posture—as of an instant in time. An alternative to this is the analysis not of the *funds* but of the *flow* of funds. This is a study of the *changes* occurring during a period of time, such as the interval between two financial statements, in the sources from which funds come into a business and the uses to which they are put. Such changes evidence to a credit analyst the movements of profits and of funds from other sources into all working capital accounts, not only into cash.

The following sources and uses of funds are identified:

Sources	Uses
Net profit	Net losses
Increase in liabilities	Decrease in liabilities
Decrease in assets	Increase in assets
Contribution of funds	Decrease in capital funds

Thus it is seen that funds flow accounting traces increases and decreases among the major balance sheet categories: liabilities, assets, and capital, and in the net profit summary of the income statement. Basic ratios show proportions, but they do not show the trends or changes which to the credit analyst represent value, liquidity, claims, equity, and efficiency. Normally, changes in these funds are shown by contrasting balance sheets of two periods. When statements are available for only one fiscal period, analysis of the flow of funds can be made if from the income statement can be obtained the net profits, dividends, and non-cash expenses such as reserves for depreciation for the year.[9]

Analysis of Small Business Enterprises

The techniques of ratio analysis are applicable to any business organization, but they are less useful for small businesses simply because their financial structures do not provide the categories with which some of the ratios are concerned. Creditworthiness depends upon the emergence, from the flow of funds, of cash which can be used to meet current obligations. In larger concerns, this evolution of funds is complicated by the diversity and liquidity of current assets (cash, receivables, and inventory), by the security and priority of creditors, by the burden of costs and restraints imposed by the absolute and relative magnitude of owners' contribution to total funds and by the portion of them which is invested in fixed assets, and by the efficiency of management expressed in sales activity and operating costs. In small concerns, the availability of funds for meeting credit obligations is related almost wholly to their sales activity and their gross profit. Small businesses (under $35,000 owners' equity) rarely have accounts receivable, notes payable, or long-term liabilities. Sales of merchandise turn into cash, and that cash is used to pay operating expenses and merchandise creditors. Any surplus beyond that is profit.

Analysis of creditworthiness of small business enterprises, therefore, made from their financial statements, is based mainly upon some facts and a few assumptions. Presumably known are accounts payable, monthly sales, cash on hand, and monthly operating costs. Assumed are that operating expenses for a month must be provided for by an equivalent amount of cash on hand, that operating expenses are met out of income before

---

[9] See Anton R. Hector, *Accounting for the Flow of Funds* (Boston: Houghton Mifflin Company, 1962), and Perry Mason, *"Cash Flow" Analysis and the Funds Statement*, Accounting Research Study No. 2 (New York: American Institute of Certified Public Accountants, 1961).

merchandise creditors are paid, and that cash on hand in excess of the required minimum can be used for immediate reduction of accounts payable. Under such factual and assumed conditions, the length of time required to pay existing debt out of sales can be determined. This is illustrated as follows:

Known:

Sales (annual)	$40,000
(monthly)	3,500
Monthly operating costs	
(30%)	1,050
Cash on hand	1,500
Accounts payable	5,000

Problem: To determine the length of time required to liquidate accounts payable out of sales.

Assumptions:

That monthly operating expenses of $1,050 determine the minimum cash on hand to be maintained.

That $450 of present cash on hand can be applied immediately to reduction of the $5,000 accounts payable. ($1,500 — $1,050 = $450). This would leave $4,550 payables remaining ($5,000 — $450).

That each month $2,450 ($3,500 — $1,050) could be used from sales to pay merchandise creditors.

That outstanding indebtedness could therefore be liquidated in 1.85 months ($4,500 ÷ $2,450 = 1.85).

That if a vendor's credit terms were 30 days net, the customer could be expected to pay in 55 days, or 25 days late. (1.85 × 30 = 55.5 — 30 = 25.5 days).

Such an analysis is a model of averages. It assumes that monthly sales are an average of monthly sales and that operating expenses equal the average or median of similar firms in the trade. Such assumptions may be altered if facts are otherwise, and corresponding adjustments made in the computations.

Another approach to analysis of the small business is the determination of its break-even point—the volume of sales required at which it operates at neither a loss nor a profit. This study is predicated upon a distinction between fixed and variable expenses and an assumption that existing operating expenses are fixed. From standard ratios or from the subject's operating statement may be determined the percentage of sales which operating expenses normally or actually are. By dividing the dollars of operating expenses by the percentage which they constitute, the volume of sales (or break-even point) can be determined which is necessary to provide for those expenses and also for payments to merchandise creditors. An illustration follows.

Known:

Fixed, operating expenses (annually)	$12,000
(monthly)	1,000
Operating expense ratio	29.2%

Derive the break-even point:

$1,000 = 29.2% of sales
$1,000 ÷ 29.2% = X ÷ 100%
29.2X = 100,000
X = $34,246 sales—break-even point.

FALSE FINANCIAL STATEMENT LEGISLATION

Because accuracy in financial statements inspires a high degree of credibility, special legal inducement, in legislation dealing with falsification of this information, is given those preparing and using financial statements for credit purposes. Both federal and state statutes define falsity in no uncertain terms and provide punishments for violators. Federal jurisdiction is provided by the Commercial Code of the United States; in addition to this, almost all states also have laws making the issuance of false financial statements for credit purposes a punishable crime.

Properly to appraise the import of such legislation, it must be recognized that both types of laws deal with the *criminal* aspects of financial statement falsification. Civil suits, under which an injured party brings action against a debtor, are wholly apart from criminal action. The latter is instigated by the government, is for punitive and preventive purposes, and may be independent of whether loss was actually suffered. Conceivably, civil and criminal actions against a misrepresenter could proceed concurrently, unrelated.

Conditions for liability under false financial statement legislation are specifically detailed.[10] They all require (1) that the financial statement in question be materially false, (2) that the person offering it know of its falsity, (3) that it be intended to be relied upon for credit purposes, and (4) that it be made in writing. Although "False Pretense Statutes" of the states, pertaining to obtaining property by means of a false financial statement, require proof that property of values was actually obtained, the special false financial statement laws enacted by states do

[10] Although provisions of the statutes should be checked in their original sources, a summary of such legislation is given in any current edition of *Credit Manual of Commercial Laws*, published by the National Association of Credit Management.

not make this a necessary condition. Neither does the Commercial Code require proof that loss be actually suffered, although it does require proof that the false statement was mailed, thus basing action on a crime against the Post Office.

Emphasis should be given the fact that each of these requirements is given special construction in the enforcement of the law. "Materially false" means that it be sufficiently false that a prudent credit manager would have decided differently had he been in possession of true facts. As some statement items are matters of opinion and estimation and not indisputable, determination of falsity is not simple. Items such as cash in banks, accounts receivable, acceptances and notes payable, tax liabilities, and mortgages are more or less provable from private or public records. Items such as cash on hand, inventory, land, buildings, machinery, fixtures and equipment; receivables due from other than customers; and sums owing to partners, friends, and relatives are more difficult to substantiate.

"Knowledge" of the falsity of a statement means constructive knowledge of it. If an officer of a company is presumed to know, or has responsibility for accuracy, he is held to have knowledge of the falsity of the statement although in fact he did not know of it.

The requirement that it be given "to be relied upon," and relied upon "for credit purposes," removes from actionability statements which may have been lost or stolen and were not intentionally given for credit purposes and statements which were prepared and given for such purposes as internal management decisions, tax determination, or stockholder or public information.

To be "in writing" a statement must be signed. Statements meeting all these requirements, whether given directly by the applicant or indirectly by an agent or representative, are actionable. The laws are equally applicable to individuals or business firms. Punishment includes fines up to $1,000 and imprisonment up to five years for federal offenses and up to one year under state laws.

DISCUSSION QUESTIONS

1. What are the theories which underlie the use of financial statement analyses as a useful basis of determining creditworthiness?

2. Compare the standards by which financial statement values and ratios may be analyzed.
3. Explain the potential contribution to or detraction from the debt paying capacity of a firm shown in each balance sheet item. Indicate the factors which cause this potential for each to be greater or less.
4. Is it possible that a subject could have assets with high debt paying potential and yet from the standpoint of a ratio analysis lack creditworthiness? Explain.
5. Contrast the merits of balance sheet ratios and flow of funds analysis.
6. Upon what bases may there be differences of opinion as to the valuation of items in a balance sheet? To what extent may values differ without being cause for liability under false financial statement laws?
7. What differences in financial statement analysis are presented by small companies, in contrast with large?
8. The financial statements of the Cotton Candy Company at the beginning and end of 19XX were as follows:

ASSETS	Jan. 1	Dec. 31
Current assets		
Cash	$ 1,250	$ 1,500
Accounts receivable	1,750	2,000
Inventories	2,750	2,500
Total current assets	$ 5,750	$ 6,000
Long-lived assets		
Building and fixtures	$10,000	$10,000
Allowance for depreciation	4,000	4,500
Undepreciated cost	$ 6,000	$ 5,500
Total assets	$11,750	$11,500

LIABILITIES AND EQUITIES		
Current liabilities		
Accounts payable	$ 1,000	$ 750
Federal taxes payable	750	750
Total current liabilities	$ 1,750	$ 1,500
Bonds payable—5½%	$ 6,500	$ 6,000
Total liabilities	$ 8,250	$ 7,500
Owners' equity		
Capital stock	$ 2,000	$ 2,000
Retained earnings	1,500	2,000
Total owners' equity	$ 3,500	$ 4,000
Total liabilities and equity	$11,750	$11,500

Sales	$33,550
Cost of goods sold	
Beginning inventory	2,750
Purchases	25,000
Less: discounts earned	(250)
Total	$27,500
Ending inventory	2,500
Cost of goods sold	$25,000
Margin	$ 8,550
Operating expenses	
Selling expenses	$ 3,000
Administrative expenses	3,200
Depreciation	500
Total operating expenses	$ 6,700
Net operating earnings	$ 1,850
Interest expense	350
Earnings before taxes	$ 1,500
Federal taxes	750
Net earnings after tax	$ 750
Retained earnings, January 1	1,000
Total	$ 1,750
Dividends	250
Retained earnings, December 31	$ 1,500
Earnings per share	$ 37.50

(a) Appraise the creditworthiness of this company. Assume that you received an order for $500 of merchandise; would you extend credit in this amount? (b) Assume that the company was operating with an operating expense ratio of 30 per cent. What sales would it have to make to break even? What sales would needed to provide the same net earnings after taxes?

9. Compute the significant ratios for The Arlington Corporation and compare them with the Dun & Bradstreet ratios given below.

The Arlington Corporation Comparative Balance Sheets

	December 31		
	19X2	19X1	19XX
ASSETS			
Current assets:			
Cash	$ 8,500	$ 7,000	$ 6,000
Receivables	20,000	15,000	14,000
Inventories	50,000	35,000	28,000
Total current assets	$ 78,500	$57,000	$48,000
Buildings and equipment	$ 60,000	$50,000	$30,000
Less: Allowance for depreciation	12,000	10,000	9,000
Buildings and equipment (net)	$ 48,000	$40,000	$21,000
Total assets	$126,500	$97,000	$69,000

The Arlington Corporation Comparative Balance Sheets (Continued)

	December 31		
	19X2	19X1	19XX
LIABILITIES AND STOCKHOLDERS' EQUITY			
Current liabilities:			
Accounts payable for merchandise	$ 10,000	$ 8,000	$ 7,000
Notes payable—bank	3,000	2,000	1,000
Federal income tax	7,000	6,500	6,000
Total current liabilities	$ 20,000	$16,500	$14,000
Bonds payable (due 10 years after issue)	40,000	20,000	–0–
Total liabilities	$ 60,000	$36,500	$14,000
Stockholders' equity:			
Capital stock (1,000 shares)	$ 25,000	$25,000	$25,000
Retained earnings	41,500	35,500	30,000
Total stockholders' equity	$ 66,500	$60,500	$55,000
Total liabilities and stockholders' equity	$126,500	$97,000	$69,000

The Arlington Corporation Comparative Statement of Earnings and Retained Earnings

	Calendar Year		
	19X2	19X1	19XX
Sales	$100,000	$90,000	$70,000
Less: cost of goods sold	60,000	52,000	38,000
Gross margin	$ 40,000	$38,000	$32,000
Operating expenses:			
Selling expense	$ 11,000	$11,000	$10,000
Administrative expense [a]	13,000	13,000	10,000
Total operating expenses	$ 24,000	$24,000	$20,000
Net earnings from operation	$ 16,000	$14,000	$12,000
Bond interest expense	$ 2,000	$ 1,000	$ –0–
Federal income taxes	7,000	6,500	6,000
Total interest and taxes	$ 9,000	$ 7,500	$ 6,000
Net earnings after interest and taxes	$ 7,000	$ 6,500	$ 6,000
Retained earnings, January 1	35,500	30,000	25,000
Total available for dividends	$ 42,500	$36,500	$31,000
Dividends	1,000	1,000	1,000
Retained earnings, December 31	$ 41,500	$35,500	$30,000
[a] Includes depreciation as follows:	$ 2,000	$ 1,000	$ 1,000

DUN & BRADSTREET, INC., FINANCIAL STATEMENT RATIOS

Manufacturing & Construction

Line of Business (and number of concerns reporting)	Current assets to current debt	Net profits on net sales	Net profits on tangible net worth	Net profits on net working capital	Net sales to tangible net worth	Net sales to net working capital	Collection period	Net sales to inventory	Fixed assets to tangible net worth	Current debt to tangible net worth	Total debt to tangible net worth	Inventory to net working capital	Current debt to inventory	Funded debts to net working capital
	Times	Per cent	Per cent	Per cent	Times	Times	Days	Times	Per cent	Per cent	Per cent	Per cent	Per cent	Per cent
273 Books, Pubshg. & Printing (36)	4.04	7.66	19.02	24.48	3.32	5.29	42	7.9	9.1	25.2	41.4	44.4	56.6	11.4
	2.97	4.95	12.49	14.53	2.23	3.14	66	6.5	25.8	45.0	62.1	60.8	83.0	17.4
	2.05	1.66	4.40	7.11	1.95	2.43	93	3.3	46.3	62.5	76.3	81.1	161.9	57.9
1711 Contractors, Plumbing Heating & Air Cond. (75)	2.56	4.04	23.95	30.75	8.88	13.19	**	**	11.4	44.1	77.9	**	**	8.8
	1.79	1.70	10.79	13.90	6.71	8.52	**	**	20.8	80.4	110.8	**	**	16.4
	1.39	0.65	4.50	4.96	3.63	4.74	**	**	40.8	167.6	231.9	**	**	79.5
283 Drugs (51)	5.09	8.69	15.00	29.47	2.97	5.24	35	7.4	24.0	19.6	34.2	49.6	37.2	7.6
	3.10	4.38	11.06	13.88	2.29	3.58	43	5.8	37.9	30.3	47.6	67.3	71.1	22.7
	2.24	1.18	3.80	4.78	1.38	2.39	54	4.1	57.4	48.3	73.5	91.2	120.2	42.8

Wholesaling

Line of Business	Current assets to current debt	Net profits on net sales	Net profits on tangible net worth	Net profits on net working capital	Net sales to tangible net worth	Net sales to net working capital	Collection period	Net sales to inventory	Fixed assets to tangible net worth	Current debt to tangible net worth	Total debt to tangible net worth	Inventory to net working capital	Current debt to inventory	Funded debts to net working capital
5072 Hardware (203)	4.73	2.39	9.06	10.95	5.56	6.59	34	6.7	5.5	22.9	43.0	68.1	36.8	4.3
	2.90	1.29	4.51	5.75	3.45	4.39	45	4.9	13.0	44.6	78.7	87.3	60.9	15.0
	2.00	0.53	1.86	2.39	2.44	2.86	54	3.7	25.5	79.4	151.6	114.3	98.8	43.7
5047 Meats & Meat Products (57)	4.12	1.28	16.78	31.52	17.50	31.93	13	81.5	11.4	20.6	57.1	19.6	102.8	19.7
	2.27	0.79	8.94	14.56	11.98	16.24	22	46.6	26.9	41.7	124.8	35.7	171.6	40.5
	1.58	0.31	4.02	8.32	6.99	11.25	30	31.2	51.6	108.3	184.0	78.5	354.6	96.0

Retailing

Line of Business	Current assets to current debt	Net profits on net sales	Net profits on tangible net worth	Net profits on net working capital	Net sales to tangible net worth	Net sales to net working capital	Collection period	Net sales to inventory	Fixed assets to tangible net worth	Current debt to tangible net worth	Total debt to tangible net worth	Inventory to net working capital	Current debt to inventory	Funded debts to net working capital
5511† Automobile dealers (133)	2.37	2.26	21.54	29.53	15.73	21.83	*	12.2	11.5	49.1	80.7	95.8	63.2	11.9
	1.78	1.28	13.12	18.02	9.88	14.70	*	9.4	22.8	91.2	132.2	160.3	84.2	26.3
	1.44	0.60	5.46	8.46	6.70	9.29	*	7.8	42.9	153.8	167.9	234.9	102.9	66.3
5212 Building Materials (110)	4.33	4.04	12.16	17.10	5.17	8.54	38	10.7	13.0	21.7	59.6	44.8	53.6	24.8
	2.79	1.74	6.06	7.67	3.27	4.71	51	6.4	26.9	36.7	84.1	65.7	87.7	43.7
	1.74	0.23	0.46	1.26	2.17	3.13	82	4.9	53.9	73.8	136.7	93.2	141.1	87.8

384

23

Non-specialized Information Sources

Although agencies and bureaus supply a vast amount of information used in the analysis of creditworthiness, additional assistance can be obtained from other sources which possess such information in the process of their other primary activities. Among them are customers themselves, salesmen, banks, and other creditors. These sources are discussed in this chapter. In addition to them are many others, which need merely be mentioned as indicative of the scope of reference material available for credit analysis: personal character references, general and trade publications carrying articles about the subject, financial analysts and their reporting services, court records, and employers of individuals. Each of these sources is somewhat unique with respect to the information it can provide. The well-informed credit manager will have among his resources both specialized and non-specialized contacts and will draw upon them individually or collectively as best serves his needs.

The credit analyst selects his information among the variety of sources available, supplementing information in some instances, complementing it in others. His selection is governed by the following factors:

Adequacy: The type of information needed is a determinant of the source from which it will be obtained. Needs sometimes call for complete reports, sometimes for selected facts relative to antecedents, character, financial condition, or operations.

Timeliness: Basically, creditworthiness is based upon facts and trends of long standing, but recent developments may outweigh other factors or alter an established credit appraisal. Some sources of information are in better position than others to be apprised of changing circumstances.

Speed: Prompt delivery of information is essential in some credit decisions but not in all. The need to authorize a credit sale, for example, may demand more speedy information assembly than the investigation of new customers or the reappraisal of an account.

Involvement: Use of some information sources presumes managerial involvement in the form of reciprocity, personal identification, and participation in the search process. This may or may not be desirable; thus selection is made among services which either avoid or require it.

Cost: Specialized sources charge for their information; non-specialized sources generally do not. Thus to avoid fees, resort may be made to information sources which cost only the involvement entailed. This, however, is not entirely without cost, when all factors are considered, and may in the long run not be the most economical form to use.

Each source of information has its own merits in terms of all these considerations. In terms of adequacy or type of information alone, a comparison of sources is given in Fig. 23–1. As a general rule, choice is based upon the policy to use those sources which best serve the need and to avoid inquiring when the information desired can better be obtained elsewhere.

CREDIT APPLICATIONS

A common source of information is the credit application, whereby facts are obtained directly from the applicant for credit himself. This source is more used in the opening of retail accounts than in mercantile credit, for in the latter essential information may be obtained better from other sources.

The credit application is a written form of credit information, designed to gather facts which the creditor thinks cannot be obtained elsewhere, or which may lead him to obtaining other facts elsewhere. In retail credit granting, applications are generally supplemented by credit reports, and they may or may not be

Check-List of Sources
And Where to find it

The Information You Want

	Salesman	Customer	Cr. Mgr's Observation	Credit Interchange	Mercantile Agencies	Bank	Other Creditors	Group Discussions	Insurance Agent	Landlord	Court Records	Newspapers	Stockholders Repts	Credit Association	Chamber of Commerce	Trade Journals	Business Journals	Economic bulletins	Other Customers	Foulke Ratios
Trade style	✓	✓		✓	✓							✓		✓						
Legal composition	✓	✓		✓	✓	✓						✓		✓						
Capital structure		✓			✓								✓	✓						
Kind of business	✓	✓			✓									✓						
Branches	✓	✓			✓									✓						
Inter-company relations		✓			✓															
Products sold	✓	✓	✓		✓		✓	✓								✓				
Selling terms	✓	✓			✓															
Selling markets	✓	✓			✓															
Buying terms		✓			✓			✓	✓											
Buying markets		✓	✓					✓	✓											
Operating details	✓	✓	✓		✓			✓	✓	✓				✓						
Community industries	✓	✓	✓		✓		✓	✓	✓	✓										
Competition	✓	✓	✓					✓	✓	✓										
Number of employees	✓	✓	✓		✓															
Labor relations		✓						✓	✓					✓						
Equipment	✓	✓	✓		✓															
Description of quarters	✓	✓	✓		✓															
Location	✓	✓	✓		✓															
Fire hazards	✓	✓	✓						✓											
Housekeeping	✓	✓	✓		✓				✓											
Display	✓																			
Real Estate owned	✓	✓			✓		✓				✓									
Landlord	✓	✓																		
Terms of lease: rental	✓	✓			✓					✓										
Insurance agent	✓	✓							✓	✓										
Insurance coverage	✓	✓			✓				✓											
Name of bank		✓					✓	✓		✓										
Loans outstanding						✓	✓													
Banking relations						✓	✓													
History of owners		✓				✓	✓	✓	✓											
Age of owners	✓	✓	✓		✓		✓	✓	✓											
Management efficiency			✓					✓	✓											
History of business		✓				✓	✓	✓	✓		✓									
Fire record							✓			✓										
Failure record							✓	✓	✓											
Mortgages; liens		✓				✓	✓				✓									
Suits; judgments				✓		✓		✓	✓		✓									
Extensions				✓		✓		✓	✓											
Other creditors	✓	✓				✓	✓	✓	✓		✓									
Payments						✓	✓	✓	✓											
Creditor satisfaction						✓		✓	✓											
Balance-sheets		✓			✓									✓						
Operating statements		✓												✓						
Sales, profits, dividends		✓			✓									✓						
Budgets		✓																		
Explanation of balance-sheet items															✓					
Estimated inventory	✓	✓	✓																	
Standard ratios																				✓
Industry practices								✓	✓					✓	✓	✓			✓	
Market trends	✓	✓						✓	✓			✓		✓	✓	✓	✓	✓	✓	✓
Industry problems	✓	✓						✓	✓					✓	✓	✓	✓	✓		✓
Local business activity	✓	✓					✓	✓	✓	✓				✓	✓	✓			✓	
General business activity								✓	✓	✓		✓		✓	✓	✓	✓	✓	✓	✓

Fig. 23–1. Checklist of Sources. (Source: H. M. Sommers, "Where Shall We Find The Answer?" *Credit and Financial Management*, August, 1950, p. 5.)

supplemented by interviews. Application forms are made available to customers in a variety of ways: in distribution boxes
located throughout the store, in newspaper advertising, and by
mail, both upon request and in promotional mailings.

Several purposes in using applications determine the information asked for. As applications are often the initial contact with
a potential credit customer, exact identification of the applicant
is essential. This is important to identify him in several con-
texts: among other customers of the creditor, in his living environment, in his employment, and as a member of a family.
Distinction among account holders with identical or similar names
must be made by correct spelling of the full name, by address,
maiden and married names, social security number, and ultimately by an account number with the creditor. Without this
exact information, investigation, authorization, billing, and adjustments cannot be made with certainty. Equally important
in the use of applications is the ascertaining of facts to be used
subsequently in collection work. When accounts are in default,
referents of different types are useful in locating individuals and
in bringing moral suasion upon them to honor their debts. Knowing the debtor's correct address, one may seek from neighbors
information concerning his living habits, removals, and employment. Knowing his employer and badge identification, one may
confirm the fact of his employment or know against whom garnishment proceedings may be initiated. With knowledge of his
kin, information may be obtained concerning his whereabouts,
or inducement may be given to encourage his making payment.
While identification for these purposes may sometimes be obtained
elsewhere, it also may not, and the voluntary submission of such
information by the applicant at a time when he is requesting
credit service is one of the best occasions for obtaining it.

Among the types of information requested in the application
from which creditworthiness may be ascertained are the following: marital status, residential ownership, length of present and
former employment, income, current indebtedness, and scheduled
payments. In applications for universal credit cards, information
is also sought as to whether billings are to be made to the individual or to the company.

In addition to providing information to creditors, applications
may serve as the form of contract between the vendor and the
applying customer. Some applications include for signed agreement such phrases as the following:

"I will pay each monthly instalment computed according to the schedule as stated above upon the receipt of each statement. If I fail to pay any instalment in full when due, at your option the full balance shall become immediately due"; or

"We are making this application and statement for the purpose of securing credit from _____ and agree to pay according to the terms of the account we establish and have requested the account to be billed in the name above."

The significance of the second statement, specifying that the statement is made for credit purposes, is that thereby the application is brought under the requirements of false financial statement legislation, intentional violation of which may prevent discharge from this particular debt in the event of bankruptcy of the debtor.

Examples of representative retail credit applications are shown in Fig. 23–2. With technical modifications, applications for personal loans follow a similar pattern.

The lesser use of credit applications in mercantile credit is due to several factors. First, applications are not the means used for solicitation of new mercantile credit customers; sales presentations and product promotion are more commonly used. Second, forms used for information sought directly from customers are often filled by salesmen and so are not applications but in-house information forms. Third, the types of information upon which such credit decisions are based are so detailed and complex that the collection of them by information specialists is preferred. Fourth, the principal information sought from prospective customers, if it is not possessed by information agencies, is the financial statement of the customer. This cannot be considered a credit application, although it may include the statement also found in the credit application and be offered for credit purposes.

APPLICANT INTERVIEWS

In contrast to applications, interviews are personal, face-to-face confrontations for the purpose of assessing creditworthiness. Several objectives lead to the use of interviews: the expectation that types of information can be obtained which cannot be ascertained from impersonal applications; desire to accommodate customers who view the opening of an account as a personal experience; willingness to assist customers to whom form filling and

SEARS
Credit
Application

(PLEASE SIGN AGREEMENT ON REVERSE SIDE)   AUTHORIZED PURCHASERS

MR.
MRS.
MISS.
(Please Print)   (Wife's Name)   1.
ADDRESS   2.
CITY   ZONE   STATE   3.
PREVIOUS SEARS ACCOUNT   (Date)   (Approx. Amount)   (What Store?)
OWN   MARRIED
HOW LONG AT   RENT   SINGLE
PRESENT ADDRESS?   BOARD   AGE   WIDOWED   DEPENDENTS   PHONE NO.
FORMER ADDRESS (IF LESS THAN   HOW
2 YRS. AT PRESENT ADDRESS)   LONG?
EMPLOYER   ADDRESS
TIME CARD OR   WEEKLY
HOW LONG?   OCCUPATION?   BADGE NO?   EARNINGS?
FORMER EMPLOYER (If less than 1 yr. with present employer)   HOW LONG?
NAME AND ADDRESS OF BANK   (Branch)   CHECKING
SAVINGS
EXPLAIN OTHER INCOME, IF ANY   LOAN
NAME AND ADDRESS   CREDIT REFERENCES   NAME AND ADDRESS

application for a
fashion charge account

name ....

wife's first name ....

address ....

city ....zip code ......state......

home phone ....

mr. employed by ....how long ....

occupation ....

mrs. employed by ....how long....

occupation ....

other accounts with ....

....

....

signature ....

Fig. 23–2. Credit applications—retail.

letter writing are unfamiliar or bothersome; and effort to serve the customer in the store whose desire to purchase leads to simultaneous request for immediate credit. When interviewing is part of the credit approval process, interviewers may supplement a customer-filled application with further interrogation, may fill a similar form while conversing with the applicant, or may make an informal record of credit qualifications after the interview.

Personal impressions are fallible, but from visual contact with applicants, creditors make useful observations of character, integrity toward debt, attitudes toward credit service, and the economic competence of the customer. Discussion may also lead to information concerning employment and indebtedness not asked for in the application. Equally important is the opportunity afforded by the interview to educate the customer in the vendor's credit terms, policies, and procedures. Interviews are the only occasion for many customers to confer with credit department representatives, and mutual benefits may be expected from the event.

Whereas in retail credit granting the interview is usually held at the creditor's place of business, mercantile credit interviews often occur through a visit of the credit manager to the customer desiring to use his credit. As applications are less used in this area of credit management, interviews often serve a useful purpose. They afford more than mere interrogation; rather, opportunity to discuss with the customer his credit needs and capabilities, to observe conditions of his establishment, to suggest means of improving tangible or intangible circumstances for the betterment of creditworthiness, and to cement a profitable understanding between the two. Difficulties of time and space in mercantile trade often militate against such interviewing, but its advantages are nonetheless to be realized. Such interviewing, moreover, is not confined to the opening of credit relations but is also profitable thereafter when the credit manager can visit customers regularly or intermittently. Visitation programs of this kind may distinguish good from superior credit management.

When personal calls are impossible, telephone communication with customers may be a satisfactory substitute. They are less expensive, yet they provide a rapport unavailable through correspondence.

THE MANAGEMENT OF CREDIT BUSINESS

SALESMEN

Of non-specialists, salesmen of a firm are particularly useful in supplying some kinds of credit information. This is not true in retailing; there salesmen view buyers in their consumption, not their credit, context, and the assembly of credit information is left to other individuals. In mercantile trade, however, where salesmen go out to call on customers with whom the credit manager may have little or no direct contact, especially when credit is initially requested, salesmen can be uniquely useful.

Their value lies in their presumed ability to view a sales situation from the combined viewpoints of sales, credit, and general management. Their superiority to a mercantile agency investigator lies in their *interested*, rather than disinterested, scrutiny of the credit customer. Both of these claimed advantages have long been debated, more so earlier when sales objectives were less integrated with over-all corporate objectives. It is questioned whether the salesman state of mind will or can assimilate the types of information, find the customer rapport, which yields essential credit information. Sales quotas, commission compensation scales, paper routines, and selling psychology impinge upon the success of a salesman as a credit manager's assistant. These obstacles, however, can be dissolved through proper arrangements between the sales and credit departments if the importance of individual contribution to corporate objectives is paramount. If that objective prevails, it then becomes the responsibility of the credit manager to determine how best to use the services of salesmen available to him.

Salesmen, in general, provide an excellent source of information concerning a customer's credit character and capacity, interpreted in the light of his own firm's interests. Salesman-customer relations can disclose much of the customer's probable willingness to pay: his integrity, earnestness, and reliability. The salesman is also in an excellent position to appraise capacity: business activity, competitive position, locality, character of trade, product lines, and adequacy of physical facilities. Moreover, he views these conditions not merely in the abstract but in the context of his own sales and the profit of his employer. On the other hand, the salesmen may be less useful in ascertainment of capital, for, even if he can appraise values of inventory, fixtures, and real estate, he has no access to financial conditions which differentiate owners' equity from simple asset values. Some credit managers use salesmen for obtaining a financial statement; others do not, preferring to obtain it through an information agency or through direct contact with the customer. Under some circumstances, salesmen assist in collection work, in both current and past-due indebtedness.

Examples of forms used by salesmen in submitting credit information are shown in Fig. 23–3.

BANKS

Banks also provide information relevant to credit investigations, provided the inquirer carefully conducts the strategy of making the inquiry and interprets correctly the information received. Banks of both the investigator and the investigated may participate in the gathering of this information.

Banks are in business for their own credit activity, and their ability to furnish information helpful to other creditors is a by-product of that activity and is directly conditioned by it. Their relationship with the subject investigated revolves around the balances which he maintains with the bank and the loans he obtains from it. In the process of dealing with him both as creditor (depositor) and debtor (borrower), the bank forms judgments of creditworthiness which are also enlightening to another creditor.

It must be within the framework of this information, however, that a credit manager resorts to banks for credit information. He must be capable of precise interpretation and application of the information which can be obtained in this way, and he cannot expect the general expository, analytical, or interpretative information that might be obtained from credit agencies or salesmen. Banks' loyalties are primarily with their depositors and borrowers and secondarily with inquiring banks and creditors. An investigator should take this into consideration in phrasing his demands. The bank can and will in most cases answer the following type of questions:

1. Has the subject an account with the bank?
   How long has it been carried?
   What are the average balances of the account?
2. Does the subject have a line of credit with the bank?
   Have loans been granted?

C. D. KENNY DIVISION
CONSOLIDATED GROCERS CORPORATION

REQUEST FOR CREDIT

Branch _____ Name of Customer_____

Date _____ Trade name _____

How long in business_____Address—Street _____

Estimated value of stock_____ City _____

Estimated value of fixtures_____Kind of business_____

General appearance of store_____

REFERENCES (GIVE AT LEAST THREE)

Branch *must* contact references and give information below

FIRM	ADDRESS	TERMS	OWES	HOW PAYS

Amount of credit requested by branch $_____   Terms_____

_____   _____
Salesman   Branch Manager Approval

GENERAL COMMENTS

_____

[For Main Office Use Only]

Date_____ Amount of Credit Approved $_____ Terms_____

_____
Credit Manager

Fill out in duplicate and send both copies to Headquarters. We will return one for your files. The above information to be submitted by salesmen and approved by branch manager.

Fig. 23–3. Salesmen's credit information forms.

NEW ACCOUNT INFORMATION

_____
(Date)

BRAND SHOES AS: _____ J. & K.   CONFIRMATION REQUIRED   _____ YES

_____ LOCKE   _____ NO

_____ UNBRANDED

BILL TO:

_____   _____
NAME   DEPT.

_____
STREET ADDRESS

_____   _____   _____
CITY   STATE   ZIP CODE

SHIP TO:
(IF DIFFERENT FROM ABOVE)   _____

_____

NAMES WE SHOULD KNOW: OWNER   _____

BUYER   _____

MANAGER   _____

ADV. MGR.   _____

OTHERS   _____

CORRESPOND WITH: _____

LINES OF SHOES NOW IN THE STORE

_____   _____

_____   _____

_____   _____

CUSTOMER'S BANK _____

USE OTHER SIDE FOR ADDRESSES
OF BRANCH STORES WHICH WILL
BE HANDLING OUR SHOES

_____
SALESMAN

Fig. 23–3. *Continued.*

What maximum loan has been made during the past year, and what is now owing?
Why has the subject borrowed?
What terms and security have been involved?
Have loans been guaranteed or endorsed? By whom?
3. What is the bank's attitude toward the subject and its appraisal of his capabilities?

Although banks possess such information, and generally are willing to cooperate with other creditors, the success of an inquiry depends much upon the strategy and etiquette employed. As this is a form of direct exchange of credit information, it should be used sparingly, judiciously, and appreciatively. The credit investigation should have been carried to an advanced stage before bank information is sought. Moreover, preparation for the inquiry should be made. Not only should specific questions be formulated; the relative merits of correspondence and telephoning should be considered. When unknown to the subject's bank, an investigator may profit by having his own bank make the inquiry. Use of an intermediary, however, requires informing him of the details of the credit investigation so that information may be requested in the context of its anticipated use. Even when direct contact is made with the bank, the investigator should, by phone, reciprocate with what he knows about the subject and, by letter, be precise enough to facilitate reply. Several calls may be necessary for establishing a relationship with the bank that will be productive of the desired information.

Above all, the inquirer should be alert to the forms of communication by which bank information is communicated. More than some other credit communications, those of banks are cryptic. Unwilling to express specific amounts, their terminology denotes general sums, yet specific enough to the trained observer. Categories are expressed as "low," "medium," or "high," or as "low," "moderate," "medium," "good," and "high." In the latter case the designations correspond to the following digits:

Low	1–3	Good	6–8
Moderate	3–4	High	8–9
Medium	4–6		

Thus a "medium five-figure balance" would be between $40,000 and $60,000. Caution impels bankers to let inquirers take the initiative in eliciting information, and they seldom volunteer what is not asked for. It therefore behooves the inquirer to ask carefully, probing by indirection if necessary to gain impressions, and to make warranted inferences from the information obtained.

The price of information obtained from banks is fixed, but seldom in terms of money. Its price is discretion in the use of this freely given service, personally written and signed letters if correspondence is used, reciprocity in information exchange, accuracy in statement of the information desired, and avoidance of deception of the bank as to the motives for the inquiry.

DIRECT TRADE INTERCHANGE

Bank experience constitutes a type of ledger information, and as such it is typical of the larger amount of such information commonly sought from other trade creditors. The Credit Interchange Bureau specializes in assembling and reporting this information, but a certain amount of it is also exchanged through direct contact among creditors. This is another source to which a credit analyst may make recourse in his investigation.

Direct interchange is an advantageous complement to information obtained from other sources, when the need calls for confirmation of a reported fact, continuation of a reported trend, verification of rumors, or conference discussion of mutual experiences. As with bank references, trade references are not intended to replace agency ratings and reports, for another's judgment or another's experience alone should not be made the basis of one's own decision. However, another creditor's experience may reveal information which no other source contains. Although credit reports are presumed to be confidential, some types of information are not entrusted to these communications. Direct contact provides a means of making them known. Personal idiosyncrasies of a debtor, changes in his condition, unpublicized arrangements, guarantees, requests for special considerations, extensions, composition settlements, and the like are subjects for beneficial direct exchange.

The means of direct interchange differ with circumstances. Need for immediate information may impel telephone inquiry, either local or long distance. Less urgent needs are served by correspondence, although unless specific points are raised these needs are often better served by agency information. Still other needs lead to creditor group discussions as a means of direct interchange. One of the most striking examples of this is the foreign credit Roundtable, monthly discussion meetings of credit conditions and problems faced by exporters in the New York area. Other similar meetings are held by both mercantile and retail credit managers, often those engaged in only a specific line of trade. On such occasions names of problem-giving credit customers may be discussed, experiences related, or information given concerning paying habits, indebtedness, and terms extended.

Direct information exchange has unmistakable advantages: it is speedy; it elicits information and interpretation not reported elsewhere; it fosters cooperation and esprit de corps among credit managers; it is undeniably inexpensive. On the other hand, it is time consuming; it accumulates obligations for reciprocity; it is supplemental rather than complete; and it discloses possibly to a competitor the name of one's own customer. The balance of these advantages and disadvantages shift, depending upon circumstances, and it is the responsibility of the credit investigator to determine the direction of the balance in individual situations.

DISCUSSION QUESTIONS

1. Compare the merits of non-specialized information sources as compared with services of credit specialists.
2. Explain the principle that any source of information should be used chiefly because of the superiority of its information, and secondarily because of cost or convenience.
3. Under what circumstances is the use of credit applications possible, advisable, imperative, or inadvisable?
4. When creditors take initiative to open unrequested accounts in a customer's name, is the lack of an application and interview necessarily a handicap? Why?
5. What contribution to successful interviewing may be made by a creditor's thinking of credit as a social process rather than merely as a technical business or economic process?
6. Discuss the use of salesmen for credit information from the standpoint of credit organization, loyalties, perception, and marketing mix.
7. What principles of personal interaction would facilitate obtaining credit information from bankers?
8. Appraise the contribution of personal and business references, insurance companies, and court clerks as non-specialized suppliers of credit information.

24

Credit Lines and Limits

Ascertainment of creditworthiness is a qualitative judgment, but it is inseparable from a quantitative determination known as the setting of credit lines and limits. So closely related are these two management decisions that distinction between them is not always made, but their differences are clear and are evident in the uses to which each is put. Determination of creditworthiness involves investigation, analysis, and appraisal of a subject's qualifications *before* a credit relationship is approved. Determination of credit lines and limits relates to the relations of creditors and customers *after* their creditworthiness has been approved.

The Meaning of "Lines and Limits"

Like other concepts, that of lines and limits has a specific technical meaning, but it also has a wider significance that needs to be interpreted. Specifically, a *line of credit* is an amount of credit service which a supplier would be willing to provide a customer. It has a positive connotation. The maximum may not always be needed, but it is an amount that is made available. Mercantile creditors and banks often extend their clients lines of credit. A *credit limit*, on the other hand, is an amount beyond which a creditor would go reluctantly, if at all, in providing credit service to a customer. It has a more negative connotation, indicating the twilight zone in which confidence turns to doubt. The line of credit is a permissive concept; the limit is restrictive.

In general, both lines and limits are guides to action in decisions which must be made by credit managers. They represent an attempt to identify a somewhat indeterminate area where the capacities of both the creditor and the debtor to participate in a credit relationship diminish to extinction. Both parties have an interest in the definition of this area, but creditors carry the responsibility for finally drawing the line. They mark the point beyond which the creditor may be unable financially to invest more in a given account or type of account. They outline the extent of the risk which, by policy, the creditor will or can accept. They reflect also the estimated credit potential of the customer, as determined by his character, capacity, and capital. In these roles, the line and limit may appear to be a precisely stated quantity, but they represent a number of considerations which cannot be so precisely evaluated. While lines and limits may not actually be negotiable, they are at least subject to a variety of factors.

More specifically, lines and limits are guides to action in the performance of the basic credit functions. They state the amount of investment that will be made in any one account. They restrict the individual risk to be taken. They facilitate numerous operational routines: credit approval, credit sales promotion, sales authorization, and collection. A line of credit provides a customer with an "open-to-buy" allowance; it furnishes a sales potential for promotional effort. A credit limit divides levels of responsibility in authorization procedures; it remands a credit risk for further investigation and appraisal; it denotes the point at which follow-up and collection activity should be initiated.

Types of Lines and Limits

There are several forms of credit lines and limits, which are generally of two types: dollar quantities and rates. Both are used for the same purposes, but they reflect different approaches to the solution of the problem.

Guides expressed in terms of absolute *dollar amounts* limit (1) the total indebtedness which a customer may accumulate and (2) the size of orders which he may place. Total debt limits are the most common. They may serve as a line of credit offered the customer, but they are also the point at which some action on the account will be taken—either trading curtailed or further consideration given it. Limits are also set in terms of order size, rather than in terms of outstanding debt. Thus authorization may be automatic for orders up to a certain amount, but larger orders are given individual consideration. Choice between debt and order limits depends upon the control which the creditor's systems afford through each. Ledger records showing cumulative indebtedness may be the more effective if order and credit records are handled together. When account records are separated from sales departments or branches handling shipments, or when sales are handled through several decentralized locations, order size may be the simpler control measure. Such measures serve primarily as credit limits, causing referral of the credit request to higher authority.

Authorization control is gained also through the use of *rates:* rates of purchase and rates of payment. Normal use of credit, once creditworthiness has been approved, is evidenced by regularity of purchasing patterns, shown in frequency and tempo. Irregularity of purchasing calls for caution in authorization. Such rate considerations enter, for example, into recommendations given by Dun & Bradstreet, Inc., in its credit advisory service, by which acceptance of specific orders is approved. Rates of payment, on the other hand, serve a similar purpose. Thereby authorization is given if payment is made satisfactorily, regardless of the amount of indebtedness, the size of orders, or the frequency or volume of purchases. So long as payments are made according to credit terms, it is presumed that a buyer is using good judgment in the use of his credit, and there is a willingness of the creditor to grant his requests. Such a form of credit limit provides flexibility and allows the introduction into the credit equation, through the buyer's judgment, of factors which, had they been known to the seller, he probably would have approved.

There is a degree of substitutability among the types of lines and limits, but there are also factors upon which the preference of one over another may be reasonably established. The following are some of them:

1. Whether the measure serves primarily as a line of credit or as a credit limit. If the former, quantitative measures of debt are most commonly used. They provide the buyer a basis for using his credit, allowing him to vary the rates and increments of his purchases as best suits his purposes.
2. The stability of the customer's business. If he is expanding on a

sound basis, a rate of payment measure allows for extension of business beyond what fixed limits would accommodate. A stable business with good paying habits would be served equally well by either quantitative or rate measures.

3. The relative importance of volume or rate as indications of normality in a customer's business activity. Apart from natural growth, changes in one or another form of behavior may first suggest conditions to which credit managers' attention should be given.

4. Decentralization of credit authorization. Centralization may occur either within a personnel structure or in a geographic area. Limits based upon paying records presume a system of record keeping in which credits and debits of individual accounts are constantly updated. Quantity debt limits depend only upon sales records and ledger debits. The centralization of these records and their accessibility to authorization personnel influence the type of limit used. Decentralized authorization is accomplished more often by reference to order size and volume; centralized, by reference to the fuller information there available.

Computation of Lines and Limits

Choice of type of measure does not prescribe the means by which it is actually determined. This requires further consideration of the variables which affect achievement of the objectives for which lines and limits are used.

Requirements. The merits of lines of credit and the need for credit limits are more variable for business customers than for personal users of credit, for the volume of credit purchases and the residual debt of businesses depend upon the competence of the managers of the business. The credit service they need is a function of their ability to use it and to liquidate the attendant debt. Thus lines of credit are related to the requirements of a business, or what they need to conduct the type of business in which they are engaged.

Requirements, however, to a credit manager reflect not only the total sales potential of the customer but also the division of this requirement among his suppliers and among the number of credit period turnovers of a year. To set a line of credit in terms of requirements necessitates estimating first the customer's probable sales of the line in question, particularly of the products of the specific supplier. This volume of sales, however, must be converted to a volume of purchases by deduction of the portion of sales represented by gross markup on the product. The portion of total purchases allocable to an individual supplier may be ascertained by an arbitrary division or by some rational deduction, giving an estimate of likely purchases during a year. However, as a line of credit is but a fraction of the annual credit volume, the line or limit depends on the credit terms and collection ratio of the supplier. Terms of 30 days would fix a line at $\frac{1}{12}$th of the annual volume, but a collection rate of 50 per cent would increase the line to $\frac{1}{6}$th of the volume. This method is illustrated as follows:

Customer's estimated sales in the line of business	$51,430.00
Customer's estimated purchases in the line of business, with 30% markup ($51,430 × (100% − 30%))	36,000.00
Division of customer's business among 3 equally patronized suppliers ($36,000 ÷ 3)	12,000.00
Division of credit volume by credit terms of 30 days ($12,000 ÷ (360 ÷ 30))	1,000.00
Division of credit volume by collection period of 60 days ($12,000 ÷ (360 ÷ 60))	2,000.00

The requirements method of establishing a line of credit is particularly applicable in mercantile credit transactions, but the logic is applicable also to a line of loan credit. It is also used in authorization of instalment purchases. Goods are usually bought on instalment in single contracts; the purchase is equivalent to a "requirement." Consolidation loans too are scaled to the debt which a borrower "requires" to be consolidated.

Income. Credit lines and limits, especially in consumer credit, are also often based upon income. The problem then is to determine what portion of income can be expected by any one creditor. Both rational and arbitrary estimates of this are made. Experience has led to the formulation of such generalizations as follows:

Debt on a personal loan repayable in one year should not exceed one month's salary.
Total personal indebtedness should not exceed
—20 per cent of one year's income
—10 per cent of income during 12 to 24 months
—$\frac{1}{3}$ of discretionary income for a year
30-day charge accounts should not exceed two weeks' salary.
Instalment debt should not exceed 12 per cent of basic monthly income, with one per cent deducted for each dependent.

No one rule is universally applicable, for limits are affected by many factors: total income, discretionary income, dependents, time period, the use to which credit is to be put, and the like.

Paying ability is generally the basis of the line of credit used in connection with revolving or budget accounts. The line is based upon the amount that the customer can pay monthly for this purpose. Depending upon the policy of the creditor, this amount is then multiplied by the number of months in the plan, whether it be 10, 12, or 24. Creditors with more extended time plans set higher limits than another vendor for the same customer. In optional accounts, both the monthly payment and the total debt are variable and are left to determination by the customer.

Conversely, some creditors make the limit a quotient of paying power dividing the total by the number of creditors. Loan companies sometimes scale their limits relative to the number and amount of existing loans an applicant has. When these are consolidated into one loan, the elimination of other creditors is a determinant of the size of the loan justified.

Net Worth. Net worth also serves as a base for credit limits. Usually the debtor's net worth is scrutinized and a fraction of it regarded as the limit of creditworthiness. Specifically, 10 per cent of his net worth as reported by Dun & Bradstreet, Inc., has been considered a reasonable limit. The whole concept of basing limits on net worth, however, should be seen as an evidence of heavy emphasis placed upon capital as a factor in creditworthiness. As this is usually a minor consideration, it seems inconsistent to base a limit on capital when creditworthiness is appraised mainly in terms of capacity and character.

Net worth not of the debtor but of the creditor is also a base for limits. Commercial banks are restricted by law from lending one borrower more than 10 per cent of the sum of their capital stock, undivided surplus, and reserves. Such a restriction impels diversification and thus accomplishes in some degree the reduction of risk expected of limits.

Legal Limits. In certain instances there are legal limits. This condition is found mainly in the consumer lending field, where loan limitations are set for different types of lenders. This form of limit serves several purposes. It helps to differentiate different segments of the loan market; it restricts the liability of borrowers; it curbs the extent to which loan promotion can be carried.

Ceilings set on loans made by consumer finance companies illustrate the legal type of limit. When first recommended by the Model Small Loan Law, in 1916, limits of $300 were proposed. The underlying thought was that this sum, then representing 20 times the weekly income,[1] would be sufficient to take care of even exceptional cases. With increases in income, inflation, and disposable purchasing power, needs have increased and with them the legal small-loan limits in most states. Common limits today are $500, $600, $800, $1,000, $1,500, $2,500, and $3,000.

Limits are set similarly by law for other institutions. The Federal Credit Union Law permits unsecured loans up to $600; secured loans may be larger. Likewise, a limit of $5,000 is common for industrial banks. While these limits do not serve all the purposes of individually determined limits, they do provide a framework in which individual limits may then be computed.

Character.   An alternative to limits is "no limit" policy in credit management. Such a policy reflects an emphasis on character as the basis of credit and results in the granting of what are known as "character loans." When it is said that a customer is good for "an unlimited amount" or "for all he wants," it is presumed that he possesses both integrity and ability to use profitably what is requested on credit. Such "limitless" credit granting occurs almost solely in business credit, where debts are "self-liquidating." In consumer credit, such a policy means that a person's creditworthiness far exceeds his likely credit requirements.

Arbitrary Limits.   In addition to the more or less rational types of limits, some simple rules of thumb are employed. For example, limits of $25 or $50 are set on new consumer accounts as a starting point, a margin in which creditworthiness can be proved. "Teen Accounts" are sometimes given limits of $15 arbitrarily, to confine use of the account to purchases of minor importance. Sales finance companies have restricted the number of times a month that a dealer may borrow or "floor plan" his inventory. Six borrowings a month have been regarded as a limit, beyond which need for more frequent financing indicates questionable risk. Mercantile creditors also set arbitrary or temporary limits until a better basis can be determined.

In the effort to express complete rationality in limit setting

---

[1] M. R. Neifeld, *Neifeld's Manual on Consumer Credit* (Easton, Pa.: Mack Publishing Co., 1961), p. 336.

and to reduce it to a fully scientific procedure, some credit managers construct weighted formulas into which they throw every factor they regard to be important. Basically, the evidences are drawn from the categories of character, capacity, and capital, each being quantified and weighted according to a plan. While such efforts are helpful to the users, they are so largely through the analysis which they impel rather than because of their exactness in arriving at a specific figure. Limit setting is not yet that exact, and, what is more, the various uses of limits do not always require minute accuracy.

Administration of Lines and Limits

The concept of lines of credit and credit limits is inherent in every credit relationship, but actual use is not always made of these devices. There are several reasons. First, knowledge that a limit has been set is believed to be a deterrent to the use of credit by a customer. It is a point beyond which he will restrain his purchases, although circumstances may warrant more extended use of credit to the benefit of all. Second, limits which have been set are not always adhered to because of the creditor's optimistic hope that he has underestimated the debtor's capacity, or that an exception to the limit will be temporary. Third, limits are violated because of the systems and policies of authorization employed. Sales are sometimes authorized without reference to account records, as a means of saving time and work. Thus while the use of limits is in keeping with the concept of taking a calculated risk, disuse of an established limit may express another phase of this concept.

In general, four principles may be adhered to in the adoption, setting, and administration of lines and limits: (1) they should be a reflection of conditions both of the creditor and the debtor; (2) whether to give notification that a limit has been set should depend upon whether it is to be used only for internal action decisions or also for self-government and self-administration by the debtor; (3) they should be regarded as the product of a number of variables and as subject to periodic reconsideration and adjustment; (4) their form is dependent upon the use to which they are put and upon the degree of centralization or decentralization of the organizational structure in which they are used.

DISCUSSION QUESTIONS

1. Is the concept of a limit always inherent in the approval of credit?
2. Give examples of credit limits based upon the buyer's character, capacity, capital; upon the seller's capital, risk policy; upon factors external to both.
3. Prepare a matrix showing along one side quantity and rate limits and along the other side forms of credit service. Explain the relationships.
4. Prepare another matrix relating types of limits to the credit functions of promotion, authorization, and collection. Show the uses of limits in each of these activities.
5. Draft the elements of a policy which might be adopted relating to the selection and use of limits in a given credit operation.
6. What differences would one observe between consumer credit and business credit in the fixing of lines and limits?
7. Of what significance are limits in the following: mercantile open accounts, letters of credit, revolving accounts, optional accounts, personal loans, commercial loans?

25

Credit Department Systems

Throughout this book the term "systems" has been used to indicate organizations of units related for the accomplishment of a purpose. Two types of systems have been discussed. First, the organizations of credit service suppliers, linked in channels for the serving of various credit markets. Second, the organizations of men within units of the credit operation, combined for the accomplishment of a corporate objective. In this chapter are considered the systems of mechanisms and devices employed within a credit department to facilitate performance of its activities.

The object of technical facilities is to improve and extend the human capacities. Ideally, the credit operation would be managed by an individual with omniscient intelligence—an intelligence which comprehended all factors related to customer's creditworthiness, knew simultaneously the probable costs and gains involved in various degrees of credit risk venture, and communicated to every department the implications of action elsewhere. No one person can know so much, and if he could, the organization would seek to reduce its dependence upon such an individual. Technical facilities offer a solution to the problem. They provide for assembly, classification, storage, and dissemination of information, after the manner of the human intellect. At the same time, they release individuals from specific posts without jeopardizing an operation. Personal performance, therefore, is reinforced by the development of technical facilities.

Being patterned after the nature of personal activity, technical facilities have a twofold character: they are operated singly, and they are linked in systems. In both capacities they augment the action and the interaction of individuals engaged in the credit work. Singly, they enlarge the efficiency of the individual, increasing speed and dexterity, saving effort, supplying information. They also facilitate the interaction among participants in the credit work, furnishing information banks to which one person adds and another withdraws, supplanting personal with impersonal cues to action, and performing some of the cogitative processes of persons in several roles. Thus technical facilities may be viewed either as operating mechanisms or as systems providing for a succession of processes and complementing the interaction of the human relationships.

Four types of technical facilities and systems are particularly important in the credit department. They and their functions are as follows:

1. Records—providing storage and availability of information
2. Identifications—cuing action
3. Communication devices—altering time and space limitations
4. Data processing equipment—analyzing, synthesizing, and reporting information

CREDIT RECORDS

The purpose of records in the credit department is to store information and to make it available in a useful manner. They represent an assemblage of facts with past, present, and possibly future relevance to the credit operation. These facts may be of different types, but those for which record keeping devices are particularly prepared are those pertaining to the individual credit accounts. For each account, information concerning creditworthiness is collected at the time of approval. This is supplemented by additional experience throughout the credit relationship. Ultimately it may be stored for historical purposes. Meanwhile, it is preserved in forms useful to the several parties whose actions are based upon such information.

Types of Records

Credit records usually contain the several types of information discussed below.

Customer Information. Customer information preserved in credit records is of four types: (1) creditworthiness evidence, (2) authorization evidence, (3) transaction evidence, and (4) postauthorization evidence. Each of these serves as a basis both for individual actions and for personal interactions.

Creditworthiness Evidence. Evidence of customer creditworthiness is an important fact to document, for it underlies initial credit approval and subsequent servicing of the account. As not all of the details of this information are in continual reference, some are often kept apart from that portion which is in more active use. Compartments known as credit folders may contain such evidences as the customer's credit application, interview notations, credit bureau reports, letters from referees, newspaper clippings, and the like. This information, filed alphabetically by customers' names, serves to substantiate the decision to approve or disapprove credit for an applicant; it chronicles change in an account; it preserves facts whose meaning may be unapparent until later in a credit relationship.

Summaries of the full evidence of creditworthiness may be kept in separate files for use in authorization. Additions to the bulk of creditworthiness evidence may be made from the running experience with the subject, thus combining initial with subsequent evidence.

Authorization Evidence. The records used as a basis of authorization consist of but a portion of the customer records: those containing cues to action at the time a customer attempts to use his account or line of credit. For this purpose, historical information is less useful than the current status of the account and guidelines set for administration of the account. If a summary of creditworthiness is provided for easy reappraisal of the account, it is usually accompanied by evidence of current use of the account, indicators of limits set on the account and guidelines to action under certain conditions, and patterns in the use of the account. Such records are working records, whereas those evidencing creditworthiness are mainly reference records.

Authorization records take many forms. They range from simply listed names to fairly full information about the customer. The simple lists are for checking when use of credit is to be made. Such lists contain names either of good accounts to be authorized, or of bad accounts not to be authorized; the former use is known as "positive authorization," the latter as "negative authorization." Economy of time and space prompts negative listings, although that practice permits authorization to *non-existing* accounts merely because they are not listed as *bad* accounts. More comprehensive authorization records generally contain the types of information mentioned above. They are maintained in variously designed "tubs," "trays," or "drawers" for convenience of authorizers. Such facilities pose space and traffic problems as the number of accounts increases.

Transaction Evidence. When credit sales are authorized, evidence of the transaction also becomes part of the credit records. Sales records in the form of invoices and sales slips, or loan records in the form of promissory notes, acceptances, drafts drawn, evidence the total credit service extended, the obligations of individual debtors, the relations of credit used to limits set, and the details of sums to be billed and collected. Sales records are incorporated into credit records through daily or periodic filing of sales documents where they may be used for several purposes. In some procedures, they are actually filed in the authorization records until they are photographed for preservation in the historic reference files of customers, or they are summarized in a bill and sent to the customer.

Postsales Evidence. Evidence of use made of an account or line of credit constitutes still another type of credit record. Unless credit terms extend from the date of invoice and no further notification of indebtedness is given, credit sales records are used for billing and ultimately for collecting. They also serve for a reappraisal of creditworthiness and for further authorization of use of the account.

Use of Credit Records

Two types of use of credit records are made. One is to facilitate the performance of certain individuals engaged in the credit processes. This is depicted in Table 25–1, wherein the usefulness of each type of records to the credit department personnel is suggested. Thus it is seen that each record must be designed to augment the capacities of the individuals using them, whether by collecting information, storing it, or classifying it.

The record use of credit records is to facilitate interaction among individuals performing the credit processes. When parties

Table 25-1. Users of Credit Records

Types of Records	Investigators	Authorizers	Billers	Adjusters	Collectors
Creditworthiness evidence	X				
Authorization evidence		X			
Transaction evidence	X	X	X		
Postsales evidence	X	X		X	X

interact face to face, there is a bidirectional exchange of information, a commanding of action between the dominant and the subordinate parties, and initiation of action and response thereto. Where in large credit operations face-to-face contact is lacking, records serve to link individuals and to produce results similar to those resulting from personal relations. Among the sets of relationships in which credit records play an important part are the following:

Relationships	*Function of Records*
Investigator—customer	To attest to creditworthiness; to evidence changing circumstances; to suggest lines of further inquiry
Investigator—information resource	To summarize evidence; to convey a flow of information
Authorizer—salesman	To encourage or restrain sales effort; to request authorization
Sales—billing	To itemize sales for billing; to summarize indebtedness for further sales effort; to identify terms of sale with sales made
Adjuster—customer	To evidence sales and purchase actions; to store and summarize evidence
Collector—customer	To interpret billings and receipts for further action; to suggest manner of collection action to take; to document use of credit for legal purposes

Serving these purposes, the credit records facilitate personal interaction and thus expedite performance of the credit processes.

CREDIT IDENTIFICATION

Another technical feature which has become part of the mechanical and human systems of the credit department is the identification provided customers whose credit has been approved. Evidence of accepted creditworthiness has long been given in the form of tokens and credit cards, mainly to facilitate authorization processes. Recently, the devices used for this purpose have been designed also to assist in record keeping and in billing.

Types of Identification

Credit customer identifications have taken many forms, although the purpose of all has been to distinguish bona fide account holders when they choose to make a credit purchase. In commercial transactions, the need for identification has presented less of a problem than in retail transactions, for when orders may be checked against credit records and sent to a known address, there is less risk than in dealing with great numbers of consumers in over-the-counter, charge-take transactions. The need for identification of commercial credit customers has been served by account numbers by which orders and payments are identified. Thus the needs of the record and billing departments, more than of authorization, are served.

In consumer credit, a greater variety of identifications has been used over the years, and most of them continue in use today. The simplest is that of identification by cognizance or recognition. Authorization was originally given by proprietors and managers as they recognized on sight their selected credit customers. Delegation of this function to floor men followed. As the number of credit customers increased, identification by recognition became more of a formality than an actual safeguard. Signatures of buyers constituted another form of identification, one which was distinctive, could be checked against authentic signatures kept on file, and had legal implications in collection.

Of less personal character were many physical devices used to facilitate authorization. Metal coins or tokens bearing the store name and customer number have been widely used, as have printed paper and plastic credit cards. Embossed and perforated cards have also had wide circulation as identification devices and have been made to serve recording and billing as well as authorization. An embossed metal plate, trademarked the "Charga-Plate," was commercially provided to stores by a company which leased hand presses by which the customer's name and address were imprinted on sales slips. Although similar plates were used by many stores, notches in the plates permitted them to be used only in the issuing stores. To economize in the issuance of such identification plates, and to avoid cumbersome multiplicity of plates held by customers with several accounts, "community" plates have been used having the notches of not one but several stores. With the development of account numbers by which customers are identified in data processing systems, identification devices again became exclusive to the individual stores. However, as creditors have become linked in vast computerized information systems, common customer identifications have again increased in use. Consideration has been given even to the possibility of universal identifying numbers for every individual, such as his Social Security number, whereby he would be identified in all transactions and relations. It must be recognized, of course, that such identification may serve billing purposes better than authorization, for which identifications were originally conceived.

Among the various forms of identification for credit purposes, several characteristics are essential. It is thought that means of identification should have the following features:

Portability—Convenient for carrying in wallet, purse, or pocket
Durability—Not easily destructible through use or non-use
Revocability—Being valid for a specified period only, after which it is renewed by replacement
Economy—Of low cost, compatible with other qualities
Personalized—Identified with the specific user, either by his identification or by creditor-given account identification
Functional—Including other features designed for whatever purposes the issuer may have

Forms of identification in use have become more varied as their use for billing, in addition to authorization, has increased. Although plastics have been widely employed, punched cards and other paper forms have also been used. Practically all have used identifying account numbers in forms suitable to the creditor. Embossing on plastic cards has provided for imprinting identification on sales invoices; perforation of machine data cards has permitted sorting of cards and transfer of data to electrical mechanisms, and magnetic inks have provided for electronic scanning processes. Embossed plastics are widely used by department stores, credit card plan companies, and petroleum companies. Perforated cards in the form of sales slips are also used by some gasoline companies. Magnetic inks are commonly used on bank checks.

Selection of a form of identification to aid in the processes of authorization, recording, and billing must be made with several considerations in mind. First, it must be known which of these processes the device is to serve. Increasingly it is serving all three, thus facilitating the interactions of customers, salespeople, authorizers, and accounting and billing personnel. Second, certain alternatives must be viewed as choices in calculated risk. If frequent replacement is made to minimize risk, costs of operations will be correspondingly increased. Likewise, if portability is increased, durability may be sacrificed. Third, the potentiality of adaptation to wider information and credit systems should not be overlooked.

CREDIT COMMUNICATION SYSTEMS

A third technical facility incorporated into credit department systems is that for communication. This extends the human capacities through saving time and overcoming space, but it is also a means by which the interaction of many participants in the credit work is affected. Three devices have been found to be of more or less use in this service: mechanical propulsion devices, pneumatic tubes, and telephones.

The first is primarily of historical interest, for early spring-propelled baskets have long been superseded by more modern means. They were, nevertheless, devices by which problems arising from the functional separation of selling and credit authorizing could be solved. As retail stores grew, multidepartmental need for conveyance of papers bearing requests, information, and responses increased. The sight of ceiling-hung tracks on which darted basket carriers was common in early years of this century. Their practical and aesthetic limitations, however, caused them quickly to yield to other inventions.

A second means of credit department communication has been the pneumatic tube system. A principal merit of this carrier is its capacity to handle both cash and credit transactions. By conveying customer-signed sales slips to the credit authorization department, it has made possible signature verification, thus reducing some risks. By transmitting cash to a centralized cashier, it has eliminated need for cash register facilities in the sales department and has concentrated money handling among responsible individuals. Tube systems have also provided the advantages of low-cost maintenance. On the other hand, tube carrier transportation is time consuming, relatively inflexible, and not conducive to easy personal interaction. Tubes have, nevertheless, continued to play an important role in credit operations, varying with the cash handling needs, type of merchandise sold on credit, volume of business handled, and other communication facilities of the establishment.

The third means of credit communication is telephonic, whereby with regular or special phone equipment the sales and authorizing departments are related. A twofold need has thereby been satisfied: the need for transmission to the credit department of information identifying the customer and the sale, and the need to return to the sales department evidence of authorization. Verbal communication each way is accomplished by ordinary telephone facilities; proof of authorization is achieved by a device, attached to the phone, which perforates the sales record in the sales department at the direction of the authorizer elsewhere. Special provision for reaching appropriate sections of authorization records is made through selected dialing.

Although both the pneumatic tubes or the telephone systems have technical intricacies, they serve a simple purpose of facilitating work which involves the interaction of people, mainly authorizers and salesmen. Both act as a substitute for face-to-face exchange of ideas. Both make possible the application of credit records information to specific credit transactions. Thus this type of facility, too, complements the work of individuals and groups in the providing of the credit service.

INFORMATION PROCESSING FACILITIES

Newest additions to the list of technical facilities applicable to credit work are the data processing equipment, both mechanical and electronic. The latter most nearly simulate the functions of human intelligence, surpassing accomplishments of the human mind in feats of memory storage, speed calculations, and combination of many variables. Phenomenal as these devices are, however, they cannot do what it is impossible for an individual to think. The mechanism is but a conception and projection of the human mind and has no intelligence of its own. Its appearance of creativity derives from the fact that new analytical conceptions have extracted from these mechanisms information hitherto untapped. The value of electronic facilities in credit administration is proportionate to the creative thinking of credit planners for the machine and to the internal and external systems of the credit organization, into which the output of the equipment is introduced.

Although several variations of basic information processing facilities are in use and applications of their services vary among credit operations, detailed description is not given here either of the technical characteristics of the equipment or its use. Rather are presented brief descriptions of types of equipment currently available, a statement of processes performed by such equipment, and their possible uses in the credit systems.

Types of Equipment

Information processing equipment currently available includes devices designed to perform an assortment or a sequence of functions. They may be grouped as follows:

Receptors. One type of facility primarily receives data fed into it and holds the information for whatever use intended. It is essentially a passive agent, not acting on its own initiative but recording information given it by punched cards, punched and magnetic tape, or other means of impression such as cash registers, counters, time clocks, and the like. The function of information receptors is to receive, record, sort, classify, and compile data.

In the credit department, receptor equipment serves as files, where the receipt of information is preliminary to the storing or analyzing of it. Information originating in credit investigation, in credit sales authorization, or in receipt of payments is typical of that introduced into this facility. As additions are made, they increase the information available and may be received into categories planned as useful for subsequent purposes.

Perceptors. Other facilities perform a more active role in the receipt of information and actually "reading data." [1] Optical

---

[1] George E. Snively, *Receivables Management Utilizing Computers and Related Devices* (New York: National Association of Credit Management, Credit Research Foundation, 1963).

scanners are capable of reading words, numbers, and punctuation marks for the purpose of sorting, summarizing, punching cards, printing, sensitizing tape, or feeding code into a computer. Similar but more sophisticated equipment is capable of reading lines of text and of selecting information which it has been instructed to ferret out. Listening devices also receive information from cues in the human voice, distinguishing numbers, words, and such signs as "plus," "minus," and "total."

Retainers.   A third type of equipment is the retainer of information for use in credit management. As seen before, many administrative processes depend upon a bank of information, much of which may have been accumulated progressively. Manual files and microfilms perform this function. In electronic equipment, magnetic tapes also store vast quantities of information and do so in such a manner that facts are recallable almost instantaneously. With proper wire connections to a computer, its memory reserve is made available to users in widely scattered locations. Several uses may be made of such stored information, but the storing of it, once it has been received into the system, is a special feature of some of the available equipment.

In credit work, reference alone to stored information is useful, as reference to information upon which creditworthiness has been judged, ledger experience with a customer, or sales experience with different types of accounts.

Analyzers.   One use made of accumulated information is for analysis of existing or prospective conditions. Computers provide for such analysis through the programming introduced into them. Many combinations of facts and the relationships among many variables may be observed, allowing for the setting of standards and policies, for their revision in terms of selected objectives, and for the making of comparisons between incidents.

A specific use made of computer analysis is in appraisal of creditworthiness by the scoring technique. As point values for given characteristics are introduced into the mechanism, representing numerous weights and variables, a summation is made and compared with a programmed standard. Thus a comparative analysis may be furnished with greater ease, speed, and objectivity than could be done by human faculties. Financial statement ratios may be determined in this way and their significance relative to a complete financial picture suggested. Credit risk levels may be set consistent with stated objectives, accounts aged, break-even points determined, and credit costs analyzed—all by the introduction into the computer of proper data. These are principal uses of the information processing equipment.

Conveyors. Finally, technical facilities join the human systems through the preparation and dissemination of information received, stored, and analyzed within them. Some of the output of computers merely produces in print such information as names, addresses, lists, statistics, code symbols, and a limited amount of text. Other equipment vocalizes rather than prints such information. Letters may be written, bills prepared, checks drawn, and entries made in ledgers as examples of the conveyor or communication function of these facilities. They also cue action such as signaling caution in credit authorization, listing sales prospects, suggesting need for further credit investigation, or recommending action to be taken in collections. Thus both the actions and the interactions of individuals are improved through the new technical systems which simulate the intelligence of the human mind.

Although computerization of the assembly, analysis, and reporting of credit data is in progress in many establishments, illustrative of its potentialities on a broad scale is the first computerized central file of credit information.[2] Organized in 1965 and subscribed by 300 merchants, the Credit Data Corporation in Los Angeles provides inquirers within 90 seconds up-to-date credit reports. Inquiries of a subscriber are telephoned to the information center, where an inquiry ticket is carried by conveyor belt to the computer. Instantly a report is typed by the mechanism and is read to the waiting subscriber. Information from the current inquiry is simultaneously added to the information retained in the computer, so that its information is always current. Reports so provided contain identifying evidence of the subject, ledger information from other creditors, and facts obtained from public records. Charges of such credit reports had been reduced by the automation to between 46 and 63 cents.

DISCUSSION QUESTIONS

1. Explain the principle that technical systems are and should be subordinate to and correlated with human systems in a business.

[2] "L. A. Merchants Dial for Data," *Department Store Journal*, February, 1966, p. 39.

2. Diagram the technical system of facilities which one might find in a credit department, showing their linkage and their relations to the human organization or system which uses the facilities.

3. Investigate the record facilities produced by several companies and observe their respective advantages and limitations.

4. Show how the "evidences" preserved in credit files may serve as evidence of creditworthiness, as explained in Chapter 20.

5. Examine several examples of credit identification and determine the extent to which they fulfill what is expected of them by the issuer.

6. Compare the merits of pneumatic tubes and telephone authorizations as they may be found in local establishments.

7. Confer with producers or users of electronic data processing equipment in credit operations, and attempt to determine the effect of such equipment on the performance of various credit functions.

26

Collecting by Commercial Processes

Collecting is a part of the credit operation which occurs between the time that a debt becomes past due and when more formal legal means are undertaken by a creditor to produce payment. Collecting is a commercial, not a legal, process; it is individually, not cooperatively, undertaken. Whatever a creditor does during this interval to induce or to assist delinquent debtors to fulfill their credit obligations constitutes his collection process.

The Collection Task

In the modern credit operation, collecting is not simply a process of money retrieval. It is rather a process so related to and interwoven with other processes of the credit operation that its border lines cannot be easily drawn. It is inseparable from the granting of credit, for many collection problems are inherent in the types and degrees of risk accepted. It is inseparable from the sales function, for an objective of collecting is to preserve relationships which will produce future patronage from debtors. It is inseparable from the cultivation of running accounts, for only judgment separates slow but satisfactory accounts from slow and unsatisfactory ones. Collecting is an activity whose roots extend throughout the credit operation and whose objectives are those of the broader credit organization.

As a process, collecting is an integral part of the credit operation, and not a sequel to it. Collecting does not occur apart from credit approval, authorization, billing, and other functions, as an attempt to succeed where they have failed. It is part of a continuing process, is planned as such, and is as essential to the total credit objectives as are credit promotion and customer counseling. When credit is accepted, a calculated risk is assumed, and it is anticipated that some debts will not be paid and more will not be paid promptly. Delinquency is a normal, not abnormal, part of the credit operation, and plans are made accordingly for coping with it. Collecting, therefore, is not simply a salvage operation; it is a constructive part of the credit function, and knowledge that skills are available for retrieval of past-due indebtedness is a stimulant to credit service and encouragement to the accomplishment of over-all credit objectives.

The specific objectives of collecting are (1) to gain payment of money due, (2) to retain, if possible, the future patronage of the customer, and (3) to do both of these with the incurrence of minimum additional expense and effort.

Organization of the collection activity includes identification of accounts needing collection, classification of customers for collection purposes, and development of collection systems appropriate for the business.

Information of Delinquency

The first requirement of a collection system is to provide information as to when and which debts are due and unpaid. This information is not always readily available when many accounts are outstanding, when due dates vary, and when billing and payment records are not synchronized. Various office systems have been devised, however, to provide this information, and increasingly it is being furnished mechanically. The following are some of the means employed:

1. Direct observation of the debtor. Landlords, for example, where there are few tenants, know that when payment is not received by a specified date, the account is in arrears. Direct observation, however, has many limitations in commercial practice and cannot be relied upon when a large number of accounts are involved.

2. Duplicate bill file. When bills are prepared, a carbon copy may be filed as evidence that it has not yet been paid. When payments are received, a deduction is made on the duplicate copy or it is removed as evidence that the debt is paid. When ar-

ranged according to maturity dates, those accounts whose due dates have passed are subject to collection activity.

3. Reference to ledger accounts at the time of a subsequent billing. When receipts are credited directly to account records, ledger files are a good source of information concerning the status of accounts. This means is particularly useful for running accounts where credit period coincides with billing periods. If not paid by the next billing, they are past due. In revolving and optional accounts, this is a signal for charging an interest rate; in other accounts, it calls forth other actions. At the second billing, duplicate copies may be filed separately as slow accounts. Thus is avoided duplicating records of the many accounts which do not become past due, yet are provided separate records which may be used exclusively for collection purposes.

4. Interim reference to ledger records. When billing dates and due dates do not coincide, periodic reference to account files provides the needed information. Such direct reference is most feasible when accounts and delinquencies are few in number, and when continual checking of the account is possible.

When non-payment is observed, judgment must still be made whether a debt is "past due" in the sense that collection should be undertaken. Mere non-payment is not always in itself a sufficient reason for action; collecting depends also upon the history of the account, leniency of credit policy, and urgency of the creditor's need for payment. To pounce upon a debtor whose record has been good might damage a relationship while gaining payment. The possibility of such ill-advised action is increased by the use of electronic billing equipment, and care must be taken to program its action so as to exclude good accounts from automatic collection procedures. Moreover, leniency may be given any debtor, good or bad, on the ground that with time most delinquents will make payment and that collection efforts are best reserved for later stages of the debt. Determination and definition of "past due" is the first step in organizing the collection process.

Characteristics of Debtors

When it is determined that a debtor is in default and warranting collection effort, the selection of appropriate action is dependent upon the circumstances of the debt and the characteristics of the debtor. Much attention has been given to understanding the debtor mentality as a means of improving meeting of the minds, and it has been learned that while debtors have some attitudes in common they also have varied reasons for delinquency which influence collection practices.

Examining overextended and delinquent families, one researcher [1] found non-payment of personal debt to be associated with both economic and social circumstances. As might be expected, payments were stymied by the disproportion of debt to income, over 50 per cent of the next year's income having been committed to credit obligations, on the average. Debt consolidation loans, common to all, attested an effort to extricate themselves from debt by further borrowing. Declining incomes, living close to the edge of earnings, and emergencies such as temporary unemployment, replacement of an appliance or car, and pregnancy accentuated the economic plight. On the other hand, proneness to buy, impressionableness, gullibility, and unsophistication in market dealings made them ready customers for "easy credit," door-to-door selling, and "bait" advertising. Thus the encumbered debtor is depicted as economically vulnerable, a condition for which both he and sellers may assume some responsibility.

Attitudes of debtors disclosed by the survey are no less revealing. Within the families there was more than expected marital stability but little indication of jointly made decisions in spending. Rather there was a tendency for both husbands and wives to spend freely without criticism or constraint of the other— "laissez-faireism parading as a sort of magnanimous democracy in the dispensing of funds." Similarity in personality traits between mates was evident, both tending to be impulsive, carefree, and easy going. By contrast, in non-overextended families, dominance of husbands was clearly evident. While some delinquent families chose bankruptcy "to get rid of" a creditor or "to get even with" him, many unable to pay their debts rejected bankruptcy as impractical, immoral, or embarrassing. They chose to repay their debts, although that imposed low living standards for some time to come. On the other hand, 10 per cent of the families who utilized bankruptcy in less than three years were back in the same condition of indebtedness. Thus the problem

[1] A study made by Milton J. Huber of 100 families in Detroit. See "A Profile of Overextended Credit Family," *Consumer Finance News*, May, 1965, p. 6.

of collecting is complicated by social relationships and attitudes formed both within and without the family.

Characteristics of the family debtor are symptomatic of all debtors. Indebtedness is not only an economic condition but a type of social relationship, and whether they be business or individual debtors their behavior patterns have similarities. Indebtedness presents for the collector the obverse of many circumstances which confront him merely as creditor. When credit is originally approved and transactions authorized, the creditor and debtor have mutual interests in the exchange. Their interactions are cooperative. They attempt to understand each other's expectations and their mutual obligations. While either may initiate the credit relationship, the creditor, by the nature of the transaction, is dominant in the relationship.

When a debt becomes past due, the creditor, as collector, often finds his role and relationship changed. Put in a position where he must initiate action for payment, the creditor is often defensive; his dominance is lost, except as he may resort to legal means. Conflict may replace cooperation. The routine transaction may become particularized and impersonal dealings give way to personal feelings. Anticipated profits are jeopardized, and worse, additional costs and efforts must be extended. Unrelated parties are brought into previously private transactions. And short-run retrieval objectives clash with long-run customer relationship objectives.

Debtors' attitudes also change. To avoid embarrassment, harassment, and the necessity to make decisions, debtors often avoid contact with creditors, even diverting cash business from them. Inability to *keep* out of debt is further compounded by inability to *get* out of debt. Resistance exaggerates conflict, inflames sentiments, evokes self-justification.

If collectors accepted delinquency as inevitable conflict, however, the principle upon which credit operations are based would be voided, i.e., the mutuality of interests in a credit transaction. This mutuality must continue throughout the credit relationship, and it is the responsibility of the creditor, even in collecting, to demonstrate this. Because of the basic integrity of human nature, debtors desire freedom from debt, and, if honest, they welcome to be shown how payment can be made and this freedom gained. Too often the conflict, rather than the concord, of the debtor–creditor relationship in delinquency is emphasized and the fact overlooked that instruction, direction, and advice are more effectual than intimidation, duress, and arrogance. However, as debtors in default present an array of attitudes, the same treatment is not appropriate for all in achieving the basic objective. For this reason, types of debtors need to be distinguished for effective development of collection procedures.

Classification of Debtors

The purpose of classifying debtors in default is to assume dealing with them appropriately. A meaningful basis of classification is the cause of their default, whether attributable to the creditor or to the debtor.

Creditor-induced Conditions. Although creditors may not acknowledge responsibility for debtors' default, a share of the cause is often theirs, and collecting should reflect this fact. Creditors' contribution to non-payment is sometimes accidental, sometimes intentional. Both occur at the approval of credit and create conditions which continue throughout a credit relationship.

Unintentionally, creditors make collection problems for themselves by improper approval of credit. Lack of skill in interpreting evidences of creditworthiness and failure to assemble representative evidence are two deficiencies. This may reflect incompetence in credit management, which is sure to breed collection problems. On the other hand, acceptance of potentially delinquent customers is sometimes intentional, based upon a liberal risk policy intended to increase sales and profits. Collections resulting from such a cause are asked for, and the handling of them must be planned in the over-all credit operation.

Behavior toward debtors whose non-payment results in some degree from creditors' own actions has certain characteristics. In general, creditors who know what they have done should act accordingly, with dispatch where deterioration of an account may be rapid, with deliberation where that is no danger. Principally, they should act with a sense of responsibility to those whom they have induced or accepted into a difficult debt situation. No single type of action is appropriate for all customers, but an attitude of patience, respect, and helpfulness, at least, would be expected. Creditors, however, do not always know that they have erred, else they would not have. Collections should be undertaken, therefore, with an initial intent to understand why a delinquency has occurred, to ascertain past and present contributing factors, to judge anew the creditworthiness of the customer, and to act in the best interests of all. To the extent that potential collection problems are voluntarily induced, warning systems should provide timely and adequate alerting so that such customers would be identified when non-payment occurs.

Debtor-induced Conditions. Other causes of delinquency arise from conditions of the debtor, particularly from changes which occur in his conditions after his creditworthiness has initially been approved. Changes occur in both his capacity and character. Too often, creditors have no knowledge of these changes until informed of them by non-payment. There are, however, other means of learning of them, as through continuing reporting services of credit information agencies, or through one's own continual efforts to update credit files, exchange information with other creditors, and maintain contact with customers.

Principal causes of inability to pay are unemployment, excessive indebtedness, and emergency expenditures. If such conditions are not accompanied by changes in character, the creditor may expect ultimately to receive payment. Such circumstances provide occasion for discussions with the debtor, who, if he is honest, may welcome a detached view of his position. Thus in collecting, creditors may perform a counseling service which contributes not only to collection but to general credit relationships.

Changes in a debtor's willingness to pay, however, pose another type of problem. Unwillingness arises usually from circumstances of the debtor rather than from basic changes in his personal character. Trade disputes, dissatisfaction with products and services, and disapproval of creditors' credit or collection policies are common causes of delay or non-payment. In personal relationships, marital difficulties of the debtor have similar effect, evidenced by repudiation of responsibility for indebtedness of a spouse. While such causes also occasion discussion, they place the creditor more on the defensive than changes in ability to pay, for attitudinal changes are often the more difficult to cope with.

In summary, collection systems are predicated upon classification of debtors reflecting causes and characteristics of their delinquency. The following are some of the characteristics commonly taken into consideration:

Creditor causes	vs.	Debtor causes
Inability to pay	vs.	Unwillingness to pay
Temporary default	vs.	Permanent insolvency
Remediable causes	vs.	Unalterable causes
Inherent circumstances	vs.	Environmental circumstances
Fixed conditions	vs.	Changing conditions
Particular default	vs.	General default
Economic situation	vs.	Attitudinal situation

The circumstances listed depict an array of characteristics, a range of degrees of willingness and ability to pay. Variously combined, they describe an assortment of debtor conditions which, when a debt is in default, require different debtor–creditor interaction patterns. As shown in Fig. 26–1, six combinations of capacity and character are suggested, each ranging from low to high.

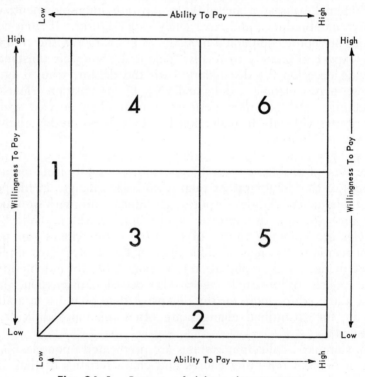

Fig. 26–1. Patterns of debtor characteristics.

Group 1 are those debtors with little capacity and a wide range of character. Group 2 have a range of capacity but little character. Both are unsatisfactory credit risks; when they are delinquent, suits, composition settlements, and bankruptcy are often the means by which their debts are settled.

Group 3 are those who are rated as "slow and unsatisfactory." Lacking both ready ability to pay and strong motivation, they are marginal accounts retained for whatever contribution they can make to sales and profits. In collecting, they are given little leeway but are subjected to the most rigid payment expectations.

Group 4 are debtors with unquestionable intentions but with capacity limited by working capital, adverse conditions, competition, etc. Collection efforts include counseling, extension of the credit period, reduction of the credit limit, and composition settlement as a last resort. These are customers rated as "slow but satisfactory."

Group 5 have high capacity and moderately low character. Neglect and carelessness distinguish them from Group 2, whose lack of character may involve dishonesty and fraud. Collection consists of efforts to motivate and impel payment.

Group 6 represent the highest type of risk, combining character and capacity. They are discounting customers, and default, which is exceptional, may reveal debate of some trade issue. Collections warrant individual attention.

Collection Message Systems

The collection task being a communications problem, the means by which payment is obtained involve message systems and media systems. The former consist of the ideas used in collection, their organization and presentation. The latter consist of the communication media by which these ideas are presented to debtors.

Delinquency represents a disparity between the expectation of a creditor and the action of a debtor; it is a fault in a structural relationship where ideas ceasing to coincide need to be brought into alignment. As the circumstances of delinquency have been shown to differ widely, however, the aligning process of collecting is highly relative. The messages by which creditors achieve collection are relative to the cause of delinquency, the class of debtor, the amount of money involved, and the costs of collection. The appeal which activates an indifferent debtor would be inappropriate for a belligerent one. That which convinces a consumer may be ineffective for an industrial buyer. Moreover, as the objective of collection is an economic one, the gains must be considered relative to the additional costs involved.

In recognition of these degrees of relativity, the organization and presentation of ideas in collecting take varied forms, proportions, sequences, and diversity. That which is appropriate for a particular task is not easily determined and less easily prescribed. It is certainly no process of applying simple rules of thumb; rather, it is the application of some fundamental principles of collection communication to the task at hand. The following are some of these principles.

Collection Appeals.   The idea of the collection message should appeal to the debtor's inclinations and counteract his resistances. This presumes what is not always valid: that a collector knows the debtor's inclinations and resistances. Often the best that can be done is to assume what they are from a knowledge of debtor behavior, individually and collectively. First, it is assumed that most men are honest, that they are embarrassed by inability to pay, and that they are responsive to offers of help; second, that in a group of debtors most of them will be delinquent for minor reasons, that few if any have fraudulent intentions; third, that some debtors will respond to one appeal, others to other appeals. Accordingly, sets of appeals may be arranged for presentation to different types of debtors.

Some common causes of delinquency and corresponding collection appeals might be paired as follows:

Oversight	Reminder
Indifference	Fair play
Procrastination	Urgency
Embarrassment	Willingness to discuss
Dilemma	Offer to help
Parsimony	Penalties
Desperation	Fear
Fraud	Threats

Several psychological theories are relevant to the choice and use of such appeals. One is that action is best achieved by repetition of an idea. Another is that variety is preferable. Still another is that appeals should be not merely varied but graduated in severity.

Graduation of Appeals. When appeals are graduated, by one plan every debtor is subjected to each successive appeal until he pays. The first communication is mild, and should produce some results. Each progressively increases in forcefulness, inducing payment by those who respond to the stronger appeals. By the time the most stern warnings are given, presumably only those receive them who warrant by continued default such messages. Such a message system is most applicable where delinquent accounts have not been classified for difference of treatment, where the majority will be reached by the milder encouragements, and where the creditor has little urgency either from danger of loss or from need of capital. Such a progression can be applied more or less automatically to each account as it becomes past due. Deviation from the plan occurs when the debtor responds, either by payment or by some communication which calls for individual attention.

Another plan for the use of graduated appeals begins a series of messages at different stages in the progression, depending upon the circumstances of the debt. This procedure requires pre-classification of accounts. Best accounts are carried through the longest series, beginning with the mildest appeals. Intermediate accounts may be given a shortened treatment, beginning with mild appeals but advancing more rapidly to serious collection efforts. The most risky accounts may be given only the stronger messages as a means of both impelling and accelerating payment. This plan of graduation of appeals is shown diagrammatically in Table 26–1. It is most appropriately used when classification of

Table 26–1. Progressive Application of Graduated Appeals in Collection

Appeals	Best Accounts	Intermediate Accounts	Poorest Accounts
Notification and reminder			
Second billing	X		
Reminder	X	X	
Discussion and request			
Fair play	X	X	X
Credit standing	X		
Penalties	X	X	
Requirement and demand			
Implied action	X		X
Specified action	X	X	X

debtors is possible and when supervision of collections can be provided to alter the appeals and progression as seems needed.

Timing the System. Collection is made more efficacious by promptness, persistence, and intelligent spacing of the collection efforts. The importance of not prolonging outstanding indebtedness is shown in an oft-cited study made by the U.S. Department of Commerce. It is found that with increasing age the value of accounts decreases. Their shrinkage is reported as follows:

Current	$1.00
2 months	0.90
6 months	0.67
1 year	0.45
2 years	0.23
3 years	0.15
5 years	0.01

To end satisfactorily, collections must begin promptly. Promptness, however, is relative, but whatever the circumstances, it is that action which gives the impression of awareness of default and earnestness to collect and which avoids the impression of indifference to or tolerance of non-payment. What would be regarded as prompt action in any particular case depends upon the length of the credit period, means by which payment is received, competitive practices, and general relations between the debtor and the creditor. The mild appeals in collecting should be initiated as promptly as the stronger appeals.

Timing the collection system relates not only to its beginning but to the spacing of efforts until payment is received or effort is discontinued. Regularity is the principal consideration. Sporadic efforts lose the cumulative effect of rhythm and repetition. Therefore, once an interval of communication is established, it should seldom be lengthened; rather, it should be decreased as urgency increases and as incentives to act become stronger. If a 30-day interval separates early communications, this may be reduced to 15, 10, or 5 days as collection effort progresses.

Finally, termination of the collection effort also should be planned. It should cease when continuation would be profitless, when cost of further effort would produce diminished returns, or when other than collection efforts are resorted to. Termination is determined frequently by the amount of the debt involved, by legal time limitations on collecting, by exhaustion of commercial collection appeals, or by foresight that further efforts may damage the creditor's public image and his future business.

Impersonalization of Collections. Effectiveness of collection work varies with the creditor's dominance in the relationship. This position is sometimes achieved by the collector's adopting a personal attitude, sometimes by the opposite, an impersonal attitude.

Inasmuch as most non-payment is due to impersonal factors, and inasmuch as the great number of debtors in default precludes creditors' knowledge of personal factors, impersonal approaches to collecting are common, particularly in the early stages. The collector gives the impression of not having singled out the debtor in reminding him of non-payment; he makes no special point of the debt, uses clear but general terminology, and assumes the debtor's intention to pay. Thus the morale of the relationship is maintained, and the debtor may act without resistance to hostile and aggressive attitudes. Impersonalization is not merely a simulated mien, it is in fact the most warranted attitude in many collection situations.

On the other hand, personal appeals are equally effective and sometimes imperative. At that stage of collections when the creditor becomes cognizant of the particular debt, proposes and discusses specific remedies, or threatens action, direct adaptation of tone and message to the individual debtor is advisable. Moreover, inasmuch as many consumers with little business contact view business relations from a personal standpoint, a personal approach from the outset is sometimes employed. Appeals to sympathy, reputation, fair play, and reciprocity elicit response from the human element in the debtor. Encouragement of him to explain his non-payment, discuss his problems, and cooperate in the indebtedness illustrates personalization of collections.

Still another approach which is human but impersonal is the humorous approach to collecting. Serious and perfunctory impersonal communications are so overused that they lose their impact, particularly upon people who are repeatedly subjected to them. Light, novel, humorous ideas for catching attention and asking for payment appeal to a debtor's sense of humor, reassure him of the humanity of the creditor, and evoke a favorable attitude which may become expressed in payment.

Collection Media Systems

Although stimulus to motivation to pay lies in the ideas of the collection system, much of its influence is attributable to the choice of the media in which it is presented. Whether collection is done by the creditor or by collection specialists, the following media are available to them: letters, telegrams, telephone calls, personal calls, and drafts.

Letters.   Letters are distinguished as a mailed medium. They include printed communications, individual and duplicated form letters, and individually written letters.

As letters permit the use of all collection appeals and are adaptable to the requirements of the collection message systems, they are perhaps the most generally used of the collection media. Their characteristics make them particularly adaptable to certain types and stages of collecting. A principal advantage of letters is their flexibility. They may be short or long, personal or impersonal, single or in series; and the timing of them is within the control of the sender. Another advantage is the ease with which they can be prepared. Any competent letter writer, if familiar with debtor psychology and creditor policy, can undertake to write such a letter. Preparation time may be short; in fact, printed copies of impersonal low-pressure messages used in early collection stages may be prepared in advance. Letters are also a medium familiar to all people; they gain access to debtors where personal collectors may not. Unless registered or otherwise distinguished, they are received in the normal course of affairs, yet they may be given emphasis through registry, special delivery, and personal addressing. Letters may also, under some conditions, be an inexpensive medium. The cost of postage, however, is not the entire cost. Composition and production costs must be included, and they often are high in the preparation of individual letters.

On the other hand, letters are not without disadvantages. The very fact of their common use dilutes the impact of their appeal. Being a one-way communication, they cannot complete the collection; they are dependent upon the debtor's acting *after* he has considered the content of the message. Like all letters, collection letters lack the visual effects of personal representation; they do not permit adjustment of the message to the debtor nor provide means of discussing the ideas involved. Neither are they always an inexpensive medium, particularly when top talent is employed in the writing of individual letters. Moreover, credit managers and their staffs do not always perform most brilliantly in writing collection letters, for the blending of message and tone in a frayed and indeterminate relationship requires expertise beyond that of the ordinary employee. Displays of creditor anxiety, false imputations of reasons for not paying, and descent into mediocrity in the attempt to be impersonal diminish the effectiveness of letters. Although these weaknesses are human and not inherent in the medium, the human element in collection is unavoidable.

In the effort to achieve through letters the maximum results possible, several tactics are widely employed in collection letters:

1. Letters are printed and processed when an impersonal relationship is preferred but are individually or mechanically typed when a personal effect is sought.
2. Unfavorable connotative words are avoided, such as "delinquent," "which you claim," "it is hard for us to understand," "your failure to comply," "per our request," "we are surprised to note," "you will force us," and the like.
3. Specific request for payment should be made. Some collectors believe that a request to "mail" payment is preferable to one "send" payment.
4. Designation of a particular time of expected payment is preferable to an indefinite expectation in "the near future."
5. Seriousness, simplicity, and sincerity should characterize all collection correspondence.

Telegrams. A second collection medium is the telegraph service in the form of the telephoned or delivered telegram.

Collection telegrams are an example of the effectiveness of understatement, and such understatement often preserves the dominance of the sender. Because of their measured wordage, telegrams carry an impression of urgency. This image is emphasized by the relative infrequency of their use as a regular medium of communication. It is augmented, too, by the fact that another person is introduced as a representative of the sender, yet the telephone or delivery representative is not an agent of the sender; thus personal contact but impersonal relationship are both achieved by use of this medium. Telegrams also have the advantages of directness and privacy, for they are seldom opened by anyone but the addressee, even in business; of economy, compared to prolonged compository efforts of a letter writer; and of responsive action, for a delivery messenger may accept payment requested by the telegram.

The following are examples of collection telegrams which have proved to be highly effective, according to Western Union:

1. "Please advise if check covering your account now due has been mailed."
2. "You have apparently overlooked your (monthly) payment. May we have your check promptly please."
3. "Only immediate compliance by letter (date) will save your credit."
4. "Must withhold shipment of order received today until past account settled. Wire remittance immediately to insure prompt delivery."
5. "Wire full payment of (date) and we will instruct attorney to withhold action. Failure to send will leave us no choice but to proceed immediately."
6. "Payment tomorrow imperative to prevent repossession of items charged your account of (date)."

Telephone Calls. Under certain circumstances, the telephone —both local and long-distance calling—is an effective collection medium. It is especially useful under the following circumstances:

1. The debtor is difficult to locate by mail or does not respond to letters.
2. Debtor–creditor relations have previously involved conversation.
3. Convenience of time and directness is essential to the creditor.
4. A surprise contact is disarming to the debtor and provides him an opportunity to explain his default and to consider a plan of payment.
5. Impersonal approaches have not produced payment.

Collecting by use of the telephone depends upon directness and clear statement of request to pay. It illustrates the creditor's attempt to maintain initiative by compelling the debtor to face his indebtedness, discuss it, and consider alternatives for paying. Experience has evolved a technology for telephone collecting which consists of the following: (1) make sure that it is the debtor speaking, (2) identify the person speaking on behalf of the creditor, (3) ask for the balance due, (4) find a solution to the problem if payment cannot be made at once, (5) have customer put in writing the understanding to which he agrees, (6) terminate the conversation decisively and positively.

Unfortunately, while telephoning provides for persuasiveness, it does not permit immediate action in response thereto. It is also sometimes difficult even by telephone to reach evasive debtors whose families shield them from collectors. Moreover, unless the telephone collector is skilled, he stands the chance of being outmaneuvered by a resistant and shifting debtor. Nevertheless, this medium has definite advantages in cutting time, costs, and uncertainties in the collection process.

Personal Calls. The advantages of direct confrontation are gained and the disadvantages of telephoning are avoided in face-to-face contact as a means of collecting.

Personal calls are the most commanding form in which the collection appeal can be made. They provide the opportunity actually to receive payment. For this reason, they are effective in certain types of consumer indebtedness, especially when small sums are owed, as instalment payments or rent, and which become cumulated unless collected regularly and promptly. In business relationships, the personal collection call not only affords an opportunity to pick up payment, but it also provides an occasion for the creditor to learn the cause of the default, to discuss the problem, and to reach some understanding with the customer which will prevent a recurrence. Salesmen are sometimes used as collectors; in some other countries, in fact, this is the principal use of salesmen.

Collection by personal calls, however, is a time-consuming and expensive process, and unless the scale of indebtedness and the number and location of debtors are favorable to this means, its disadvantages may exceed its advantages. Other means of collecting having failed, if a debt reaches the stage where only personal calls are effective, many creditors prefer to concentrate on their credit activity and delegate further collecting to professional collectors, who in turn, often use the medium of the personal call, going even to other cities to obtain payment from debtors. Unless a debtor is completely insolvent, there is usually some means of arranging for payment when the collector takes this kind of initiative.

Collection by Drafts. Still another medium for collecting is the use of commercial drafts drawn by the creditor and submitted to the debtor through his bank.

Collection drafts are used differently from those discussed in an earlier chapter as a credit instrument. The collection draft resembles the other in form but is used at a late stage in commercial credit relations. The debtor is ordered by it to make payment to the creditor or his bank. Being presented to the debtor through his own bank, it either gains payment or exposes to his bank the debtor's credit position. His unwillingness to jeopardize his bank line of credit may induce him to honor the draft when it is presented. It may also induce him to use his credit with the bank to pay the draft. Inasmuch as this medium is regarded as forceful and is not generally resorted to unless other means have failed, it is a courtesy to the debtor to forewarn him of intentions to submit a draft unless payment is received by a stated date. The warning may achieve payment; or it will provide time to arrange for payment upon presentation of the draft.

Illustration of Collection Systems

Seldom are all of the collection principles applied either in one collection case or in the collection systems of one creditor. A number of them are illustrated, however, in the systems used by a large branch of the American Telephone and Telegraph Company. Providing a service rather than a product and being interested in continuity of customer relations, the company had some unique requirements in its collection system. It could require advance payment before service was provided and protect itself against use of the service beyond the payment date. It could disconnect the service, yet use the facilities for reaching the customer by phone. It could sever relations with the subscriber, yet being a public utility it sought to maximize its market and to serve as widely as possible. The company classified its customers on the basis of their creditworthiness, and this classification served to differentiate its collection systems, shown in Table 26–2.

Legal Aspects of Collecting

Although collecting is a commercial and not a legal process, it involves management relationships with other economic participants on whose behalf society has established some legal controls. Creditors have a dominance through their legal rights, but the efforts of creditors to appear dominant, without having to

Table 26–2. Collection Systems Based upon a Classification of Customers

Business Accounts	Personal Accounts		
	Good	Fair	Poor
	Collection Procedure		
All accounts in this category are handled individually by the credit manager.	1st bill—30 days	1st bill—25 days	1st bill—15 days
	2d bill—5 days	Formal reminder—5 days	Suspension warning—5 days
	Formal reminder—5 days	2d bill—5 days	
	Suspension warning—5 days	Suspension warning—5 days	

Telephone call to notify of disconnection or to make arrangements for payment

Disconnection if no arrangement could be made—5 days

Disconnection notice expressing regrets and inviting further discussion—5 days

Personal visit by representative to attempt to ascertain reasons for non-payment

Telephone call by special sales representative

Personal visit by special sales representative

Termination Procedure

Disconnection

Final bill sent—10 days

First form collection letter, sent to all

Second form collection letter, sent to debtors with balances above $1 but below $5

Third form collection letter, sent to debtors with balances above $5. Further effort dependent upon the nature of the account

First attorney letter threatening to bring suit

Second attorney letter inviting settlement out of court:
    Letter A: Suit not intended
    Letter B: Suit intended

exercise those legal rights, has sometimes led them to actions relative to debtors for which there is neither legal nor social sanction. In this way, the entire credit system has been opened to criticism, debtors have been abused, and collectors in particular have earned a low esteem. Among the practices of collectors producing this effect has been the representing of themselves as something which they were not—as independent collection agencies, public agencies, public authorities, and legal agencies; as credit bureaus and other information-gathering organizations.

Thus socially accepted standards of fairness in competitive practice and trade representation have been violated, a breach of commercial ethics which has long been under the jurisdiction of the Department of Justice and the Federal Trade Commission. At the same time, the right of creditors to collect by fair means, free from legal obstructions interposed by debtors, has also faced the test of court decisions. Of particular significance, therefore, are these two areas in which the legal implications of collecting need to be understood.

Guides Against Debt Collection Deception.   Pursuant to its statutory prerogative to maintain fair competition and to prevent customer deception, the Federal Trade Commission adopted June 30, 1965, to become effective September 20 of that year, six "Guides Against Debt Collection Deception." It was hoped that these guides would encourage voluntary compliance with the law by industry members, although mandatory proceedings to prevent deceptive practices in the collecting of debts may be brought under the Federal Trade Commission Act against those whose practices are subject to the jurisdiction of the Commission. These Guides are as follows:

Guide 1.

Deception (General)—"An industry member shall not use any deceptive representation or deceptive means to collect or attempt to collect debts or to obtain information concerning debtors."

In connection with this provision, the Commission has prohibited, among others, the following misrepresentations: [2]

a. That an industry member was seeking information in connection with a survey.
b. That an industry member is in the business of a casting service for the motion picture or television industry.
c. That an industry member has a prepaid package for the debtor.
d. That a sum of money or valuable gift will be sent to the addressee if the required information is furnished.
e. That accounts have been turned over to innocent purchasers for value.
f. That debts have been turned over to an attorney or an independent organization engaged in the business of collecting past-due accounts.
g. That documents are legal process forms.

[2] Bureau of Industry Guidance, Federal Trade Commission, Washington, D.C., as reported in *The Credit World,* September, 1965, pp. 8–10.

Guide 2.

Disclosure of Purpose—(a) An industry member shall not use or cause to be used in his behalf in connection with the collection of or the attempt to collect a debt or in connection with obtaining or attempting to obtain information concerning a debtor, any forms, letters, questionnaires, or other material printed or written which do not clearly and conspicuously disclose that such are used for the purpose of collecting or attempting to collect a debt or to obtain or attempt to obtain information concerning a debtor, when the communication suggests that its objective is other than to collect or to obtain information concerning a debtor. (This affirmative disclosure also applies to all forms of communications, oral or otherwise.)

(b) An industry member shall not, through sale or otherwise, place in the hands of others for use in connection with the collection of or attempt to collect a debt or in connection with obtaining or attempting to obtain information concerning a debtor, any forms, letters, questionnaires or other material printed or written which do not clearly and conspicuously reveal thereon that such are used for the purpose of collecting or attempting to collect a debt or to obtain or attempt to obtain information concerning a debtor, when the communication suggests that its objective is other than to collect a debt or to obtain information concerning a debtor.

Guide 3.

Government Affiliation—An industry member shall not use any trade name, address, insignia, picture, emblem, or any other means which creates a false impression that such industry member is connected with or is an agency of government.

Guide 4.

Organizational Titles—An industry member shall not use the term "Credit Bureau" or any other term of similar import or meaning in its corporate or trade name, or in any other manner, when such member is not in fact a "Credit Bureau" as defined in these Guides.

Guide 5.

Trade Status—In collecting or attempting to collect debts due him, an industry member shall not, through the use of any designation or by other means, create the impression that he is a collection agency, unless he is such as defined in these Guides.

Guide 6.

Services—In the solicitation of accounts for collection or for ascertainment of credit status, an industry member shall not directly, or by implication, misrepresent the services he renders.

Collection Procedures and Right of Privacy. Another aspect of collection practice which has been subject to legal interpretation concerns the real and imagined violation of a debtor's rights by collectors. Protection from damage through disclosure to the public of one's indebtedness has long been sought through the law of libel and slander. Redress has also been sought at times on the basis of the principle of "intentional infliction of mental disturbance." But increasingly in recent years debtors have turned to the less well-known principles of tort legally classified as Invasion of the Rights of Privacy.[3]

It has been held to be slanderous, for instance, to imply publicly that a debtor has committed larceny, that he is not an honest person, or that he is a deadbeat. It has been held to be an invasion of privacy when, even though true, disclosure to the public of facts about a debtor's private affairs are detrimental to his reputation, or expose him to embarrassment or ridicule.

Claiming such rights, however, debtors have attempted to estop creditors from taking reasonable action to collect what is due them. Disclosure by a creditor of an employee's indebtedness to his employer is a particular point in issue. Courts have generally held, in favor of creditors, that such disclosures are a private, not a public, disclosure, even though the creditor's communication reaches a fellow employee while being transmitted to the employer in the ordinary course of business. Such communications to employers made both by letters and by telephone calls have been sanctioned, assuming that they are businesslike, informative, and properly addressed. Moreover, such communications are not barred on the grounds that the delinquency is disputed or completely denied, nor is the creditor precluded from contacting the employer before the dispute is resolved. The intent of the creditor in approaching the employer may be to seek aid in collecting the particular debt. Care should be exercised by the creditor to present the facts accurately, and the employer should be careful to keep confidential such information communicated to him.

DISCUSSION QUESTIONS

1. How valid is the absence of collection problems as evidence of the success of a credit operation?

[3] William R. Smith, Jr., and Paul A. Straske, "Collection Procedures and Right of Privacy," *Personal Finance Law Quarterly Report*, Winter, 1962, reprinted in *Credit World*, April, 1963, p. 6.

2. The offering of credit service and the performance of many related activities involve a calculated risk-taking or an expenditure measured against expected gain. What are the variables against which the collecting of delinquent accounts is measured?

3. Why is it difficult to determine when a debt has become an occasion for collection effort?

4. Research the literature of business, economics, psychology, and sociology to ascertain what is known (or assumed) about the behavior of people in debt. What application has this to determining a profile of creditor behavior?

5. Outline collection systems based upon the classification of debtors shown in Fig. 26–1.

6. Write sample collection letters appropriate for different stages of the collection effort.

7. How is impersonalization of the collection effort achieved? What are its merits?

8. Explain the strategy of using drafts, telegrams, telephone calls, and personal visits in collecting.

9. Make a list of the types of actions or statements in collections which might be regarded as illegal.

27

Legal Processes and Credit Management

A creditor's right to receive payment is a legal right inherent in his sales contracts and agreements. The means by which creditors exercise this right are both legal and extra-legal. The latter include means in ordinary commercial practice, discussed in the preceding chapter. They are determined by creditors' policies and are employed more or less arbitrarily. Legal means, on the other hand, are provided by law, to which strict conformity is required in safeguard of both creditors' and debtors' interests. Commercial collection practices are individual, voluntary, and primarily a creditor–debtor interaction. Legal means involve formal processes and court proceedings, which may force involuntary participation of another party, and often depend upon the joint action of a number of creditors. In the course of collecting, creditors usually resort to commercial means first, presuming to gain payment through cooperation and through their role dominance. Failing this, legal means are resorted to, social institutions, values, and customs being brought to bear upon the private transaction.

Both common and statutory laws pertain to the credit relationship. A comprehensive statement of creditors' and debtors' rights and obligations is found in the Uniform Commercial Code. Endorsed by the American Bar Association in 1951 and enacted first by Pennsylvania, where it became effective in 1954, it has subsequently been adopted by more than 47 states. The Code is thus gradually replacing the Uniform Sales Act, which previously had set forth much of the law pertaining to credit relationships. Even the Code, however, is not a complete body of credit law, nor is it assurance of uniformity. Where the Code is not yet adopted, the Act is likely to apply. The Code, not being regulatory, does not pertain to such matters as usury, consumer loans, or sales financing. Furthermore, revision of the Code in its adoption by states has perpetuated some of the diversity and uncertainty which antedated it. Nevertheless, it is a major piece of credit legislation and expresses current social philosophy concerning credit and collecting.

The right of creditors to act under law is based generally upon a debtor's *insolvency*. As defined by the Code, three tests of insolvency are that a debtor has "ceased to pay his debts in the ordinary course of business," that he "cannot pay his debts as they become due," or that, in the meaning of the federal bankruptcy law, his liabilities exceed his assets (UCC §§ 1–203,23). Bankruptcy proceedings alone require the extreme degree of insolvency; other legal actions may be based upon the lesser conditions of non-payment.

The fact of insolvency is more or less readily ascertainable in terms of the aforementioned behaviors, although insolvency is sometimes difficult to distinguish from default in payment, such as that resulting from a trade dispute. Behavior of a debtor toward *any* creditor may establish the fact of his insolvency, and knowledge of insolvency may be learned from either public or private sources. If the credit period extended in a particular transaction has expired without payment, that creditor may conclude that insofar as *he* is concerned the debtor is insolvent. Failure of the debtor to pay *other* creditors also indicates his insolvency, and knowledge of this by a creditor to whom payment was not yet due would be justification for his acting on the basis of insolvency relative to *his* relationship with the debtor.

The fact of insolvency, however, does not alone determine the action to be taken by a creditor; that is dependent also upon the *degree* of insolvency. Its degree relates to the probability of payment in the light of the debtor's circumstances. Some causes of insolvency are minor and temporary; evidence of them is found in the illiquidity of working capital—in the deficient quick ratio, as against a normal current ratio, for example. A greater degree of insolvency is not necessarily an extension of the same causes and conditions. A more serious degree of insolvency depicts a depletion of *all current* assets, not only of the liquid ones, and may be expressed in a current ratio weakened by destruction of inventory values through loss of fire, or of receivables through destruction of records or failure of key accounts. The most extreme form of insolvency is that in which not only current assets but *all assets* are less than debt and from which recovery is unlikely. While these conditions of insolvency permit taking a variety of legal actions, they also require, from the creditor's standpoint, determination of the most appropriate *commercial* action that should be taken within the provisions of the law. The credit objectives of cash recovery, future business, and minimization of expense relative to both must all be considered. Then the appropriate legal action based upon the fact of insolvency can be determined.

In general, creditors take two types of legal action: those in which they act alone in the proceedings, and those in which they act or share collectively with other creditors.

LEGAL RIGHTS OF CREDITORS ACTING INDIVIDUALLY

Acting independently upon knowledge of his debtor's insolvency, a creditor may take several courses of action, depending upon the location of the goods involved in the debt, whether they be (1) yet in the hands of the seller, (2) en route to the assignee in the hands of a carrier, (3) in the buyer's possession, or (4) in the hands of another party to whom the buyer has conveyed them. The object of action based upon any of these conditions is to preserve the creditor's interests: to maximize the possibility of his being paid, to minimize his dependence upon an insolvent debtor, and to establish his claim relative to the claims and interests of other parties.

Goods in the Hands of the Seller

Before goods have even left the hands of the seller, it is sometimes found that the buyer to whom they were sold on credit terms is insolvent. If, therefore, the buyer fails to make a payment due on or before delivery (if he also would wrongfully reject or revoke acceptance of the goods), the aggrieved seller may withhold delivery of such goods (UCC § 2–703) and refuse delivery except for cash (UCC § 2–702). So long as the buyer does not obtain lawful possession of the goods, the seller has a security interest in them; no agreement is necessary to make the security interest enforceable nor is filing of an agreement essential to perfecting the interest (UCC § 9–113). Contrary to previous requirements, the rights of the seller under the Code are not determined by when, or whether, title to merchandise has passed. Instead, specific rules are set forth for each problem depending upon trade and business custom.[1]

Seller's Resale.   Having stopped delivery of goods for reasons of the buyer's insolvency, the seller may resell the goods. He *must* in fact, resell them, for his recovery of damages from the buyer is limited by the Code to the difference between the resale price and the contract price (UCC § 2–706). Before the Code, the seller could "hold" the goods for the buyer and sue him for the entire contract price. Under the Code, the seller must first sell the goods at the best price and sue for the difference. The seller is not accountable to the buyer for any profit made on any resale. A person in the position of a seller, however, such as an agent, must account for any excess over the amount of *his* security interest.

Goods in Transit

Insolvency is reason also for the seller's stopping the delivery of goods in the possession of a carrier or other bailee (UCC § 2–705). "In transit," however, is not limited to a period of physical movement but is a state which continues until (1) the goods are received by the buyer, his representative, or sub-purchaser; (2) acknowledgment is given to the buyer by any bailee except a carrier that he holds the goods for the buyer; (3) such acknowledgment is given to the buyer by a carrier for reshipment or warehousing; or (4) negotiation gives to the buyer any negotiable document of title covering the goods. To stop delivery, the seller must give the bailee sufficient time to prevent delivery, surrender necessary documents connected with the shipment, and bear responsibility for ensuing charges and damages. Goods recovered from in-transit are subject to the seller's right of resale.

[1] Leon S. Forman, "Credit Implications of the Uniform Commercial Code," *Credit and Financial Management,* January, 1965, pp. 1 f.

Goods in Hands of the Buyer

Where goods sold have been delivered to an insolvent buyer, the seller upon learning of this insolvency may, under certain circumstances and within stated periods, reclaim the goods. If the circumstances under which replevin action is brought are subject to doubt, it should be remembered that while the seller has a right to the price, the buyer has a right to the goods.

If the buyer has received goods while insolvent, the seller may within ten days of their receipt demand return of the goods (UCC § 2–702). The ten-day limitation does not apply, however, if misrepresentation of solvency has been made to that particular seller in writing within three months before the delivery. Except for these two conditions, the seller has no right of replevin under the Code. The seller's right to reclaim goods under the Code is independent of whether title has or has not passed, or whether a chattel mortgage or conditional sales contract has been used, but it is subject to certain limitations. Reclamation is as possible under outright sale as under sale on consignment. Consignment sale is no longer a special protection of a vendor's interests, for, unless the buyer is commonly known to sell the goods of others or unless the vendor files a security interest in such goods, they are subject to claims of security parties, of buyer's lien creditors, and of his purchasers in good faith (UCC § 2–326 and § 2–702).

Claims superior to that of an unpaid seller are of several types. One type of prior interest is that held by other creditors whose security interest affords them a claim against after-acquired assets of the debtor (UCC § 9–204). Such security interest based on future advances is, of course, subordinate to conflicting interest in the same collateral. Another prior interest is that of the "lien creditor," who acquires, by means of attachment, levy, or the like, a lien on the property involved. Assignees in an assignment for the benefit of creditors, trustees in bankruptcy, or receivers in equity are among such lien creditors (UCC § 9–301). Another prior interest is that of a purchaser of stock in trade in bulk when creditors have been duly notified of the transfer ten days before the transferee takes possession of the goods (UCC § 6–105). Still another prior claim is that of a buyer in ordinary course or other good faith purchaser (UCC § 2–702).

If the unpaid seller acts within ten days to recover the goods from an insolvent buyer, or if the buyer has made misrepresentation of solvency in writing within three months, and if no prior claim is outstanding, the seller may reclaim the merchandise.

Goods in the Hands of Buyers in Course

When in the course of business a buyer, who becomes insolvent, has sold the goods in question to another party, the right of the first buyer's creditor to replevin the goods is affected. Subsequent purchasers have a prior right to the goods, to which the first creditor's right is subordinated (UCC § 2–702). However, a creditor of the seller may treat a sale as void if retention of possession by the seller is fraudulent (UCC § 2–502).

Because the right of the seller to reclaim goods under the Uniform Commercial Code constitutes preferential treatment as against the buyer's other creditors, reclamation of the goods excludes all other remedies with respect to them (UCC § 2–702).

Replevin Under the Uniform Conditional Sales Act [2]

Because many states have not yet adopted the Uniform Commercial Code and therefore the enforcing provisions of the Uniform Conditional Sales Act, and because replevin thereunder is an important legal means of collecting for creditors, a brief statement of its provisions may be useful.

When sales are made with recognition of the fact that nonpayment may require reclamation of the goods, the question of whether title to the goods has passed is essential. Under the Conditional Sales Act retention of title by the seller is basic to his right of replevin, and conditions for passing of title upon payment by the buyer are detailed carefully. A sale made with such stipulated conditions imposes some restrictions upon the buyer's reselling, although in most instances resale is an absolute and not a conditional sale. Upon default of the buyer, the seller under a conditional sale may (1) forfeit the goods and sue for the price, (2) replevin the goods and forfeit right of suit, (3) both retake the goods and sue for damages; state laws differ as to which of these actions may be taken.

If the seller repossesses the conditionally sold property, he

[2] See *Credit Manual of Commercial Laws, 1966*, New York: National Association of Credit Management, 1965, pp. 187–90, 282–83.

may do so usually either with or without legal process. When the latter means is used, the goods may be taken wherever they may be found, even with the use of reasonable force. However, a conditional seller cannot repossess without legal process, if doing so would result in a breach of peace. Depending also upon the law of the state, the seller who retakes goods may be obligated to refund to the buyer some portion of what he may have paid, or may be privileged to keep both payments and goods. The terms of the contract, the percentage of price paid, and the extent of damages and costs involved in repossession are determinants of the seller's obligation.

Security of a conditional vendor against claims of third parties depends mainly upon his compliance with the statute. Third parties include purchasers, creditors, trustees and receivers in bankruptcy; and certain statutory receivers. If the conditional vendor has not complied with the law, a purchaser who has given value for the goods usually has a superior right to the goods. On the other hand, if the conditional seller has complied with the law, the conditional vendee can convey only such title and interest as he has received, and rights of a purchaser from him would be subordinate to the rights of the conditional seller. The seller is entitled to recover the goods from such purchaser.

At the time of sale, choice is sometimes made between (1) conveyance of goods and title with reversion of title in the form of a mortgage and (2) conditional sale with retention of title by the seller until specified conditions have been fulfilled. Only under the latter terms has the seller right to replevin the goods. Possession of a chattel mortgage makes him a preferred creditor, but it does not confer right of replevin.

Sale of Stock in Trade in Bulk

Sale by a debtor of his stock in trade in bulk was cited above as one means by which an interest superior to that of one of his unpaid creditors might be established. While that protection is afforded a third party who purchases in good faith and in compliance with legal requirements, the principal intent of laws pertaining to bulk transfers is to protect creditors against fraudulent conveyance of property by an insolvent debtor. The Uniform Fraudulent Conveyance Act, the Uniform Commercial Code, and other state laws set forth creditors' rights in such circumstances. These statutes are not intended to prevent a merchant from selling his merchandise and fixtures, but only to require that the intention to make such a sale shall be made known in time to give creditors of the seller an opportunity to protect themselves against possible fraud. This fraud generally consists of a merchant selling in bulk to a friend for less than the assets are worth, hoping to re-enter business later at some advantage, or of pocketing the proceeds from such a sale and disappearing.

The principal requirement under the Code is that the transferor is obliged to furnish the transferee a list of his creditors, and the transferee is required to notify those creditors of the intended transfer. This notice must be given at least ten days prior to his taking possession of the goods or paying for them, and unless the transferee does this the transfer is ineffective against creditors (UCC § 6–105).

When a transferee, having duly notified creditors, takes possession of the goods, the consideration for the transfer is paid to creditors in several possible ways. First, the transferee may apply such consideration, so far as necessary, to pay the debts of the transferor. If the consideration payable is not enough to pay all of the debt in full, distribution shall be made pro rata (UCC § 6–106). Second, the transferee may pay the consideration into a court, which in turn orders distribution of it to the listed creditors. Third, if the sale has been by auction, auctioneer becomes responsible for such distribution of proceeds from the sale (UCC § 6–108).

Creditors of the transferor to protect their right of payment must comply with the statutory provisions with respect to filing their claims. They then may receive full or pro rata payment from the consideration or seek an injunction to stop the transfer. If a creditor's name has been omitted from the list but the transferee has acted without knowledge of this and has complied with the statute, he is absolved from liability to the creditor. When the title of a transferee to property is subject to a defect by reason of his non-compliance with the requirements of the Code, a subsequent purchaser for value in good faith and without such notice takes the goods free of such defect (UCC § 6–110).

Collection by Suit

The actions heretofore discussed which are available to creditors acting independently under legal rights have been for the retention or repossession of the goods in question. When the unpaid seller no longer has such right to the goods, his line of recourse is generally through the legal process of suit. The object of bringing suit is to obtain a judgment or legal recognition of the creditor's claim, and therewith to proceed by one of several means to attempt to gain payment.

The process by which a judgment is obtained consists of a series of steps in legal procedure:

1. Institution of suit by the creditor's attorney filing charges with the court, along with supporting evidence.
2. Service upon the debtor of a summons together with a statement of the claim.
3. Receipt from the defendant of such defenses as he may have, along with any new matter which he believes to be germane.
4. Filing of a reply by the plaintiff.
5. Trial of the case before a judge or jury when pleadings of the plaintiff and defendant have been completed. The judge passes upon questions of law; the jury considers issues of fact. The decision rendered is the judgment in the case, for the plaintiff or for the defendant. In suits involving cognovit or judgment notes, the procedural steps between filing of the claim and issuing of the judgment are omitted, made necessary by the waiver of notification and confession of judgment by the debtor.
6. Entry of the judgment in records of the court. In some jurisdictions this constitutes a lien upon property of the debtor.
7. Request for "execution" of the judgment, whereby a lien on the debtor's assets is obtained. This consists of a direction of an officer of the court to seize the property and make demands upon the debtor for payment. Actions requested of the court may consist of attachment, garnishment, or replevin.
8. If in levying upon the debtor the officer finds no property, he returns the execution to the court unsatisfied. If he levies upon property and the debtor fails to make payment, the property is sold, proceeds less the officer's charges and expenses are turned into the court, payment is made to the creditor, and, if payment is made in full, a form of receipt known as a "satisfaction piece" is given to the debtor.

Replevin. Under certain laws and circumstances, replevin of goods for which the unpaid debt was incurred depends upon establishment of a legal claim through court action. When judgment is given in favor of the creditor, execution of it in replevin of the goods is one form of satisfaction of the creditor.

Attachment. When reclamation of the specific goods is impossible—because of failure of the creditor to act within time limitations, because the debtor has made no untrue claims about his solvency, because the goods have lost their identity or have been sold, or because under the Uniform Sales Act title has passed to the buyer by attachment—other property of the debtor may be seized. The right of attachment, however, differs widely in different jurisdictions. Most favorable to creditors are those whereby a writ of attachment may be executed simultaneously with service of notice of suit, before judgment is given. More commonly, attachment is limited to circumstances where the debtor is a non-resident or a foreign corporation, has absconded, conceals, or hides himself, or is about to dispose of property to the detriment of creditors. Release of attached property may usually be obtained by the debtor's filing a bond. Attaching creditors may also be required to post bond for the payment of damages which the attachment may occasion.

Garnishment. When debtors have no property in their possession, claims against them can sometimes be satisfied by levying upon property of theirs in the hands of others. This action is the process of garnishment. Thereby, when a judgment is executed against a debtor, the debtor's property in the hands of the party receiving the notice of garnishment is to be held subject to claim or seizure. Tangible goods of, accounts payable to, and wages due the debtor are the properties most commonly garnisheed. When ordered to make payment to the court, parties holding property of the debtor must do so. In the collection of wages due the debtor, as this is a nuisance service on the part of the employer, it is often cause for warning or disemployment of the debtor and this is a strong persuasive influence for direct payment.

Exemptions. Notwithstanding the several protections to creditors' rights, creditors are limited in satisfaction of some claims by exemptions provided debtors. In all states, statutes of exemption specify the types and amounts of properties of debtors which are excluded from attachment and garnishment.

Property exemptions are generally classified as homestead exemptions and personal property exemptions. Homestead exemptions are variously stated, often depending upon whether the state is predominantly agricultural or urban. In agricultural areas, exemption is commonly given to a number of acres of land, up to 160 acres, with values ranging up to $12,500 in California. Values of from $1,000 to $2,500 are usual, and it is often required that the exemption be established by declaration and recording. The claiming of exemption is usually reserved to householders and heads of families. Personal property exemptions are of less value and include such items as household goods, wearing apparel, tools to carry on a trade, and specified livestock. In most states, any resident may apply for such exemptions.

Exemptions from garnishment are also provided, consisting generally of a specified amount of earnings within a recent stated period of time which cannot be seized. The exemption in Georgia, for example, is up to $3 per day and 50 per cent of excess thereof; in Ohio, 80 per cent of the first $300 and 60 per cent of balance earned within 30 days preceding issue of process, with minimum exemption of $150; in Rhode Island, not exceeding $30.

Considering the extent of such exemptions, it behooves a creditor to appraise the prospects of recovery before instituting proceedings which call for execution upon the properties of a debtor.

Limitations.   Whereas statutes of exemption vouchsafe to debtors minimal personal and business effects, statutes of limitation provide them ultimate release from debts which have been uncollected for specified lengths of time. The concepts of forgiveness, settlement of debt, or release from debt have deep historical roots and are characteristic for many peoples. In our society it takes the form of legal time limitations upon different forms and evidences of indebtedness. While limitations differ widely among the states, from 3 to 15 years for promissory notes, 6 years is a model period of time. The collectibility on open accounts is generally less, with 3, 4, and 5 years being most common. Limitations are also set for domestic and foreign judgments, and for instruments and contracts. In some states, judgments must be kept alive by execution every 5 years. After the expiration of the period of limitation, creditors may no longer pursue collection of a debt.[3]

---

[3] A summary of state statutes concerning both exemptions and limitations will be found in the *Credit Manual of Commercial Laws,* published annually by the National Association of Credit Management.

LEGAL PROVISIONS FOR CREDITORS ACTiNG COLLECTIVELY

Inasmuch as the plight of one unpaid creditor is often the plight of others, fair and just treatment of any one of them may best be achieved by treating all alike. Achievement of this, however, may require that the creditors coordinate, if not consolidate, their collection effort. Such action is not reserved for cases of extreme insolvency, although it is applicable there, but is appropriate in all degrees of insolvency. The collective actions most commonly used are debt pooling, composition settlement among creditors, assignment for benefit of creditors, appointment of an equity receivership, and petition in bankruptcy.

Debt Pooling

One form of collective action of creditors is known as debt pooling. It consists of creditors subordinating their individual claims to a general plan whereby the debtor may eventually pay all of his debts. This is also known as the granting of an extension to a debtor. It involves insolvency of the lesser types.

The occasion for debt pooling usually arises when a debtor is in temporary financial difficulties, but when there is no reason to doubt that with time he will solve his problem. Presumably, with patience, creditors will be satisfied. Until they are appraised of the circumstances, however, commercial collection efforts continue, with more or less harassment of the debtor as pressure is increased. If he communicates with one or more of his creditors, the debtor may request an extension of time. If agreed to individually by creditors, the agreement is not binding upon the creditor unless consideration is given. This may occur in one of two ways.

One form of consideration for an extension is the giving of a promissory note by the debtor in lieu of his account. Thus the creditor has a more tangible evidence of the debt, and the debtor has a period of grace in paying it.

The other form of consideration is the mutual agreement of creditors to forbear in their pressing of the debtor for payment. As all cannot be paid fully at once, each weighs the improbability of full payment against the possibility of no payment and shares with others pro rata payments and prolongation of the debt. The mutual concession of all constitutes consideration, and participation in the agreement is binding upon a creditor.

The request for such a settlement originates with the debtor, but coordination of the creditors is the responsibility of someone else. That may be an attorney representing one or several of them, a trade association, or some other debt adjuster or debtor advisor. The function of such an individual is to arrange with creditors a plan whereby they may share equally in payments made by the debtor. The adjuster may periodically receive from the debtor lump payments which are then divided pro rata among the creditors. Inasmuch as this form of service has been subject to some abuses, particularly in consumer debt adjustment, many states have enacted laws requiring licensing of agencies engaged in such practice and the posting of bond by them and limiting their charges for the service.

Composition of Creditors

With more than the mildest type of insolvency, the prospect of full payment of all creditors diminishes. At some point, it may be advantageous to creditors to accept less than full payment and cancel the remainder of the debt. When creditors enter into such a settlement through mutual agreement among themselves and with the debtor, this practice is known as settlement by composition.

The circumstances warranting acceptance of partial payment in full satisfaction of a claim are those of moderate insolvency but reasonable prospects for the survival of the debtor's business. The principal expectation in a composition is that the debtor will be able to continue in business following whatever adjustment in his financial condition must be made. Improbability of being able to pay results from permanent disappearance of values of inventory and receivables, usually due to conditions beyond the debtor's control. Incompetence or lack of character should not be a contributing factor, or else other means of collection would be more appropriate.

When terms of a composition have been arranged, they are binding upon all creditors who agree to them, and the debtor is thereby discharged from the remainder of his debt to those parties.

Equity Receivership

A presumption implicit in composition, namely, that the debtor is capable of rehabilitating his business if relieved of a portion of his debt, is not always valid. Outside assistance is sometimes necessary, and this may be obtainable through appointment of an equity receiver. This action results usually from the filing of a petition of a *creditor* on behalf of himself and all other creditors, requesting the appointment of a receiver by the court.

The receiver is appointed to solve the immediate problems arising from the debtor's default, to continue operation of the business on behalf of both creditors and debtor, and either eventually to liquidate the business or to return the assets to the debtor. Being an officer of the court, the receiver cannot be sued, and neither creditors nor others can interfere with assets in the hands of the receiver. Creditors are usually not entitled to participate in the proceedings; the entire matter is under the supervision of the court which appointed the receiver. No discharge of the debtor from his liabilities is obtainable through receivership proceedings.

Assignment for Benefit of Creditors

The state of affairs which suggests termination of an insolvent debtor's business also leads to several possible collective actions of creditors. One is the receipt of the assets of the debtor through his assignment of them to creditors collectively. Assets are thereafter liquidated, and proceeds are distributed pro rata to the creditors.

The degree of insolvency provocative of an assignment may or may not be that which would warrant termination of the business in bankruptcy. It is at least a degree of insolvency sufficient that either the debtor or his creditors may doubt the advisability of continued operations. After the initiation of assignment proceedings, it may be found that composition settlement or extension of paying time is better for the interests of all concerned; on the other hand, as assignment constitutes an act of bankruptcy, it may lead also to dissolution of the business through bankruptcy proceedings. Whatever the circumstance, assignment by the debtor evidences his willingness to turn his assets over to creditors for their mutual advantage.

Liquidation through assignment may be achieved under either common law or statutory provisions; the latter differ somewhat among the states. Common law assignment, sometimes termed "friendly adjustment," is conducted under the supervision of a committee of creditors, is not supervised by the court, and is not filed. Powers of the assignee under common law assignment are usually limited to the express terms of the instrument of assignment. Validity of the common law assignment rests upon the consent of the creditors. Its advantages over liquidation through court action are that it is quicker, less complex, and less costly, inasmuch as it avoids court costs, attorneys' fees, and fees of numerous officials in bankruptcy. On the other hand, friendly adjustment does not provide creditors opportunity to examine the debtor under oath, to benefit from preferential claims (unless specifically stated by the assignor), or to prevent liquidation from ending up in bankruptcy proceedings. Moreover, assignment, whether by common law or statutory procedures, provides the debtor no discharge from his debt, except by unanimous consent of creditors.

Wage Earners' Plans

Short of bankruptcy, another means by which creditors may collectively receive payment from a debtor is through Wage Earners' Plans, Chapter XIII of the Bankruptcy Act. Payments are made from a debtor's earnings to the court, which in turn distributes the money to his creditors. Creditors thereby receive payment, albeit slowly, and the debtor is relieved of certain executory contracts and lien executions.

Provisions of Chapter XIII are available to individuals whose income is derived principally from wages, salary, or commissions. Initiative for election of this form of settlement is taken by the debtor, who may file for this action either before or after adjudication in a pending bankruptcy proceeding, or when no such proceeding is in process. The petition, stating the inability of the debtor to pay his debts as they mature, may express his desire to effect either a composition or an extension, or both, out of his future earnings. Such a filing acts to stay adjudication or administration of the estate in bankruptcy proceedings.

Upon receipt of a petition for settlement under the Wage Earners' Plan, the judge or referee proceeds to act. The debtor submits a list of his creditors, who are invited to furnish proof of their claims; he also submits his plan for future payment to creditors. If they accept the plan in writing, a trustee is appointed by the court to receive and distribute monies paid by the debtor under the plan. Exemptions of the debtor are the same as those provided in bankruptcy.

In the debtor's plan, provision is made for dealing with *both secured and unsecured* debts, and a priority of payments may be established. Provision may be made for submission of future earnings or wages to the control of the court, who may also vary the amount or time of instalment payments arranged under the plan. Acceptance of the plan by the court is contingent, among other things, upon the debtor's freedom from guilt of any acts which would bar a discharge in bankruptcy. Confirmation of a plan by the court makes it binding upon all creditors.

During the period of extension, the court retains jurisdiction over the debtor's property for all purposes of the plan and may direct an employer of the debtor to make such payments as could be required through enforcement of judgments. If within three years of confirmation of the plan the debtor has failed to discharge his debts, because of circumstances for which he is not accountable, the court may discharge him from all debts provided for by the plan, excepting those which are not dischargeable. If, however, the debtor defaults in compliance with the requirements of the petition or the plan, the court may (1) dismiss the case, (2) with the debtor's consent, adjudge him bankrupt, or (3) if he is so adjudged, proceed with bankruptcy proceedings.

Thus is provided a means by which a conscientious employed debtor may stay other legal actions of creditors while attempting to make equitable payment of their claims.

Arrangements

Creditors of individuals or corporations may also be affected by the petitioning of those parties for settlement by arrangement, under Chapter XI of the Bankruptcy Act. Provision is thereby made for court administration of an insolvent debtor's plan for paying his creditors, whereby he desires to obtain a discharge from his *unsecured* debts.

It should be noted that arrangement settlement is applicable only to the *unsecured* liabilities of a debtor. If a debtor's proposal is accepted in writing by his creditors and confirmed by the court, he is discharged from those debts except as payment is provided for in the plan. If it is not confirmed, or if the debtor fails to act according to the requirements, the court may dismiss the case, adjudicate bankruptcy, or proceed with a previous adjudication.

Initiation of an arrangement may be made only by a debtor, without regard to whether a petition in bankruptcy has been filed or whether he has been adjudged a bankrupt. The filing of such a petition does not automatically stay adjudication of bankruptcy, although the same may be stayed upon application of the debtor and notice to all interested parties. Receipt of the petition also empowers the court to reject executory contracts of the debtor, authorize an agent to lease or to sell the debtor's property, extend the time for performance of any duties under Chapter XI, or stay the commencement or continuation of suits against the debtor.

In connection with the petition, a statement of provisions of the arrangement proposed by the debtor is made. The arrangement *must* include provisions modifying or altering the rights of unsecured creditors generally, or of some class of them, upon any terms or for any consideration. In addition, it *may* include provisions for the treatment of unsecured debts on a parity one with the other, for rejection of an executory contract, for payment on account during the term of the arrangement, for continuation of the debtor's business with or without supervision, and for payment of debts incurred after filing the petition. If circumstances warrant it, the proceedings may be referred to a referee and a receiver or trustee appointed.

In the hands of the court, the terms of a confirmed arrangement may be altered or modified. Confirmation, however, makes the arrangement binding upon the debtor and all persons affected by the arrangement, whether or not they have filed claims or whether or not their claims have been scheduled or allowed. Confirmation discharges the debtor from all his unsecured debts and liabilities provided for by the arrangement, except those not dischargeable.

If the arrangement is withdrawn or abandoned prior to acceptance, if it is not accepted, or if it is not confirmed, and if the arrangement proceeding has superseded a pending bankruptcy proceeding, the court must enter an order dismissing the arrangement proceeding and directing that the bankruptcy be proceeded with. If no bankruptcy proceedings are in process, unless the arrangement proceedings are dismissed, the debtor is adjudicated a bankrupt and appropriate action follows.

Through this plan is thus provided a stay of bankruptcy in the hope of a more favorable solution for continuing the business under court supervision, with modification of the unsecured indebtedness.

Bankruptcy

As a last resort in recovering their credit investment, creditors may participate in bankruptcy proceedings. This is a procedure whereby under court supervision an insolvent debtor's assets are liquidated, money realized is distributed among creditors, and the debtor is discharged from his debt.

Bankruptcy, as a means of protecting interests of both debtors and creditors, has deep historical and social roots. The ancient Hebrews were governed by a law requiring creditors to release neighbors indebted to them every seven years. This meant that loans made should not be exacted of them again. Also, Hebrew men and women bought for servitude were released after six years, and they were released from bondage with sufficient flocks, grain, and wine to give them a new start (Deut. 15). Non-Hebrews, however, were not so treated; their indebtedness was not forgiven. Subsequently, imprisonment for debt was common, and debtors were held until redeemed by relatives or friends. More recently has prevailed the philosophy of the Hebraic laws: that no one should be required to remain permanently in debt and that in payment of debt he should not be made absolutely destitute. These ideas are embodied in legislation pertaining to limitations, exemptions, and bankruptcy.

Contemporary bankruptcy legislation in the United States dates from 1898, when an Act was passed to establish a uniform system of bankruptcy throughout the States. Repeatedly amended, this legislation provides protection to both creditors and debtors. To creditors of an insolvent debtor it provides a means of terminating his failing operation and sharing in the remainder of his assets before they are completely dissipated.

To insolvent debtors, it provides a means of relief from the harassments and varied collection efforts of creditors. Thus provision is made for both involuntary and voluntary—creditor-initiated and debtor-initiated—bankruptcy proceedings.

Beneficiaries of Bankruptcy. Bankruptcy, however, is not a blanket remedy for all debtors and creditors. Not every debtor may resort to bankruptcy. Not every debtor may be forced into bankruptcy by his creditors. And not every debt may be discharged through bankruptcy. (See § 4 of the Bankruptcy Act.) Railroad, insurance, and banking corporations, and building and loan associations may neither petition voluntarily for bankruptcy relief nor be forced into bankruptcy involuntarily through a petition of creditors. Insolvency of those organizations is dealt with not under the provisions of straight bankruptcy, but by special legislation and administrative agencies.[4] On the other hand, wage earners earning less than $1,500 annually and farmers, while they may voluntarily petition for bankruptcy, may not be filed against by creditors.

The following, moreover, are debts which are not subject to bankruptcy discharge (§ 17):

1. Taxes due the United States, and State, county, district, or municipality.
2. Liabilities for obtaining money or property obtained by false pretenses or representations or upon a materially false statement in writing respecting his financial condition, made with intent to deceive, or for alimony, maintenance and support of wife and child, seduction of an unmarried female, breach of promise of marriage accompanied by seduction, or for criminal conversation.
3. Debts not scheduled in time for proof and allowance, if known to the bankrupt, unless such creditor had notice or actual knowledge of the proceedings in bankruptcy.
4. Debts created by his fraud, embezzlement, misappropriation or defalcation while acting as an officer or in any fiduciary capacity.
5. Wages earned within three months before the date of commencing of the proceedings in bankruptcy due to workmen, servants, clerks, or traveling or city salesmen, on salary or commission basis, whole or part time, whether or not selling exclusively for the bankrupt.
6. Moneys of an employee received or retained by his employer to secure the faithful performance by such employee of the terms of a contract of employment.

[4] Section 77 of the Bankruptcy Act pertains to Reorganization of Railroads Engaged in Interstate Commerce.

Conditions Requisite for Bankruptcy. Before bankruptcy proceedings may be undertaken, there must be a presumption of two conditions: (1) insolvency of the debtor whereby his liabilities exceed his assets and (2) commission of an act by bankruptcy on the part of the debtor. If allegations of either of these conditions are disputed, responsibility for proof of solvency or innocence of an act rests upon the debtor.

The six acts of bankruptcy detailed in the law consist of a debtor's having done any of the following:

1. Fraudulently conveyed, transferred, concealed, or removed any part of his property with intent to hinder, delay, or defraud creditors.
2. Transferred, while insolvent, any portion of his property to one or more creditors with the result that the creditor receives a greater percentage of his claim than other creditors of the same class.
3. Suffered or permitted, while insolvent, any creditor to obtain a lien upon his property through legal proceedings, and failed to vacate or discharge the lien within thirty days from the date thereof, or at least five days before the date of any sale or other disposition of the property.
4. Made a general assignment for the benefit of his creditors, whether or not the debtor was insolvent.
5. While insolvent, permitted or suffered, voluntarily or involuntarily, appointment of a receiver or trustee to take charge of his property.
6. Admitted in writing his inability to pay his debts and his willingness to be adjudged a bankrupt.

Acts numbered 1, 2, and 4 must have been committed within four months prior to the filing of the petition. Acts 2, 3, and 5 must have been committed while the debtor was insolvent. A voluntary petition may be filed by a debtor whether or not he is insolvent. An involuntary petition, presuming insolvency, may be filed by three creditors having provable claims against the bankrupt amounting to $500 or more, unless the total number of creditors is less than twelve, when any one creditor may file.

Bankruptcy Participants and Procedure. Bankruptcy procedures, which are precisely defined by the Act, are set up within the system of the United States district courts, with a referee designated by the presiding judge to have responsibility for administering the cases. Depending upon circumstances involved, a receiver and a trustee may be appointed to assist the court in the interest of fairness and impartiality to the debtor and creditors. A close similarity exists between the procedure involved in straight suit of a debtor and that of bankruptcy. The two are illustrated diagrammatically in Fig. 27–1 and explained in the following text.

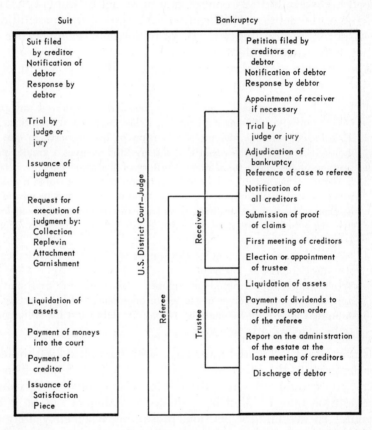

Fig. 27–1. Comparison of legal procedures in suit and bankruptcy.

FILING OF PETITION. Like the filing of a suit, a petition in bankruptcy initiated by creditors is followed by notification of the debtor that allegations have been made. The debtor may then (1) ignore the claims and be adjudged a bankrupt by default, (2) acknowledge the pretentions and cooperate with the court, or (3) refute the imputations and contest them. If the latter attitude is taken, whereby the debtor may deny his insolvency or that he has committed an act of bankruptcy, the case may be tried by the judge or by a jury to establish the facts. If satisfied that bankruptcy is warranted, the judge gives an adjudication to that effect. The debtor has thereafter five days in which to file a schedule of his property showing its kind, amount, location, and money value; a list of his creditors, showing their addresses, amounts due, the security held, and what claims are contingent, unliquidated, or disputed; and a claim for such exemptions as he may be entitled to.

If the debtor voluntarily files a petition, it is accompanied by these same schedules. The procedure under the jurisdiction of the District Court judge, however, is short-circuited, and adjudication follows more or less automatically.

During this interval of initial investigation, if the judge deems it advisable in the interests of creditors, he may appoint a receiver, whose duty is to preserve the state until the appointment of a trustee. No-asset cases warrant no receiver; others sometimes also may not.

ESTABLISHMENT OF CLAIMS. Following adjudication, the case is usually referred to a referee, an officer of the court who has jurisdiction over the liquidation of the estate and the settlement of claims.

The referee notifies all creditors and invites them to submit proof of their claims. If a list of creditors has not been prepared by the debtor, it is the responsibility of the referee to prepare or cause to be prepared such a list. He examines schedules filed and claims submitted. Precise instructions for handling different classes of claims, for allowing and disallowing, are set forth in § 57 of the Act.

MEETING OF CREDITORS. Not less than 10 nor more than 30 days after adjudication, the first meeting of creditors is held, presided over by the referee and attended by the bankrupt. Principal purposes of this meeting are to allow claims of creditors present, to interrogate the bankrupt, and to elect a trustee if there are assets to be disposed of. Any creditor may nominate a candidate for trustee, and the candidate receiving the majority of votes is to be appointed. Creditors holding secured or priority claims are not entitled to vote unless the amounts of such claims exceed the values of the securities or priorities, and then only for such excess. Creditors at this first meeting may also appoint a committee of not less than three creditors to consult with and advise the trustee in connection with the administration of the estate. Upon proper petition of creditors, additional meetings may be called. Also, when the affairs of the estate are ready to be closed, a final meeting of creditors is held. This meeting, however, may be omitted in no-asset cases.

LIQUIDATION OF ESTATE. It is the duty of the trustee to reduce the property of the estate to money, to deposit the funds in his keeping, to pay dividends, and to account and to report to the referee and all creditors for the details of his administration.

Taking over the properties from a receiver, if such was appointed, the trustee obtains an appraiser's valuation of them and proceeds to sell the property. Sale for less than 75 per cent of appraised value may not be made without approval of the court. Sale may also be made at auction if that seems expeditious. The trustee is responsible for setting aside and reporting upon the bankrupt's allowable exemptions. He examines the bankrupt at hearings upon objections to discharge and may himself oppose the discharge if he deems it advisable to do so. His jurisdiction continues through the final meeting of the creditors.

DISCHARGE OF THE DEBTOR. An end objective of bankruptcy is the discharge of the debtor from his obligations. Adjudication as a bankrupt of any person except a corporation operates automatically as an application for a discharge. In the case of a corporation, an application for a discharge must be filed within six months after adjudication. Discharge may be opposed by the trustee, by any creditor, or by the United States Attorney. Grounds for objection are based upon the bankrupt's having done any of the following:

1. Committed an offense, punishable by imprisonment, under Title 18 U. S. C. § 182.
2. Destroyed, mutilated, falsified, or failed to keep books of account, unless the court finds such failure justified.
3. Obtained property on a materially false statement in writing while engaged in business as a sole proprietor, partnership, or as an executive of a corporation.
4. Made a fraudulent transfer within twelve months before the petition, with intent to defeat the provisions of the Act.
5. Been granted a discharge, or had a composition or an arrangement by way of a composition, or a wage-earner's arrangement plan by way of a composition confirmed within six years.

6. Refused to obey orders of the court or answer material questions.
7. Failed to explain the deficiency of assets to the satisfaction of the court.

In the absence of sustained objection to discharge, and at the expiration of the required time, the court discharges the bankrupt.

DISCUSSION QUESTIONS

1. Distinguish between commercial, legal, and "friendly" collection efforts.
2. Define "insolvency." Explain how the fact of insolvency is ascertained. Explain also the significance of the degree of insolvency.
3. Identify the rights of unpaid vendors which are dependent upon the physical location of the goods in question and in whose possession they are.
4. To what extent is a creditor's recovery dependent upon resale value, replevin, or other equities of the debtor?
5. What are "superior claims" and what safeguards must a creditor take to protect himself against them?
6. What are the status and rights of third parties to a debtor–creditor relationship?
7. Distinguish between the procedures of obtaining and of executing a judgment.
8. In which legal situations is the debtor obligated to submit a plan for the paying of his debts?
9. What alternative actions are available to a private individual who could qualify for adjudication as bankrupt?
10. Explain the relevance of the various Chapters of the Bankruptcy Act to solution of the debt problem.
11. What justification is there for the following: statutes of limitation, exemptions, priority claims, undischargeable debts, discharge in bankruptcy?

28

Appraisal of Credit Management

Following the foregoing detailed consideration of credit and credit management, it is appropriate that attention be turned to an evaluation of them. In a free-market society, with initiative given to private enterprise, it is reasonable that divergence of interests should appear and that appraisal of credit should be possible from several viewpoints. It is increasingly evident that society at large is appraising credit, adopting its offerings yet pressing for conformity to society's values and standards. Entrepreneurs are also appraising credit management, setting new goals and creating measurements of management efficiency. At this stage of development, no simple judgment can be offered; not only is society's judgment still formative, but the criteria for judgment are also yet debatable. In the following pages, therefore, are presented some criteria by which credit and credit management may be appraised, that individuals may better draw their own conclusions concerning them. The criteria are classified as to their relevance to the general aspects of credit and to its managerial aspects.

SOCIAL APPRAISAL OF CREDIT

From the standpoint of society in general, several questions might be asked suggesting the nature of public interest: Is the credit system providing the types of service needed in our society? Is free enterprise compatible with the interests of the public in its uses of credit? Is the credit system responsive to social change? Answers to these questions are suggested by several evidences.

Adequacy

Favorable judgment of credit might be made if provisions for the use of credit were deemed adequate. Adequacy, however, presumes agreement concerning the needs. In the past, credit service was considered adequate if it met the needs of parties with unquestionable creditworthiness. Today, one may consider whether meeting needs of virtually *everyone* for credit service might not be expected, and whether adequacy should be judged by the degree to which this is achieved. It has been seen that forms of credit have been devised whereby less and less credit-worthy risks can be accommodated through the use of appropriate terms and instruments, as well as with the aid of credit specialists and technical facilities. As our economy becomes increasingly service-oriented, adequacy may be judged in terms of the capacity of the credit system to serve simply convenience rather than credibility. The needs of business users of credit, too, must be adequately provided for, and it has long been the experience of small businesses that credit services are inadequate for their needs. Where private enterprise has not supplied these needs adequately, cooperative and governmental institutions have sometimes stepped in to fill the gap. Thus government agencies have given loans and guarantees of loans to small-business proprietors, agriculturalists, homeowners, veterans, and others.

Whether credit facilities are yet adequate may be judged by whether everyone who would use credit may do so. If not, old concepts of credit may be challenged; the discovery of new means of serving additional markets may be required.

Some critics conclude that the supply of credit services is more than adequate and that their superfluity results in terms which are unworkable in our present stage of technological development, in competition which violates sound standards of credit management, and in a volume of debt which jeopardizes economic stability. Resolution of these differences will depend upon more careful determination of the role which credit is *expected* to serve in our society and of the means by which this goal can best be achieved.

Specialization

Judgment of the credit system may also be made in terms of specialization found within it. Specialization has long been accepted as evidence of economic efficiency, as division of labor and reduction of compound functions to elemental tasks have progressed. In a marketing economy, specialization of institution and service offering also connotes adaptation of function to market demand.

It is apparent that in the supplying of credit service there is much specialization, evidenced in the variety of institutions comprising the credit structure and in the forms of credit service offered to business and personal users of credit. Such specialization is conducive to expertness. It also provides society with a range and assortment of credit services.

As in any field, the advantages of specialization in credit may reach a point of diminishing returns, where proliferation and fragmentation of offering exceed the maximum economy. At that point a reversal of trend sometimes occurs, and integration, combination, and merger of functions and institutions take place. This, too, has occurred in credit service as institutions have provided more diversified offerings, combining sale and loan credit service to both business and personal clients. Such a departure from specialization, however, is no certain evidence of economic retrogression; rather it may evidence changing market conditions and habits to which the entrepreneur is adapting himself. Thus both specialization and diversification may be laudable, depending upon the conditions which have produced them.

Competition

In a free-market society, one is disposed to regard competition as contributory to social and economic progress. Non-capitalistic societies believe otherwise: that competition is destructive and that state planning is conducive to the maximum progress. Which of these viewpoints is valid depends upon the nature of the competition which the environment creates. Competition in our society is a constructive force, for gradually and increasingly it has offered society the benefits of the creativity of many participants. Under state planning, no incentive produces this result. Consequently, we have experienced in credit, as in other fields, a great amount of competitive enterprise which has tended to keep the credit offering adapted to the market demand.

Competition in credit service, however, has not been all of one type. There have been both price and service, or product competition. That based upon product or service differentiation has become expressed in the diversity of institutions in the credit structure and in efforts for betterment of their offering by individual enterprises. Differences in counseling, convenience, personal relations, contract terms, security requirements, and the like, have resulted. On the other hand, differences in terms and credit charges have also indicated some price competition. As differentiated credit offerings nevertheless serve overlapping markets, their different rates constitute a type of price competition among them.

It appears that price competition has been less vigorous in this field than in others. This has been due in part to the fact that much credit service is bought as adjunct to obtaining commodities or other satisfactions. Clear distinction has not been made between the total charge and the charge for credit service; therefore the purchaser has not always been critical of price or aware of competitive practices. Concurrently, suppliers of credit service do not, nor have been required to, state their charges in such ways that price comparisons can be easily made. Consequently, in some instances competition on the basis of price has not been vigorous. This partial absence of price competition has defeated, in part, realization of the benefits of the competitive system and has resulted in agitation for social regulations enforcing such competition.

Change and Innovation

Another basis of merit in credit offering is the extent to which change occurs. Change for its own sake is of no particular importance, but change which represents innovation is important. Such change, often stimulated by competitive efforts, may represent what is called "adaptive behavior"—the tendency of the business system to adapt itself to environmental changes. That such change has taken place cannot be questioned.

One evidence of this is the innovation which has occurred in consumer credit to provide credit service to the ever broadening middle-income class of our society. This has taken form in revolving and optional credit plans serving markets other than those supplied by regular charge accounts; in the development of universal card plans serving a very itinerant population; in various forms of instalment payment catering to purchasers of high-priced durable goods; in auxiliary credit facilities meeting needs of vendors and lenders who are unable to perform some of their own credit functions; and in adoption of physical facilities and equipment expediting performance of the credit work. In all these ways, it would seem that the credit system has kept abreast of the times, passing to users of credit the advantages of change and the fruits of entrepreneurial creativity.

Technical Facilities

In this day of rapidly changing state of technology, credit management is expected to adopt means which lower costs, improve service, or both. A far-reaching development along this line has been the computer. Progress in credit management will be measured in coming years by use made of this facility in compiling, analyzing, and disseminating information. Isolation of credit operations, whether in credit bureaus or in credit operations, has many disadvantages in duplication, fragmentation, and disintegration of activities. The fact that many other technical devices and facilities have been employed by credit managers attests their receptiveness to modernization.

Research

Still another criterion of service to the general public is the extent to which research in credit is carried on. In industry, the allocation of funds to product research is an indication of effort to explore new opportunities. Market research allocations have similar implication. In credit, rarely is such use made of funds. Comparable fertility of opportunity may not exist, but on the whole less attention is given to research and development of new ideas for the offering of credit services.

As evident in credit periodicals, thought about credit relates mainly to technical considerations, to processes and problems of the credit manager. Some attention is given to interpreting the use made of credit in our economy, to social problems attributable to credit practices, to stratification of credit markets, and to summation and comparison of credit legislation. Academicians engage in both theoretical and empirical research; credit associations compile experiences and opinions of their members; behavioral scientists study psychological and sociological influences on the use of credit; and credit managers themselves analyze their experiences and those of others. Notwithstanding all these efforts, one is not impressed with much volume of scientific findings advancing thought and practice in the field. One is rather aware of the tardiness with which research into credit costs has been undertaken, or the integration of credit functions into formal corporate organization, or the shiftability of credit functions, or the human aspects of the behavior of credit participants. Many opportunities exist for further development of credit through research along such lines.

Education

Fields of economic behavior are advanced through knowledge and education. Progress is indicated by refinement and development of thought, keeping it contemporary with conceptual developments and with current practice.

Credit thought has been relatively stable for many years and has been slow to assimilate some new ideas which impinge upon it. Education for credit work, as provided for by the typical literature in the field, has prepared individuals for the position of credit manager. It has given less help to preparation of individuals in higher managerial positions for participation in or appraisal of credit work in its broader aspects. It has seldom incorporated into credit management theory concepts drawn from marketing theory, such as concepts of market segments, product differentiation, or price and product competition. A cause for this has been preoccupation with credit as a finance function, as the management of money or a type of investment, rather than as the providing of an economic, marketable service.

Delay in development of credit theory has jeopardized the position of education for credit management in the course structure of schools. Discrimination against functional courses of a low technical order, in preference for broader management training and more liberal business education, has crowded courses in credit out of some business school curricula at a time when the credit function in business and society is more vital than at any previous time. Professional courses and training programs are designed mainly according to traditional patterns to prepare managers for operational levels; few provide the insights needed for dealing with credit in its broader dimensions. Nevertheless, alterations of credit thought are in progress, and with new views it may be expected that a renaissance of this field of management will be experienced.

Social Regulation

Still another criterion of the stature of credit in our economy is the extent and manner in which it has been subjected to social regulation. This is an indication of the esteem in which it is held and of the disrepute which it has attained.

The credit system seems to have sprung from the very roots of our economy, i.e., free enterprise, capitalism, and competition. The specialized economy, the exchange market, and the medium of money have been natural stimulants to the use of credit. More than that, we have devised institutional systems, like the Federal Reserve Bank, to facilitate a complex system of credit. Recognizing growing need for both commercial and personal use of credit, we have given legal sanction to credit institutions, rates, and practices, providing for commercially profitable performance of the credit functions. Where private enterprise has faltered, cooperative sponsorship of credit activity has been encouraged. The federal Government has also directly and indirectly engaged in the supplying of credit service. Thus a strong inclination of our society has been toward support of credit, toward, the evolution of it under the direction of forces which characterize our economy.

On the other hand, society has recognized the necessity for restricting as well as encouraging use of credit. Lending, particularly, has always been exposed to derogation because of abuse of positions in the debtor–creditor relationship. Similar abuses have entered into use of credit in selling. Consequently, the rights of both parties have been protected through laws fixing interest rates and credit charges; requiring licensing and inspection of credit agencies; basing entry into the field upon proof of necessity; and prescribing and prohibiting certain practices in the promotion of credit business, preparation of contracts, and collecting of debt. Restraints have been imposed upon the volume of credit in presumed protection of the economy against inflation, excessive debt, and debtor illiquidity. Thus one may conclude that, while much confidence has been placed in credit, precautions have been taken to keep its use within bounds deemed socially appropriate.

From these several criteria, one may answer affirmatively the question: Has credit had a salubrious role in our society? It has been a changing role, with the standards of appraisal evolving with social change. Critics differ in detail and in degree as to its merit in particulars, but there is assent to the fact that the use of credit has enabled us as a society to achieve some of our contemporary aspirations. This has been accomplished without excessive cost to society. Truly, the charge for credit service is appreciable, but such service has a marketable value in an advanced and affluent market. Also, credit practices have exposed both debtors and creditors to unexpected losses, but the plaudits of successful uses of credit are far more impressive.

APPRAISAL OF CREDIT MANAGEMENT

Apart from the question of whether credit has made its maximum contribution to society, that of whether credit management has made a maximum contribution to the firm is equally important. Management appraisal is perhaps the more common of the two, for the expectations of managerial performance have been the more precisely stated. Consequently, there have evolved measures of performance and efficiency for credit management, many of which have already been stated in this book. For present purposes, some of them are reconsidered in the context of the total behavioral and technical aspects of management.

Measures of management stated in earlier chapters were grouped according to the three basic credit functions, thereby providing a basis for appraising functional performance. There is merit also in considering together measures of performance which relate to the human relationships in which management acts. Actions alone can be measured, and such measures are compared with standards of performance, but the ultimate standard of judgment is the socially sanctioned expectations held by others with whom managers interact in the credit processes. Expectations are the basic motivations; measures of performance are guidelines indicating whether expectations are fulfilled and suggesting action to be taken for better fulfillment of them. Both qualitative and quantitative standards for appraising credit management, therefore, are meaningful as guides to action of managers, in their relations with consumers, owners, and government.

Management—Consumer Relations

The point of view maintained throughout this book has been that the supplying of credit services begins with consideration of markets and consists of effort to provide the services desired, under the circumstances and at the prices preferred. Whether management is satisfying these expectations of its market may be learned in several ways.

Market Analysis. One source of evidence for judging credit management is analysis of the market for credit service. This may be done by direct interrogation and study of motivations and habits in the use of credit by those who constitute one's market. It may also be approached by honest appraisal of one's offering in terms of what is already known about the market. Self-questioning along the following lines is a useful guide to management appraisal:

Are terms of credit service compatible with the quality of merchandise sold on credit?

Are the forms of credit service adapted to needs of the market served?

Is the credit service offered competitive with or differentiated from other services in the same market?

Is credit policy flexible to meet changing conditions of the market?

Is the image of the service offered consistent in the minds of customers with their expectations, and is it consistent with the image it is intended to create?

Relations of credit management with customers are a point of interest to top management of a firm and should not be confined to the level of representatives of the firm who are in contact with customers. Top management has responsibilities for the determination of market segments to be served and for success in achieving its objectives. It may periodically, therefore, consider such questions in its appraisal of the role of credit in the entire organization.

Applications and Acceptances.   Another evidence of management–customer relations is the attraction of potential credit customers to the business and the measure in which their applications are approved.   Promotional activity is initiative taken by the creditor; submittal of applications is the response of customers.   Both the credit offering and the merchandise offering are inducements to the use of credit.   Therefore, measures of applications received, their source, and their quality indicate the effectiveness of management's promotional effort.

Approval and rejection of applications is another useful measure.   If the objective is to stimulate credit business through affiliation of credit customers, acceptance of applications should reflect whatever policy of calculated risk assumption management adopts.   An index or ratio of applications approved to applications received, therefore, guides management in its initial contacts with credit customers.

Account Activity and Dormancy.   Another measure of management useful in guiding management–customer interaction is that of account activity.   This is shown by use made of accounts.   It is also shown by disuse of them, indicating attrition, dissatisfaction, apathy, and lack of promotion on the part of management.

Each of these criteria is useful in the appraisal of management's behavior relative to customers.

Management–Owner Relations

When management's obligation to customers, to provide them desired credit service, is fulfilled, management's next obligation is to owners of the enterprise, to produce for them a profit.   Commitment to capitalism places this priority on profit, but the privilege of earning profit carries responsibilities to employees, government, the community, and others.   Consequently, measures of profitability are extremely important, for they show fulfillment of manager's obligations to owners and the related potentiality of their fulfilling expectations to others.   The following are some useful measures of profitability.

Income from Credit Service.   Credit service is a productive factor in the sales effort of a firm.   It is offered either to produce an indirect stimulant to income through the increase of product sales, or a direct addition to income through the sale of credit services.

In either case, the effect of credit service upon income may be observed through such measures as the following:

Credit sales, past period : credit sales, present period
Credit sales : total sales
Credit sales : market for credit sales

The volume of sales and loans made, however, does not alone satisfy owner's expectations; profits are even more important. Making credit for the sake of credit sales is no longer regarded as sufficient justification for credit activity. Profitability must be demonstrated. Consequently, margins and costs which combine to yield profit are taken into consideration in management appraisal through such measures as the following:

Profit on credit-stimulated sales : cost of credit service
Cost of credit service : credit sales
Costs of funds : credit sales
Cost of funds : average receivables outstanding
Receivables outstanding : average daily credit sales
Profit on credit sales : funds invested
Bad debt loss : credit sales
Cost of performing credit functions : cost of shifting same functions

From such measures it may be ascertained whether management performance compares favorably with past performance, with planned performance, and with the performance of others in the industry. Whatever norm is employed, appraisal of management from owners' standpoint may be made along these lines.

Management–Government Relations

The obligations of credit management to both consumers and owners fall within the private sectors of the economy. Some measure may also be taken of management's relations with the public regulatory sector, namely, government.

In this area, it may be thought that the least interaction is best. One cannot believe today, however, that interaction of management and government is solely defensive or a one-way relationship. It is true that in credit fields government has had to initiate interaction in many instances, because the expectations of others, mainly consumers, were unsatisfied. The function of government in a society like ours is to act as intermediary or arbiter between contending or injured parties, to undertake action in the general welfare, and to enforce law and order. Contacts of credit managers with government, however, are not merely defensive. The integrity of credit depends upon honesty in credit transactions. To encourage this quality, credit managers through their national association have promoted enactment of false financial statement laws. They have also promoted laws providing differential credit charges and loan ceilings to accommodate various needs, legislation prescribing disclosure of credit terms and contract requirements, bankruptcy law amendments, and anti-discriminatory taxation and regulation among credit agencies. Thus it is apparent that fulfillment of the expectations of government and of the community in general is shown both by compliance with law and by cooperation in the formulation of credit law.

As the role of credit in our society is influenced by the role of credit management in the credit institution, appraisal of the one is inseparable from appraisal of the other.

DISCUSSION QUESTIONS

1. Reconsider the four concepts of credit discussed in Chapter 1, and indicate their relevance to appraisal of credit.
2. The bases of credit appraisal lie, in general, in the social circumstances and attitudes concerning this process. Show the circumstances and attitudes of American society, in particular, which affect our appraisal of credit, and indicate the means by which these factors find expression.
3. A credit system which would be regarded "adequate" at one time or place might not at another. What determines "adequacy"? What relation has the stage of economic development to it? Is "adequacy" a condition to be left to private enterprise?
4. Evaluate the element of time lag between management innovation and social control as found in the field of credit.
5. Show how differently appraisal of credit management would be approached from a functional standpoint and from a behavioral standpoint.
6. Relate the concept of credit objectives discussed in Chapter 5 to that of management appraisal.
7. At what points do the social appraisal of credit and the managerial appraisal of credit management coincide?

Index